Romanticism, Enthusiasm, and Regulation

Romanticism, Enthusiasm, and Regulation

Poetics and the Policing of Culture in the Romantic Period

JON MEE

OXFORD
UNIVERSITY PRESS

OXFORD

UNIVERSITY PRESS

Great Clarendon Street, Oxford OX2 6DP

Oxford University Press is a department of the University of Oxford.
It furthers the University's objective of excellence in research, scholarship,
and education by publishing worldwide in

Oxford New York

Auckland Bangkok Buenos Aires Cape Town Chennai
Dar es Salaam Delhi Hong Kong Istanbul Karachi Kolkata
Kuala Lumpur Madrid Melbourne Mexico City Mumbai Nairobi
São Paulo Shanghai Taipei Tokyo Toronto

Oxford is a registered trade mark of Oxford University Press
in the UK and in certain other countries

Published in the United States
by Oxford University Press Inc., New York

The moral rights of the author have been asserted
Database right Oxford University Press (maker)

First published 2003

British Library Cataloguing in Publication Data
Data available

Library of Congress Cataloging in Publication Data
Data available

ISBN 0-19-818757-2

1 3 5 7 9 10 8 6 4 2

Typeset by Hope Services (Abingdon) Ltd
Printed in Great Britain
on acid-free paper by
Biddles Ltd,
Guildford and King's Lynn

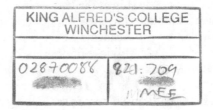

Acknowledgements

THE IDEA OF writing this book was prompted by the workshop on Enthusiasm organized by Laurence E. Klein and Anthony J. La Vopa and sponsored by the UCLA Center for 17th and 18th-Century Studies and the William Andrews Clark Memorial Library, held on 3–4 May 1996. Prior to this event the sheer diversity of the trajectories of 'enthusiasm' in the eighteenth century had escaped me, although I had given the subject some thought in my first book: *Dangerous Enthusiasm: William Blake and the Culture of Radicalism in the 1790s* (1992). The proceedings for the conference subsequently appeared in the form of a book and a special issue of the *Huntington Library Quarterly*. My contribution provides the basis of Chapter 3 of this book, but I am grateful to the encouragement given to me more generally by the participants at the conference, and especially Tony and Larry. Some of my early thinking about Wordsworth and enthusiasm appeared in an article entitled 'Apocalypse and Ambivalence: The Politics of Millenarianism in the 1790s' in a special edition of *South Atlantic Quarterly* edited by Thomas Pfau and Rhonda Ray Kercsmar in the summer of 1996. *Romanticism, Enthusiasm, and Regulation* has taken a long time to write, partly because my ideas on many aspects of the subject have been constantly evolving, and partly because of a major upheaval in moving back to England from Australia. Many people must be thanked for their contributions to this enriching process. Undergraduates at the Australian National University and University College, Oxford, have helped me think through many of the basic ideas during tutorials on a range of different topics. More materially a Visiting Fellowship at the Humanities Research Centre of the Australian National University in 2001, and the extended sabbatical provided by the Academy of the Humanities Research Leave Scheme created the conditions of time and space that enabled me to translate the thinking into words. Among others who have contributed specific ideas and information and made the whole thing so much fun over almost a decade of thinking about this topic are: Stuart Allen, Judie Barbour, John Barrell, Marilyn Butler, Luisa

Calè, Phil Cardinale, Dipesh Chakrabarty, Jim Chandler, Frances Chiu, Timothy Clark, Deirdre Coleman, Pete de Bolla, David Goldie, Harriet Guest, Ranajit Guha, Helen Irving, Simon Jarvis, Nigel Leask, Emma Major, Emma Mason, Saree Makdisi, Susan Matthews, Iain McCalman, Peter McDonald, Jeff Mertz, Leslie Mitchell, Lucy Newlyn, Tim Morton, Kaz Oishi, Mark Philp, Sebastian Kalhat Pocicovich, Rajeswari Sunder Rajan, Isabel Rivers, Robert Rix, Gillian Russell, Michael Scrivener, Nigel Smith, Neelam Srivastava, Fiona Stafford, Clara Tuite, John Walsh, Marcus Wood, and Robert Young. Seminars at the Universities of Sussex, Chicago, and Cambridge helped refine many of the ideas. The response of 'the Unconfined Seminar' at Oxford was encouraging as the project started to be drawn together at the end. Rebecca Rees, Kate Williams, and Alicia Black were great helps in the later stages of preparing the manuscripts. Christine Ritchie helped in innumerable ways in University College Library. Being teased by Vera Ryhajlo and Helen Rogers in the Upper Reading Room of the Bodleian made even checking the most arcane references something of a pleasure. Clare Drury, Jane Vicat, and Linda Cousins in the College Office helped me keep things in perspective. Sophie Goldsworthy, Frances Whistler, and Edwin Pritchard at OUP provided wonderful editorial help and encouragement. It goes without saying that none of these persons or institutions are responsible for the places where my enthusiasm was not able to find appropriate forms of expression. Lastly I would like to thank Leila Jordan and Sharmila Jordan-Mee for putting up with so much. Without their patience this book would not have been possible. The book is dedicated to them in the hope that they will forgive all the unwordliness and distraction.

J.M.

University College,
Oxford
October 2002

Contents

Abbreviations   viii

Introduction: Situating Enthusiasm   1

PART I: THE DISCOURSE ON ENTHUSIASM

1 Commanding Enthusiasm through the Eighteenth
   Century   23
2 Enthusiasm, Liberty, and Benevolence in the 1790s   82

PART II: THE POETICS OF ENTHUSIASM

3 Coleridge, Prophecy, and Imagination   131
4 Barbauld, Devotion, and the Woman Prophet   173
5 Wordsworth's Chastened Enthusiasm   214
6 Energy and Enthusiasm in Blake   257

   Conclusion: Enthusiastic Misreadings   294

Select Bibliography   297

Index   315

Abbreviations

Aids	S. T. Coleridge, *Aids to Reflection*, ed. John Beer (Princeton: Princeton University Press, 1993).
Anno.	Annotations
BL	S. T. Coleridge, *Biographia Literaria*, ed. James Engell and W. Jackson Bate, Bollingen Series, 2 vols. (Princeton: Princeton University Press, 1983).
BP	*The Poems of Anna Letitia Barbauld*, ed. William McCarthy and Elizabeth Kraft (Athens: University of Georgia Press, 1994).
CCS	S. T. Coleridge, *On the Constitution of Church and State*, ed. John Colmer, Bollingen Series (Princeton: Princeton University Press, 1976).
Characteristics	Anthony Ashley Cooper, Third Earl of Shaftesbury, *Characteristics of Men, Manners, Opinions, Times*, ed. Lawrence E. Klein, Cambridge Texts in the History of Philosophy (Cambridge: Cambridge University Press, 1999).
CPW	S. T. Coleridge, *Poetical Works*, ed. J. C. C. Mays, Bollingen Series, 3 vols. (Princeton: Princeton University Press, 2001).
E	William, Blake, *The Complete Poetry and Prose of William Blake*, ed. David V. Erdman, rev. edn. (New York: Anchor-Doubleday, 1988). References to poems give an abbreviated title followed by a plate and line number, references to prose simply give the page number in Erdman after an abbreviated title. The relevant abbreviations are: *BU*, *The Book of Urizen*; *DC*, *A Descriptive Catalogue*; *J*, *Jerusalem*; *M*, *Milton*; *MHH*, *The Marriage of Heaven and Hell*; *VLJ*, *Vision of the Last Judgment*.
EY	*The Letters of William and Dorothy Wordsworth: The Early Years, 1787–1805*, ed. Ernest de Selincourt, 2nd edn. rev. Mary Moorman (Oxford: Clarendon Press, 1969).
Friend	S. T. Coleridge, *The Friend*, ed. Barbara E. Rooke, Bollingen Series, 2 vols. (Princeton: Princeton University Press, 1969).

Godwin Works   Political and Philosophical Writings of William Godwin, gen. ed. Mark Philp, 7 vols. (William Pickering, 1993).

Griggs   *The Collected Letters of Samuel Taylor Coleridge*, ed. E. L. Griggs, 6 vols. (Oxford: Oxfordd University Press, 1956–71).

H   Leigh Hunt, *An attempt to shew the folly and danger of Methodism. In a series of essays first published in the . . . Examiner, and now enlarged with a preface and . . . notes. By the editor of the Examiner* (1809).

L1795   S. T. Coleridge, *Lectures 1795 on Politics and Religion*, ed. Lewis Patton and Peter Mann, Bollingen Series (Princeton: Princeton University Press, 1971).

LB   William Wordsworth and Samuel Taylor Coleridge, *Lyrical Ballads*, ed. R. L. Brett and A. R. Jones (Methuen, 1963; repr. 1968).

LCS   London Corresponding Society

Life of Wesley   Robert Southey, *The Life of Wesley; and the Rise and Progress of Methodism*, 2 vols (London, 1820).

LLit   S. T. Coleridge, *Lectures 1808–1819 on Literature*, ed. R. A. Foakes, Bollingen Series, 2 vols. (Princeton: Princeton University Press, 1987).

LPhil   S. T. Coleridge, *Lectures 1808–1819 on the History of Philosophy*, ed. J. R. de J. Jackson, Bollingen Series, 2 vols. (Princeton: Princeton University Press, 2000).

LY   *The Letters of William and Dorothy Wordsworth: The Later Years 1821–1853*, ed. Ernest de Selincourt, rev. Alan G. Hill, 4 vols. (Oxford: Clarendon Press, 1978–88).

MY   *The Letters of William and Dorothy Wordsworth: The Middle Years, 1806–1811*, ed. Ernest de Selincourt, 2nd edn. rev. Mary Moorman (Oxford: Clarendon Press, 1969), part 1.

Notebooks   *The Notebooks of Samuel Taylor Coleridge*, ed. Kathleen Coburn, Bollingen Series (Princeton: Princeton University Press, 1957–).

PB   William Wordsworth, *Peter Bell*, ed. John E. Jordan (Ithaca, NY: Cornell University Press, 1985).

Prelude   William Wordsworth, *The Prelude: The Four Texts (1798, 1799, 1805, 1850)*, ed. Jonathan Wordsworth (Harmondsworth: Penguin, 1995). Year will follow title in italics.

Rutt   *The Theological and Miscellaneous Works of Joseph Priestley*, ed. J. T. Rutt, 25 vols. (1871).

SM   S. T. Coleridge, *The Statesman's Manual, Lay Sermons*,
             ed. R. J. White, Bollingen Series (Princeton: Princeton
             University Press, 1972).
TT   S. T. Coleridge, *Table Talk*, ed. Carl Woodring,
             Bollingen Series, 2 vols. (Princeton: Princeton University
             Press, 1990).
Watchman   *The Watchman*, ed. Lewis Patton, Bollingen Series
             (Princeton: Princeton University Press, 1970).
WP   *The Prose Works of William Wordsworth*, ed. W. J. B.
             Owen and J. W. Smyser, 3 vols. (Oxford: Clarendon
             Press, 1974).

Introduction: Situating Enthusiasm

THE PURPOSE OF this book is simple. It aims to renew our sense of the cultural importance of 'enthusiasm' in the Romantic period. The word is far from being an unfamiliar one, but this familiarity contributes to a blindness that obscures its complex centrality to the period. For all its simplicity of purpose, this book is also perhaps itself a work of reckless enthusiasm as it attempts to track the multiple and various meanings of the term as they develop and recur across a range of discursive networks. The result is a reassessment of some of the governing concepts of Romantic criticism. In some respects, the spirit of the study is in line with recent New Historicist approaches that have represented 'Romantic ideology' in terms of its displacements and denials of history. Enthusiasm was involved in such a series of displacements, as we shall see, but I want to begin with a caveat in regard to this study's relationship to New Historicism in Romantic studies. Several critics have recently registered a concern at the way that New Historicism tends to make an *abstract* appeal to history',[1] that is, one that represents history as always already complete to itself and only mystified by Romanticism's deployment of categories such as 'imagination', 'vision', 'prophecy', and even 'affect' itself. 'Enthusiasm' ought to be listed among these categories too, for it was not only displaced but also desired in Romantic writing, yet its inclusion can perhaps serve to highlight the complexity of the historical relations of this grouping. If it does oppose these terms to history, New Historicist criticism is in danger of replicating the binaries that it critiques. Affect in this case can become a mere fiction (in a negative, limited sense) against which the truth of history can be revealed. Such a view ignores the fact that affect too has a history, a history crucial

---

[1] Simon Jarvis discusses the '*abstract* appeal to history' in 'Wordsworth and Idolatry', *Studies in Romanticism*, 38 (1999), 24. See also Gregory Dart, *Rousseau, Robespierre and English Romanticism* (Cambridge: Cambridge University Press, 1999), 8–9.

to the development of the idea of the literary in the period covered
by this book, even if the Romantic ideology can present literariness
as beyond such claims. Beginnings have been made to understanding this history of affect and its relation to the aesthetic, but too
often they become fixated on familiar literary terms such as 'sensibility' or 'the sublime.'[2] 'Enthusiasm' as a concept ranged more
awkwardly across discursive boundaries than either of these terms.
Both the fleshly seeing of the crowd and the highest flights of poetic
inspiration were identified with the word. Part of its productive
potential as an object of study is that it was (and is) not a term that
had been fully recuperated by the ideology of the aesthetic. Schiller
claimed that 'in the realm of Aesthetic Semblance, we find that ideal
of equality fulfilled which the Enthusiast would fain see realized in
substance'.[3] Standing at the boundaries between literary ideas of
affect and the more unruly spectacle of the crowd, caught within a
complex patterning of desire and disavowal, enthusiasm serves to
highlight the entangled historicity of affect. As a beginning to a
historical understanding of enthusiasm, this book is necessarily
incomplete, perhaps overblown, and sometimes contentious; I hope
in a stimulating way. Some of its claims may be just plain wrong,
but if the endeavour means that enthusiasm emerges as a new category of serious analysis for the writing of the Romantic period then
(as all enthusiasts believe) the gains are worth the risks.

The primary meaning of the word enthusiasm for about two
centuries or more in English defined a specifically religious error:

To equal the *imaginations of men* to the *holy scripture of God*, and think
them as much the *inspiration of God*, as what was dictated as such, to the
holy prophets and apostles, is strictly and properly *Enthusiasm*.[4]

---

[2] Peter de Bolla's *The Discourse of the Sublime: Readings in History, Aesthetics, and the Subject* (Oxford: Basil Blackwell, 1989) ranges across discursive boundaries, but I take 'enthusiasm' to be a larger category than 'the sublime', one even
more loosely identified with aesthetics, and one for which issues about the relationship between aesthetic discourse and other forms of social behaviour were much
more fraught, mainly because of the historical relationship with the social upheaval
of the Civil War and the spectre of the energized crowd it evoked.

[3] Schiller, 'On the Aesthetic education of man', quoted in M. H. Abrams, *Natural Supernaturalism: Tradition and Revolution in Romantic Literature* (New York: W. W. Norton & Company, 1981), 352.

[4] M[artin] M[adan], *A Full and Compleat Answer to the Capital Errors, Contained in the Writings of the Late Rev. William Law* (1763), quoted in Susie I. Tucker, *Enthusiasm: A Study in Semantic Change* (Cambridge: Cambridge University Press, 1972), 27.

Martin Madan's definition from 1764 was much the same as the one Hobbes was working with in the 1650s and Locke in the 1670s, but it was also still the one used by Leigh Hunt writing against what he perceived as the excesses of Methodism in 1809. The regularity of these statements concerning enthusiasm is such that they constitute a discursive formation in Foucault's sense.[5] I'll be calling this formation 'the discourse on enthusiasm'. The kinds of statements that constitute this discursive formation will be outlined below, and take up most of Part I of the book. They operated across the long eighteenth century to identify something that was taken to transgress the boundaries of the emergent bourgeois public sphere, although, as we shall see, enthusiasm became less something to be prohibited and excluded than regulated and brought inside the conversation of culture.[6] The word 'regulation' points one toward Foucault's ideas on the kind of disciplinary procedures that produce in order to control, and certainly from early on the term regulation appears in writing such as Shaftesbury's associated with the promise of winning something great from what had been a scandal.[7] The journey towards the modern meaning of the word (*OED*: 'passionate eagerness in any pursuit, proceeding from an intense conviction of the worthiness of the object') was one then that produced enthusiasm as an object of discursive practices of regulation, but another caveat needs registering here. Foucault's followers, and Foucault himself in the early work, are often accused of a tendency 'to stabilize the object of study'.[8] One of the key discoveries of this study is the instability or 'play' involved in the disciplinary activity surrounding enthusiasm. The regulation of enthusiasm, say, in the aesthetic sphere, never quite convinced itself that what it produced was any better than its vulgar avatar in religious enthusiasm. What

---

[5] See *The Archeology of Knowledge*, trans. Alan Sheridan Smith (Routledge, 1991), 107.

[6] On the trope of conversation in the period, see Stephen Copley, 'Commerce, Conversation, and Politeness in the Early Eighteenth-Century Periodical', *British Journal for Eighteenth-Century Studies*, 18 (1995), 63–77.

[7] From early on, *Characteristics* addresses the question of how 'to regulate men's apprehensions and religious beliefs' (*Characteristics*, 11). There the emphasis is on how to control and respond to popular panics. It is in 'Soliloquy, or Advice to an Author' that Shaftesbury turns his attention to 'the way of private exercise, which consists chiefly in control', 75. On production and control, see, for instance, Michel Foucault, *The History of Sexuality: An Introduction*, trans. Robert Hurley (Harmondsworth: Penguin, 1981), ch. 1, 'The Incitement to Discourse'.

[8] See de Bolla, *Discourse of the Sublime*, 11.

was sometimes brought forward as a cultural cure for a society becoming mechanistic and spiritually empty was also feared as a poison that would dissolve the subject it was saving into the ocean of his or her passions.[9]

Projecting the modern meaning of enthusiasm and its relatively positive valency back on to the earlier period, most literary critics have implied that it had come to be regarded as no bad thing by the late eighteenth century.[10] Such a view, after all, fits nicely into a generally accepted common sense narrative that moves us from a cold classicism to a passionate romanticism in the course of the eighteenth century. This book takes a contrary view, however, in so far as it emphasizes striking and important *continuities* in the attitudes expressed towards enthusiasm. These continuities, I argue, constituted a discourse on enthusiasm that shaped the way people thought, wrote, and behaved as late as the early nineteenth century (and perhaps beyond in the development of disciplines such as crowd psychology). Hunt, for instance, can sound remarkably like Jonathan Swift a hundred years earlier on the subject of religious enthusiasm. Indeed the notes of Hunt's *Folly and Dangers of Methodism* are full of references to Swift.[11] How do these continuities square with Shaun Irlam's claim that they 'gradually gave way, among poets in the eighteenth century, to a passion for divine inspiration, epiphanic experiences, apocatastatic [sic] ambitions, and poetic Enthusiasm'?[12] For Irlam the narrative of Romanticism as a species of rehabilitated enthusiasm is very much in place, it just gets

---

[9] Jacques Derrida's work has influenced my thinking on this matter, see his *Of Grammatology*, trans. Gayatri Chakravorty Spivak (Baltimore: Johns Hopkins University Press, [1974] 1976) and *Writing and Difference*, trans. Alan Bass (Routledge, [1967] 1978). Not that this 'trace' of the pathological variant of enthusiasm is simply to be regarded as a textual effect; rather, I understand such effects as gravitating towards anxieties surrounding the challenge of the counter-public of enthusiasm to the enlightened public sphere. See 'A Counter-Public of Enthusiasm?' in Chapter 1.

[10] See, for instance, Abrams, *Natural Supernaturalism*; Timothy Clark, *The Theory of Inspiration: Composition as a Crisis of Subjectivity in Romantic and Post-Romantic Writing* (Manchester: Manchester University Press, 1997); and Shaun Irlam, *Elations: The Poetics of Enthusiasm in Eighteenth-Century Britain* (Stanford, Calif.: Stanford University Press, 1999). Clark's excellent study, as its title suggests, is aware of the anxieties surrounding the idea of 'poetic enthusiasm' and more committed to exploring the problematic aspect of the rehabilitation of enthusiasm than either Abrams or Irlam.

[11] See, for instance, H 86–7.   [12] Irlam, *Elations*, 24.

under way earlier, and is effectively completed by Wordsworth.[13] There is little doubt that what Irlam thinks of as the 'rehabilitation' of enthusiasm was an aspect of eighteenth-century literary culture, but I believe it was neither as comprehensive nor as innocent as he suggests. In terms of the latter, of course, I see this rehabilitation as centrally concerned with Foucauldian issues of power and cultural authority, but, ironically without recourse to Foucault, Irlam goes too far towards stabilizing his own object of study. Although his book does not put it in Foucauldian terms, Irlam seems rather too confident that disciplinary practices brought the play of enthusiasm to historical closure in the eighteenth century. The example of Hunt, for instance, helps us see that enthusiasm was never successfully rehabilitated. It remained haunted by the fear of the combustible matter within both the individual and the body politic. If one is tempted to align enthusiasm with Romanticism as part of a binary opposition with, say, Reason and Enlightenment, as Irlam implicitly does, one will miss the fact that, throughout the eighteenth century and beyond, enthusiasm remained as suspect as it had always been, if not properly regulated. If literature was a cultural space where enthusiasm gained a relative toleration, it was only because literariness itself came to be seen as part of the process of regulation. To transform enthusiasm into art was to make it relatively safe, but even then, as we shall see, questions of what constituted art rather than rant and who was capable of regulating whom remained at issue.

Why was it that 'enthusiasm' specifically was such a fraught issue? What were the origins of the anxious associations of the word that I have so far only hinted at? The answer I think is one that helps us understand broader anxieties surrounding emergent ideas of subjectivity. Once thinkers began to found 'their accurate disquisitions of human nature intirely upon experience', as Hume put it, enthusiasm became available as a way of describing perversions of feeling and experience.[14] Not that this book is concerned to trace the specifically philosophical trajectory of the word alone. Philosophy was just one of many discourses involved with defining its grounds of knowledge by way of contrast to enthusiasm. Religion remained among the most important of these. Such

---

[13] See ibid. 239.
[14] David Hume, *A Treatise of Human Nature*, ed. L. A. Selby-Bigge and P. H. Nidditch, 2nd edn. (Oxford: Clarendon Press, 1978), 646.

anxieties are often associated by modern critics with the emergence of the secular subject; I believe they were deeply conditioned by the religious discourses surrounding the Reformation and its consequences in England.[15] Although there was a trajectory for the word 'enthusiasm' in the classical languages that meant 'the reformulation of positive estimations [of the word] remained a standing option', its English usage was primarily concerned with erroneous conceptions of man's relation to God.[16] Strongly identified by Hume and others before him as a Protestant error, in contrast to Catholic 'superstition', 'enthusiasm' defined the error of finding God everywhere and justifying one's own impulses as his Word. More broadly this development did quickly provide a language for speaking about the dangers facing the self-authenticating subject that had to look at personal experience as the basis of identity and knowledge. Various philosophical and other kinds of solution to this problem were proposed during the period covered by this book, but ultimately none of them could point to a way of distinguishing authentic knowledge or feeling from mere enthusiasm with entire security. Enthusiasm appears in Locke's *Essay on Human Understanding* as 'a perswasion of an immediate intercourse with the Deity . . . ,which though founded neither on Reason nor Divine Revelation, but rising from the Conceits of a warmed or over-weening Brain, works yet, where it once gets footing, more powerfully on the Perswasions and Actions of Men, than either of those two'.[17] Enthusiasm was the arch-enemy of proper human understanding then for Locke, but even he could not entirely quell the fear that the sensorium was merely another theatre for enthusiasm:

[15] See Andrew Ashfield and Peter de Bolla's introduction to de Bolla and Ashfield (eds.), *The Sublime: A Reader in British Eighteenth-Century Aesthetic Theory* (Cambridge: Cambridge University Press, 1996), 1, where they claim that eighteenth-century aesthetics articulated 'the complexities of affective experience . . . in the context of an emerging new understanding of the construction of the subject'. They see at the heart of this new subject a transition from 'an epistemology based in theological belief and debate to one in which man must find from within himself the grounds of knowledge'. Attending to 'enthusiasm' rather than the more 'safely' aesthetic category of the 'sublime' in the context of these changes makes the secularist teleology of Ashfield and de Bolla look rather too confident.

[16] Lawrence E. Klein and Anthony J. La Vopa, 'Introduction', *Huntington Library Quarterly*, 60 (1998), 1.

[17] John Locke, *An Essay Concerning Human Understanding*, ed. Peter H. Nidditch (Oxford: Clarendon Press,1979), 699.

If it be true, that all Knowledge lies only in the perception of the agreement or disagreement of our own *Ideas*, the Visions of an Enthusiast, and the Reasonings of a sober man will be equally certain. 'Tis no matter how Things are: so a Man observe but the agreements of his own imaginations and talk conformably, it is all Truth, all Certainty.[18]

For Locke the 'restraint of Reason, and check of Reflection' could provide a corrective against such enthusiasm, but the anxiety raised by his question was never quite put to bed, and for some of those who followed him, most famously Hume, his faith in Reason could seem simply a latter-day variety of enthusiasm.[19]

What I call a more regulatory response developed to the problem of enthusiasm as a challenge to the modern subject. If the passions and affections seemed increasingly to have an unavoidable and even necessary role in the formation of knowledge as identity, then this regulatory discourse attempted to incorporate them into the picture without abandoning the desideratum of coherent self-identity. My account of the regulation of enthusiasm parallels Irlam's account of the term's rehabilitation insofar as it represented an attempt to incorporate what Locke excluded. If various kinds of affect were increasingly brought into accounts of human identity and know-ledge, however, there was also a constant drive to distinguish authentic affect from mere enthusiasm. Shaftesbury went so far as to suggest that the former was only qualitatively different from the latter. What he perceived as the rough and vulgar longings of the crowd were, he claimed, unrefined versions of a natural human impulse to get beyond the self and ultimately to God.[20] Yet if human beings were increasingly defined as sympathetic creatures across a whole range of discourses and practices in the period, there remained an anxiety about where such sympathies led. If the eigh-teenth century was a clubbable century, should anyone be allowed into the club? What was the difference between the club and the crowd who seemed the very type of disorganized enthusiasm? In more theological and aesthetic terms, if transport out of the self offered itself as a way of authenticating individual experience in terms of some higher ontological arena, providing a corroborating ground for subjective experience, whether Christian or theist, there

---

[18] Ibid. 563.   [19] Ibid. 699.
[20] Lawrence E. Klein, 'Introduction' to id. (ed.), *Characteristics of Men, Manners, Opinions, Times* (Cambridge: Cambridge University Press, 1999), pp. xxx–xxxi.

remained the nightmare of losing the self on the journey. What if one could not get back down to earth after the transports of the sublime? To ask the question in a more narrowly literary context, what if people came to believe that 'there is nothing to stop anyone who can feel from springing into verse'?[21]

Of course, the eighteenth century was not in a constant funk about the nature of identity, but it was alert to behaviours and forms of speech that seemed to put its idea of a coherent subject into jeopardy. To this extent, the subject was never allowed to be self-authenticating, even in the Romantic period. Indeed, from one conservative point of view, claims to self-sufficiency, whether religious, literary, political, philosophical, or otherwise, were always taken as signs of a dangerous enthusiasm. Faced with the uncertainty of empirical knowledge, manners and other socially coded forms of behaviour provided observers with an index of what coherent identity might be. Burke, for instance, held Reason to be no better than what Locke called 'perswasion' when it claimed to be able to reveal truth entirely by its own lights. To be able to see the truth transparently and spontaneously without mediation was construed as enthusiasm across a range of discursive fields.[22] Rousseau became the representative figure of this latter-day enthusiasm for Burke, an idea that Coleridge perpetuated when he compared the Swiss philosopher to Luther in *The Friend*. Coleridge deemed both 'in their *radical* natures' types who 'referred all things to [their]

[21] Judith Pascoe, *Romantic Theatricality: Gender, Poetry, and Spectatorship* (Ithaca, NY: Cornell University Press, 1997), 79.

[22] See J. G. A. Pocock's 'Edmund Burke and the Redefinition of Enthusiasm: The Context as Counter-Revolution' in *The Transformation of Political Culture, 1789–1848*, vol. iii of François Furet and Mona Ozouf (eds.), *The French Revolution and the Creation of Modern Political Culture* (Oxford: Oxford University Press, 1989), 19–43, and 'Enthusiasm: The Antiself of Enlightenment', *Huntington Library Quarterly*, 60 (1998), 7–28. Pocock's view is that the doctrine of *transparence* promulgated in the French Revolution under the name of Rousseau was immediately understood in Britain in the terms of the discourse of enthusiasm already in place: 'Redefinition of Enthusiasm', 25. The classic study of Rousseau and *transparence* is Jean Starobinski's *Jean-Jacques Rousseau: Transparency and Obstruction*, trans. Arthur Goldhammer, with an introduction by Robert J. Morrissey (Chicago: University of Chicago Press, 1988). For an interesting discussion of the idea of *transparence* within the context of Jacobin developments of Rousseau's thinking in the 1790s, see also Marie-Hélène Huet, 'The Revolutionary Sublime', *Eighteenth-Century Studies*, 28 (1994), 51–64. English responses to Jacobin developments of Rousseau on this score are central to Dart's, *Rousseau, Robespierre, and English Romanticism*. I am extremely grateful to Luisa Calè for sharing her thoughts on this subject with me.

own Ideal'. Only the fact that Luther had 'derived his standard from . . . the inspired Writings' provided his enthusiasm with 'an object out of itself, on which it may fix its attention, and thus balance its own energies' (*Friend*, ii. 113). Few commentators, including sometimes Coleridge himself, rested easily on the thought that the Bible alone, without external support, could provide such an anchor.[23] After all, enthusiasm, as it had been from the seventeenth century, was still primarily in circulation as a pejorative term describing an excess of religious zeal. The uneducated reader left alone with the Bible was in certain respects at the bottom of the problem. As such, as I have already suggested, it was regarded as a particularly Protestant failing. If Catholicism was regarded as tending towards superstition and idolatry, abasing the individual in fear and trembling before a distant God, interposing ceremonies and rituals between Creator and created, then the reforming churches were thought to be drawn to enthusiasm in their desire to bring man and God closer together.[24] Coleridge saw in Luther 'a language so inflammatory' that it was barely saved from declaring a 'holy right of Insurrection' (*Friend*, ii. 116). To believe oneself to have an immediate relationship with one's God, to believe oneself able to apprehend his will directly, or be his peculiar favourite was to be guilty of enthusiasm. Prophetic pretensions, therefore, were always associated with the word, especially where those pretensions, as they did during the Civil War, claimed to be the basis of interventions in the public and political worlds. The sectaries of the English Civil War remained for the succeeding two centuries the primary examples of enthusiasm in English history. To declare the end of the state on the basis of the immediate apprehension of God's will was the ultimate folly of the doctrine of *transparence* for the English imagination, only to be matched a century later by Robespierre's claim to have unmediated access to the will of the people. Pocock believes that the experience of the Civil War fundamentally conditioned the subsequent development of Anglicanism in this respect. Enthusiasm was associated with the sectarian belief that 'the Spirit might at any time be active in the congregation or even in the individual and stood in no need of the authority of hierarchy or

[23] See Chapter 3 for a fuller discussion of this point.
[24] The classic statement of this idea for the period is David Hume's essay 'Of Superstition and Enthusiasm' in *Essays Moral, Political, and Literary*, ed. T. H. Green and T. H. Grose, 2 vols. (Longmans, Green & Co., 1875), i. 144–9.

magistrate'.[25] For this reason the latitudinarian tradition within the Church at least worked hard 'to reduce spiritual authority without at the same time reducing the divine person itself'.[26] Compared to the ubiquity of the divine presence proclaimed by enthusiastic sectarians, this tradition favoured, so Pocock claims, 'an independently existing God, who made himself known by the wonders of his works, seldom by direct revelation, and never by his immanence or inherence, which he had made the human mind incapable of grasping'.[27] Its definition of piety tended towards depth and stillness and away from the controversialism and crowds that were associated with enthusiasm.

The primary associations of enthusiasm for the seventeenth century were all certainly still present for Samuel Johnson in the eighteenth, but now with a few signs of further developments thrown in: '1. A vain belief of private revelation; a vain confidence of Divine favour or communication . . . 2. Heat or imagination; violence of passion, confidence of opinion . . . 3. Elevation of fancy; exaltation of ideas'.[28] Note, however, the development of the dangers of enthusiasm out of the purely religious context here. 'Confidence of opinion' and 'exaltation of ideas' picks up on phrases of Locke's on prophetic enthusiasm, but points towards the Burkean definition of enlightenment itself as a strain of the virus. If these definitions, like Hume's, identify enthusiasm with an exorbitance of ego (as against the abjection of superstition), there was also a great stress on the sociable nature of enthusiasm. An emphasis purely on the epistemological foundations of the term's trajectory, such as Pocock's ideas on *transparence*, is liable to miss this aspect of the discourse on enthusiasm. 'Enthusiasm is indeed sufficiently contagious', Samuel Johnson noted; and as the eighteenth century went on the word was increasingly used to describe kinds of social behaviour that placed one beyond the pale of the emergent bourgeois public sphere (as well as those codes of Anglican religiosity outlined above).[29] Although it was often associated with the sort of implosion of the self that came from the prophet retiring into the

[25] Pocock, 'Antiself of Enlightenment', 12.   [26] Ibid. 9.   [27] Ibid. 17.
[28] Samuel Johnson, *A Dictionary of the English Language: in which the WORDS are deduced from their ORIGINALS, and ILLUSTRATED in their DIFFERENT SIGNIFICATIONS by EXAMPLES from the best WRITERS*, 2 vols. (1755), 'enthusiasm'.
[29] Johnson, *Works*, ed. A. Murphy (1806) xi. 329. For a discussion of the trope of contagion in relation to enthusiasm, see Tucker, *Enthusiasm*, 145–8.

wilderness, a species of melancholia and gloomy introspection, it was also routinely construed in terms of the delirium of the senses that manifested itself in the mania of the crowd. Developing out of its initially strictly religious usage, enthusiasm came to be understood as a way of describing what Walter Benjamin's translators call the 'distraction' of the nineteenth-century crowd. If the eighteenth century had no developed discipline of crowd psychology as such, enthusiasm was one of the words whose usage developed as part of an explanation of such phenomena. Johnson's own definition points towards the migration of the term away from a strictly religious usage towards an understanding of the way the passions could communicate themselves without resort to rational articulation. Enthusiasm was taken to avoid reflection and meditation. These were the behavioural qualities that linked the crowd to the theological and philosophical *transparence* of Luther and Rousseau in the discourse on enthusiasm. The crowd hurried to translate words into actions and to elide the gap between things and their representations: 'When the Imagination is so inflam'd, as to render the Soul utterly incapable of reflecting, there is no difference between the Images and the Things themselves.'[30] These words belong to John Dennis. Despite the warning note they sound, Dennis was a writer whose career and reputation were ruined by the imputation that he was mired in the enthusiasm of the crowd.[31] Dennis's fate cannot simply be understood as the result of his coming before his time. Again let me reiterate that I don't believe that this attitude can simply be filed away under an idea about the Augustan suspicion of Imagination, for I will be arguing that literature in the Romantic period continued to define itself against the dangers of enthusiasm. Nathan Drake, for instance, writing in the year that Wordsworth and Coleridge published *Lyrical Ballads*, shared their sense of the 'IMAGINATION' as a 'fruitful source of the beautiful and sublime', but associated 'enthusiasm' with the degeneration of this potential precisely into 'distraction':

[30] *The Critical Works of John Dennis*, ed. E. N. Hooker (Baltimore: Johns Hopkins University Press, 1939), i. 363.
[31] On Dennis and enthusiasm, see Brean Hammond, *Professional Imaginative Writing in England 1670–1740: 'Hackney for Bread'* (Oxford: Oxford University Press, 1997), 9–10 and 169–71; Irlam, *Elations*, 60–79; and Lawrence E. Klein, *Shaftesbury and the Culture of Politeness: Moral Discourse and Cultural Politics in Early Eighteenth-Century England* (Cambridge: Cambridge University Press, 1994), 5 and 165.

But should this brilliant faculty be nurtured on the bosom of enthusiasm, or romantic expectation, or be left to revel in all its native wildness of combination, and to plunge into all the visionary terrors of supernatural agency, undiverted by the deductions of truth, or the sober realities of existence, it will too often prove the cause of acute misery, of melancholy, and even of distraction.[32]

Coleridge's need to distinguish between Imagination and Fancy perpetuates this long-standing need to cordon off certain areas of affective experience from the dangerous extremes of enthusiasm. Even as he desired 'enthusiasm and feeling profound or vehement', Coleridge insisted that the Imagination, unlike the Fancy, was regulated by 'judgment ever awake and steady self-possession' (*BL* i. 17).

If Drake's passage suggests that an important disciplinary distinction between the authentic imagination and enthusiasm was coming into being at this time, it should be acknowledged, of course, that the latter had previously more often been defined in a binary opposition to 'enlightenment'. Locke's *Essay* is an obvious case in point, but the contrast was a pervasive one in philosophical writing of the period. In Germany, for instance, the definition of enlightenment proposed by Kant and others opposed both '*Enthusiasm*' and its virtual synonym '*Schwärmerei*' to 'philosophy's effort to establish itself as the public voice of reason'.[33] Philosophers of the Scottish Enlightenment such as David Hume and Adam Smith had made it clear that the spread of enlightenment (and commercial society) depended on the eradication of enthusiasm in the general population. What these philosophical attacks on enthusiasm often had in common with the older religious discourse was the suspicion of the passions intruding themselves on to the purity of rational discourse. For the impulses that the enthusiast mistook for the voice of God were widely identified with the excitements of the body, especially given that classic enthusiastic behaviour was identified with the shaking and quaking of religious sects. Kant's belief that '*Enthusiasm*' was a lesser evil than '*Schwärmerei*'

---

[32] Nathan Drake, *Literary Hours, or Sketches Critical and Narrative* (1798), 29.
[33] Anthony J. La Vopa, 'The Philosopher and the *Schwärmer*: On the Career of a German Epithet from Luther to Kant', *Huntington Library Quarterly*, 60 (1998), 86. See Kant, *Critique of the Power of Judgment*, ed. Paul Guyer, trans. Paul Guyer and Eric Matthews (Cambridge: Cambridge University Press, 2000), 156, and the commentary in Jean-François Lyotard, *Lessons on the Analytic of the Sublime*, trans. Elizabeth Rottenberg (Stanford, Calif.: Stanford University Press, 1994), 153–6.

was founded on the idea that the former was further from the sensuality of the crowd (a distinction that Coleridge probably picked up on and developed in the desynonimization of 'enthusiasm' from 'fanaticism').[34] If through Methodism and the Evangelical movements, for instance, affect came to play an increasing role in eighteenth-century religion, that role was carefully envigilated to make sure that it did not degenerate into enthusiasm. Practices such as Methodist 'love feasts' were always suspected of being outlets for incompletely sublimated sexual feelings.[35] Warmth in matters of religion remained an object of regulatory discipline, especially where its effects were written on the body. This disciplinary gaze can be regarded as part of the more general preference, identified by Barbara Stafford, for conceiving truth in terms of 'spirit' or 'idea' as opposed to the grossness of the body.[36] The data of the senses might be the prerequisite for truth to emerge, but the truth itself was often granted a transcendent status. Within the aesthetic sphere the same distinction as in the religious was made. Joseph Addison, for instance, made it clear that 'the pleasures of the Imagination . . . are not so gross as those of Sense'.[37] To use William Galperin's terms, tensions between the 'visible' and the 'visionary' in the Romantic period perpetuated this same division.[38] What has become known as the Romantic ideology looked for a realm of Imagination beyond the exigencies of the senses, even if it also sought to anchor itself in them as an insurance against the dangerous 'unworlding' aspects of enthusiasm.[39] Coleridge looked for 'something *great*—something *one & indivisible*' beyond the 'immense heap of *little* things' (Griggs, i. 349). Whether in philosophical, religious, or aesthetic

[34] See Kant, *Critique of the Power of Judgment*, 156. Kant defines '*Schwärmerei*' as the 'delusion of being able to see something beyond all bounds of sensibility'.

[35] See, for late instances of this kind of analysis, Hunt's comments on 'the influence the body has upon this kind of devotion' (H 55) and Southey's *Life of Wesley*, i. 224–5.

[36] Barbara Stafford, *Body Criticism: Imaging the Unseen in Enlightenment Art and Medicine* (Cambridge, Mass.: MIT Press, 1997).

[37] *The Spectator*, ed. Donald F. Bond, 5 vols. (Oxford: Oxford University Press, 1965), iii. 537 (No. 411, 21 June 1712).

[38] William H. Galperin, *The Return of the Visible in British Romanticism* (Baltimore: Johns Hopkins University Press, 1993) detects a division in Romantic ideas of subjectivity 'between the visible and the visionary', that is, between the material world and one '*no sooner seen* than imaginatively appropriated', 3. The former he describes as 'the central and unrivaled repressed of romanticism', 3.

[39] For a useful account of the role of 'unworlding' in 'poetic enthusiasm', see Irlam, *Elations*, 7–8.

discourse, the confusion of the bodily and the spiritual was liable to be identified with an improperly regulated enthusiasm.

Possibly I may have hitherto been representing the discourse on enthusiasm too much as a technology of denial rather than production and regulation; for enthusiasm *was* desired as well as disavowed. Indeed literature and other forms of aesthetic production were granted a special status in relation to this process. Before moving on to say more about the specifically literary aspects of this desire for enthusiasm, however, I would like to say a little more about its role in relation to religion. Although the evangelical revival did witness a revision of the latitude granted to affect in religion, very few evangelicals were ready to use the word enthusiasm in a positive sense in this context. A partial exception is William Law, who seriously influenced Wesley, but his relative tolerance of enthusiasm was often blamed for those features of Methodism deemed excessive: 'it is said that few books have', wrote Robert Southey, 'ever made so many religious enthusiasts as his Christian Perfection and his Serious Call' (*Life of Wesley*, i. 57). Wesley himself felt constantly impelled to distinguish 'real experimental religion' from enthusiasm.[40] One thing that needs to be recognized is that what was described as enthusiasm in religion as in all the other spheres covered by this book depended upon who was looking and at whom. Some kinds of people were deemed to be incapable of conforming to proper codes of behaviour whatever their actual practise. Crudely put, for some Anglicans, particularly those of a High Church orientation, merely to be a Methodist (even before its schism from the Church) or Dissenter was to be tainted with enthusiasm. Prejudice this may have been, but it was structured by the cultural logic of the discourse on enthusiasm: only the delirious enthusiast was so committed to the self-sufficiency of his or her persuasion that he or she could abandon the tried and tested institutions of the Church. For if the Church of England could not provide truth, it could at least offer itself as a safe haven of tradition with tried and tested limits. The more 'rational' the behaviour of the Dissenter or Methodist, the harder it was to make the charge of

---

[40] See, for instance, *A Second Letter to the Author of the Enthusiasm of Methodists and Papists Compar'd* (1751) in *The Works of John Wesley*, ed. F. Baker et al. (Oxford: Oxford University Press, 1975–84; Nashville, Tenn.: Abingdon, 1984–), vol. xi, *Appeals*, ed. Gerald R. Craggs (Oxford: Oxford University Press, 1975), xi. 380.

enthusiasm stick perhaps, but many tried, especially in times of political and social uncertainty. When Dissenters such as the respected scientist Joseph Priestley pressed for the abolition of the Test and Corporation Acts, they were liable to be pictured as ranting enthusiasts, however much their case was couched in the language of the Enlightenment. Style, written and personal, was one barometer of self-regulation. When Priestley used the vehement language of the biblical prophets, he was making himself particularly vulnerable to the charge. When a woman used this language, as Anna Letitia Barbauld did in poems and pamphlets of the early 1790s, she was even more open to the accusation, because women were taken to be peculiarly vulnerable to mistaking their physical desires for illapses of the spirit. But many Dissenters too, of course, were keen to define themselves against enthusiasm. Broadly speaking, as Daniel White has said, the circle of Rational Dissenters with which Barbauld was associated affirmed much the same idea of the public sphere as the Anglican mainstream.[41] Priestley and other liberal Dissenters were always keen to represent themselves as guardians of enlightenment principles in Britain. Many Dissenters explicitly distanced themselves from the gloomy enthusiasm of their seventeenth-century forebears on the basis of an ecumenical idea of politeness, even to the point of looking to an eventual reunion with the Church. Barbauld in the 1770s saw such a reunion as part of a general progress of Dissent towards the manners associated with polite sociability.[42] If Dissenters were interested, for instance, in the relationship between biblical prophecy and contemporary politics, they tended to present their interest as the product of scholarly research and not any appeal to the sudden illumination of the spirit. Barbauld even thought that Priestley was coming dangerously close to enthusiasm when he insisted on the theological differences between Dissent and the Church rather than their practical similarities. Broadly speaking, many Anglicans and Dissenters shared the idea of 'practical piety' underlying Pocock's account of the development of Church of England theology. Much of this practical piety, as R. K. Webb has argued, placed a premium on moral improvement in the world-as-it-is rather than sudden and absolute

---

[41] Daniel E. White, 'The "Joineriana": Anna Barbauld, the Aikin Family Circle, and the Dissenting Public Sphere', *Eighteenth-Century Studies*, 32 (1999), 511–33.
[42] See below, Chapter 4.

transformations of either self or society.[43] John Wesley too, for all that he wanted to reanimate religious feelings and keep open the possibility of justification by the inner light of the believer (the foundation of the accusation of enthusiasm for Locke and most others), was careful to distance Methodism from enthusiasm. Both Wesley and Priestley were readier in their different ways to flirt with being accused of enthusiasm, as we will see, than accept empty conformity, but both were sensitive to the point at which unworlding the way-things-are might lead to unworldliness or fruitless speculation.[44] The Evangelical Hannah More's *Practical Piety* (1811) denounced 'dry specularists, frantic enthusiasts' for being enemies to 'active virtue' and 'subverters of the public weal'.[45] More's sense of practical piety was contrasted with 'boundless liberality', that is, those radical ideas of universal benevolence that were the targets of Edmund Burke's redefinition of enthusiasm.[46] Yet for all their emphasis on practicality, and despite the fact that both kept within the bounds of the Church of England, Wesley and even More were accused of enthusiasm at different times. For unbelievers and various kinds of freethinkers, as well as paradoxically enough for the dry men of the High Church tradition, just about any kind of overly demonstrative religious belief was enthusiasm.

To shift from religion back to philosophy, one must acknowledge the important role of Shaftesbury in this study as a rare example of someone prepared to rehabilitate the word 'enthusiasm' itself. Shaftesbury's ideas were deeply influential on the 'moral sense' philosophy developed by Francis Hutcheson, but just as Wesley, who was impressed by Law, did not seek to develop a case in favour of 'enthusiasm' as such, so Hutcheson tended to drop Shaftesbury's attempt to develop a positive use of the word ('benevolence' effectively took its place).[47] The fact was that the word brought with it too much baggage, especially where it was associated with either

---

[43] R. K. Webb, 'Rational Piety' in Knud Haakonssen (ed.), *Enlightenment and Religion: Rational Dissent in Eighteenth-Century Britain* (Cambridge: Cambridge University Press, 1996), 287–311.

[44] For more detail on Wesley see Chapter 1 and on Priestley Chapter 4.

[45] Hannah More, *Practical Piety; or, The Influence of the Religion of the Heart on the Conduct of Life*, 2 vols. (1811), i. 13.

[46] *Thoughts on the Manners of the Great* in *The Works of Hannah More*, 8 vols. (1801), vi. 13.

[47] See the discussion of these two relationships in Chapter 1.

popular participation or innovating attempts to transform the world. When ideas of universal benevolence became associated with radical ideology in the 1790s, however, Burke and others quickly labelled them a species of enthusiasm. So is there any basis left to Irlam's claim that during the eighteenth century attitudes towards 'enthusiasm' as such became softer? There is, in the poetic sphere that is Irlam's main interest. Shaftesbury's ideas, for instance, were influential on a 'line' of poets, including James Thomson and Mark Akenside, who all represented 'enthusiasm' as a necessary part of poetic composition.[48] Independently from Shaftesbury, John Dennis also proposed an idea of the greatest kind of poetry as a form of enthusiasm, but faced severer problems than his aristocratic contemporary in distancing himself from the image of enthusiasm in the broadest pejorative sense. His is a classic example of someone whose practice was deemed insufficiently regulated to protect his poetic enthusiasm from the rougher passions of the crowd. The attempt to separate poetic from religious enthusiasm remained haunted by the latter. This haunting meant that if within the aesthetic sphere enthusiasm was desired as the basis of poetic inspiration, it was also disavowed where it seemed to lead to 'distraction'. The enlightened public sphere could make room for feeling, but only—to use Shaftesbury's term redolent of Foucault—if it was 'regulated' into a healthy form. Expressions of enthusiasm even within poetry were regularly scrutinized to see if they were properly part of the aesthetic sphere.

Discourses are always under construction and never complete, and literature can only really be thought of very loosely as a discourse in the disciplinary Foucauldian sense, notwithstanding Clifford Siskin's recent emphasis on the covert deployment of such boundaries in the period. Indeed its special kind of authority, as Siskin himself has noted, was predicated precisely on being beyond such local disciplinary interests. Yet paradoxically the insubstantiality of its disciplinary boundaries also seemed to leave it open to infection from the currents of languages that swirl around in any society. So while it seemed to offer a safe haven wherein the

---

[48] On Shaftesbury's influence on eighteenth-century poetry, see C. A. Moore, 'Shaftesbury and the Ethical Poets in England, 1700–1760', *PMLA*, 31 (1916), 264–325, and Michael Meehan, *Liberty and Poetics in Eighteenth Century England* (Beckenham: Croom Helm, 1986).

dangerous energies of enthusiasm could be regulated into aesthetic form, it was also potentially a treacherous inlet for 'the combustible matters' that 'lie prepared and within ready to take fire at a spark' (*Characteristics*, 23). Encouraging all kinds of people to write on the basis of their enthusiasm by presenting itself as beyond any particular interest, the language of enthusiasm in the poetry of the period seemed to be encouraging the very delirium it was meant to be a protection against. This book then is concerned both with the discourse on enthusiasm and enthusiastic discourse. The former comprises the discursive construction of enthusiasm as both a dangerous excess of social energy and also a restorative draft of emotion. The latter indicates those practices, including poetry, but also the habitus of the Methodist chapel and the field meeting, that to a greater or lesser degree manifested this enthusiasm. Chapter 1 outlines the development of the discourse on enthusiasm from the seventeenth into the eighteenth century, looking at the way this discourse migrated from a strictly religious context and how that transformation was complicated by a more tolerant attitude to affect and sympathy (sometimes even named 'enthusiasm'). At the same time it is concerned with the relationship between this discourse and the various practices of enthusiasm. These range from the poetic tradition that attempted to rehabilitate the term after Shaftesbury to the counter-public of chapels and field meetings that asserted the sufficiency of the inner light against the conventions of the classical public sphere. Chapter 2 takes a more detailed look at the context of the 1790s, a crucial period in the development of the idea that enlightenment *transparence* itself might be a species of enthusiasm, but also the testing-ground for the poets whose writing provides the focus for the second half of the book. Novelists such as Fielding in *Joseph Andrews* and Tobias Smollett in *Humphry Clinker* on to Maria Edgeworth in *Belinda* could be more unequivocally hostile to enthusiasm in religion, and its secular variants, perhaps because their literary territory was coming to be defined precisely in contrast to the unworlding effects that poets increasingly claimed as their own. Indeed, the prominent attacks on Methodism in Fielding and Smollett could be seen as part of the covert struggle for authority between the novel and poetry. In this respect, there is a link between Smollett's attack on Methodist preachers and their female adherents in *Humphry Clinker*, and his dislike of the frothiness of Shaftesbury expressed in *Peregrine*

Pickle.[49] The novel's commitment 'to describe life or manners in real or probable situations' as Mary Hays put it, meant that its disavowal of sudden transports was less haunted by a desire for their unworlding effects, although this perhaps was relatively less true of those novelists (such as Hays herself) whose primary concern was with sensibility and sympathy than the realistic representation of society.[50] Certainly the cultural problem of enthusiasm was most acute in poetics.

The poets who provide the focus for the second part of the book emerged from a context wherein ideas of universal benevolence and sympathy had been put to a severe examination by the lights of the discourse on enthusiasm (from inside as well as outside the radical movement itself). The second half of the book looks at four writers in detail as test cases for the claim that a revivification of the critical purchase of the term enthusiasm can help us understand nuances in their writing that have become dead to us. Each of the writers contributed to the discourse on enthusiasm, and each of them contributed to the discursive practice of enthusiasm in more or less regulated ways, although the choice of these particular writers also has to do with their current high status in the academy. Their centrality for us as readers now allows us to see very vividly how important enthusiasm was as a problem then. At one extreme stands Blake's faith that 'Mere Enthusiasm is the All in All!' (E 645). Usually poets at the time were caught in a more ambivalent position. They sought after a power that they feared might destroy them. Coleridge's desynonymization of enthusiasm from fanaticism was one attempt to separate out these conflicting aspects. Yet even he could not quite convince himself that the former's 'endless power of semination' (*SM* 16) was any different from 'the contagious nature of Enthusiasm, and other acute or chronic diseases of deliberative Assemblies' (*Friend*, ii. 127).

[49] For attacks on enthusiasm in the eighteenth-century novel, see S. J. Rogal, 'Enlightened Enthusiasm: Anti-Methodism in the Literature of the Mid and Late Eighteenth Century', *Enlightenment Essays*, 5 (1974), 3–13. For Smollett's view of Shaftesbury's frothiness, see *The Adventures of Peregrine Pickle*, ed. James L. Clifford (London: Oxford University Press, 1964), 232.

[50] Mary Hays, 'To the Editor of the Monthly Magazine', *Monthly Magazine*, 4 (1798), 180–1, reproduced in *Memoirs of Emma Courtney*, ed. Marilyn L. Brooks (Peterborough, Ont.: Broadview, 1999), 284–6.

PART I

The Discourse on Enthusiasm

CHAPTER ONE

Commanding Enthusiasm through the Eighteenth Century

Enthusiasm's the best thing, I repeat;
Only, we can't command it; fire and life
Are all, dead matter's nothing, we agree.[1]

BISHOP BLOUGHRAM IN Browning's poem is complaining about the scarcity of religious feeling in what he perceives to be a commercial and godless society. Two centuries had passed since Britain had been ripped apart by religious enthusiasm spilling over into the political arena. Something happened between the middle of the seventeenth and the middle of the nineteenth in terms of attitudes towards enthusiasm, but it did not happen suddenly, nor did it represent a complete rupture with what had gone before. Although enthusiasm in religious and other spheres did come to be increasingly valued as a humanizing and even healing power in the eighteenth century, the fear that the cure could become a poison remained. Commanding enthusiasm seemed to be a question of regulating a dangerously unstable internal force that threatened the integrity of both the individual and society as a whole. This chapter tries in its own way to command enthusiasm too; that is, it attempts an overview of the development of the discourse on enthusiasm from the late seventeenth to the early nineteenth centuries and charts the tense relationship it had with certain kinds of newly enthusiastic discourse. The recurrent and sustained interest in the term 'enthusiasm' across all kinds of discourses throughout the period indicates that it was foundational to the mentality of the long eighteenth century. The political settlement of 1688, partially dissolved in 1832, was conditioned by the experience of the Civil War.

[1] Robert Browning, 'Bishop Bloughram's Apology', in *Poetical Works 1833–1864*, ed. Ian Jack (Oxford: Oxford University Press, 1970), ll. 556–8.

The 1640s and 1650s were widely regarded in the eighteenth century as the product of religious enthusiasm run riot. A historical memory of uneducated prophets and tub preachers rushing into print to announce the rule of the Saints, however vague and imprecise its grasp of the historical facts, provided the *locus classicus* of enthusiasm for the century that followed. While freedom of the press was perhaps the most vaunted of the liberties of the eighteenth-century Englishman, the very engine of enlightenment, these historical associations meant that the press was always suspected of betraying itself to enlightenment's chaotic nemesis.[2] This relationship between liberty and anarchy—in which enthusiasm frequently played a defining role—was at the centre of a century of thought about the nature of civil society inaugurated by the settlement of 1688.

Enthusiasm was the monstrous alter ego of eighteenth-century civility. My particular interests here are oriented towards the literary, but only insofar as the idea of literariness itself was defined in relation to ideas of politeness that depended on their difference from enthusiasm. Enthusiasm was the very anti-self of enlightenment notions of civility, partly because in order to prevent a recurrence of the violence of the seventeenth century, it was deemed necessary to discipline spiritual agency. Spiritual matters were preferably excluded from the public sphere. Even to dispute religious matters in public, as we will see throughout this book, could be represented as enthusiasm. Rancour in religion was a charge regularly laid against Methodism. Even the great scientist and Dissenter Joseph Priestley could be accused of enthusiasm when he insisted on the importance of candour in religion. Many even of Priestley's fellow Dissenters agreed with Edmund Burke that 'politics and the pulpit are terms that have little agreement'.[3] Literature came to be seen by many as a space where religious 'feelings' could be aired without the violent passions of controversy being provoked. Geoffrey Hartman has even gone so far as to trace the

---

[2] On anxieties surrounding the proliferation of print towards the end of the eighteenth century, see Jon Klancher, *The Making of English Reading Audiences, 1790–1832* (Madison: University of Wisconsin Press, 1987) and Paul Keen, *The Crisis of Literature in the 1790s: Print Culture and the Public Sphere* (Cambridge: Cambridge University Press, 1999).

[3] Edmund Burke, *Reflections on the Revolution in France* (1790), in *The Writings and Speeches of Edmund Burke*, gen. ed. Paul Langford, viii: *The French Revolution 1790–94*, ed. L. G. Mitchell (Oxford: Oxford University Press, 1989), 62.

origins of modern literary criticism in English to a tradition of 'civility' designed as a defence against 'enthusiasm, religious or secular, private or collective'.[4] Using Addison and Steele's essays from the *Spectator* as his prime examples, he suggests that literariness came into being at the turn of the eighteenth century as a category defined against the intemperate ranting and preaching of hacks and evangelists.[5] His primary concern is to defend the disinterestedness of literary criticism from the incursions of latter-day hacks and evangelists. I suspect he would number myself among these. For what I want to do in this study is to treat Hartman's historical claims seriously, examine why and how enthusiasm was regulated, and explore the ways in which this discourse of regulation structured the literature of the Romantic period. Against Hartman's perspective has to be weighed the one put forward by critics such as Irlam, outlined in my opening chapter, that sees enthusiasm as becoming increasingly desirable at least within literary culture. The unworlding of enthusiasm from the perspective of these critics was increasingly valued as a means of returning an alienated society to values that were seen as more essentially human. In fact I will argue that these two attitudes to enthusiasm remained in an uneasy tension throughout the period covered by this book. Even poetic enthusiasm was regarded as dangerous if it did not regulate itself sufficiently against the danger that it would drown the very subjectivity that it was meant to be buoying up.

THE DISCOURSE ON ENTHUSIASM

This section will offer a more detailed account of the discourse on enthusiasm adumbrated in my Introduction. While it cannot hope to provide a full account of the development of that discourse in the wake of the Interregnum, it does try to demonstrate the continuities that stretched from the late seventeenth century to the early nineteenth. What did the word 'enthusiasm' originally mean in English usage? The Greek original was associated with the inspiration of the poet and the seer. For the classically educated elite, this origin always kept open the possibility of thinking of a noble enthusiasm

---

[4] Geoffrey H. Hartman, *Minor Prophecies: The Literary Essay in the Culture Wars* (Cambridge, Mass.: Harvard University Press, 1991), 177.
[5] Ibid. 78.

connected with the greatness of the Ancients. In its English form, however, without entirely ever losing the connection with classical inspiration, the word's primary function was a technical and religious one, denoting the delusion that one was possessed by the Holy Spirit. For most people in the eighteenth century and for some decades afterwards, enthusiasm continued to mean something excessive and erroneous by definition.[6] In Protestant Britain, the term had initially become important as a means of describing and thereby controlling excessive zeal. John Douglas writing *An Apology for the Clergy* in 1755 described enthusiasts as the 'spurious children of the reformation'.[7] 'Theologically speaking', as Michael Heyd puts it, the discourse of enthusiasm 'centred around the question of the working of the Holy Spirit and the role it played in leading the individual Christian to Truth and Salvation.'[8] For most Anglican theologians, prophecy and the gifts of the spirit were taken to have ceased after the apostolic age. Writing in 1795, the clerical author of *Memoirs of Pretended Prophets* argued that 'since the sacred canon was completed, no person has given satisfactory evidence of his being a prophet'.[9] The 1640s and 1650s were widely regarded as a period when enthusiasm had taken possession of the body politic. Above all else, enthusiasm was associated in Britain with the 'the fury of the millenial sects'.[10] Although he praised the emergence of toleration and liberty of the press in the Interregnum, David Hume's *History of England* (1754–62) played an important part in keeping this view of events before the eyes of the general reading public of the late eighteenth century. Consequently, prophesying continued to be seen as a sign of a dangerous enthusiasm, especially where it seemed designed to stir up popular unrest or ventured into the political arena. The late eighteenth century retained a firmer and more detailed memory of the prophets of the Civil War as examples of the dangers posed to the stability of

[6] For an invaluable exposition of the development of the semantic range of the word 'enthusiasm' over this period, see Susie I. Tucker, *Enthusiasm: A Study in Semantic Change* (Cambridge: Cambridge University Press, 1972).

[7] Douglas, *An Apology for the Clergy* (1755), 2.

[8] Michael Heyd, 'The Reaction to Enthusiasm in the Seventeenth Century: Towards an Integrative Approach', *Journal of Modern History*, 53 (1981), 260.

[9] *Memoirs of Pretended Prophets. Who have appeared in different ages of the World, and especially in Modern Times* (1795), 20.

[10] J. G. A. Pocock, 'Enthusiasm: The Antiself of Enlightenment', *Huntington Library Quarterly*, 60 (1998), 10.

Church and State by popular religious enthusiasm than is often allowed. *Memoirs of Pretended Prophets*, for instance, contains a list of examples stretching back as far as the Middle Ages.[11] During the controversy surrounding the Paddington Prophet Richard Brothers in 1794–5 frequent mention was made of the millenarians of the previous century. Perhaps rather more surprisingly, the judge who presided at the Treason Trials of 1794 compared Thomas Hardy, secretary of the London Corresponding Society, to Thomas Venner, who had led the rising of the millenarian Fifth Monarchists against the Restoration over a century before.[12] My next chapter will develop the connections between the popular radical movement of the 1790s and the discourse on enthusiasm. Suffice to say at this stage that enthusiasm had become available for making sense of any popular phenomenon, religious or otherwise, deemed threatening by the cultural hegemony of the Anglican Church and the broader culture of politeness in the eighteenth century.

Although the political settlement after 1688 came to guarantee freedom of worship to Trinitarian Protestants, most Dissenters were still liable to be regarded as tainted with enthusiasm. Even Joseph Addison, a man far from being a High Church bigot, could claim that all sects outside the Anglican fold had 'strong Tinctures of Enthusiasm'.[13] During the campaign for the abolition of the Test and Corporation Acts at the other end of the century, opponents of the Dissenters routinely represented them as zealous enthusiasts eager to blow up the established order of civil society.[14] The association was not simply historical. J. G. A. Pocock seems to think that the light of Reason cherished by Rational Dissenters such as Richard Price really was little more than a transmogrified version of the inner-light theology of the seventeenth century. There is no need to go that far to see that there was a coherent structural logic at work in such accusations. Certainly many Anglican contemporaries thought confident assertions of the right to free enquiry in matters of religion looked like a casting off of the mediations of the national

---

[11] *Memoirs of Pretended Prophets* ranged from the sixteenth-century Anabaptists on the continent right up to the contemporary example of Richard Brothers.

[12] See the discussion of Hardy's trial in Chapter 2.

[13] *The Spectator*, ed. Donald F. Bond, 5 vols. (Oxford: Oxford University Press, 1965), ii. 289 (No. 201, 20 Oct. 1711).

[14] My accounts of Coleridge and Barbauld in Chapters 3 and 4 effectively provide detailed case studies of the way this set of associations worked in their careers.

Church of the kind always taken to be a defining feature of enthusiasm. Earlier in the century Hume had made a distinction between enthusiasm and superstition. The former was associated with anti-clericalism and an antagonism towards religious institutions, the latter with priestcraft. Whereas superstition abjected the self, enthusiasm, for Hume, had its origins in 'presumptuous pride and confidence'.[15] In its most extreme manifestations, 'the inspired person comes to regard himself as a distinguished favourite of the Divinity'.[16] This influx of divine power was also seen to involve a dangerous dissolution of subjectivity in which, as Nigel Smith puts it, 'the distinction between individual utterance and Scriptural authority dissolves'.[17] Thus, paradoxically, the arrogance of the enthusiast involved the destruction of his or her proper self. The apocalyptic ecstasies of the prophet threatened the continuous self-identity that so much eighteenth-century writing sought to affirm. Enthusiasm threatened a stable subjectivity as much as it did the stability of the body politic.

It was in the aftermath of the Civil War that 'enthusiasm' really developed its own discourse, a network of associations that articulated a powerful cultural logic for describing certain kinds of religious and other forms of behaviour in terms of deviance. A language of pathology soon developed to explain enthusiasm's explosive presence in the body politic.[18] Anglican writers developed the idea of enthusiasm as the product of vapours clouding the brain. Two texts published in 1656, Meric Casaubon's *Treatise Concerning Enthusiasm* and Henry More's *Enthusiasmus Triumphatus*, began the process of understanding enthusiasm as a product of diseased minds. Enthusiasm was increasingly seen as a pathology of the individual and society, rather than a heresy: a 'Distemper' which 'disposes a man to listen to the Magisterial Dictates of an over-bearing *Phansy*, more then to the calm and cautious insinuation of free *Reason*'.[19] Psychological explanations of

---

[15] Hume, 'Of Superstition and Enthusiasm', in *Essays Moral, Political, and Literary*, ed. T. H. Green and T. H. Grose, 2 vols. (Longmans, Green & Co., 1875), i. 148.

[16] Ibid. 145.

[17] Nigel Smith, 'Introduction', in Nigel Smith (ed.), *A Collection of Ranter Writings from the 17th Century* (Junction Books, 1983), 31.

[18] See Michael Heyd, *'Be Sober and Reasonable': The Critique of Enthusiasm in the Seventeenth and Early Eighteenth Centuries* (Leiden: E. J. Brill, 1995), 92–108.

[19] Henry More, *Enthusiasmus Triumphatus* (1662) quoted in Lawrence E. Klein, *Shaftesbury and the Culture of Politeness: Moral Discourse and Cultural Politics in*

this distemper were increasingly supplemented by physiological accounts. Overheated by the 'Phansy' the animal spirits responsible for transmitting impressions to the mind were believed to give off vapours, which clouded their passage and allowed the vagaries of the imagination to be mistaken for external reality. The anonymous author of *A Dissuasive against Enthusiasm* (1708) gave a typical account of the relationship between the imagination and the animal spirits in producing enthusiasm:

> A Delirium, or Natural Enthusiasm arising from a disorder'd Brain, occa-sion'd by great Fervency of Temper, or violent Agitations of the animal Spirits, will necessarily impregnate the Fancy, cause the Images of Things to come into it very fast, and produce a very ready Invention of matter, and copious Fluency of Words.[20]

Notions of the 'animal spirits' as a 'subtle liquid' were later dis-placed by the nerve paradigm, but the basic medical account of enthusiasm as interference in the processing of sensations remained in force. Enthusiasm was commonly thought of as either a species of mania or delirium throughout the period. 'Distraction' became a key word in describing its psychological effects. Oscillating between the gloominess of the Puritan and the sensuality of the antinomian (often in the same person), it came to be regarded as a form of madness.

At the beginning of the nineteenth century, Leigh Hunt thought that the fiery popular preacher William Huntington and the poet William Cowper were both the victims of enthusiasm. Their different responses, he explained, were due to their different physical and psychological constitutions: so that 'HUNTINGTON laughs, COWPER goes mad' (H 53). Social class was at the bottom of Hunt's distinction. The nervous and genteel poet Cowper collapses in upon himself. The coarse former coal-heaver turned preacher Huntington is inspired with the energy to spread the Word, dissolving himself back into the crowd whence he came. The one was subjectivity devouring itself. In the other subjectivity is never even really achieved. From the elite perspective of Hunt, delirium *is* consciousness for someone such

Early Eighteenth-Century England (Cambridge: Cambridge University Press, 1994), 162.

[20] *A Dissuasive against Enthusiasm. Wherein the Pretensions of the Modern Prophets to Divine Inspiration and the Power of Working Miracles are Examined and Confuted by Scripture and Matter of Fact* (1708), 45.

as Huntington. Whatever the model accounting for its progress within the individual, the fear of contagion remained central to the discourse of enthusiasm. Michael Heyd has shown that several writers in the late seventeenth and early eighteenth centuries subscribed to the idea that the effluvia produced by the animal spirits were capable of literally infecting others. An essay on the subject printed in the *Gentleman's Magazine* in 1735 was titled 'Enthusiasm as Catching as the Plague'.[21] Enthusiasm was regarded as violent and disruptive, it was the product of vulnerable minds, readily transmitted by the irrational mob, its ecstasies were to be contrasted with a reasonableness which was increasingly used to define a politeness appropriate to the development of what after Habermas we have come to call the 'bourgeois public sphere'.[22] Insofar as this ideal of a modern public was advocated in the eighteenth century, it depended on the ideal of a communion of autonomous readers, a position between self-absorption and dissemination, and assumed a regulated conversation between stable subjects given neither to sudden transports or irrational swarming together nor to a gloomy isolationist retreat into the self.

Any form of religious zeal that threatened the orderliness of society was likely to be identified with enthusiasm throughout the period covered by this book.[23] By 1735 this threat did not even need to be religious. Once the term was medicalized, it was free to be attached to any kind of socially disruptive mania. The *Gentleman's Magazine* defined 'enthusiasm' as 'any exorbitant monstrous Appetite of the human Mind, hurrying the Will in pursuit of an Object without the Concurrence, or against the Light of Reason, and Common Sense'.[24] Enthusiasm of this kind was especially associated with innovation. Swift saw it in any desire to 'advance new systems with such an eager Zeal'.[25] When Henry Sacheverell linked '*any Upstart Novelist* [innovator] with the '*Self-conceited*

[21] *Gentleman's Magazine*, 5 (1735), 203.

[22] See Jürgen Habermas, *The Structural Transformation of the Public Sphere: An Inquiry into a Category of Bourgeois Society*, trans. Thomas Burger with Frederick Lawrence (Cambridge, Mass.: Polity Press, 1989).

[23] Although sobriety itself, taken to excess, was, of course, a hallmark of Puritan enthusiasm.

[24] *Gentleman's Magazine*, 5 (1735), 203.

[25] Jonathan Swift, *A Tale of the Tub: To which is Added The Battle of the Books and The Mechanical Operation of the Spirit*, ed. A. C. Guthkelch and D. Nichol Smith, 2nd edn. (Oxford: Clarendon Press, 1958), 166. See also, Heyd, 'The Reaction to Enthusiasm in the Seventeenth Century', 266–7.

Enthusiast', he was identifying a pairing that was a staple of Swift's writing and one which was to endure throughout the century (with a spectacular renaissance in Burke).[26] My next chapter will deal with the coalescence of philosophical system-building and emotional and religious fervour under the rubric of enthusiasm, but it is worth pointing out now how early this elision occurs in the writing of Swift and other High Church polemicists. What these more general understandings of the dangers of enthusiasm tended to retain from the primary religious discourse was the idea of the peculiar vulnerability to it of the masses. Enthusiasm comes to name the tendency within the population to be swept by crazes. Reflecting the still strong association with Presbyterianism, the *Gentleman's Magazine*, for instance, printed an opinion that 'the lowest Class of People' in Edinburgh had 'generally speaking, a turn to Enthusiasm, and so strong is its Influence, such is the force of delusion, that they can work themselves up to a firm Persuasion and thorough belief that any Mischief they are able to do is not only lawful but laudable'.[27]

Against this expansion of the negative reach of the idea of enthusiasm has to be weighed early signs of a relative tolerance to it in religious discourse. Faced with the deadening effects of rational religion, clergymen such as the Dissenters Isaac Watts and Philip Doddridge as well the non-juror William Law started to urge a renewed sense of the role of the affections in religion. Both Law and Watts even entertained the possibility of a positive definition of the word 'enthusiasm' in religion, but generally speaking little latitude was given to such suggestions. Although Doddridge and Watts were careful to distinguish 'affectionate religion' from the rough passions usually associated with enthusiasm, both were attacked for opening a door to popular licentiousness.[28] Almost a century later, Robert Southey could still castigate Law for trying to rehabilitate the word: 'it is said that few books have ever made so many religious enthusiasts as his Christian Perfection and his Serious Call' (*Life of Wesley*, i. 57). By the time Southey was writing, faced with the dangers of

[26] Henry Sacheverall, *Perils of False Brethren* (1709) quoted in Tucker, *Enthusiasm*, 32.
[27] *Gentleman's Magazine*, 7 (1737), 458.
[28] See Isabel Rivers, *Reason, Grace, and Sentiment: A Study of the Language of Religion and Ethics in England, 1660–1780*, 2 vols. (Cambridge: Cambridge University Press, 1991–2000), i. 192–3.

infidelism and atheism associated with the French Revolution, religious warmth was frequently invoked as a bulwark against popular unrest. One might, therefore, expect more latitude to have been granted to attempts to revalorize the word 'enthusiasm' in its religious circumstance. Several writers, including Coleridge, did make the attempt.[29] Through a process of desynonymization, ignoring more general usage, 'enthusiasm' was defined strictly in contrast to 'fanaticism'. The inner light of enthusiasm was being quarantined from its long association with the passions of the multitude or the dissolution of the self (Law too had stressed a quiet mysticism rather than missionary fervour).[30] A few years before Coleridge made his attempt, Thomas Ludlam distinguished enthusiasm from fanaticism as an error of '*knowledge*' or perception rather than the claim to receive '*directions*' from God.[31] The latter instead of channelling religious feelings inward and upward, as it were, was generally construed as less forgivable for urging them outwards and downwards towards the mob. Any Christian attempt to disparage too much warmth in religion, however, always had to be chary of bringing religion per se into disrepute. Ludlam shared with Isaac Taylor the sense that for cynical freethinkers 'any degree of feeling in matters of religion is enthusiasm'.[32] Wesley had made a similar complaint in his *Journal*: 'Whatever is spoke of the religion of the heart, and of the inward workings of the Spirit of God, must appear enthusiasm to those who have not felt them.'[33] While prophecy and direct inspiration may have stopped with the last page of the Bible, the Holy Spirit could not be dispensed with entirely by Christians, even by Anglicans. Attacks on enthusiasm by Christians had to be careful not to sound like Hobbes: 'when it is said, that God *inspired* into man the breath of life, no more is meant then that God gave

[29] Coleridge shared Law's interest in Jacob Boehme. See Chapter 3 for a discussion of Coleridge's ambivalence about the latter's enthusiasm.

[30] See his *An Appeal to All that Doubt or Disbelieve the Truths of the Gospel* (1740), especially the appended 'Some Animadversions upon Dr. Trapp's Reply'. I am grateful to Professor Isabel Rivers for these references, and for the opportunity to look at her forthcoming *DNB* article on Law.

[31] Thomas Ludlam, *Four Essays on the Ordinary and Extraordinary Operations of the Holy Spirit; on the Application of Experience to Religion; and of Enthusiasm and Fanaticism* (1797), 68.

[32] Isaac Taylor, *The Natural History of Fanaticism* (1833), quoted in Tucker, *Enthusiasm*, 61.

[33] *The Journal of the Rev. John Wesley, A.M.*, ed. N. Curnock, 8 vols. (1909-16), ii. 319.

unto him vitall motion'.[34] Faced with the emergence of a popular deism influenced by Thomas Paine at the end of the eighteenth century, Thomas Thomason imagined infidels exclaiming 'against the prophets for encouraging enthusiasm by their sublime descriptions of the deity'.[35] 'Every good Christian is indeed inspired,' wrote one clergyman in 1799, but true spirituality was distinguished from enthusiasm in that the former was 'of a more private nature'.[36] Great store was set by steady spiritual growth that suggested the coherent development of the whole being. Sudden transformations, the 'extraordinary calls', for instance, associated with Methodism throughout the eighteenth and early nineteenth centuries, were always likely to be satirized as enthusiasm.[37] Well aware of the disruptive nature of claims to direct illumination, and without giving way to deism or the materialism of Hobbes, the Church looked for a mediated concept of the divine, a theology which affirmed the presence of God, but never his immanence.[38] Revealed religion was defended, but only the labours of scholarship or disciplined devotion could come to an understanding of the divine nature, and even that was more by the way of a glimpse of its workings than an immediate apprehension of its essence. Only those who 'best understand those Scriptures' are fitted to be 'spiritual Instructors and Guides'.[39]

'For most of the eighteenth century' as R. K. Webb puts it, 'one of the highest compliments that could be paid to a minister was to say that he was a practical preacher, that is, that his sermons led his hearers to a wide range of reflections on living a Christian life. The compliments did not extend to the preaching of strictly political sermons—apart from exhortations to patriotic or dynastic loyalty in times of crisis—or to pointed injunctions about the daily conduct of

---

[34] Thomas Hobbes, *Leviathan*, ed. with an introduction by C. B. Macpherson (Harmondsworth: Penguin, 1985 repr.), 440. On Hobbes's role in the development of the discourse on enthusiasm, see Pocock, 'Antiself of Enlightenment', 12–14.

[35] Thomas Thomason, *An Essay Tending to Prove that the Holy Scriptures, Rightly Understood, do not give Encouragement to Enthusiasm or Superstition* (1795), 5.

[36] *A Treatise on Inspiration; in which the Pretence to Extraordinary Inspiration, is Considered, and Clearly and Fully Refuted* (York, 1799), 5.

[37] See below for the Bishop of Exeter's attacks on 'extraordinary calls'; and for the significance of the phrase to *The Prelude*, see Chapter 5.

[38] See Pocock, 'Antiself of Enlightenment', 8–9 and 17.

[39] *A Treatise on Inspiration*, a2.

business or the relations of one social group to another.'[40] Practical or rational piety was a cross-denominational aspiration throughout the century. If devotion conflicted too much with everyday life or led to religious disputatiousness on matters of theology, it was likely to be charged with enthusiasm. Of course, as we shall see, different religious groups had particular opinions on what qualified as 'practical' or 'rational' belief. For all his stress on Reason as the core of Christian life, it was easy for Joseph Priestley to be represented as a throwback to the enthusiasts of the seventeenth century when he mixed religious prophecy with political radicalism. Even so, most religious groups agreed that devotion without some sort of disciplinary element or 'practical' outcome opened the door to enthusiasm. Part of the scandal of enthusiasm, as we shall see, was that it seemed to offer the prospect of something for nothing. That is why it was more often attached to doctrines, antinomianism being the extreme example, which privileged faith over works. Figures such as Jacob Boehme and George Fox were regarded as notorious enthusiasts in part because they shunned rigorous study and abandoned their trades. When in 1723 a freethinker wrote to the *British Journal* accusing the Christian martyrs of a 'crackt Enthusiasm', a pious correspondent reminded him that their zeal had been accompanied by 'Real Wisdom, Excellent Learning, and cool and solid Virtue'. Even the Old Testament prophets, it seems, could barely be allowed a view of God unmediated by hard work and practical virtue.[41]

True or 'practical' piety to the eighteenth century was not just the product of wisdom and learning, it was often defined by a modest restraint which kept its revelations to itself, and, in the process, preserved the unity of that self. 'There is not only more reverence in still adoration, but there is more real feeling; the voice has nothing to do with the expression of ineffable sentiments,' wrote Leigh Hunt in 1809 (H 56). Enthusiasm, in contrast, was defined by its pressing desire to broadcast its spiritual discoveries and so thin the substance of real piety. Despite the efforts of some writers, such as Law, Ludlam, and Coleridge, to distinguish 'enthusiasm' as a private feeling of religious warmth from crowd-inciting 'fanaticism', James

---

[40] R. K. Webb, 'Rational Piety', in Knud Haakonssen (ed.), *Enlightenment and Religion: Rational Dissent in Eighteenth-Century Britain* (Cambridge: Cambridge University Press, 1996), 289.

[41] See Tucker, *Enthusiasm*, 39–40.

Lackington acknowledged that few of his contemporaries in practice respected the distinction:

Was it possible to keep the enthusiast at all times free from fanaticism, I believe the mischief to society would not be so great, as in that case, enthusiasm would be a more harmless madness; but it seems impossible to keep the two characters separate, which is the reason that the terms are often used by writers indiscriminately.[42]

The terms he pointed out could not be kept separate because in practice introverted religious warmth all too quickly led to extroverted missionary zeal. Taken up by an ecstasy of religious experience, ravished in the spirit, the rational self abdicated responsibility and either dispersed itself into the crowd or imploded into itself. The buttoned-in, rational subjectivity beloved of the eighteenth century is washed away in the 'copious fluency of words'.

This abdication of the properly bounded self was also thought to involve the dissolution of gender boundaries. The male prophet was often presented as unmanly in his failure to control the self. Addison represented enthusiasm as the degeneration of masculine reason:

Nothing is so glorious in the Eyes of Mankind . . . as a strong, steady, masculine Piety; but Enthusiasm and Superstition are the Weaknesses of Human Reason, that expose us to the Scorn and Derision of Infidels, and sink us below the Beasts that perish.[43]

Behind Addison's opinion lies the widespread assumption that women were extraordinarily open to the experience of enthusiasm. The prophetess was a standard figure brought forward in discussions of female hysteria, a figure in which femininity engulfed the regulated subjectivity of the proper lady.[44] In a parody of the Quaker practice of letting women preach, Swift made the female genitalia the oracle of enthusiasm.[45] A century later Hunt was still using the same terms, though more politely veiled, to deride popular Methodism:

---

[42] Lackington, *Memoirs of the Forty-Five First Years of the Life of James Lackington*, 7th edn. (1794), 166.

[43] *Spectator*, ii. 290.

[44] See Deborah M. Valenze, *Prophetic Sons and Daughters: Female Preaching and Popular Religion in Industrial England* (Princeton: Princeton University Press, 1985) for an extended account of reactions to female prophecy and preaching in the period.

[45] Swift, *Tale of the Tub*, 157.

We may see directly what influence the body has upon this kind of devotion, if we examine the temperament of its professors. The female sex, for instance, are acknowledged to possess the greater bodily sensibility, and it is the women who chiefly indulge in these love-sick visions of heaven. (H 55)

Too much emphasis in religious discourse on the ravishment of the spirit was always suspected of confusing literal and metaphorical applications of its terms. Hunt condemned Methodism for being 'full of amatory complaint and bridal sensuality' (H 55). Wesley himself had come to suspect the Moravians who had influenced his early thinking of the same error.[46] Such grossness was associated by Hunt and many before him with an arrogant self-sufficiency that thought itself qualified to approach God without any institutional mediation. Eighteenth-century notions of politeness often appealed to a process of self-division as a necessary step in the construction of the polite and self-controlled individual. Even after a century of so-called rehabilitation, enthusiasm is repeatedly the focus of such disciplinary scenes in Wordsworth's poetry.[47] What is often called Romantic irony in relation to figures of revelation and apocalypse could be construed as another manifestation of the cultural anxiety surrounding unmediated claims to prophetic vision.[48] Claims to the immediate apprehensions of the truth were charged with enthusiasm not only in religious contexts. Coleridge's comparison of Luther's enthusiasm with Rousseau's doctrine of *transparence* is a reflex of the same discourse.[49] Enthusiasm was derided for claiming to be able to see the divine vision with the fleshly senses. The 'visionary' Romanticism of Wordsworth and Coleridge tends to disclaim such power, preferring 'intimations', and frequently in Wordsworth's case, privileging the aural over the visual. Contrary-wise, Blake was accused of madness by Robert Hunt precisely because he eschewed such regulatory precautions. Blake believed after all that the divine could be seen in its 'minute particulars'.[50]

---

[46] L. Tyerman, *The Life and Times of the Rev. John Wesley M.A., Founder of the Methodists*, 3 vols. (1870–1), i. 561–2.

[47] See the discussion of Wordsworth's 'emotion recollected in tranquility' in Chapter 5.

[48] For a reading of the apocalypticism of the poetry of the period in terms of Romantic irony, see Greg Kucich, 'Ironic Apocalypse in Romanticism and the French Revolution', in Keith Hanley and Raman Selden (eds.), *Revolution and English Romanticism: Politics and Rhetoric* (Hemel Hempstead: Harvester, 1990), 67–88.

[49] See Chapter 3.   [50] See Chapter 6.

His version of the sublime was very different from that of many of his Romantic contemporaries in this respect at least.

REGULATION AND REHABILITATION

Having sketched some of the general continuities and developments in the discourse on enthusiasm over the eighteenth century, let me turn now to the question of the rehabilitation of the term. I will start predictably enough with one of the classic pronouncements on enthusiasm. John Locke's *Essay Concerning Human Understanding* had a chapter 'On Enthusiasm' added to its 1700 edition. The text is a defining one in the construction of enthusiasm as the antithesis of enlightenment. The improvement of knowledge for Locke depends on us getting and fixing '*in our Minds clear, distinct, and complete* Ideas' and annexing '*to them proper and constant Names*'.[51] Enthusiasm was the product of 'laying by Reason' and substituting for it 'the ungrounded Fancies of a Man's own Brain'.[52] Rather than sensations grounded in objective causes, the enthusiast was deluded by 'a strong, though ungrounded perswasion of their own Minds that it is a Truth'.[53] 'Demonstration' to others rather than personal 'perswasion' was crucial to Lockean psychology as the means of proving the truth of one's sensations. The idea of enthusiasm as resistant to the kind of public dialogue that demonstration entailed was a recurrent theme of eighteenth-century writing on the matter. What this appeal to demonstration failed to quell, however, was the Humean charge that Reason was incapable of distinguishing between true and false sensations, and indeed was itself only a slave to the passions. Locke, as we have already seen, had articulated the anxiety himself. At least, he anticipated the charge that a philosophy grounded in the sensations might open the door to a situation wherein 'the visions of an enthusiast and the reasonings of a sober man will be equally certain'.[54] Others who came after him, including Coleridge, arraigned Locke and his followers for reducing ideas of consciousness to a 'delirium' in which an insecurely moored Reason struggled not to be overwhelmed by the tides of enthusiasm. There was no real difference between the

---

[51] John Locke, *An Essay Concerning Human Understanding*, ed. Peter H. Nidditch (Oxford: Clarendon Press, 1979), 642.
[52] Ibid. 698.   [53] Ibid. 702.   [54] Ibid. 563.

vulgar prophet and the polite philosopher, the 'enthusiast' and the 'sober man', if sensation and enthusiasm could not be properly distinguished. Nor in the political sphere would the sober deliberations of a Whig politician be differentiated from the prophetic radicalism of the Civil War era. All would be simply the victims of 'perswasion'. The ubiquitous and troubling presence of enthusiasm represented a standing denial of the idea of continuous and unified identity that was the bedrock of emergent liberal-bourgeois ethics.

One influential philosophical attempt to solve the problem was to bring enthusiasm in from its liminal position, imbue it with a moral sense, and lock it into the very centre of consciousness and identity. The attempt was made in the work of Anthony Ashley Cooper, the third Earl of Shaftesbury, ironically, a former pupil of Locke's. Shaftesbury was concerned that Locke's epistemology presented human nature as a mere machine.[55] No less than Locke, Shaftesbury was a philosopher of the Whig settlement, who wished to limit the power of the Crown, encourage a commercial society, and guarantee freedom of worship. Where he differed from Locke was in his stress on human sociability. Shaftesbury thought Locke guilty of the epicureanism of Hobbes in his individualist emphasis on rational self-interest. Shaftesbury used a language of sensations derived from Locke, but made room among them for a 'moral sense' that came from within and sought echoes of itself without. Locke proscribed such inner voices as mere 'perswasion', banished to the margins of philosophy as fantasies of the mind that threatened the foundations of objective knowledge. Shaftesbury agreed with Locke that enthusiasm could be and had been dangerous, as listening to the inner voice had been in the Civil War, but viewed it not only as inescapable but also as fundamental to what it was to be human. He appropriated from Anglican attacks on enthusiasm the idea that it represented a going-out-of-self, but gave the notion a positive spin; enthusiasm was a sociable passion, founded in the desire to join with others, and ultimately with God. Whereas for Locke enthusiasm represented the result of an unnatural process that obscured the light of Reason, for Shaftesbury nothing could be more natural than enthusiasm: 'So far is he from degrading enthusiasm or disclaiming

---

[55] For Shaftesbury's critique of Locke, see G. J. Barker-Benfield, *The Culture of Sensibility: Sex and Society in Eighteenth-Century Britain* (Chicago: University of Chicago Press, 1992), 107–8, and Klein, *Shaftesbury and the Culture of Politeness*, 64–9.

it in himself that he looks on this passion, simply considered, as the most natural, and its object as the justest, in the world' (*Characteristics*, 353). Much of Shaftesbury's writing in *Characteristics*, especially in *The Moralists*, apostrophized Nature.[56] These ascents of the soul were 'natural' enthusiasm, but Shaftesbury did concede that it could be debased into the form feared by Locke. True enthusiasm had to be cultivated and regulated if it was not to degenerate into the vulgar enthusiasm of the crowd.[57] Whereas Locke's view of enthusiasm had been proscriptive, Shaftesbury's was regulative. Natural enthusiasm, this noble passion, was the product of 'self-knowledge and self-possession'.[58]

Shaftesbury's discussion of enthusiasm begins with the case of the so-called French prophets—Huguenot refugees from Louis XIV—who were causing popular unrest in London at the beginning of the eighteenth century. Contrasted to these archetypal victims of religious enthusiasm, Shaftesbury thought of the properly sociable self as the product of a process of division in which one controlled one's own affections. He claimed that the ancient injunction 'Recognize yourself!' should in fact be rendered 'Divide yourself!' (*Characteristics*, 77). The only way to deal with the 'combustible matters' which 'lie prepared and within ready to take fire at a spark' (*Characteristics*, 23) is to subject them to self-regulation before they enter into the public sphere. He recommends soliloquy as a technology of discipline, testing the passion to communicate against one's own understanding before it is brought before the public. He suggests that authors ought to retire to solitary places, 'woods and river banks', to test their work against themselves so that the 'fancy' may 'evaporate' and the 'vehemence' of the 'spirit and voice' may be reduced (*Characteristics*, 73). Isolation in itself is negative, it is unnatural not to be sociable, in fact the withdrawal of the hermit is another vulgar form of enthusiasm, but retirement in its proper place is a necessary preparation for integration into the polite world.[59] Already one might glimpse the emergent outlines of a Wordsworthian definition of poetry as 'emotion, recollected in

---

[56] On this aspect of Shaftesbury, see Pat Rogers, 'Shaftesbury and the Aesthetics of Rhapsody', *British Journal of Aesthetics*, 12 (1972), 244–57.

[57] Barker-Benfield, *The Culture of Sensibility*, 67.

[58] See Klein, *Shaftesbury and the Culture of Politeness*, 27.

[59] On Shaftesbury's attitude to solitariness and its relation to politeness, see Lawrence E. Klein, 'Sociability, Solitude, and Enthusiasm', *Huntington Library Quarterly*, 60 (1998), 153–77.

tranquillity' (*WP* p. i) here. The properly social self is a formerly divided self reconstituted or re-collected, 'as in a looking-Glass, [we] discover ourselves' (*Characteristics*, 87) and made autonomous by this very act of self-division. This process depends in part on 'taste', a faculty which 'lies somewhere between nature and art, between the internal principles given to man and their external improvement, practised in society'.[60] Taste allows the individual to move from the private to the public, but its nature is complex and even contradictory. Sometimes it seems a rational faculty; elsewhere, Shaftesbury identifies it with the classical education available to the gentleman. At other points in his argument, however, it appears as an innate sense capable of regulating both the wilder social passions and the calculations of self-interest.

The elusive nature of Shaftesbury's writing was one of the reasons why it was able to inspire so many different opinions of its importance and meaning in the eighteenth century. A Scottish tradition primarily associated with Francis Hutcheson developed the idea of the moral sense as an affection, although it continued to wrestle with the problem that the affections might actually come into conflict with the demands of universal benevolence, whereas an English tradition, within which Dissenters such as Philip Doddridge and Richard Price loomed large, emphasized the role of reason as the reflective capacity that could regulate the senses.[61] Neither tradition was complacent about the possibility that Shaftesbury's noble enthusiasm might only be a variant of the passions of the crowd. One thing that *Characteristics* did make clear, however, was that, where the 'popular fury . . . called "panic" . . . [or] the rage of the people' (*Characteristics*, 10) does burst out, not persecution and repression but 'raillery' was the appropriate means of social control. Shaftesbury's High Church opponents were furious at his refusal to provide a role for the Church in patrolling such phenomena.[62] Regulation rather than persecution is Shaftesbury's response

---

[60] Peter de Bolla, *The Discourse of the Sublime: Readings in History, Aesthetics, and the Subject* (Oxford: Basil Blackwell, 1989), 77.

[61] See Rivers, *Reason, Grace, and Sentiment*, ii. 211.

[62] Shaftesbury's *Sensus Communis* was written largely in response to attacks on *A Letter Concerning Enthusiasm* for its lax attitude towards religious enthusiasm and mockery of religious intolerance. These attacks include Mary Astell's *Bart'lemy Fair* (1709), Edward Fowler, *Reflections on a Letter Concerning Enthusiasm, to Lord **** (1708), and *Remarks upon the Letter Concerning Enthusiasm* (1708). Revealed religion plays little part in *Characteristics* overall. Indeed Divinity figures

to enthusiasm on the social as well as the personal level. His recommendation of raillery and ridicule as a corrective to popular religious frenzy is the corollary of the toleration of religious Dissent in the Whig state. Indeed in one of the trademark rhetorical loops typical of *Characteristics*, Shaftesbury identifies religious persecution itself as a form of enthusiasm. The refusal of High Church bigotry to respect the autonomy of other selves and the reciprocal or conversational nature (to use one of Shaftesbury's favourite tropes) of true sociability corresponds to the refusal of vulgar enthusiasm to make concessions to dialogue or demonstration. Shaftesbury believed the magistrate faced with popular enthusiasm 'instead of caustics, incisions, and amputations' ought to use 'the softest balms. . . taking, as it were, their passion upon him . . . divert and heal it' (*Characteristics*, 10–11). This Whig tolerationist tradition was absolutely central to the emergence of what I have been calling the discourse of regulation. To a century obsessed with ideas of sympathy and conversation, regulation offered a way of confirming the fundamental importance of sociability without abandoning society to the crowd, but the nature and extent of the regulation was endlessly contested as groups well beyond those Shaftesbury himself imagined capable of self-regulation clamoured to be let into the polite public sphere. It would also be a mistake to suggest that the Whig discourse of regulation remained unchallenged even in its fundamental assumptions. Throughout the long eighteenth century, for instance, there were plenty of high churchmen for whom Dissent ought not to be tolerated at all. Other commentators of all kinds of religious persuasion took the idea that enthusiasm was essential to morality as an affront to Reason. The Dissenter Richard Price was among these.[63] He thought Shaftesbury more of a rationalist than his disciples in Scotland

mainly as a sense of the harmony of nature and the sublimity of human feelings in response. This omission *inter alia* meant that Shaftesbury was widely regarded as an apologist for deism. As late as 1790 the *Critical Review* (69), 5 noted that his zeal for virtue 'overlooked, or seemed to overlook . . . the dictates of Christianity'. The same *Critical Review* article, providing a list of latitudinarian divines of whom Shaftesbury wrote in 'terms of applause or of respect', took the balanced view that 'he cannot be styled an infidel, or, uniformly, a Deist' (ibid.). In fact Shaftesbury seems to have been wary of early eighteenth-century deists such as John Toland for their ability to stir up popular passions and regarded the national Church as a necessary hindrance to fanaticism and social disorder. See Klein, *Shaftesbury and the Culture of Politeness*, 157, and Barker-Benfield, *The Culture of Sensibility*, 108.

[63] See Rivers, *Reason, Grace, and Sentiment*, ii. 171–3.

allowed. For some of these thinkers, such as, we shall see, the Anglican-turned-Unitarian Gilbert Wakefield, just about any sign of affect in relation to religious worship was tainted with enthusiasm. In times of crisis, such as the 1790s, Shaftesbury's faith in self-regulation, even among the educated elite, seemed rather too liberal a notion. Even so, whether directly indebted to Shaftesbury or not, a discourse of regulation became fundamental to conceptions of enthusiasm in the period. It was a discourse that embraced the human possibilities created by the going-out-of self, but remained aware that without discipline such transports could be destructive of the very identity they promised to fulfil.

Although he was increasingly chided for his aristocratic preciousness, Shaftesbury opened up an idea of the social affections that was to appeal to deists, Dissenters, and Anglicans alike throughout the century that followed. There were at least ten editions of *Characteristics* between 1711 and 1790, and its ideas were extended and debated by others who often wished to make its model of politeness less socially exclusive.[64] Aided by the fact that Shaftesbury's elitism was cloaked in the language of a generic human nature, *Characteristics* fed into the literature of bourgeois sociability.[65] The first issue of *The Spectator* was published soon after *Characteristics*. Shaftesbury argued only for the 'liberty of the Club, and of that sort of freedom which is taken amongst gentlemen and friends who know one another perfectly well' (*Characteristics*, 36). The *Spectator*, to repeat its own boast, took this politeness into the coffee houses and less exalted sites of the urban renaissance of the eighteenth century. Nor was the influence of Shaftesbury's 'noble enthusiasm' confined to moral philosophy and the practice of sociability. It was also directly identified with the Whig tradition of liberty or 'patriot enthusiasm'. In 1790 the *Critical Review* remem-

[64] For the influence of Shaftesbury and the diffusion of his ideas, see Rivers, *Reason, Grace, and Sentiment*, vol. ii, and 'Shaftesburian Enthusiasm and the Evangelical Revival', in Jane Garnett and Colin Matthew (eds.), *Religion and Revival since 1700: Essays for John Walsh* (Hambledon Press, 1993), 21–39, Barker-Benfield, *The Culture of Sensibility*, 137–8, Klein, *Shaftesbury and the Culture of Politeness*, 2 and 36–7, and Ernest Tuveson, 'The Importance of Shaftesbury', *ELH* 20 (1953), 267–99; for his influence on eighteenth-century poetry, see C. A. Moore, 'Shaftesbury and the Ethical Poets in England, 1700–1760', *PMLA*, 31 (1916), 264–325, Rogers, 'Shaftesbury and the Aesthetics of Rhapsody', and Michael Meehan, *Liberty and Poetics in Eighteenth Century England* (Beckenham: Croom Helm, 1986).

[65] Barker-Benfield, *The Culture of Sensibility*, 119.

bered him as 'in politics . . . the enthusiast of liberty'.[66] Hume's
History had specifically related the British appetite for liberty to
enthusiasm in the religious sphere. The Reformation was the great
original of political freedom from this point of view. For Whiggish
historiography the association of 'enthusiasm' with innovation and
liberty, which for Swift had been a sign of fanaticism, was often
understood in terms of a noble passion for freedom. Wotton had
rejoiced in that 'true Enthusiastick Rage which Liberty breathes
into their Souls who enjoy it'.[67] Only in a free society, Shaftesbury
believed, could the enthusiasm flourish that would lead men to a
perception of the sublimity of the order of the universe. Without
enthusiasm, commented the Oxford clergyman George Nott,
repeating a proverbial saying, 'nothing great or noble amongst men
can ever be produced' (although Nott was less sure that this applied
to matters of religion).[68] Enthusiasm was potentially a paradigm-
busting force responsible for historical progress in this Whig appropriation of the term to the political sphere.

The possibility of a positive definition of enthusiasm oriented
towards the unworlding of things-as-they-are remained available,
but always haunted by a fear that unworlding was at best unworldly
and at worst subversive. Fears over the limits of enthusiasm continued to be articulated in relation to 'patriot enthusiasm'. The pairing
of liberty and enthusiasm betrayed the irresponsibility of Whig
apostrophes to 'Liberty' for Hume. He mocked those panegyrists
who turned a blind eye to the excesses of the Civil War as enthusiasts whose fervour for liberty had blinded their judgement. The
execution of Charles I was a disgrace to the cause of liberty, perpe-
trated by those who had distracted themselves with politico-
religious delusions. He accepted that without Puritan zeal Britain
might never have regained its political liberties, but even so thought
that it had not been 'necessary to pass through the fires of enthusiasm'.[69] Underlying his view of British history was the idea that this
spirit of enthusiasm had to be constantly regulated by the external
authority of the Crown as part of the 'perpetual intestine struggle,
open or secret, between AUTHORITY and LIBERTY'.[70] Hume's was a

[66] *Critical Review*, 69 (1790), 5.
[67] Quoted in Meehan, *Liberty and Poetics*, 6.
[68] George F. Nott, *Religious Enthusiasm Considered* (Oxford, 1803), 5.
[69] Pocock, 'Antiself of Enlightenment', 22.
[70] David Hume, 'Of the Origin of Government', in *Essays Moral, Political, and
Literary*, i. 116.

Tory version of a more general concern about limits when it came to the ardour of enthusiasm. He shared Shaftesbury's sense of the power of enthusiasm, and even its potential for good, but he had a more developed sense of its ceaseless desire to elude regulation, and the need for external powers to be brought to bear on controlling its excesses. Where Shaftesbury saw enthusiasm as the reflection of a divine spark that animated the universe, Hume was more concerned about it as a sociological and historical phenomenon that 'only runs along the earth; is caught from one breast to another; and burns brightest where the materials are best prepared'.[71] Hume's were ideas that were to have an important influence, as we shall see, on Burke's response to the French Revolution as a new form of dangerously contagious enthusiasm. Revolutionary *transparence* for Burke becomes a new strain of the old virus that refused to limit its passion for liberty with a concern for worldly affairs.

Eighteenth-century moral philosophers were deeply influenced by Shaftesbury's attempt to place the social affections at the centre of morality, but like Hume they often remained sceptical about his view of the relation of such sentiments to enthusiasm. Whereas Shaftesbury left open the possibility of defining his moral sense as a kind of passion, leaving open the frightening possibility that it was at least related to the vulgar enthusiasm of the crowd, later moralists, no less interested in the ideal of sociability, tended to argue that it was the conformist pressures of opinion and culture that might usefully moderate the passions into a polite concern for others. 'The ambiguity of sympathy in Shaftesbury's account', as John Mullan has noted, 'proceeds from an uneasy sensitivity to the limitations of such "Company" and "mutual Converse", from an awareness of the necessary separation of polite society from society at large.'[72] Most of those who followed Shaftesbury wanted to make the distinction between sociability and enthusiasm a more certain one. Even a philosopher such as Francis Hutcheson, who popularized some of Shaftesbury's key ideas, developing the notion of an innate moral sense, dropped his predecessor's attempt to give the word 'enthusiasm' a positive valency. Hutcheson was a philosopher of 'benevolence' not 'enthusiasm'. Indeed Hutcheson complained that: 'Many

---

[71] 'Of the Rise and Progress of the Arts and Sciences' in Hume, *Essays Moral, Political, and Literary*, i. 177.
[72] John Mullan, *Sentiment and Sociability: The Language of Feeling in the Eighteenth Century* (Oxford: Clarendon Press, 1988), 29.

have been discourag'd from all Attempts of cultivating Kind generous Affections in themselves, by a previous notion that there are no
such Affections in nature, and that all Pretence to them was only
Dissimulation, Affectation, or at best some *unnatural Enthusiasm.*'[73]
For all Shaftesbury's stress on regulation, Hutcheson was far more
sensitive to the dangers of construing the social affection as the product of the senses. Linking sociability to 'enthusiasm', as Shaftesbury
did, was to give a hostage to fortune when the dominant connotations of the latter still conjured images of the sectaries of the
Commonwealth. Hutcheson located the moral sense in the reflective
faculties, making it more like conscience, as Chris Jones points out,
and less open to being regarded as a sense in itself.[74] For Hutcheson
the love of mankind in general provides a balance to other more partial feelings, and he carefully counselled his readers against thinking
that the lower-class characters they pitied shared their sensibility.[75]
Benevolence was the product of a properly regulated sensibility, not
something that the crowd, more often than not slaves to their passions, could muster. 'Meditation' and 'Reflection', as Jones points
out, are key words for Hutcheson, as they had also been, despite
other differences, for Shaftesbury.[76] Even so, despite the various
barriers Hutcheson put in place to prevent benevolence being
mistaken for enthusiasm, other readers of Shaftesbury, such as
Richard Price, disparaged Hutcheson for perpetuating an idea of
the moral sense that seemed to give too much of a role to the
affections and too little to reason.[77] Others even within the Scottish
tradition also had a more circumspect view of the extent of benevolence than Hutcheson. Hume bluntly stated 'there is no such
passion in human minds, as love of mankind, merely as such.'[78] For
Hume morality was relative to the sentiment or taste of the individual. This discovery he attributed to Hutcheson, but denied the

[73] Francis Hutcheson, *An Essay on the Nature and Conduct of the Passions and Affections* (1728), p. v.
[74] Chris Jones, *Radical Sensibility: Literature and Ideas in the 1790s* (New York: Routledge, 1993), 24 and 62.
[75] Ibid. 67.   [76] Ibid. 24–5.
[77] On Price, see Rivers, *Reason, Grace, and Sentiment,* ii. 227–37.
[78] David Hume, *A Treatise of Human Nature,* ed. L. A. Selby-Bigge and P. H. Nidditch, 2nd edn. (Oxford: Clarendon Press, 1978), 481. Lord Kames criticized Shaftesbury for refusing 'to admit of any thing like partial benevolence; holding, that if it is not entire, and directed to the whole species, it is not benevolence at all', *Essays on the Principles of Morality* (1751), 121.

existence of an authorizing moral sense that could provide any kind
of objective ground for these affections.[79] Indeed he implied that the
yearning for such an authority within the self was really no better
than the enthusiasm of the Puritans that he had disparaged throughout the *History*: 'Any warm Sentiments of morals, I am afraid wou'd
have the air of Declamation amidst abstract Reasonings, & wou'd be
esteemed contrary to good Taste.'[80] Only calm reflection could be
relied on to control the passions 'in their most furious movements';
there was no higher form of regulation beyond the pragmatics of living in the world as it is.[81] Only the pressures of conformity with the
society around one, the influence of manners, the power of authority
and inertia of church establishments, could provide a bridle for these
dangerous passions. Both Hume and Adam Smith thought that
benevolence was and should be founded on more tangible objects
than the potentially combustible matter of the moral sense. Smith's
Theory of Moral Sentiments regards religious fanaticism as 'pernicious to society' and destructive of 'all industry and commerce'.[82]
Sociability for Smith was about a regulation of the passions to bring
the individual into consensus with the polite Scottish burghers
around him. Such convergence 'checks the spirit of innovation' associated with enthusiasm, and helps 'preserve . . . the established
balance'.[83] Earlier editions of his *Theory of Moral Sentiments* placed
a great deal of stress on the power of public opinion to bring about
that regulation of selfish passions, but as his ideas evolved this
seemed too unstable, too open to the enthusiasm of the crowd, and
the concept of the 'impartial spectator', the authority of the man
within the breast, a regulatory principle which was taken to correct

[79] David Hume, *Philosophical Essays Concerning Human Understanding*, 2nd
edn. (1750), 15 n.
[80] 'To Francis Hutcheson, July 1739', in *The Letters of David Hume*, ed. J. Y. T.
Greig, 2 vols. (Oxford: Clarendon Press, 1932), i. 33.
[81] *Treatise*, 438.
[82] Adam Smith, *The Theory of Moral Sentiments*, ed. D. D. Raphael and A. L.
Macfie (Oxford: Oxford University Press, 1976), 313. See also *An Inquiry into the
Nature and Causes of the Wealth of Nations*, gen. eds. R. H. Campbell and A. S.
Skinner, textual editor W. B. Todd (Oxford: Oxford University Press, 1976), 788–9.
[83] *Theory of Moral Sentiments*, 230–1. See also John Dwyer, *Virtuous Discourse:
Sensibility and Community in Late Eighteenth-Century Scotland* (Edinburgh: John
Donald, 1987) and Evan Ratcliffe, 'Revolutionary Writing, Moral Philosophy, and
Universal Benevolence in the Eighteenth Century', *Journal of the History of Ideas*,
54 (1993), 221–40.

vehemence of the passions, increasingly separates itself from the opinions of any empirical community of spectators.[84]

Although the idea of the impartial spectator developed across several editions after 1759, its differentiation from public opinion was only fully secured in the sixth edition of 1790, perhaps by Smith's response to the French Revolution. To the moral imagination concerned with regulating enthusiasm into a polite form of sociability, the Revolution must have seemed like the fulfilment of all its nightmares of the excesses of the crowd. Burke's attack on the French Revolution and its allies in Britain exploded the distinction between universal benevolence and enthusiasm insisted upon by Hutcheson and others in the British tradition. Although it was more often the more recent and importantly foreign version of such ideas associated with Rousseauvian *transparence* that he used as his target, universal benevolence to Burke was simply a dangerous form of enthusiasm, opposed to the common sense and natural sociability of local attachments.[85] In some respects, Burke offered a hysterical version of Hume, insisting that universal benevolence was a mere chimera that distracted from the 'little platoon we belong to in society'.[86] However much they might represent themselves as properly regulated enquirers after truth, radicals were little better than the playthings of enthusiasm to Burke, men who were sacrificing a proper sense of self and the stability of the commercial and social order to their improbable visions of futurity. My next chapter will explore these issues in more detail, but what needs to be stressed at this point in mapping out a tradition of regulation is that it never freed itself of the anxiety that it was encouraging what it sought to discipline. Hutcheson, Hume, and Smith in their different ways were all beset by the fear that sociability could easily dissolve and slip into the barbarism of the crowd. Burke moved this anxiety to the very centre of political discourse in the 1790s.

---

[84] For a discussion of the developments of Smith's idea of the 'impartial spectator' across the different editions, see the introduction to *Theory of Moral Sentiments*, 15–16, and Dwyer, *Virtuous Discourse*, 169–70.

[85] See Ratcliffe, 'Revolutionary Writing'; J. G. A. Pocock, 'Edmund Burke and the Redefinition of Enthusiasm: The Context as Counter-Revolution', in *The Transformation of Political Culture, 1789–1848*, vol. iii of François Furet and Mona Ozouf (eds.), *The French Revolution and the Creation of Modern Political Culture* (Oxford: Oxford University Press, 1989), 19–43; and the discussion of Burke in my next chapter.

[86] Burke, *The Writings and Speeches*, viii. 97–8.

The discourse of regulation needs to be considered in relation to Michel Foucault's account of the internalization of disciplinary power in the eighteenth century.[87] Foucault argues that modern power is the product not of the prohibition but of the production of knowledge. Shaftesbury and his followers seem like harbingers of this modernity in that enthusiasm is moved from its liminal position in Locke's psychology into a central position in which regulatory work can be done on it. Clifford Siskin has made a similar claim for Romantic psychology (a psychology, I would argue, that was deeply indebted to Shaftesburian ideas) for which he claims 'a self-made mind, full of newly constructed depths, is an object of the new knowledge of those depths and therefore subject to professional power'.[88] In Shaftesbury's writing, the topography of the psyche is relatively undeveloped. The new depths Siskin describes were to be the product of the extension of the insights of Shaftesbury and others into various disciplines, including medical knowledge of the nervous system, the moral philosophy of Hutcheson, Hume, and Smith, and the psychology of Hartley. Literature and even aesthetic theory became a professional site (fiercely hostile to the unqualified) in which such regulatory work was done, a point Siskin himself has been exploring in his more recent work, but I should here like to enter a caveat against rushing into the arms of an overly deterministic reading of Foucault's ideas. Clifford Siskin says of this disciplinary power that 'it always opens deeper depths to surveillance and invites more and more specialized intervention'.[89] What this only implicitly acknowledges is that disciplinary power in fact chases an ever-receding shadow. The discourse of regulation produced a supplement, an anxiety that regulated enthusiasm could always transmute back into its vulgar alter ego. The curative potential of enthusiasm if not correctly prescribed could become a poison. The amiable sympathies that seemed to be the basis of civic society

---

[87] See, especially, *Discipline and Punish*, trans. Alan Sheridan (Harmondsworth: Penguin, 1979).

[88] Clifford Siskin, *Historicity of Romantic Discourse* (New York: Oxford University Press, 1988), 13.

[89] Ibid. For more recent work on professionalism in relation to these issues of discipline, see Siskin's *The Work of Writing: Literature and Social Change in Britain 1700–1830* (Baltimore: Johns Hopkins University Press, 1998). Klein, *Shaftesbury and the Culture of Politeness*, 83, suggests that it was in his notebooks that Shaftesbury devoted time to the 'expansion and elaboration of human interiority'.

teetered on the edge of the unruliness of the crowd. The difference between the two was never felt to be stable.[90]

ENTHUSIASM, SENSIBILITY, AND THE SUBLIME

An emergent consumer society could hardly afford to do otherwise than seek a positive role for the feelings. Developing Colin Campbell's ideas about Romanticism and the ethics of consumption, G. J. Barker-Benfield has made an impressive case for regarding eighteenth-century Britain as a 'culture of sensibility', a culture in which feelings were aggrandized and invested with moral value as a justification of the appetite for consumption.[91] Though its view of the feelings often rested on materialist assumptions about the nervous system, sensibility invested sensation with spiritual and moral value, but it also perpetuated Shaftesbury's concern with self-fashioning, the need to shape and be shaped by this inner feeling. Sensibility as a cultural movement derived from Shaftesbury and others the belief that human beings were united by sensations beyond the merely rational, but it was always anxious about being mistaken for enthusiasm. This anxiety was characterized by an unstable economy of desire and disavowal. The emotions might be regarded as virtuous, but they might also be feared as inflationary, flooding the market with cheap passions, which threatened to drown real values and stable identities. When the word 'enthusiasm' does occur in a positive sense in the eighteenth-century discourse of sentiment and sensibility, it is usually hedged about with terms such as 'delicacy' and 'refinement'. Not all writers were careful to take such precautions, but in general the discourse of sensibility deserves to be understood as a process for regulating enthusiasm. 'Benevolence' was routinely distinguished in it from what Hume called the 'rougher and more boisterous emotions'.[92] 'Enthusiasm' was a term that could not easily shake free its associations with the latter, especially when it came to popular religious

[90] On the 'supplement', see Jacques Derrida, *Of Grammatology*, trans. by Gayatri Chakravorty Spivak (Baltimore: Johns Hopkins University Press, [1974] 1976).

[91] For an elaboration of this idea, see Barker-Benfield, *The Culture of Sensibility*.

[92] 'Of the Delicacy of Taste and Passion', in *Essays Moral, Political, and Literary*, i. 193.

sentiment. Entrepreneurs of taste and politeness, even as late as Leigh Hunt, for this reason tended to be particularly hard on religious enthusiasm. He believed that 'the vulgar admire Methodism just as they do violent colours, violent noise, and violent swearing' (H 12). The strong links between 'enthusiasm' and the vulgar culture of the crowd meant that it was a word that could be used only with discretion in the discourse of sensibility.

Hunt was in no doubt that Methodism seethed with barely suppressed sexuality, in which proper female refinement was extinguished in women, and so could scarcely begin to do its work of softening rough male habits. If a feminized idea of domesticity was regarded as a prime agent in the reformation of male manners, female enthusiasm opened up a nightmarishly deformed side of a process that might corrode where it was meant to soften. Joanna Southcott, for instance, seemed to travesty the maternal affections when she claimed to be pregnant by the Holy Spirit. Male enthusiasm was often demonized precisely in terms of its antagonism to domesticity. Case histories abounded detailing the scandal of inspired prophets who abandoned their work and their families to follow their inner light.[93] Although such things are not easily quantified, eighteenth-century discourse on enthusiasm does seem to become increasingly concerned with the privileging of production (not only in a religious context either, as Francis Jeffrey's comments on enthusiastic but uneducated poets, discussed below, reveal). Certainly Adam Smith represents enthusiasm as an impediment to trade and commerce in *The Wealth of Nations*. Enthusiasm either swept away domesticity and work discipline into the inchoate passions of the crowd, or, at the other extreme, tempted the prophet into an unsociable and unworldly isolation. The discourse of sensibility more often presented itself in terms of a productive dialectic between retirement and sociability. The cultural phenomenon scouted by Barker-Benfield was intent on separating the middling sort both from the enthusiasm of the crowd and from what Shaftesbury represented as the empty formality of royal courts.

Such distinctions can be seen clearly at work in the writing of one of the entrepreneurs of sensibility, Henry Mackenzie, author of the

---

[93] See, for instance, Southey's comment on the damage done to the families of working men by Brothers, discussed in Chapter 3; and on Southcott, see James K. Hopkins, *A Woman to Deliver her People: Joanna Southcott and English Millenarianism in an Era of Revolution* (Austin: University of Texas Press, 1982).

sentimental best-seller *The Man of Feeling*. Mackenzie's essay on
'The Effects of Religion on Minds of Sensibility' (1779) first published in *The Mirror* begins by noting that his periodical followed a
policy not to discuss matters of religion, especially when it was
'mystical or controversial'.[94] Periodicals throughout the eighteenth
century in their roles as guardians of the civility of the public sphere
routinely bypassed or even sneered at religious controversialism.
The latitudinarian tradition of practical piety that fed into sensibility always sought to 'de-emphasize dogma for the sake of peace'.[95]
Mackenzie allows religion into the public sphere only when it is
'introduced as a feeling, not a system, as appealing to the sentiments
of the heart, not the disquisitions of the head.'[96] Protestant clergyman La Roche, the hero of Mackenzie's essay, 'possessed devotion
in all its warmth, but with none of its asperity'.[97] 'Asperity' implies
the Puritan ardour of the saints of the commonwealth, driven by
their enthusiasm to bring their religious convictions into the heart
of the public sphere (indeed to make them the basis of the public
sphere). Mackenzie is aware that to a sceptic La Roche will still look
like a victim of his emotions, but he is quick to make a distinction
between such feelings and enthusiasm: 'A philosopher might have
called him an enthusiast; but if he possessed the fervour of the
enthusiast, he was guiltless of their bigotry.'[98] The unfeeling philosopher—the Lockean reasoner or Hobbesian epicurean despised by
Shaftesbury—does not differentiate between true feelings and
enthusiasm, both are simply against Reason. Mackenzie's story is
designed to show that the difference is real and as such capable of
being demonstrated (as Locke would have required). It goes on to
reveal the superiority of the religion of the heart over the coldness
of the philosopher, but takes care to demonstrate that La Roche's
warmth is tastefully regulated. Mackenzie steers a course here
between overheated enthusiasm and cold philosophy that was the
heart's desire of the eighteenth-century idea of sensibility. Even the
death of his daughter does not discompose La Roche. Instead of
paroxysms of grief, which would intrude the body on to an affair of

[94] Henry Mackenzie, *Works*, 8 vols. (Edinburgh, 1808), iv. 175. Note that Adam
Smith was involved in the Mirror Club that produced Mackenzie's journal. See
Dwyer, *Virtuous Discourse*, 168.
[95] Pocock, 'Antiself of Enlightenment', 15.
[96] *Works*, iv. 175. The same values inform Anna Letitia Barbauld's attack on her
erstwhile friend and fellow Dissenter Joseph Priestley. See Chapter 4.
[97] *Works*, iv. 182.   [98] Ibid. 195.

the heart, we are presented with a pious tableau of stillness. 'Bending gently forward, his eyes half-closed, lifted up in silent devotion,' La Roche's religious warmth is self-contained and definitely not infectious.[99] Nor does it go to the other extreme of enthusiasm and implode into melancholy. The death of his daughter only reveals the depth of his self-command. Sensibility for Mackenzie was about refinement and discernment. Enthusiasm was more often associated with obsession, the mania that allowed individuals or the crowd to be swept up in a single idea. Delicacy meant a polite veiling of the body. Enthusiasm was apt to confuse agape and eros, imaging Christian love in gross terms, and barely managing, if at all, to sublimate sexual desire into religious devotion.

The repetitive energy that went into drawing these distinctions in novels, poems, and many other aspects of the culture betrays a fear within the culture of sensibility about its own excess and degeneration into enthusiasm. Once sensibility became identifiable as a popular movement (even a fashion) then it was liable itself to be represented as enthusiasm in the worst sense. Mackenzie's distinction between La Roche's religious warmth and enthusiasm precisely recognizes the dangers of the one translating into the other. Indeed in a later essay on novel writing, he explicitly compared the ways that sensibility courted many of the dangers associated with religious enthusiasm:

In the enthusiasm of sentiment there is much the same danger as in the enthusiasm of religion, of substituting certain impulses and feelings of what may be called a visionary kind, in the place of real practical duties, which in morals, as in theology, we might not improperly denominate good works.[100]

The culture of sensibility attempted to identify a restorative sphere of feeling that would provide a positive basis for 'real practical duties'. Female novelists such as Ann Radcliffe continually represented their heroines as capable of transport but ultimately able to regulate their feelings into a pious sense of the divine order in nature. The passions could be benevolent from this perspective, but it could not entirely convince itself that sensibility would not degenerate into enthusiasm. Literature had come to be seen as the place in which the restorative of feeling could be safely handled by the middle of the eighteenth century, but Mackenzie reveals an anxiety

[99] *Works*, iv. 202.   [100] Ibid. v. 182–3.

that even here fingers might be burnt. Indeed it might even be doing more extensive damage, taking enthusiasm out of the religious sphere, and encouraging those incapable of regulation to be believe that their vulgar enthusiasm was artistic genius. Hence the criticism that even someone as careful in her regulation of the emotions as Radcliffe could meet, but for the poet the stakes were even higher. Poetry was coming to have an increasing investment in the unworlding possibilities of transport, but in the process making itself ever more vulnerable to the accusation that it was encouraging an enthusiasm it could not contain.

The idea of poetry as a sphere in which the emotions could be regulated into a natural harmony became widespread in the eighteenth century, and preceded most discussions of sensibility in its more limited historical sense. Shaftesbury was not the only source for such ideas. In his insightful account of Romantic and post-Romantic theories of inspiration, Timothy Clark points out that John Dennis had a pioneering role in promoting 'a view of poetic creativity as a carefully-regulated form of frenzy, analogous to the delirium of religious enthusiasm but capable of acceptable insight into the cosmic order'.[101] Clark's perspective anticipates in a very different academic register Irlam's claims about the line of poetic enthusiasm that emerged in the first decades of the eighteenth century. An English tradition which viewed 'enthusiasm' as essential to poetry dates back at least as far as John Dryden.[102] More to the point, however, Clark claims that after Dennis 'enthusiasm' was increasingly valued as 'an ideal of natural communication, transcending the arbitrariness of signs'.[103] His claim seems to be corroborated by the sheer number of poems published in the eighteenth century with titles like Joseph Warton's 'The Enthusiast' (1744).[104]

---

[101] Timothy Clark, *The Theory of Inspiration: Composition as a Crisis of Subjectivity in Romantic and Post-Romantic Writing* (Manchester: Manchester University Press, 1997), 65.

[102] See Tucker, *Enthusiasm*, 88, who credits Dryden with being 'the first on record to use Enthusiasm of poetic fervour', but significantly in terms of the ambivalences traced in this book she also credits him with being the first to use 'Enthusiast' to imply 'general irrationality', 2.

[103] Clark, *Theory of Inspiration*, 65.

[104] For a general survey see M. Kevin Whelan, *Enthusiasm in the English Poetry of the Eighteenth Century (1700–1774)* (Washington, DC: Catholic University of America, 1935); see also Shaun Irlam, *Elations: The Poetics of Enthusiasm in Eighteenth-Century Britain* (Stanford, Calif.: Stanford University Press, 1999).

Warton himself was in the vanguard of those who believed enthusiasm to be essential to 'PURE POETRY'. 'Poetry, after all, cannot well subsist, at least is never so striking, without a tincture of enthusiasm' was Warton's judgement on the matter.[105] What Clark's version of this process of rehabilitation perhaps underestimates is the significance of his own phrase 'carefully-regulated'. How and who could properly regulate the spirit of enthusiasm remained key questions even in relation to poetry. Indeed, regulation was what qualified mere expression to be regarded as poetry. Enthusiasm was desired and disavowed in the eighteenth century, never free from anxieties and qualifications even in its most positive poetic expressions. Poets might increasingly seek to transport themselves into a realm of authentic communication beyond a fallen world of signs, as Clark suggests, but such rhetoric operated in ways that tried to carefully distance the poetic from the visionary pretensions of vulgar enthusiasm. William Duff's *Essay on Original Genius* (1767) made a clear distinction between the classical enthusiasm that inspired Shaftesbury and the modern enthusiasm that was the stuff of religious fanaticism:

ENTHUSIASM . . . is almost universally taken in a bad sense; and, being conceived to proceed from an overheated and distempered imagination, is supposed to imply weakness, superstition, and madness. ENTHUSIASM in the modern sense, is in no respect a qualification of a Poet; in the ancient sense, which implied a kind of divine INSPIRATION, or an ardour of Fancy, wrought up to a Transport, we not only admit, but deem it an essential one.[106]

'Transport' out of the self was what one gained for poetry from enthusiasm, but there was always an anxiety that it might not come with a return ticket. Eighteenth-century aesthetics was specifically oriented towards circumscribing the power of 'transport'. Theories of the sublime sought to reaffirm rather than simply disperse the subject, bringing him or her back to a true sense of the self within a

---

[105] Joseph Warton, *Essay on the Writings and Genius of Pope* (1756), i. pp. iv and 320. Pope himself had in fact been willing to commend his own poem's 'Enthusiastick spirit'. See 'To Dr William Cowper, 5 Feb. 1732', in *The Correspondence of Alexander Pope*, ed. George Sherburn, 5 vols. (Oxford: Clarendon Press, 1956), v. 269; and also Abigail Williams, 'The Poetry of the Un-enlightened: Politics and Literary Enthusiasm in the Early Eighteenth Century', forthcoming in *History of European Ideas*, Spring 2003.

[106] William Duff, *Essay on Original Genius* (1767), 170.

divine hierarchy, but this process of regulation often served only to reintroduce continually the dangerous excesses of enthusiasm.[107]

A brief look in more detail at the case of John Dennis, in fact, confirms Peter de Bolla's claim that this kind of anxiety haunted the discourse of the sublime from the very beginning of the eighteenth century, and should enable us to see the difficulties and contrary tensions in the cultural phenomenon described by Clark. Dennis did stress the regulated nature of the religious sublime. He wished to see it made the basis of a poetic renaissance, carefully distancing such poetry from the prophetic rantings of the vulgar, and sometimes sounding in the process very like Shaftesbury. Even so, Dennis was successfully impugned by the Scriblerians as 'one of the most impolite men who ever lived', his reputation as a serious critic destroyed, and even now barely recovered.[108] It is true that the Scriblerians were often suspicious of Whig notions of self-regulation in any form. Although they believed that their own genteel circle could manage enthusiasm properly, too much latitude smacked to them of the self-righting confidence of the market place or the impudence of Dissent. The established discourse of enthusiasm provided a ready language for pillorying both its secular and religious mutations. Yet even for those more committed to the expansion of print culture and the free play of enthusiasm under liberty than the Scriblerians, there remained a conviction that enthusiasm ought to be demonstrably brought within the pale of politeness. The success of Pope's demonization of Dennis lay not only in the individual brilliance of *The Dunciad*, but also in the fact that its victim's definition of the religious sublime left the boundaries between poetry and prophecy too porous for most polite eighteenth-century readers. Bringing Milton forward as the prime model of the religious sublime only fifty or so years after the execution of Charles I, as Dennis did, was to flirt with the memory of the religious enthusiasm of the commonwealth. Moreover his descriptions of the Miltonic sublime sounded more like the gross enthusiasm of the impolite; 'those happy Enthusiasms, those violent Emotions, those supernatural transports . . . [which]

---

[107] For discussion of the anxieties surrounding the idea of transport, see de Bolla, *The Discourse of the Sublime*. He describes the major achievement of eighteenth-century aesthetics as its construction of 'an adequate legislative able to police the transport of the sublime experience', 37, but its boundaries remained a source of anxiety throughout the eighteenth century and well into the nineteenth.

[108] Brean Hammond, *Professional Imaginative Writing in England 1670–1740: 'Hackney for Bread'* (Oxford: Oxford University Press, 1997), 305.

shake and ravish a Poet's soul with insupportable pleasure', than the decorous politeness of a Shaftesbury.[109] The latter was much less taken with such eroticized displays as a feature of enthusiasm. Nor did his idea of enthusiasm readily admit the Miltonic example of the poet-prophet or republican pamphleteer. Dennis's version of Milton was too close to what Shaftesbury, looking back to the 1640s, called the 'saint-author' to be generally acceptable (*Characteristics*, 75). Addison's essays on *Paradise Lost*, unlike Dennis, offered a more politely literary version of Milton's poem, that is, one that stressed the classical Milton rather than the poet-prophet. Milton was, in Nicholas von Maltzahn's words, 'constrained to the diminished sphere of poetic discourse' by Addison and safely placed in the 'ancient' rather than 'modern' category of Duff's distinction of enthusiasms.[110] What von Maltzahn may underestimate, however, is the extent to which drawing distinctions between the two or between poetry and prophecy remained a fraught and uncertain business. 'Literariness' may have come into being in order to regulate enthusiasm, but the difference between the two was not transparent and constantly had to be demonstrated. Few of those who followed Dennis along the path of the sublime could afford to celebrate enthusiasm without demonstrating the politeness of their feelings.

Those poets who participated in the rehabilitation of enthusiasm were rarely praised by reviewers without at least some warning about the dangers involved. Even the excitable Della Cruscan poet Edward Jerningham thought it necessary to stage a celestial courtroom drama to adjudicate between the good and bad effects of enthusiasm.[111] Despite the fact that he had submitted the word to a judicial process, intending 'to display the good and bad effects occasioned by Enthusiasm', the *Critical Review* still found his praise of its virtues too complacent: 'Enthusiasm, it is well known, when not founded in virtue, nor guided by understanding, is violent

[109] *The Critical Works of John Dennis*, ed. E. N. Hooker (Baltimore: Johns Hopkins University Press, 1939), ii. 379. Although Shaftesbury, too, of course, was attacked in Book IV of *The Dunciad*, his reputation sustained less lasting damage, presumably in part because as an aristocratic Whig he was less easy to assimilate to the idea of the uneducated ranter.
[110] Nicholas von Maltzahn, 'The Whig Milton, 1667–1700', in David Armitage et al. (eds.), *Milton and Republicanism* (Cambridge: Cambridge University Press, 1995), 229–53.
[111] Edward Jerningham, *Enthusiasm: A Poem in Two Parts* (1789); on Jerningham and the Della Cruscans, see W. N. Hargreaves-Mawdsley, *The English Della Cruscans and their Time, 1783–1828* (The Hague: Martinus Nijhoff, 1967), 182–3.

and erroneous, producing the most famous effects.'[112] These 'effects' were frequently evoked as the signs that distinguished poetic enthusiasm from its vulgar sibling. Disciplining of these effects had to be demonstrated if the poet was to be accepted into the aesthetic sphere. The parallel regularly drawn between poetry and prophecy in the late eighteenth century remained similarly fraught. Twentieth-century critics have made the idea of the Romantic prophet a familiar one to us, but even after Robert Lowth's lectures on the sacred poetry of the Hebrews made the identification of poetry and prophecy a commonplace, the idea of the latter appearing in the eighteenth century was still tainted with enthusiasm.[113] Lowth's historicism provided a protective barrier between the Bible and contemporary enthusiasm. Obviously influenced by historical research such as Lowth's, Thomas Thomason urged his readers to take account of 'the climate, manners, and figurative style of the East', when considering the Bible, its words 'otherwise appear to be the offspring of a overheated imagination'.[114] William Duff's distinction is clearly in force here. Where poets laid claim to the ancient enthusiasm, they had always to be careful that they were not being drawn into its modern pathology. Writing in the same year, 1795, and puzzled at the appearance and popularity of an uneducated prophet, Richard Brothers, in a sophisticated, modern metropolis like London, a reviewer in the *Analytical* commented:

Prophecy and poetry are so nearly allied, that in most nations they have been more or less confounded. In some languages, the same term denotes both a prophet and a poet . . . Both use a bold metaphorical style; both utter their oracles in verse, or in a sort of prose resembling verse; both claim the gift of inspiration; and both are, or at least were once, believed to be inspired.[115]

The word 'confounded' here sounds a note of warning that always echoed around the equation between poetry and prophecy. To

---

[112] See Jerningham, *Enthusiasm*, 1, and *Critical Review*, 67 (1789), 249.

[113] See the accounts of Lowth's lectures on the poetry of the Hebrews in M. H. Abrams, *Natural Supernaturalism: Tradition and Revolution in Romantic Literature* (New York: W. W. Norton & Co., 1971; repr. 1973), 398–9, and Murray Roston, *Poet and Prophet: The Bible and the Growth of Romanticism* (Faber & Faber, 1965).

[114] Thomason, *An Essay*, 16–17. Thomason is writing to protect the scriptures from populist deists exclaiming 'against the prophets for encouraging enthusiasm by their sublime descriptions of the deity', 5.

[115] *Analytical Review*, 21 (1795), 213.

continue to believe that the poet and the prophet are identical is to be guilty of a misguided literal-minded primitivism. The regression would be social and historical. Historically and geographically, it would be to regress to the practices of the 'barbarous' oriental culture of the Hebrews. Socially, it would be to regress to the enthusiasm of London's deluded masses. The *Analytical Review* suggests that two quite different kinds of inspiration are at stake in poetry and prophecy. They can appear similar, both could even take the form of verse, but they should not be 'confounded'. To mistake one for the other is to sin against polite definitions of literariness and, more fundamentally, to surrender the advances of civilized society.

'COPIOUS FLUENCY OF WORDS'

Literariness was thus a key site wherein the shaping of the self through disciplining enthusiasm took place, but it was not one that could be hermetically sealed from other aspects of culture, especially since the authority of literary discourse was partly predicated on its openness. Clark sees the attraction of enthusiasm to eighteenth-century literary culture in terms of a preference for an authentic orality over the alienation of print culture.[116] The 'voice' of enthusiasm suggests that the poet is present to the reader in a way that the commodity of the printed page does not. There is no doubt that the immediacy associated with enthusiasm was often figured in terms of a nostalgic orality. Shaftesbury and Hunt both thought of noble enthusiasm in terms of a still small voice.[117] Speaking in tongues and prophetic utterance were the extreme cases of the same idea, but their extremity should alert us to a cultural logic Clark's opposition between orality and writing overlooks. This other cultural logic feared the loss of self-presence in the chaos of the crowd. The rantings of the street prophet and the hysteria of Joanna Southcott were scarcely conceived as promising a salvation from the mechanisms of print. A simple binary opposition between orality and writing obscures these complications. In fact, for both theoretical and historical reasons, print culture itself was often represented

---

[116] Clark, *Theory of Inspiration*, ch. 2.
[117] See Shaftesbury 39 above and Hunt 34 above.

as a latter-day variant of enthusiasm. It might actually be more useful for our purposes to split off writing from print in discussing these associations and anxieties. The narrator of Swift's *A Tale of a Tub* tells the reader that he is a former inmate of bedlam who has been urged to write to keep up his mental health.[118] Writing from this point of view is a form of healthy regulation, because it could be regarded as easily monitored and passed around in manuscript to a circle of friends. To commit one's writing to print is more dubious. It allows inspiration out of a more regulated environment and into the faceless and inflationary world of the crowd. Part of the irony of Swift's pamphlet is that the narrator himself may not have been careful enough of this distinction.[119]

This claim may seem perverse. Print was often conceived in enlightenment terms as a crucial mediation between self and society. In Habermas's terms, print was a medium of regulation by which autonomous readers could transform their private thoughts into public opinion. By the later eighteenth century, however, the medium was starting to seem more ambiguous. Print might allow the endless repetition of ungoverned enthusiasm. 'Electrick communication everywhere,' Edmund Burke's nightmare of the proliferation of print, seemed to offer no room for mediation at all, but the instantaneous dissemination and desiccation of knowledge.[120] By the 1790s it was conventional opinion in Germany that modern print culture, and especially prose fiction, was a secular mutation of 'Schwärmerei' (Luther's term for the swarming effects of enthusiasm).[121] Looking back on the expansion of print culture from the vantage point of Britain in 1820, one writer in the *Retrospective Review* coined the term 'bibliomaniacs' to describe those professors who, 'with an enthusiasm not unworthy of a higher calling', sought to keep pace with the dizzying nature of book production.[122] Half a century earlier, Oliver Goldsmith had described print as 'that fatal

[118] Swift, *Tale of the Tub*, 35.
[119] See his summary of the maxims of the ancient Aeolists, especially the idea that inspiration 'ought not to be covetously hoarded up, stifled, or hid under a Bushel, but freely communicated to Mankind', ibid. 152.
[120] Burke, *The Writings and Speeches*, viii. 97–8. See also Keen, *The Crisis of Literature in the 1790s*, esp. 57–8.
[121] See Anthony J. La Vopa, 'The Philosopher and the *Schwärmer*: On the Career of a German Epithet from Luther to Kant', *Huntington Library Quarterly*, 60 (1998), 86.
[122] *Retrospective Review*, 1 (1820), pp. vii–viii. See the discussion of 'bibliomania' in Keen's *The Crisis of Literature in the 1790s*.

revolution whereby writing is converted to a mechanic trade'.[123] Although such sentiments may look like a direct affirmation of Clark's thesis, they also participate in a different trajectory whereby 'mechanic' was linked to the compulsive spasming of popular enthusiasm. This sense of the word was exploited by Swift's *Mechanical Operation of the Spirit* (1710) and later echoed by Wollstonecraft when she warned of not confounding 'mechanical instincts with emotions that reason deepens, and justly terms the feelings of humanity'.[124] Philip Doddridge directly aligned such instinctual spasming with the 'distraction' of enthusiasm:

Should we place [the experience of regeneration] in any mechanical trans-ports of animal nature, in any blind impulse, in any strong feelings, not to be described, or accounted for, or argued upon, but known by some inward inexplicable sensation to be divine; we could not wonder, if calm and pru-dent men were slow to admit the pretension to it, and were fearful it might end in the most dangerous enthusiasm.[125]

Here enthusiasm is being defined not as Clark's authentic orality, but as a mere instinct that is mechanical in its enslavement to the combustible matter within. These were concerns that informed the doubts of both Coleridge and Wordsworth about the relationship between poetic enthusiasm and the individual will as we shall see. Much earlier in the century writers such as Swift and Pope always associated the drones of an expanding print culture with religious Dissent precisely for these reasons. They saw both print and non-conformity as species of endless mechanical repetition. Their Dissenters are slaves to their sensations. Print culture dispenses such sensations—whether religious or poetic—without allowing space or leisure for the kinds of reflection that might shape them into polite form. Brean Hammond paints a picture of the expanding print mar-ket place as one of happy democratization:

Literature could be *created* by writers who had nothing but their genius to recommend them, and, as the 'polite' literary periodicals of the early

[123] Quoted by Raymond Williams in *The Long Revolution* (Harmondsworth: Penguin, 1961; repr. 1981), 183.

[124] Wollstonecraft, *Vindication of the Rights of Woman* (Harmondsworth: Penguin, 1975), 141. See also her attack on Burke's 'romantic enthusiasm', which she compares to 'the blind impulse of unerring instinct', in *A Vindication of the Rights of Men*: Mary Wollstonecraft, *Political Writings*, ed. Janet Todd (Oxford: Oxford University Press, 1994), 30. And see below, Chapter 2, note 7.

[125] Doddridge, 'Of the Nature of Regeneration', quoted in Rivers, *Reason, Grace, and Sentiment*, i. 199.

eighteenth century taught their readers, it could also be *consumed* by members of the literate middle class who had some leisure time rather than any extensive training or cultural pedigree.[126]

Yet the literary market place continued to be riven by concerns about the grounds of cultural value. The *Dunciad* offers an account of a market incapable of reflection. Instead print culture endlessly echoes its own empty impulses. Even those much more frankly committed to the idea of the market than Pope could still be concerned about this inflationary potential. Outside the literary, 'enthusiasm' had always functioned as a figure for the scandalous belief that the workings of the spirit were cheaply available and brought with it a discourse for explaining how the disease propagated itself. Enthusiasm seemed to brook no restraint in its minting of the coin of grace. If a Cobbler could preach the Word, what was the Word worth? Print culture looked like enthusiasm when it too seemed to stretch the value of writing. If one only needed to be (barely) literate to be published, what was literature worth? Shaftesbury was committed to 'the open and free commerce of the world' (*Characteristics*, 405), but he assumed a cultural conversation made up of gentlemen with education and taste to regulate themselves. Others who followed him were keen to erect more visible barriers.[127] Popular enthusiasm in religion or poetry was feared as an exorbitant expression of the freedom Shaftesbury propounded, wherein the movement of the spirit was rushed mechanically into print to infect other equally unregulated readers. Enthusiasm is both impulsive and mechanical, because it overleaps the space of reflection essential to Shaftesbury's notion of self-fashioning, the space which can convince the writer either not to publish or at least to shape inspiration into a polite form.

Given this set of assumptions, it became increasingly important to control the distribution of texts to those who were deemed incapable of regulating their reading. When Thomas Paine was tried for publishing *Rights of Man* it was because, so the Attorney-General alleged, the second part had been sold at such a price that it was available to readers 'whose minds cannot be supposed to be conversant with subjects of this sort, and so cannot therefore correct as

---

[126] Hammond, *Professional Imaginative Writing*, 83.

[127] On the role of the periodicals in erecting these limits, see Stephen Copley, 'Commerce, Conversation, and Politeness in the Early Eighteenth-Century Periodical', *British Journal for Eighteenth-Century Studies*, 18 (1995), 63–77.

they go along'.[128] Even Hannah More could be accused of 'enthusiasm' when she set about teaching her poor neighbours in Somerset
to read between 1800 and 1804.[129] This tendency to see in the
expansion of the reading public a new strain of an old virus raises
the question of how reading was understood to be infectious in such
a way as to make it a dangerous enthusiasm? Wasn't reading
necessarily a form of reflection? Because sympathetic identification
was regarded as the very basis of the reading experience in the
eighteenth century, this was not always the assumption. William
Godwin believed the success of the writer depended on the ability
to create such an identification in the reader: 'He must sympathize
with my passions, melt with my regrets, and swell with my enthusiasm' (*Godwin Works*, vi. 198). Imaginative identification with the
passions of the author was deemed necessary if communication was
to take place, but it was important to regulate the identification, not
to lose hold of oneself, if the process was not to be destructive.
Predictably, reading zealous religious pamphlets and, especially,
prophecy was widely regarded as opening oneself to the most dangerous of enthusiasms. Shaftesbury himself wrote in the shadow of
the enthusiasm of the 1640s and 1650s when press freedom seemed
to licence all kinds of ranting:

A *saint-author* of all men least values politeness. He scorns to confine that
spirit in which, he writes to rules of criticism and profane learning. Nor is
he inclined in any respect to play the critic on himself, or regulate his style
or language by the standard of good company and people of the better sort.
(*Characteristics*, 75)

The prophetic author refuses to regulate his inner light and its
unconfined passion spreads itself to readers, ultimately producing
tumults and civil unrest. The memory of the Puritans of the
Commonwealth using the press to promulgate the rule of the Saints
stands behind Shaftesbury's 'Advice to an Author'. One stage of
self-regulation in Shaftesbury's model operates specifically between

---

[128] *A Complete Collection of State Trials*, compiled by William Cobbett and
T. B. Howells, 34 vols. (1818–20), xxii. 381. For a full discussion of the trial and
these attitudes in general, see Keen's *The Crisis of Literature in the 1790s*, esp.
42–75.
[129] The episode was known as the Blagdon controversy. See M. A. Hopkins,
Hannah and her Circle (New York: Longmans, Green, and Co., 1947), 194, and for
one of More's responses to the charge, see *The Letters of Hannah More*, ed.
R. Brimley Johnson (1925), 185–6.

the moment of inspiration and committing copy to the press. He recommends retirement and soliloquy as a technology to retard the rush into print. Even for those more firmly committed to the eighteenth-century market place for books, print culture could look like an endless and bewildering nexus of exchanges unmoored from any certainty of inherent value. Peter de Bolla has claimed that there was an emphasis on the public reading of books to regulate 'the private consumption of romances and novels'.[130] He tells only half the story. The place of reading was a key eighteenth-century problem, but the 'public' space was not simply defined against the private. The crowd, for instance, was not the public. Field preaching and other secular sorts of reading aloud were regarded as being perhaps even more scandalous than the secretive consumption of novels in private. Both were transgressions of notions of polite sociability which stand behind eighteenth-century notions of the public. Reading aloud in fact was associated with places that seemed to be almost parodic inversions of the polite public sphere. The conversation of culture, which was the fruit of considered reading by reasonable men, seemed to be mocked by the pretensions of dissenting congregations in crowded chapels, the field meetings of Methodists, and, on a secular level, the debating clubs which took place in taverns and other dubious sites all over London. When the spectre of a popular radicalism emerged in the 1790s, it was its contagious propagation in places such as these that caused the government most alarm.

A COUNTER-PUBLIC OF ENTHUSIASM?

Throughout the eighteenth century readers were represented again and again as requiring the luxury of leisure and retirement to pursue the kind of self-reflection advocated by Shaftesbury. 'The pleasures *The Spectator* advocated', as Barker-Benfield points out, 'were largely those of relief, complacency, and a sense of safety.'[131] At the other end of the century, Godwin was still stressing the importance of leisure and reflection to the proper consumption of literature. Although he believed that in theory 'every individual

---

[130] De Bolla, *The Discourse of the Sublime*, 254.
[131] Barker-Benfield, *The Culture of Sensibility*, 63.

should have leisure for reasoning and reflection', the present state of society determined that the benefits of literature exist 'only as the portion of a few' (*Godwin Works*, iii. 16). Romantic ideas of retirement were often predicated on the same set of assumptions about reflection and leisure. It is little wonder, then, that both Coleridge and Wordsworth were hostile to the idea of the emergent literary market place, inhabited, they believed, by writers and readers who had neither the time nor the capacity for such acts of reflection. Coleridge complained that 'in these times, if a man fail as a tailor, or a shoemaker, and can read and write correctly (for spelling is still of some consequence) he becomes an author' (*LLit* ii. 463). His fears of the journeyman cobbler clearly appeal to the prototype of the ranting tub-preacher of the discourse on enthusiasm. This kind of identification was reinforced by the fact that a large quantity of the eighteenth century's print production was taken up with religious disputation or often-lurid accounts of conversion experiences. Methodism, for instance, was very much a print phenomenon, one that encouraged converts to translate their feelings into words. From 1778 Wesley's *Arminian Magazine* and its successor the *Methodist* provided autobiographical narratives that he regarded as 'the marrow of experimental and practical religion'.[132] Many of the attacks on Methodism complained of the proliferation of enthusiasm in print.[133] Women in particular contributed to a 'steady stream of hymns and devotional verse', a stream which most reviewers regarded as incapable of entering the aesthetic sphere.[134] Reviewers as guardians of taste, guiding readers and banishing interlopers, were always particularly hard on religious enthusiasm. Remember Mackenzie's concern about religious matters being discussed in *The Mirror*. Discourses on the prophecies, sermons,

---

[132] *The Letters of the Rev. John Wesley, A.M.*, ed. J. Telford, 8 vols. (1931), vi. 295.

[133] John Styles, *Strictures on Two Critiques in the Edinburgh Review on the Subject of Methodism and Missions; with Remarks on the Influence of Reviews in General on Morals and Happiness in Three Letters to a Friend* (1808), complained of the *Edinburgh* that 'the Evangelical and Methodist magazines were chosen as objects of its sarcastic ridicule, on account of their wide and increasing circulation among the populace' (28). For a discussion of the *Edinburgh*'s attitude to enthusiasm, see below.

[134] Margaret Maison, ' "Thine, Only Thine": Women Hymn Writers in Britain 1760–1835', in Gail Malmgreen (ed.), *Religion in the Lives of English Women: 1760–1930* (Croom Helm, 1986), 11–40.

conversion narratives, hymns, and other kinds of devotional verse accounted for a significant proportion of the expansion of print culture, but the reviews were apt to represent this deluge of religious experience as an infection abroad in the republic of letters. The *Edinburgh*, for instance, complained that 'for the swarm of ephemeral sermons which issue from the press, we are principally indebted to the vanity of popular preachers, who are puffed up, by female praises, into a belief, that what may be delivered, with great propriety, in a chapel full of visitors and friends, is fit for the deliberate attention of the public.'[135] Here the print phenomenon of experimental religion is firmly placed in the discourse on enthusiasm. The product of self-deluding egotism and unregulated female admiration, enthusiasm is threatening to overwhelm the reading public.

The periodicals were eager, of course, to celebrate the circulation of what they regarded as proper forms of knowledge. Their problem was that large sections of the population, keen to join in this expansion of print culture, seemed to be operating with a very different account of what constituted knowledge. This was an audience only too eager to read, where they could, the latest accounts of spiritual awakening or disputes about the nature of grace. Prophecies were especially popular, much to the chagrin of journals such as the *Analytical Review*, which in the summer of 1795 felt reluctantly obliged to devote several review pages to the controversy surrounding the so-called Paddington Prophet, Richard Brothers.[136] The superiority of the British as a 'polite and commercial people' implied a contrast with what James Lackington called 'the enthusiast on the banks of the Ganges'.[137] The interest shown by the populace in prophets such as Brothers threatened to subvert these distinctions and allow the kind of comparisons between Methodism and Hinduism implied by Lackington here. Leigh Hunt, for instance, compared the ecstasies of Methodist women with 'the East Indian widow, who devotes herself to the flames in order to accompany her husband into bliss' (H 94). Anxieties about enthusiasm undermining such differences are evident even in Robert Southey's praise for the Baptist missionaries to India in the *Annual*

---

[135] *Edinburgh Review*, 1 (1802), 128.
[136] For more detail on the *Analytical* and Brothers, see Chapter 2.
[137] Lackington, *Memoirs*, 154.

Register of 1802.[138] Southey wrote a review extolling the virtues of
the former shoemaker turned missionary William Carey. Despite
his lack of education and the fact that he was a Dissenter, Southey
assured his readers that Carey was guilty of nothing 'enthusiastic or
declamatory', but his confidence soon shrivels to acknowledge a
fear that Carey might be little better than those he wished to convert.[139] Although ostensibly written in defence of Carey and the
Baptist missions, Southey's review ends with a call for the Church
to involve itself in missionary work. The Calvinism of the Baptists
is potentially even worse than Hinduism, Southey finally admits,
because of its vulgar need to see signs of 'grace' and 'new birth': 'If
the mission to Hindostan were connected with nothing but the
propagation of such a faith, we should hope the natives would
continue to worship Veeshnoo and Seeva, rather than the demon
whom Calvin has set up!'[140] The *Edinburgh Review* was much
more forthright on the matter: 'if no other instruments remain than
visionary enthusiasts, some doubt may be honestly raised whether
it is not better to drop the scheme entirely.'[141] Its discussion of the
missionaries was predicated on a view that the inner light was a
dubious foundation on which to erect any religious belief. Sounding
a familiar note, it suggested that the missionary fanaticism was the
traditional *ignus fatuus* of the crowd: 'if a tinker is a devout man,
he infallibly sets off for the East.'[142] Southey and many of his contemporaries implicitly feared that the enthusiasm of the seventeenth
century was alive and well all around them. His *Letters from
England* (1807) is almost a guidebook to the enthusiasm (both religious and secular) of his fellow countrymen, though written in the
voice of a bemused Portuguese visitor. Enthusiasm seemed constantly to be bubbling up from below in both religious, secular, and

---

[138] Robert Southey, 'Art. LXXI: Periodical Accounts Relative to the Baptist
Missionary Society, for Propagating the Gospel among the Heathen', *Annual
Review*, 1 (1802), 207–18. Southey used much the same material in another review
of the same material in the *Quarterly Review*, 1 (1809), 193–226. Although it man-
ifests some of the same ambivalence, the *Quarterly* piece is less critical. His review
of William Myles's *A Chronological History of the People called Methodists* (1802)
had called Methodists 'literally and precisely speaking, an Ecclesiastical
Corresponding Society' (165). By 1809 he was more clearly evolving the position set
out in his *Life of Wesley*. On the former, see *Annual Review*, 2 (1803), 201–13. For
an account of the change in Southey's attitudes, see Mark Storey, *Robert Southey: A
Life* (Oxford: Oxford University Press, 1997).

[139] *Annual Review*, 1 (1802), 208.
[141] *Edinburgh Review*, 12 (1808), 180.

[140] Ibid. 216–17.
[142] Ibid.

even scientific forms. In 1802 Southey had claimed 'a worse danger than the spread of Methodism can scarcely be apprehended for England'. The threat was much more dangerous than what he called the 'those enemies of straw' infidelity and atheism.[143]

To represent the fear of vulgar enthusiasm only as a discursive 'trace' or textual effect within polite culture would be to miss this point. The repressed of Shaftesbury's politeness seemed to be continually returning and proclaiming its right to a place in the public sphere on the basis of the inner light. The Gordon Rioters of 1780, who went on a rampage through London in defence of Protestant religion, looked to Edward Gibbon like 'forty thousand Puritans such as they might be in the time of Cromwell . . . started out of their graves'.[144] Nowhere, however, was this spectre of popular religious enthusiasm more often seen and feared by Gibbon's contemporaries than in the phenomenon of Methodism. Eighteenth-century Methodism has been the site of a long-standing debate among historians over whether or not it inhibited an English Revolution on the French model. Bernard Semmel claimed that the Methodists saw themselves not as a threat to the established order, but as a catalyst for its revivification, asserting what Isabel Rivers calls 'the essential place of feeling and experience in religion'.[145] A related approach has seen Methodism as playing an important role in the coming of time-work discipline.[146] What these approaches underestimate is the extent to which Wesley was attacked for encouraging a dangerous enthusiasm that undermined morality and an unworldliness that was 'the bane of industry'.[147] The Bishop of Exeter saw Wesley's movement as old enthusiasm writ large in the licence it granted 'inspirations, revelations, illuminations, and all

---

[143] *Annual Review*, 2 (1803), 207 and 213.

[144] 'To Dorothea Gibbon, 8 June 1780', in *The Letters of Edward Gibbon*, ed. J. E. Norton, 3 vols. (London: Cassell, 1956), ii. 243.

[145] Bernard Semmel, *The Methodist Revolution* (Heinemann, 1974), 4–5, and Rivers, *Reason, Grace, and Sentiment*, i. 207. For a critique of Semmel's view that places more stress on the political and social ambiguities of the movement, see David Hempton, *Methodism and Politics in British Society 1750–1850* (Hutchinson, 1984).

[146] See Edward Thompson, *Customs in Common* (Harmondsworth, Penguin, 1993), ch. 6. My thinking about this subject has been greatly helped by conversations with John Walsh. See his ' "The Bane of Industry"? Popular Evangelicalism and Work in the Eighteenth Century', in R. N. Swanson (ed.), *The Use and Abuse of Time in Church History* (Woodbridge: Boydell & Brewer, 2002), 223–41.

[147] *Norwich Mercury*, 18 Jan. 1752, quoted in Walsh, ' "The Bane of Industry"?', 225.

the extraordinary and immediate actions of all the persons in the sacred Trinity'.[148] It was regularly accused of giving an undue emphasis to matters of salvation and inward religious experience rather than the common duties of practical Christianity. Justification by faith was seen as a dangerous creed in this respect. Although part of the Thirty-Nine Articles of the Church, in the wrong hands the doctrine could lead to the presumption that 'everything is represented to be done for them by the all-sufficient merits of a saviour'.[149] Wesley strongly denied the Bishop's charge that '*Impulses*, Impressions, Feelings, Transports of sensible Joy, etc.' had been advanced into 'certain Rules of Conduct' or that he neglected 'the means of salvation', but he was aware of dangerous tendencies among his own followers that he attempted to regulate.[150] He wrote to Thomas Maxfield in November 1762 to explain what he understood by enthusiasm and why he disliked it:

I dislike something that has the appearance of enthusiasm: overvaluing feelings and inward impressions: mistaking the mere work of imagination for the voice of the Spirit; expecting the end without the means, and undervaluing reason, knowledge and wisdom in general.[151]

What is striking about this letter is that it defines enthusiasm not so much as false inspiration, but more as the claim to grace without dignifying labour. Present pardon might be assured in the intensity of religious feeling, Wesley told his followers, but these feelings offered no guarantee of future salvation. Believers ought not to judge 'by their own inward feelings'.[152] '*Deep* repentance' and '*thorough* conviction' (my emphasis) were his watchwords against enthusiasm.[153] The increasingly Arminian emphasis of his theology insisted on works as a necessary condition of salvation, even if the

---

[148] George Lavington, Bishop of Exeter, *The Enthusiasm of Methodists and Papists Compared*, 3 parts (1759–61), i. 15

[149] J. Green, *The Principles and Practices of the Methodists Considered* (London, 1760), quoted in Walsh, ' "The Bane of Industry"?', 231.

[150] Lavington, *Enthusiasm*, ii. 104–5. Wesley directly denied the charge, see, for instance, *The Works of John Wesley*, xi: *The Appeals to Men of Reason and Religion*, ed. Gerald R. Cragg (Oxford: Oxford University Press, 1975), 399. On the neglect of the 'means of salvation', see Lavington, *Enthusiasm*, ii. 146, and for Wesley's rebuttal, see *Appeals*, 414.

[151] *Letters of Wesley*, iv. 193.   [152] Wesley, *Appeals*, 399.

[153] *The Works of John Wesley*, i–iv: *Sermons*, ed. A. C. Outler (Nashville: Abingdon, 1984–7), ii. 50.

individual could not be saved by the merits of his works alone.[154]
Wesley later condemned those preachers in his own movement who
trusted the Spirit and did not prepare their sermons. Only diligent
scholarship could communicate the divine message. Those 'who
expect to understand the Holy Scriptures without reading them and
meditating thereon' and those 'who *designedly* speak in the public
assembly without any premeditation' were laying themselves open
to the pretensions of enthusiasm.[155] Yet he was more tolerant of
'extraordinary calls' than many in the church hierarchy for all that
such calls had to be tested against experience, reason, and scripture.[156] Too many of his fellow churchmen, he believed, were quick
to identify all 'experimental religion' with enthusiasm. His sermon
on *The Nature of Enthusiasm* (1755) suggested the possibility of a
positive meaning of the word 'enthusiasm' applied to the behaviour
of the prophets and apostles.[157] Wesley's position on these matters
was no less complex than Shaftesbury's (whom he quoted in his
sermon on the possibility of a positive meaning for the word). He
accepted that the usual meaning of 'enthusiasm' referred to a
genuine 'disorder of the mind', but if he reluctantly gave up on the
word itself he refused to accept that all of the usual behaviour associated with it was simply madness or imposture.[158] His theology
like Shaftesbury's philosophy wanted to celebrate the power of the
inner light, while remaining suspicious of the inflationary potential
of something for nothing or 'for the end without using the
means'.[159] He ended his sermon on enthusiasm by defending 'that
pure and holy religion which the world always did, and always will,
call enthusiasm; but which to all who are saved from real enthusiasm—from merely nominal Christianity—is . . . a fountain of water,
springing up with everlasting life!'[160] Such language may have
seemed to Robert Southey—even in 1820, when his position on
religious warmth had relaxed—to come too close to 'making the
outward Christ an enemy to the Christ within' (*Life of Wesley*, i.

---

[154] Rivers, *Reason, Grace, and Sentiment*, i. 212.

[155] Wesley, *Sermons*, ii. 56.

[156] Wesley correctly ascribes to Shaftesbury the idea that 'there is no man excellent in his profession, whatsoever it be, who has not in his temper a strong tincture
of enthusiasm', ibid. 49.

[157] See ibid. 47–9.   [158] Ibid. 49.

[159] *The Works of the Rev. John Wesley*, ed. T. Jackson, 14 vols., 3rd edn. (1831),
viii. 316.

[160] Wesley, *Sermons*, ii. 60.

173), but the unworlding of the conversion experience was essential to Wesley's idea of moral transformation. Little wonder that one of his earliest publications was a pirated version of Young's *Night Thoughts*, a key text in Irlam's account of the rehabilitation of enthusiasm in early eighteenth-century poetry.[161]

'Extraordinary calls' were possible, Wesley believed, if not sufficient to the believer's salvation. Indeed he scoffed at those for whom a believer was to be charged with enthusiasm 'if he continually sees him that is invisible, and accordingly walks by faith and not by sight'.[162] How were such experiences different from mere 'delirium'? Richard Brantley has suggested one of the ways Wesley tried to legitimate such experiences was by analogy with Locke's ideas of sensations.[163] By stressing his admiration for Locke, Brantley argues, Wesley was attempting to suggest affective religion could be an object of knowledge. Religious feeling was a genuine sense experience, not at all the same thing as enthusiasm, if based on genuine sensations that left real impressions on the mind, but here he ran into another problem. Experimental religion had to be distanced from the grossness of the senses. The spiritual eye was not fleshly or what his opponent 'John Smith' condemned as 'perceptible inspiration'.[164] That mistake Wesley too believed was the error of enthusiasm. Faith provided 'a more extensive knowledge of things invisible, showing what eye had not seen, nor ear heard, neither before could it enter into our heart to conceive'.[165] The analogical nature of the claim to spiritual knowledge had always to be respected. Metaphor was not to be mistaken for a sensory apprehension of divinity.[166] Thus Wesley's wariness of 'overvaluing *feelings* and inward impressions'.[167] Yet many still thought Wesley was playing with fire by placing too much emphasis on these spiritual

---

[161] Irlam discusses Young at length in *Elations*, chs. 6 and 7. For Wesley's version of the poem, see *An Extract from Dr Young's Night Thoughts on Life, Death, and Immortality*, ed. John Wesley (Bristol, 1770).

[162] Wesley, *Sermons*, ii. 47. See Richard E. Brantley, *Wordsworth's 'Natural Methodism'* (New Haven: Yale University Press, 1975), 71, on Wesley's defence of the possibility of extraordinary calls.

[163] Brantley, *Locke, Wesley, and the Method of English Romanticism* (Gainesville, Fla.: University of Florida Press, 1984), esp. chs. 1 and 2.

[164] *The Works of John Wesley*, xxv–xxvi: *Letters*, i–ii, ed. F. Baker (Oxford: Oxford University Press, 1980–2), ii. 170.

[165] Wesley, *Appeals*, 56–7.

[166] Brantley, *Locke, Wesley, and the Method of English Romanticism*, 31–3.

[167] Wesley, *Appeals*, 399.

impressions, and that he could not really maintain the distinctions he was making. 'Insisting too strongly even on Scripture metaphors has something in it misguiding to the reader,' wrote 'John Smith', 'Thus the hanging so much on faith being the eye, the ear, the finger, the palate etc. of the soul, inclines a reader to think that you mean something more than mere metaphor.'[168] Failing to understand the figurative nature of metaphor, as we have seen, was regarded as a common failing of uneducated readers. By taking such language to the masses, whether or not he had driven himself to 'distraction', Wesley was deemed to be encouraging enthusiasm. Even Robert Southey, who by the time he wrote his *Life of Wesley* was increasingly impressed by the disciplinary success of Methodism on the masses, remained concerned that 'like Mesmer and his disciples, he had produced a new disease, and he accounted for it by a theological theory instead of a physical one. As men are intoxicated by strong drink affecting the mind through the body, so are they by strong passions influencing the body through the mind. Here there was nothing but what would naturally follow when persons, in a state of spiritual drunkenness, abandoned themselves to their sensations, and such sensations spread rapidly, both by voluntary and involuntary imitation' (*Life of Wesley*, i. 239). Certainly many of Wesley's followers refused to practise the kinds of restraints their leaders encouraged. Plenty of those in the crowds who gathered to hear Wesley, Whitefield, and their preachers seem to have agreed with Blake's Isaiah against Locke that 'a firm perswasion that a thing is so, make[s] it so' (*MHH* 12: E 38).

Barker-Benfield stresses the connections between sensibility and Methodism, but his account focuses on the delicate tears of politeness rather than the violent paroxysms of its popular manifestations.[169] Methodism was particularly strong among the artisan occupational groups from whom most was feared in times of political excitement and public disorder.[170] For Leigh Hunt and for many others within the educated elite, the term 'Methodist' could be used to refer not only to the followers of Wesley and Whitefield, but to any group outside the established Church given to religious fanaticism, 'all that enthusiastic multitude who in the spirit of Christian modesty call themselves the Godly, whether Arminians or

---

[168] Wesley, *Letters*, ii. 167.
[169] Barker-Benfield, *The Culture of Sensibility*, 71–5.
[170] Hempton, *Methodism and Politics*, 12

Calvinists, or the innumerable divisions of these sects, who all claim the miracles of the Apostolic age, the immediate interference of the Deity, and the holy ecstasies of the blessed' (H 2). The doctrine associated with religious enthusiasm above all else was the abuse of the doctrine of justification by faith alone, an abuse that Wesley's Arminian emphasis on the fruits of salvation was meant to ameliorate. The message that grace was available to all who repented and believed may well have had a key role in the success of the Methodist movement among the lower classes.[171] The more orthodox on the Calvinist wing of the movement were often shocked by a hyper-Calvinism whose confidence in salvation could verge on antinomianism in the strength of its feeling of liberation from the Moral Law. The respectable Dissenters James Bennett and David Bogue regarded this failing as the besetting sin of uneducated men who had never read Calvin. They described it in 1800 as 'the popular poison, a bastard zeal for the doctrine of salvation by grace'.[172] Such zeal was feared, whether Arminian or Calvinist, because it was regarded as the preparation for the disregard for respectable morality and social deference. Sarah Trimmer was in no doubt that this stress 'on the inward feeling alone' was at the core of the Methodist's success. 'Flattering to the baseness and Depravity of the human Heart', she believed such preaching 'opens a door of hope even to the most ignorant and illiterate'.[173]

What did such beliefs offer to the mob feared by Bennett and Bogue? My answer to that question starts by thinking in terms of the existence of a popular culture of religious enthusiasm with its own institutions and distinctive practices. Habermas's notion of the bourgeois public sphere, with its newspapers being discussed in coffee houses and clubs, its periodicals encouraging the circulation of sound knowledge and banning disputation in religion from its pages, had an alter ego in the heterotopia of chapels, field meetings, and the huge circulation of popular religious pamphlets and ser-

---

[171] John Walsh, '"Methodism" and the Origins of English Speaking Evangelicalism', in Mark A. Noll, David W. Bebbington, and George A. Rawlyk (eds.), *Evangelicalism: Comparative Studies of Popular Protestantism in N. America, the British Isles, and Beyond, 1700–1900* (New York: Oxford University Press, 1994), 31.

[172] David Bogue and James Bennett, *History of the Dissenters, from the Revolution in 1688, to the Year 1808*, 4 vols. (1808–12), iv. 39.

[173] *A Review of the Policy, Doctrines and Morals of the Methodists* (1791), 13 and 8.

mons.[174] Eighteenth-century notions of civility were almost defined by the exclusion of this kind of religious literature with its tendency to rancour, disputation, and ecstasies. Henry Mackenzie's policies on religion in his periodicals, for instance, were designed to promote the conversation of culture, but not the rancorous mental warfare associated with enthusiasm. Especially where it produced mass open-air meetings, physical and other kinds of bodily displays of divine ecstasy, or violently figurative and inflammatory language, such enthusiasm looked like the grotesque other of the polite public sphere to many eighteenth-century observers, but equally the authority of the inner light remained powerfully attractive to sections of the population excluded by those invisible barriers of the enlightenment based on education, manners, and taste. Without access to the leisure necessary to reflection or the economic means to acquire taste, the crowd was barred from the theoretically level playing-field of the bourgeois public sphere. Justification by the immediate experience of God's grace was a means of transcending these worldly disadvantages. Leigh Hunt complained that 'among the Methodists every body teaches, man and boy, learned and unlearned' (H 3). Enthusiasm, whether politically inflected or otherwise, was one language by which those who were outside the conversation of culture could assert their right to be heard.

Clement Hawes sees the continuing attractions of enthusiastic discourse in terms of E. P. Thompson's 'class struggle without class'.[175] He goes so far as to identify a tradition of self-consciously 'manic' writing which employed its own rhetoric of enthusiasm to distance itself from the corruption of learning and reason. Extreme manifestations of this kind of literature did often support their claims to be inspired by pointing to their own lack of regulation; that is, they used their own transgressions of ideas of decorum and educated style to prove that they had found their authority beyond the categories of human 'reason'. 'Every man who writes and preaches without any knowledge of common English is evidently an inspired preacher, for what but inspiration could induce him to speak,' asked Hunt mockingly (H 9). Hunt was parodying those less circumspect than Wesley, who made no bones about claiming to

---

[174] See Michel Foucault, 'Of Other Spaces', *Diacritics* 16 (1986), 22–7.
[175] See Clement Hawes, *Mania and Literary Style: The Rhetoric of Enthusiasm from the Ranters to Christopher Smart* (Cambridge: Cambridge University Press, 1996), 2–3, and Thompson, *Customs in Common*, chs. 1 and 2.

experience the divine presence immediately, often literally proclaiming their ability to see God. Such texts might talk of spiritual eyes, and seem to be respecting the kind of distinction between the spirit and the flesh insisted on by Wesley, but the sheer availability of illumination seemed to undermine any idea of a regulated traffic between the human and divine. When such ecstasies were accompanied by claims that the experience of conversion or other kinds of spiritual communication rendered the mediations of the established Church and its scholarly apparatus unnecessary, they were particularly alarming to Anglicans. Whereas Samuel Johnson claimed that the Bible could not 'be understood at all by the unlearned,' others seemed only too eager to dispense with the mediations of scholarship:

> The scriptures are plain and easy—as is Christ's example clear and obvious to view: he is no hard master, nor are the scriptures a sealed book to you, but a plain clear guide, and easy to be understood, written to suit the meanest capacities, independent of the glosses of mercenaries who would make us believe to the contrary.[176]

The writer of these words, the engraver Garnet Terry, had been the publisher of the former coal-heaver turned preacher William Huntington for much of the 1780s and 1790s. Huntington was probably the most infamous popular preacher at work in the metropolis at the end of the century: the embodiment of what the elite considered religious enthusiasm. Luridly violent and emotional in their language, the sermons Terry published for Huntington were attacked again and again for trying to induce transport in a congregation considered beyond the kind of reflection required to regulate themselves.[177]

The idea that such performances and their transcriptions in print were part of a public sphere of enthusiasm can be extended to the secular versions of the inner-light theology which appear in the poetry of the period. No less than the hundreds of anonymous hymn writers whose effusions flooded religious magazines that opened their pages to the public, the so-called 'peasant poet', whose

[176] Onesimus [Garnet Terry], *Letters on Godly and Religious Subjects*, 2 vols., 2nd edn. (1808), p. iii.

[177] For more detail on the relationship between Terry and Huntington, see Jon Mee, 'Is There an Antinomian in the House: William Blake and the After-Life of a Heresy', in Steve Clark and David Worrall (eds.), *Historicizing Blake* (Basingstoke: Macmillan, 1994), 43–58.

'native genius' was paraded in print throughout the century, was bringing his or her self before the public on the authority of inner feelings. Where the poet could demonstrate through the appropriate accommodations to the codes of deference and/or politeness that he or she knew his or her place, such writing might be accepted as a properly regulated manifestation of enthusiasm and could be shown off to the public by polite patrons. Robert Southey offered a historical survey of what he called 'our Uneducated Poets' in 1831 that provides a useful cameo of attitudes to such writing. While he complained that he had been inundated by such productions since his appointment as Laureate, he also claimed to be enchanted by 'the natural feelings and natural images in these poor verses'.[178] What attracts Southey to the poets is 'a charm of freshness as well as truth'.[179] 'Charm' is a condescending word in this context, the poetry is charming, an object of interest, rather than poetry in its own right—the verses, after all, are 'poor'. The charm fades for Southey, 'when they begin to form their style upon some approved model', that is, effectively when the uneducated writer aspires to be a poet as such.[180] Southey's reaction to unlearned enthusiasm, his objection to their natural enthusiasm conforming to an 'approved model', was related to another kind of response which might seem its opposite, that is, the claim that enthusiasm had to be appropriately shaped if it were to become poetry. These are two sides of the same coin of regulatory discourse. Seeing the uneducated poet as prone to mechanical contrivance is the corollary of regarding him as incapable of the 'natural' shaping of the self imagined by Shaftesbury. 'Taste' plays the same kind of role in Wordsworth's Preface to the *Lyrical Ballads*, it is what makes him capable of recollection of the feeling subject in tranquillity. Others without taste reduce feeling to a 'mechanic' contrivance.[181] In Southey's 'Essay' the social ramifications of this idea are more clearly laid out. His taste is being privileged over the unsatisfying conjunction of feeling and 'approved models' in the uneducated poets he judges. They might have genius of a kind, but they cannot provide it with the regulation necessary to make it into literature. Where they try self-regulation, they fall into empty mechanical contrivances.

---

[178] Southey, 'Lives and Works of our Uneducated Poets', in *Attempts in Verse, by John Jones, an Old Servant* (1831), 8.

[179] Ibid. 118.   [180] Ibid.

[181] For a discussion of this relationship in Wordsworth, see below Chap 5.

Consequently, the uneducated ought to apply for his advice, Southey's essay implies, because he can supply the taste which they cannot generate for themselves. Only the man of taste has had the opportunity through education and habitual reflection to transform empty contrivances into a second nature.

The reviews of the period are littered with this kind of exercise in regulation. Francis Jeffrey's attack on John Thelwall's poetry, discussed in my next chapter, provides one example. Jeffrey's account of Thelwall as a shopman who abandons his counter to pursue his inner light ought to be read in the context of the *Edinburgh*'s contemporary campaign against religious enthusiasm (just as Southey's comments on uneducated poets ought to be read alongside his comments on the Methodist's use of 'ignorant' itinerants governed by 'sympathy' rather than 'intellect' in *The Life of Wesley*). The shopman-poet and the cobbler-preacher were regarded as parallel phenomena in the *Edinburgh Review*. Both gave way to 'extraordinary calls' they were unable to properly shape into an identity. For both Jeffrey and Southey large parts of the population are deemed incapable of regulating their enthusiasm for themselves. In Part II of this book, I will be arguing that Coleridge's distinction between the Fancy and the Imagination works in a similar way. His account of Imagination stresses volition in a way that implies the power of the true poet to regulate himself. The Fancy has all the passivity associated with enthusiasm. It is the product of mechanical impulses, a spasmodic faculty tending towards delirium and distraction. Wordsworth may have written of poetry as the spontaneous overflow of powerful feeling, but only certain kinds of men have the power to regulate it into poetry. They need not extraordinary calls, because their taste has the habitual facility of plumbing the depths of their feelings. The rest is the temporary enthusiasm of magazine verse. Wordsworth and Coleridge's defence of a professionalized poetry, recently outlined by critics such as Goldberg and Siskin, is part and parcel of the reaction against enthusiasm in the Romantic period, a reaction whose terms were inherited from the discourse of regulation outlined in this chapter.[182] No less than those Anglican divines who resented popular religious enthusiasm as an assault on the professional

---

[182] See Brian Goldberg, ' "Ministry More Palpable": William Wordsworth and the Making of Romantic Professionalism', *Studies in Romanticism*, 36 (1997), 327–47, and Clifford Siskin, *The Work of Writing*.

mediation they offered, Southey, Jeffrey, Coleridge, and Wordsworth all wrote as part of an emergent clerisy, eager to ring fence literariness from the enthusiasm of the crowd. Thelwall's poetry provides a useful contrast that runs through much of the rest of this book. He was not without ambivalence of his own about the enthusiasm of the crowd, but he was much more willing to conceive of the possibility of it regulating itself. One of the differences between Jeffrey and the three Romantic poets may lie in the fact that the latter were readier to see enthusiasm as in some ways essential even if it had to be carefully regulated. Jeffrey continually suspected that Wordsworth, for instance, was only repeating and virtually encouraging the enthusiasm of the Methodists in his desire for a poetry and religion of affect.[183] Even so, for these poets, as for Wesley in religion, the spontaneous overflow of feelings was a necessary but not sufficient condition for poetry.

EXUBERANT FANCY AND UNEDUCATED MINDS

I would like to close this chapter with an extended example that more fully illustrates the intertwining of religious and more narrowly literary discourses in relation to enthusiasm. It is drawn from the pages of the February 1794 issue of the *Evangelical Magazine*, and brings together the uneducated poet and religious seeker in the person of Richard Lee. This number of the *Evangelical Magazine* contains a review of a collection of poems by Lee. In fact many of them had already been published in the magazine over the previous year (pseudonymously under the name 'Ebeneezer').[184] The whole exercise would seem to promise an example of potential enthusiasm sublimated into poetry. A worthy magazine encourages an unknown poet by publishing his works, a volume follows, the volume is given a (largely) positive review by the magazine. Under the regulating influence of its patronage, Ebeneezer can emerge blinking into his place into the sun as the poet Richard Lee, or, at

---

[183] See the discussion of Jeffrey's attitude to Wordsworth's enthusiasm in Chapter 5.

[184] See Jon Mee, 'The Strange Career of Richard "Citizen" Lee: Poetry, Popular Radicalism, and Enthusiasm in the 1790s', in T. Morton and N. Smith (eds.), *Radicalism in British Literary Culture, 1650–1830: From Revolution to Revolution* (Cambridge: Cambridge University Press, 2002), 153–5, for further details.

least, in the properly compliant sub-category of 'uneducated poet'.
Lee seems to signal the necessary humility in his preface:

It is not from a vain Supposition of their Poetical Merit, that the ensuing
Sheets are offered to the Public; but from a Conviction of the Divine Truths
they contain; Truths which, I own, fallen and depraved Reason will always
stumble at; and which the unregenerate Heart will never cordially receive;
they are too humbling for proud Nature to be in love with;—too dazzling
for carnal Eyes to behold. But they are Truths which the CHRISTIAN
embraces, and holds fast as his chief treasure.[185]

Yet although this passage was reprinted in the review, which praises
the genuine feeling of the poetry, the reviewer simultaneously registers a concern over the presumption that incorrectness could be
overlooked in favour of the authenticity of religious feeling:

This is perhaps more than a writer is entitled to expect, when he claims the
public attention; especially as defects in grammar, accent, rhyme, and
metre, might have been removed by the previous correction of some judicious friend. However, these poems, published, apparently, 'with all their
imperfections on their head,' afford the stronger evidence of being genuine;
and many of them are superior, even in correctness, to what is naturally
looked for in the production of so young a person, who has received little
assistance from education, and whose occupation we understand to be that
of a laborious mechanic.[186]

Self-taught poets could be valued for their 'genuine' effusions of the
heart, but this was not quite the same thing as valuing them as
'poets' or 'writers' in their own right. Such a valuation would have
meant encouraging the uneducated to abandon what polite commentators perceived as their proper position within the social hierarchy, a fear repeatedly sounded in critical assessments of so-called
'uneducated' poets in the period.[187] The friendly reviewer is
'judicious' insofar as he possesses the necessary taste to regulate
Ebeneezer's enthusiasm, the laborious mechanic cannot be expected
to regulate himself and needs to be mildly censured for not seeking
the help of his more tasteful superior. Perhaps the reviewer should
have been firmer, for his doubts were more than confirmed in the

[185] Richard Lee, *Flowers from Sharon; or, Original Poems on Divine Subjects*
(1794), Advertisement [p. iii].
[186] *Evangelical Magazine*, 2 (Feb. 1794), 82–3.
[187] For a useful discussion of this issue, see Annette Wheeler Cafarelli, 'The
Romantic "Peasant" Poets and their Patrons', *Wordsworth Circle*, 26 (1995),
77–87.

following year when Ebeneezer , once again transported, became the radical activist Richard 'Citizen' Lee, 'one of the few English Jacobins who referred to the guillotine in terms of warm approval'.[188] Lee fulfilled the dreaded extreme feared by the discourse on enthusiasm: the religious 'fanatic' who believed God had directly validated the overthrow of things-as-they-are.

Here in the pages of the *Evangelical Magazine* we have encountered the micro-dynamics of Hartman's idea of literariness as a regulation of enthusiasm. Ebeneezer does not have the 'judicious' taste required to complete the process of turning prophecy into poetry. The reviewer fears that he has not quite transformed himself into the poet, or, more specifically, Ebeneezer has failed to acknowledge that as an uneducated man such a transformation is impossible without consulting a gentleman of taste. Yet there is a relative complacency in the review, perhaps rooted in the fact that enthusiasm has at least entered the realm of literature. In what seems to be an allusion to the popularity of Huntington, the very first issue of the *Evangelical Magazine* described its purpose as the protection of 'true believers, exposed to the wiles of erroneous teachers who endeavour to perplex their minds, and subvert their faith'.[189] At its very inception, then, the *Evangelical Magazine* was concerned to channel popular religious feeling into courses properly secured against enthusiasm. Its poetry and review pages, as we have seen in relation to Lee, were central to the project, but in the process of drawing out enthusiasm in order to regulate it there was the danger of aiding its proliferation. The *British Critic* claimed that 'Lee has suffered his muse (who is uniformly spiritual) to carry him to the grossest violation of Poetical decorum.'[190] From its point of view, the politeness of poetry was being destroyed by religious enthusiasm. Others were also sceptical about the role of magazines such as the *Evangelical*. In 1800 the cure promised by them was denounced as poisonous by William Hamilton Reid.[191] A few years

[188] This description of Lee is Edward Thompson's. See *The Making of the English Working Class*, rev. edn. (Harmondsworth: Penguin, 1968), 155.

[189] 'Preface', *Evangelical Magazine*, 1 (1793), 2.

[190] *British Critic*, 3 (1794), 690.

[191] See W. H. Reid, *The Rise and Dissolution of the Infidel Societies in this Metropolis: Including the Origin of Modern Deism and Atheism; the Genius and Conduct of those Associations; their Lecture-Rooms, Field-Meetings, and Deputations* (1800), 6. See also Donald Davie, *A Gathered Church: The Literature of the English Dissenting Interest, 1700–1930* (Routledge & Kegan Paul, 1978), 61,

later, Leigh Hunt joined in with his own attack on the *Evangelical*, suggesting that the vulgar were incapable of tastefully regulating their feelings:

People of exuberant fancies and uncultivated minds cannot think too highly of themselves, when they hear the refuse of society claiming familiarity with all the persons in the Trinity and talking of going to heaven as they would of the one-shilling gallery: they are led on therefore from familiarity to confidence, and from confidence to a sense of equality, and thus become gods themselves. (H xiii).

He could easily be commenting directly on Lee's volume (he wasn't). The involvement of literary figures such as Hunt and Southey in the crusade against popular religious excesses should alert us to the particularly anxious associations between literary culture and enthusiasm. From their perspective the *Evangelical Magazine* was not an aesthetic site at all. Literature needed to separate itself from the kind of vulgarity that brought the religious feelings of the lower classes so directly before the public. No less than Addison and Steele earlier in the century, periodical essayists such as Hunt were involved in a process of gentrification through taste, that is, they were expanding the circles within which self-regulation was regarded as capable of success.[192] Nevertheless there were limits even for 'Cockneys' such as Hunt. Popular religious feeling was too turbulent to be part of the process for him: they remained the *ne plus ultra* of enthusiasm. Useful recent work done on the Hunt circle by critics such as Nicholas Roe and Jeffrey Cox has familiarized the idea of the Cockney School as a grouping of freethinkers, attacking religious bigotry in the name of liberal principles, but along with such attitudes could go a certain condescension about popular belief.[193] For enthusiasm to rear its head in public in the early decades of the nineteenth century was an outrageous contradiction of Hunt's own faith in the civilizing progress of taste. Hunt regarded Methodism as a throwback to 'the fanatics

for the magazine's wide circulation and the hostility of those concerned at its Calvinistic enthusiasm.

[192] See Ayumi Mizukoshi, *Keats, Hunt, and the Aesthetics of Pleasure* (Basingstoke: Palgrave, 2001).

[193] See Nicholas Roe, *John Keats and the Culture of Dissent* (Oxford: Oxford University Press, 1997), and Jeffrey N. Cox, *Poetry and Politics in the Cockney School: Keats, Shelley, Hunt, and their Circle* (Cambridge: Cambridge University Press, 1998).

of the commonwealth' (H p. ix). His feelings about religion reveal the bottom line of his extension of the cultural franchise. Despite Hunt's liberalism, he was convinced that only men 'whose education has enabled them to search into the original languages of the scriptures and the antiquities of the church [were qualified] to search into the truth of what they teach' (H 3). Such sentiments reveal that it was not just superstition as such that Hunt feared. He was disgusted by the fact that 'among the Methodists every body teaches, man and boy, learned and unlearned' (H3).

Clement Hawes sees the appeal to the authority of the inner light as a form of resistance taken up by those excluded from the conversation of culture by guardians of culture such as Hunt. Those who did not have the cultural capital to acquire taste continued to appeal to their own feelings, religious and otherwise, as the basis of participation in the public sphere. Hawes is perhaps hasty to overlook the role enthusiasm increasingly played in elite poetic discourse.[194] He may also implicitly privilege the manic style of enthusiasm over more 'enlightened' discourses as the authentic version of popular resistance. Enlightenment notions of reasoned exchange between autonomous, self-regulated subjects were to be essential to the popular radical movement of the 1790s. Radicals put a great deal of pressure on the invisible barriers of the Enlightenment in the process. Reason for them was often regarded as being as universally available as the religious enthusiast often believed the inner light to be. Tensions between these two positions also produced severe problems within the London Corresponding Society. For Burke the distinction hardly mattered. Both reified persuasion over experience to make the Jacobin an avatar of the Ranter. From this perspective both the Enlightenment of the Rational Dissenter such as Richard Price and the visionary pretensions of a Methodist such as Richard Lee were simply species of enthusiasm. These different conflicts over the nature of enthusiasm in the 1790s will be the focus of the next chapter, which in turn provides a more local context for the readings of Romanticism that form the second part of this book.

---

[194] See Irlam, *Elations*, 237, for a critique of Hawes in this respect.

CHAPTER TWO

Enthusiasm, Liberty, and Benevolence in the 1790s

THE 1790S WAS a decade in which many of the aspirations and anxieties bound up with the discourse on enthusiasm intensified and burst into political debates. These developments provide an important context for the poets whose engagement with enthusiasm takes up the second part of this book. None of them could avoid the spin put on the discourse on enthusiasm by the whirlwind of the French Revolution. From as early as 1789 the word was being used to make sense of events in France. For Edmund Burke, the whole enterprise was vitiated by the 'errors and excesses of enthusiasm'.[1] Thomas Paine, on the other hand, looked to align the Revolution with the nobler associations of the word in the Whig tradition of liberty. He believed that the 'Bastile was attacked with an enthusiasm of heroism, such only as the highest animation of Liberty could inspire'.[2] The English closely identified 'enthusiasm' with what they believed to be their own innate propensity towards liberty, but always with a disturbing awareness that this tendency could also degenerate towards anarchy. Few of those who wished the French Revolution success wanted to raise the spectre of the English sectaries of the 1640s as an antecedent. For radicals there remained a fraught relationship between the 'enthusiasm of the popular mind' and the passions of the 'undisciplined multitude'.[3] Their opponents usually simply collapsed the two into each other, often taking the Swiftian route of presenting any proposal for innovation as a species of enthusiasm. Both were deemed manifestations of utopian specula-

[1] Edmund Burke, *The Writings and Speeches of Edmund Burke*, gen. ed. Paul Langford, viii: *The French Revolution 1790–94*, ed. L. G. Mitchell (Oxford: Oxford University Press, 1989), 208.
[2] Paine, *Rights of Man*, ed. Eric Foner (Harmondsworth: Penguin, 1985), 56.
[3] *Some Remarks on the Apparent Circumstances of the War* (1795), 6.

tion opposed to common sense and what were deemed the real
social duties of men and women.

The high-profile involvement of Dissenters in supporting the
French Revolution made this conflation easier, especially where
politically minded ministers, such as Richard Price and Joseph
Priestley, appealed to biblical prophecy to support their views.
Although it made little difference to an opponent such as Burke,
Price and Priestley both related their millenarianism to a discourse
of enlightenment Reason. They claimed not the unmediated access
to truth associated with enthusiasm, but validated their view of
history through careful historical and textual scholarship. Radicals
more generally—whether religious or otherwise—reiterated that
they were not seeking to unleash a torrent of popular enthusiasm.
Indeed they often defined themselves as the true heirs of a process
of enlightenment of which enthusiasm was the explicit antithesis.
From their point of view, vulgar enthusiasm was the product of
ignorance, but an ignorance that could be ameliorated by greater
cultural and political participation. It was not an irremediable
condition of the people. The popular radical movement associated
from 1792 with the Corresponding Societies, seeking to ameliorate
ignorance by a more vigorous dissemination of knowledge across
classes, constantly stressed its commitment to 'reform not riot', distancing itself from the passions of the crowd, but there were also
those who seemed to pay scant regard to the question of regulation,
and even some who proclaimed political change to be directly
ordained by God. Their eager expectations of an imminent political
millennium intensified fears even inside the radical movement about
the unstable nature of popular enthusiasm. Such enthusiasm seemed
a dubious ally to those such as William Godwin and John Thelwall
who represented reform as the evolutionary product of a process of
rational enquiry. Both men recognized the power of enthusiasm in
the broadest sense of its link with heroic acts, acknowledged
Shaftesbury's enthusiasm for liberty and virtue, aligned their own
enquiries with its ability to see beyond the present order of things,
and accepted that it might be a necessary (precursive) feature of
change, but they also feared that they themselves might not be able
to regulate its infectious nature (even sometimes within their own
discourse). Before turning to discuss the problem of enthusiasm in
radical and reforming circles, however, the case of their nemesis
Edmund Burke has to be addressed. For it was his brilliant if deeply

prejudiced development of the eighteenth-century discourse on enthusiasm that made those problems so much more acute.

EDMUND BURKE AND TRANSPARENCE

Horace Walpole regarded the spectacle of 'enthusiasm without religion' as the great novelty of the French Revolution, ignoring the fact that from at least Swift onwards the word had also attached itself pejoratively to schemes of innovation or improvement however 'rational' or scientific their rhetoric.[4] By the end of the decade the Anti-Jacobin could take as proven what to Horace Walpole seemed a strange and almost unbelievable idea: 'the French Revolution has proved that Enthusiasm does not belong only to Religion: that there may exist as much zeal in blaspheming God as in praising him'.[5] A great deal of the credit (or blame) for cementing this understanding of radical discourse into the vocabulary of political conservatism must go to Edmund Burke. Burke's Reflections on the Revolution in France is a text which is often rightly taken to have set the terms of the Revolution controversy that dominated British culture in the 1790s, but until recently 'enthusiasm' has not often been nominated among them.[6] Burke's text is often represented as proto-Romantic in its own appeal to feelings over Reason. From this perspective Burke might seem to be an apostle of enthusiasm writing against the cold abstractions of the Enlightenment. Some of his radical adversaries tried to represent Reflections as the errant product of an overheated mind; Godwin described Burke's reverence for the ancien régime as 'enthusiasm' (Godwin Works, iii. 275), but those more

---

[4] 'To Lady Ossory, Tuesday 16 July 1793', in The Yale Edition of Horace Walpole's Correspondence, ed. W. S. Lewis, 48 vols. (New Haven: Yale University Press, 1937–83), xxxiv. 182, but see A Letter to the Rt. Hon. Charles James Fox (1793) and its distinction between genuine enthusiasm and the visions of the revolutionaries, both equally pernicious. The French, unlike Muhammad and Cromwell (the other two examples brought forward), are judged to have 'no principle which is likely to support them under defeat, disgrace, or disappointment'. The author concludes, 'enthusiasm and atheism are irreconcilable terms' (44).

[5] Anti-Jacobin, 2 (1798), 562.

[6] Recent exceptions include Pocock, 'Edmund Burke and the Redefinition of Enthusiasm: The Context as Counter-Revolution', in The Transformation of Political Culture, 1789–1848, vol. iii of François Furet and Mona Ozouf (eds.), The French Revolution and the Creation of Modern Political Culture (Oxford: Oxford University Press, 1989), 19–43, and Chris Jones, Radical Sensibility: Literature and Ideas in the 1790s (New York: Routledge, 1993).

sensitive to the subtleties of Hume's distinction between the terms preferred 'superstition' (and made constant references to his Catholic background).[7] Burke insisted that human nature needed to be controlled by a power out of itself, and construed the Revolution's thirst for innovation and immediacy as classic examples of the egotism Hume found in 'enthusiasm'.

Burke took 'enthusiasm' to have nothing to do with religion as such. The *First letter on a Regicide Peace* (1796) reads almost as if it were a direct rejoinder to Walpole's perception of the novelty of the Revolution on this point:

They who have made but superficial studies in the Natural History of the human mind, have been taught to look on religious opinions as the only cause of enthusiastick zeal, and sectarian propagation. But there is no doctrine whatever, on which men can warm, which is not capable of the very same effect. The social nature of man impels him to propagate his kind. The passions give zeal and vehemence. The whole man moves under the discipline of his opinions.[8]

Here the optimistic linking of enthusiasm to the social instincts found in someone like Shaftesbury is inverted to produce a monstrous image of revolutionary zeal, one which appeared first in *Reflections*, and was bequeathed to anti-Jacobin thinking more generally thereafter. There are two key assumptions at work in Burke's definition of enthusiasm. The ability of opinions to turn into indiscriminate zeal is acknowledged as part of secular as well

---

[7] Mary Wollstonecraft attacked Burke's 'romantic enthusiasm' in her *Vindication of the Rights of Men*, but noted that 'had you been a Frenchman, you would have been, in spite of your respect for rank and antiquity, a violent revolutionist; and deceived, as you now probably are, by the passions that cloud your reason, have termed your romantic enthusiasm an enlightened love of your country, a benevolent respect for the rights of men. Your imagination would have taken fire, and have found arguments, full as ingenious as those you now offer, to prove that the constitution, of which so few pillars remained, was not a model sufficiently noble to deserve close adherence' (*Political Writings*, ed. Janet Todd (Oxford, Oxford University Press, 1994), 44). Jones, *Radical Sensibility*, 104, notes that Wollstonecraft sometimes thought of the feelings of the heart as an animating force that would stop reason lapsing into passive acceptance, but usually differentiated passion and (mechanical) instinct from legitimate products of feeling and reason. See Chapter 1, n. 124 above. Jones suggests that she saw mere habit behind Burke's emotional enthusiasm for the crown, but in the passage just quoted Wollstonecraft implies that Burke would be guilty of a tendency towards emotionalism without the disciplinary reins of reason, whatever the cause.

[8] Edmund Burke, *The Writings and Speeches of Edmund Burke*, ix: *The Revolutionary War 1794–7*, ed. R. B. McDowell (Oxford: Oxford University Press, 1991), 278–9.

as religious discourse, and, secondly, this ability is defined by its
need to propagate itself. Concentrating on the first of these assumptions, Pocock believes that Burke crystallized a definition of enthusiasm as the inclination of the mind to privilege its own productions
over the world, or, more specifically, 'any attempt to establish the
reasoning mind's ascendancy over the contexts in which it reasoned'.[9] From this kind of perspective, the claims of radicals such
as Godwin to an absolute freedom of enquiry in pursuit of truth
were just as much guilty of enthusiasm as the wildest Methodist.
Pocock's point returns us to the issue of mediation raised in my first
chapter. Revolutionary *transparence*, including the claim to know
and represent the will of the people, was a latter-day enthusiasm to
someone such as Burke, but perhaps too much stress on epistemology may distract us from other elements of the discourse on enthusiasm that structured his thinking. In explaining how enthusiasm
for Burke could describe the reasoning of philosophers as well as the
passions of the crowd, Pocock rather loses sight of the primary fear
of the latter. The whole point of Burke's polemic was to stop philosophers and the literati more generally from playing with what was
regarded as the flammable enthusiasm of the masses. His fear was
that they would transmit their imaginative warmth to a crowd all
too ready to be ignited into enthusiasm and translate imperfectly
understood ideas immediately into violent action.

Burke's initial target in the *Reflections* was the dissenting minister Richard Price's sermon welcoming the French Revolution, published as *A Discourse on the Love of our Country* (1789). Critics
often claim that Burke represents Price as a rational projector whose
cold calculations leave aside issues of tradition, family feeling, and
patriotism, but part of the brilliance of the attack comes in the way
he folds this image of Price into a memory of the Civil War. At the
heart of his representation of Price is the attempt to plant in the
reader's mind the spectre of Hugh Peter, the Puritan minister who
presided over the execution of Charles I:

That sermon is in a strain which I believe has not been heard in this king-
dom, in any of the pulpits which are tolerated or encouraged in it, since the
year 1648, when a predecessor of Dr. Price, the Reverend Hugh Peters,

---

[9] Pocock, 'Redefinition of Enthusiasm', 26. See also his 'Enthusiasm: The Antiself
of Enlightenment', *Huntington Library Quarterly*, 60 (1998), 7–28.

made the vault of the king's own chapel at St. James's ring with the honour and privilege of the Saints, who, with the 'high praises of God in their mouths, and a *two*-edged sword in their hands, were to execute judgment on the heathen, and punishments upon the people, to bind their kings with chains, and their nobles with fetters of iron.'[10]

When he goes on to describe Price in terms of a prophet whose 'enthusiasm kindles as he advances', Burke is appealing to two distinct, but overlapping ideas of enthusiasm present in Hume's *History*, that is, the concept of the zealot who will sacrifice everything to the dominant productions of his brain (here the products of Reason) and the simpler but more long-standing identification of religious Dissent of all kinds with enthusiasm.[11] Although Burke did represent reformers as cold system-builders, cut off from feeling and experience by 'the nakedness and solitude of metaphysical abstraction', he also succeeded in establishing an image of them as the over-zealous heirs of the fifth monarchy men and other sectarian enthusiasts of the seventeenth century.[12] They were at one and the same time too cold and unfeeling and too warm and zealous in their enthusiasm for change. Burke plays on the ready equation between Dissent of any kind and enthusiasm discussed in my previous chapter, but he was helped by the fact that the language of Price's sermon was fiery and warm, full of the figurative language associated with prophetic enthusiasm, and pervaded by an air of millenarian expectancy. Merely using the pulpit to discuss politics could make one the target for accusations of enthusiasm in the eighteenth century, and Burke was quick to point out that 'politics and the pulpit are terms that have little agreement'.[13]

In conjuring this image of Price's enthusiasm, Burke had to be careful not to travesty the vaunted liberties of the freeborn Englishman. Enthusiasm was often seen as the prerequisite of political liberty in the Whig tradition from which Burke himself came. Progress needed the heroic self-sacrifice that enthusiasm encouraged. Against Burke's attack on enthusiasm, James Mackintosh launched the defence that 'all improvements in human life have been deviations from experience'.[14] Burke had asserted his own

---

[10] Burke, *The Writings and Speeches*, viii. 62.
[11] Ibid. 115.   [12] Ibid. 58.   [13] Ibid. 62.
[14] James Mackintosh, *Vindiciae Gallicae* (1791), 111. Mackintosh saw the importance to any fundamental political reform of the unworlding power of enthusiasm: 'If the effervescence of the popular mind is suffered to pass away

'love' for 'a manly, moral, regulated liberty' against an enthusiasm that tended towards anarchy.[15] He put forward a Humean view of the dangers of such innovations proceeding in an unregulated fashion, the dangers of 'harsh, crude, unqualified reformations'.[16] Regulation, morality, and manliness were touchstones of Shaftesbury's *Characteristics* and Burke seized on another when he suggested that English liberty differed from the excesses of France and the enthusiasm of Price in its concern with manners. Politeness was both the process and the product of a self-fashioning to which the discourse of regulation looked. Politeness meant adapting oneself to 'circumstances' for Burke, as it did for the tradition of British moralists including Hume and Adam Smith. Circumstances determine for Burke whether any scheme of improvement will be 'beneficial or noxious to mankind'.[17] The antithesis of politeness was 'a systematic unsociability' that privileged the obsessions of the zealot over the surrounding world, but Burke also supplemented the familiar Whig discourse of manners with a respect for tradition embodied above all else in the compact of Church and State.[18] Tradition represents for Burke a force external to the individual which can further regulate his or her speculations: 'Always acting as if in the presence of canonized forefathers, the spirit of freedom, leading in itself to misrule and excess, is tempered with an awful gravity.'[19] Manners are bound up with tradition for Burke in a way they are not for Shaftesbury or most of the British moralists who followed him. Without tradition one is open to the delirium of individual consciousness. Tradition is a second nature that ought to be internalized as a safeguard against the enthusiasms of the moment. The Bill of Rights was not framed 'by warm and inexperienced enthusiasts' for Burke, rather it was the product of a Humean weighing of the practical demands of government against the zeal for liberty with an additional reverence for precedent.[20] Both

---

without effect, it would be absurd to expect from langour what enthusiasm has not obtained', 106. Compare Daniel Isaac Eaton's understanding of the role of enthusiasm in the Civil War, below, 106. Both of these writers, like Wollstonecraft, see a necessary political role for the 'unworlding', as Irlam calls it, associated with enthusiastic passion. See n. 7 above.

[15] Burke, *The Writings and Speeches*, viii. 57.   [16] Ibid. 86.

[17] Ibid. 58. On the role of circumstance as a corrective against the transports and utopianism of enthusiasm, see Pocock, 'Redefinition of Enthusiasm'.

[18] Burke, *The Writings and Speeches*, ix. 257.   [19] Ibid. viii. 85.

[20] Ibid. 67.

Wordsworth and Coleridge were to adopt from Burke the idea of tradition as a means of providing a necessary ballast for the uncertainties of enthusiasm. For these poets, tradition buttresses a sense of self that might otherwise be drowned in the visionary excesses of enthusiasm. But tradition for Burke—and increasingly for Wordsworth and, especially, Coleridge as their careers developed—was not only an internal force. It was also embodied in the external forms of the Constitution and the Church, neither of which ought lightly to be tampered with by reformers:

Society requires not only that the passions of individuals should be subjected, but that even in the mass and body, as well as in individuals, the inclinations of men should frequently be thwarted, their will controlled, and their passions brought into subjection. This can only be done by a power out of themselves.[21]

Burke identifies disestablishment as a highly dangerous element in the revolutionary agenda, both in Britain and in France, precisely because it aims at the destruction of the most important of these powers out of the self. He presents Price as a man who believes that anyone who cannot find a form of public worship that suits them should 'set up a separate worship for themselves'. Rational Dissent is 'remarkable in its zeal for any opinion'.[22] Revolutionary enthusiasm in Burke's eyes argues not for any particular set of principles, but for enquiry without the encumbrance of tradition. 'Candour' made into a principle of *transparence* for Burke always ends up as mere enthusiasm.

Compared to the weighty presence of tradition embodied in the external institutions of the Church and State, enthusiasm represents a 'dreadful energy', one which Burke sees as a defining trait of men of letters.[23] Living by the productions of their brain, Burke believed such men were necessarily committed to believe in what Pocock calls 'the freedom of discourse to create the world unilaterally'.[24] They are by their very nature enthusiasts in that they locate cultural value in the power their own ideas can extend over circumstance:

These philosophers are fanaticks; independent of any interest, which if its operated would make them much more tractable, they are carried with

[21] Ibid. 113.   [22] Ibid. 63 (the first time quoting Price's *Discourse*).
[23] Burke, *The Writings and Speeches*, ix. 289.
[24] Pocock, 'Redefinition of Enthusiasm', 20.

such an headlong rage towards every desperate trial, that they would sacrifice the whole human race to the slightest of their experiments.[25]

For Burke, Rousseau becomes the chief representative of such men. Only fleetingly mentioned in *Reflections*, Burke's later writing against the Revolution developed the image of Rousseau as the high priest of *transparence*. Gregory Dart has recently emphasized the difference between Rousseau and the more sceptical tradition of French enlightenment thought in this respect.[26] Certainly within Britain, as Dart shows, Rousseau was perceived as a writer who consulted his own heart above all other authorities (a reception prepared for by the tradition of Shaftesbury as Chris Jones has suggested).[27] Early reviews had stressed the 'heat of enthusiasm' in *Émile* and often represented him as a brave (Protestant) defender of religious freedom of conscience. Even in the 1790s Richard 'Citizen' Lee could publish a pamphlet made up of a passage from *Émile* presenting Rousseau as a radical apostle of Protestant enthusiasm. If Lee wanted to radicalize and re-sacralize the positive reception of Rousseau's enthusiasm, Burke's version of Rousseau cunningly develops the negative connotations of this association between religious and political enthusiasm.[28] The 'oracle of the Jacobins', Rousseau is a man who believes his own prophetic visions of mankind, abandoning received wisdom to 'the infinite void of the conjectural world', and disseminating a 'restless, agitating, activity'.[29] Developing the long-standing association of enthusiasm with the abandonment of domestic roles, Mackenzie's 'real practical duties', Burke's version of Rousseau is also drawn in terms of the prophet who, fascinated by visions of universal benevolence,

---

[25] Burke, *The Writings and Speeches*, ix. 176.

[26] See Gregory Dart, *Rousseau, Robespierre and English Romanticism* (Cambridge: Cambridge University Press, 1999), 1–2; and see also Marie-Hélène Huet, 'The Revolutionary Sublime', *Eighteenth-Century Studies*, 28 (1994), 51–64, for the influence of Rousseau's thinking on revolutionary rhetoric in France itself in this respect.

[27] On the reception of Rousseau in England, see Dart, *Rousseau, Robespierre and English Romanticism*, 11–13; Chris Jones, *Radical Sensibility*, 61; and Edward Duffy, *Rousseau in England: The Context for Shelley's Critique of the Enlightenment* (Berkeley and Los Angeles: University of California Press, 1979).

[28] See Jon Mee, 'The Strange Career of Richard "Citizen" Lee: Poetry, Popular Radicalism, and Enthusiasm in the 1790s', in T. Morton and N. Smith (eds.), *Radicalism in British Literary Culture, 1650–1830: From Revolution to Revolution* (Cambridge: Cambridge University Press, 2002), 164–5.

[29] Burke, *The Writings and Speeches*, ix. 7, 188, and 224.

abandons his own domestic responsibilities. Rousseau according to Burke is 'a lover of his kind, but a hater of his kindred,' a man who 'melts with tenderness for those only who touch him by the remotest relation, and then, without one natural pang, casts away'.[30] Human sociability is predicated on the importance of local and above all domestic attachments: 'The little platoon we belong to in society, is the first principle (the germ as it were) of public affections.'[31] Victims of enthusiasm abjure such a mediated view of human sociability, according to Burke, in favour of a vision of universal benevolence that believes it possible to love the whole without progressing through the links of more local human affections.

The infectious nature of such enthusiasm is captured most of all for Burke by the workings of the press and its ability to 'make a kind of electrick communication every where'.[32] In Burke's hands the idea of the press as the means by which enthusiasm can be transmitted instantaneously reaches its apotheosis. Printing becomes a technology that facilitates not reflection but the 'mechanic' spasming of enthusiastic philosophers. Forgoing the opportunity for reflection and self-command, in hurrying to the presses, these philosophers lose themselves in their own fantasies of benevolence: 'Confounded by the complication of distempered passions, their reason is disturbed; their views become vast and perplexed; to others inexplicable; to themselves uncertain.'[33] Caught up in a world of ideas, the revolutionaries are losing all sense of their own identity, but their ecstasies are not purely philosophical. Burke makes full use of the Swiftian idea of enthusiasm as the product of sexual drives. Even Price is made to seem like a tub preacher, overwrought by 'fervent prayer and enthusiastic ejaculation'.[34] Certainly from Burke's point of view, Price and other fellow travellers have fallen victim to 'unhallowed transports'—sexual or otherwise—which threaten to unhouse their own identity. It is the Church and other powers beyond the self that can offer a ceiling for inflationary rapture, a stable identity, can securely sit. Under what Burke took to be its capacious roof, a stable identity could sit secure in its sense of self.[35]

---

[30] Ibid. viii. 314–15. [31] Ibid. 97–8. [32] Ibid. ix. 292.
[33] Ibid. viii. 98. [34] Ibid. 122. [35] Ibid. 117 and 152.

Fundamentally Burke's definition of enthusiasm rests on his disapprobation of 'personal self-sufficiency and arrogance'.[36] 'Self-sufficiency' is a phrase that links revolutionary *transparence* to the inner light of religious enthusiasm. Such self-sufficiency, whether grounded in religious fanaticism or enlightenment candour, is typified for Burke by a fanatical confidence that the individual can discover truth without the aid of the wisdom of ages. Coleridge later compared Protestant enthusiasm and revolutionary *transparence* in 'their radical natures'. Only Luther's faith in the Bible, Coleridge claimed, saved him from the distraction of Rousseau. Increasingly, however, Coleridge was to make the Burkean move of supplementing the Bible with the institutions of the Church.[37] In Burke's writing on revolutionary enthusiasm the combination of Rousseau's *transparence* and seventeenth-century enthusiasm finds its perfect articulation in Rational Dissent (significantly, an intellectual formation that Coleridge also abandoned). Contemporary reformers such as Price and Priestley are heirs to the Puritans of the seventeenth century, from Burke's perspective, because they privilege their own visions over 'old prejudices'. They refuse to see that only a 'small stock of reason' is given to man and that in the vulnerable human situation external supports and regulations are necessary.[38] Many opponents of Burke in the radical movement and beyond regarded his representation of the spirit of enquiry as a form of enthusiasm as ridiculous. Many simply regarded enthusiasm as having nothing to do with the hardheaded questions of politics. Others, such as Mackintosh, and even Hume, thought some version of enthusiasm necessary to the idea of progress. For them, Burke had failed to see the deep differences between the world in 1790 and the world of 1648. This difference became an important theme in radical writing. John Thelwall, for instance, turned to it several times. No longer in thrall to religious fanaticism, he believed that the people were now capable of regulating their sympathies for themselves. Their enthusiasm for liberty could now be trusted to find its

[36] Ibid. 145. See also Thomas Gisborne, *An Enquiry into the Duties of Man in the Higher and Middle Classes in Britain*, 2 vols., 2nd edn. (1795), ii. 170, who also warns his readers against 'extravagant ideas of the sufficiency of human reason'. I am grateful to Gillian Russell for pointing out Gisborne's work to me.

[37] For a fuller account of Coleridge's comparison of Luther and Rousseau in relation to the discourse on enthusiasm, see Chapter 3.

[38] Burke, *The Writings and Speeches*, viii. 137–8.

own limits. Yet Thelwall and others within the radical movement never entirely exorcized their own fear that the Burkean scenario might be true in a number of ways. At times they seemed to fear that the spirit of enthusiasm in the people had not and even could not be regulated by a process of general enlightenment, and, worst of all, that their own writings and speeches might actually be provoking this infection in the body politic.

RADICAL ENTHUSIASM

Before turning to discuss the specifics of the problems faced by Thelwall and William Godwin, the validity of Burke's representation of the radical movement as a culture of enthusiasm needs to be examined more closely. How far was radical ideology committed to a form of *transparence* that was little different from enthusiasm? Is there, alternatively, any sense in which the popular radical movement could be understood as a counter-public of enthusiasm? My aim is not to suggest, as Burke suggested, that 'the people' were somehow not capable of rational behaviour. Far from attempting to belittle popular consciousness, I want to take seriously the possibility that it produced its own forms of knowledge that provided a basis for political intervention and public utterance. This approach obviously flirts with the danger of playing into the hands of a Burkean perspective, and perpetuating an idea of the irrationality of the masses. The alternative, however, is even more condescending. To present the LCS as an organization of sober working-men seeking an extension of the franchise, not only distorts the available historical evidence, but presents an all-too-respectable version of popular culture in the period. Too often in seeking to refute the aspersions of Burke or modern conservative historians, Marxist and left-oriented cultural historians have reproduced a remarkably bourgeois version of popular radicalism. This response is too defensive, and too closed to the complicated nature of popular culture and the radical movement in the period. Discussing the role of religious thinking in Indian society, Dipesh Chakrabarty has recently argued that 'we do not have the analytical categories in academic discourse that do justice to the real, everyday and multiple connections we have to what we, in becoming modern, have come to see as "non-rational." '[39] In this respect, as we might expect, the modern historiography of British popular radicalism has too often been caught up in the dialectic of enlightenment, abolishing in the name of progress what does not conform to its idea of Reason. Notwithstanding the influence of E. P. Thompson's interest in the politics of popular religious traditions, the modern historian usually finds it easiest to identify the main current of the radical movement in the 1790s with men such as John Thelwall who were confident that enthusiasm was steadily retreating in the face of the inevitable progress of truth and reason. I have no wish to disparage Thelwall, he has an important part to play in this chapter, or to suggest that religious enthusiasm was in some way more inherently 'radical' than his commitment to an extension of enlightenment principles; Thelwall's defence of enlightened principles was fought in the face of intense scepticism about the possibility of such a man conforming to them. What I do want to do is examine the role of enthusiasm in the radical movement, unpack the complex tensions between these two strands within the movement, and, in the process, show that they were not always as distinct as they might seem.

The question of enthusiasm in relation to popular politics was brought into sharp relief for the 1790s by the emergence of someone who quite literally claimed to be in direct communication with the divine will in interpreting contemporary political events. That person was Richard Brothers, the Paddington Prophet, and his popularity shocked a periodical press that desperately wanted to believe in its own narratives of progress as proof of the superiority of British manners. Conservative commentators, it is true, sometimes found the emergence of latter-day prophets useful corroboration for their view of the unstable and untrustworthy nature of the masses. The Brothers phenomenon in that sense confirmed part of Burke's thesis about the dangers of enthusiasm, but more liberal opinion—whether supportive of the Revolution or not—was shocked to see such a public refutation of its faith in progress. A typical example of its attitude can be found in the *Analytical Review*'s bewildered account of the widespread interest in Brothers mentioned in my previous chapter:

[39] Dipesh Chakrabarty, 'Radical Histories and the Question of Enlightenment Rationalism: Some Recent Critiques of Subaltern Studies', *Economic and Political Weekly*, 8 Apr. 1995, 753.

Facts sometimes occur, which, though not miraculous, almost as much astonish the philosopher, as if he saw a miracle. Such a fact is the recent attention, which at the close of the 18th century, and in the metropolis of one of the most enlightened nations of Europe, has been paid by people of all ranks to a mad prophet.[40]

The outlines of the Brothers story is quite well known by now. A number of critics and historians have recently examined his case from various perspectives.[41] To state the basic facts as far as they are known, Brothers was a former naval lieutenant who had been discharged on half pay at the end of the American War. In 1790 he had refused on religious grounds to swear the oath of loyalty to the King required for him to draw his pay. The result was a period in a workhouse, followed by a brief stay in Newgate. When he was released in 1792, Brothers began writing prophetic letters to the government claiming that God had revealed to him that the French Revolution was the fulfilment of biblical prophecy and should not be challenged by force of British arms. His prophecies became the centre of a very public controversy when he published *A Revealed Knowledge of the Prophecies and Times* (1794–5), a text that quickly proliferated in different editions. Although this kind of prophecy was a staple of popular literature in the eighteenth century, the Brothers controversy witnessed an outpouring of enthusiasm not seen for many decades. Anthologies, such as George Riebau's *God's Awful Warning* (1795) and Garnet Terry's *Prophetical Extracts* (1794–5), filled with visionary material, much of it reprinted from what we might call the canon of seventeenth-century enthusiasm, quickly appeared, bewildering the press with their zealous predictions of the imminent fulfilment of biblical prophecy. It was in response to these 'motley collections of extracts' that the clerical author of *Memoirs of Pretended Prophets* felt obliged to issue a review of all the false prophets of modern times.[42]

[40] *Analytical Review*, 21 (1795), 318.

[41] See, for instance, John Barrell's authoritative account in *Imagining the King's Death: Figurative Treason, Fantasies of Regicide 1793–6* (Oxford: Oxford University Press, 2000), 504–47, and also Morton D. Paley, *Apocalypse and Millennium in English Romantic Poetry* (Oxford: Clarendon Press, 1999), 26–30.

[42] *Memoirs of Pretended Prophets, who have Appeared in Different Ages of the World, and Especially Modern Times* (1795), p. i. The pamphlet was a Joseph Johnson publication, and predictably was favourably reviewed in the *Analytical*, 22 (1795), 284. The *Analytical* usually displayed the hostility to popular religious (and, indeed, secular) enthusiasm typical of Rational Disssent, see the discussion below.

While that pamphlet mocked the possibility of genuine prophecy in modern Europe, it did reflect a widespread sense among the educated elite that the crowd were all too ready to believe the opposite. The prophecies of Richard Brothers looked like a virus peculiarly suited to 'gratify the multitude' and potentially to destabilize the social order. Henry Spencer, the Foxite-Whig author of *A Word of Admonition to the Rt. Honourable William Pitt* (1795), making use of the traditional metaphor of infection, mocked the government's failure to take action against 'the poison prophetic that is infused and making rapid progress through the great body of society'.[43] Though not sharing Spencer's anti-ministerial politics, the *Gentleman's Magazine* echoed this point of view when it argued that the enthusiasm of Brothers' books together with their cheapness made them particularly attractive to 'the bulk of the people, whose minds in these days do not need disquiet'. Both were making assumptions about crowd psychology intrinsic to the long-standing discourse on enthusiasm. The government finally listened and arrested Brothers on suspicion of treasonable practices. He was subsequently interrogated by the Privy Council and then confined to a madhouse until Pitt's death in 1806. This decision suggests that they did not believe Brothers himself was involved in the radical movement, but it does not discount the possibility that they were still wary of the unwitting effects of his enthusiasm on a population that many believed were all too open to such influences. Trying to make sense of the dangers of a popular uprising, their decisions must have been structured in some way at least by the assumptions of the discourse on enthusiasm that was imbibed as part and parcel of elite education in the eighteenth century.

There is no doubt that a more respectable, scholarly tradition of millenarianism did play its part in the radical response to the French Revolution. The scientist and dissenting minister Joseph Priestley can be counted among the number of those Rational Dissenters who applied biblical eschatology to contemporary political events. Samuel Taylor Coleridge, who came under the sway of the Rational Dissenter William Frend while at Cambridge in the early 1790s,

---

[43] See *A Word of Admonition to the Right Hon. William Pitt* (1795), 49, and Barrell's discussion of the pamphlet, *Imagining the King's Death*, 513–18, including its gentle correction of my failure to see its irony in *Dangerous Enthusiasm: William Blake and the Culture of Radicalism in the 1790s* (Oxford: Clarendon Press, 1992), 49.

was deeply affected by this eschatological view of history. For all the power of Burke's polemic, and the traditional association between enthusiasm and Dissent, for all that in the pulpit men such as Price and Priestley sometimes let their biblical rhetoric exceed their professed political principles, there were serious obstacles to establishing an image of them as crazy fanatics. Priestley retained a reputation as a key player of the Enlightenment in England—his scientific discoveries if nothing else at least ensured him of that. Brothers, on the other hand, was widely regarded as a crazed product of popular enthusiasm. He was represented as a throwback to an age of irrationality in religion. Priestley was a commentator and interpreter for whom reason—as he sharply informed Edmund Burke—was 'the umpire in all disputes' (Rutt, xxii. 240). Burke himself, of course, regarded such a faith in the candle of Reason as simply a transmutation of the faith in the inner light, but the distinction was not necessarily so easily collapsed. Priestley looked to the fulfilment of the events in history as proof of the Bible's veracity. Brothers, as the *Analytical Review* put it, was a 'prophet commentator' who claimed to interpret and *add to* the biblical canon through his own visions.[44] One of the followers of Brothers, Benjamin Prescot, argued that the prophecies 'cannot be interpreted *by the will or wisdom of man*'.[45] The only alternative to human wisdom was direct inspiration. Priestley, in contrast, claimed to use generally agreed rational methods of research. Hardly a radical journal, nor a friend of Priestley's Unitarianism, the *Evangelical Magazine* too still wanted to distinguish between those whose 'hope that a glorious period is at hand' had 'led to study' and those who 'not content with so sober and commendable inquiry, have been bold enough to boast of a prophetic spirit'.[46] Men and women such as Brothers, who boasted of their own ignorance as proof of their inspiration, were readily consigned to the former category. What was more of a matter for dispute was whether the millenarianism of Rational Dissenters of Priestley's ilk deserved the same disapprobation. In the *Analytical Review* the Dissenters James Bicheno and

[44] *Analytical Review*, 21 (1795), 216.
[45] Benjamin Prescot, *An Explanatory Address to the Public on the Character & Prophecies of Richard Brothers and his Mission to Recall the Jews* (Liverpool, 1798), 39.
[46] The *Evangelical* joined with the *Analytical* in praising *Memoirs of Pretended Prophets* for condemning those latter-day prophets who laid claim to divine inspiration. See *Evangelical Magazine*, 4 (1796), 303.

J. L. Towers were both praised for the sober nature of their scholarly arguments in favour of a millenarian reading of contemporary political affairs.[47] Towers had specifically dissociated himself from Brothers, and stressed his scholarly debt to Newton's *Dissertations*, but the *Gentleman's Magazine* was less inclined than the *Analytical* to accept such distinctions. Its judgement on Bicheno was pithy: 'he has studied the prophetic parts of Scripture till he has bewildered himself'.[48] Bicheno believed that the Reformation, 'partial and very defective as it was', 'originated from Christians assuming the right of searching the scriptures, and of judging for themselves, as to the mind of Christ taught in them'.[49] To conservatives such as Burke, and it seems the reviewer at the *Gentleman's Magazine*, such bold assertions of the unlimited right to freedom of enquiry in matters of religion were simply a late variant of enthusiasm.[50] Dissenters were now simply passing off the inner light of the seventeenth century as the enlightenment of Reason at the end of the eighteenth.

When Dissenters such as Priestley were at their most indignant in the cause of freedom, their rhetoric could and did often take on the full fury of prophetic discourse and use a violence of language readily identified by their political opponents as a sign of enthusiasm.[51] Moreover the radical movement more generally was not completely devoid of religious enthusiasm in the older sense. At least there were those much less concerned than Priestley and his associates to underpin their millenarian fervour with a foundation of Reason. Caution is necessary, as this material is sometimes difficult to interpret. John Barrell has rightly warned against assuming that Brothers, for instance, was personally committed to the radical movement.[52] The government may even have linked him with the

---

[47] See the reviews of J. L. Towers, *Illustrations of Prophecy* (1796) in *Analytical Review*, 26 (1797), 372–82; and James Bicheno, *The Probable Progress* (1797), in the same volume of the *Analytical Review*. The review praises Bicheno's earlier *Sign of the Times* (1793) as 'ingenious, liberal, and pious'.

[48] *Gentleman's Magazine*, no. 65 (1795), 759.

[49] James Bicheno, *A Glance at the History of Christianity, and of English Nonconformity* (1798), 14–15.

[50] Even a fellow Dissenter and friend Anna Letitia Barbauld could suggest that Priestley's zeal for the truth was a form of enthusiasm in the 1770s. In the 1790s her perspective changed. See Chapter 4 below.

[51] See for example Priestley's *Sermon Delivered at the Gravel Pit Meeting, in Hackney, April 10, 1793, being the Day Appointed for a General Fast* (Rutt, xv. 494–8), *The Present State of Europe Compared with Ancient Prophecies* (1794: Rutt, xv. 519–52), and Barbauld's *Sins of the Government, Sins of the Nation* (1793).

[52] Barrell, *Imagining the King's Death*, 522–5.

movement to discredit it. The radical press, for their part, often treated him as a lunatic or impostor. Sometimes it used him as an example of the irrationality of religion in general as part of a campaign supporting the infidel views of Paine's *Age of Reason* and Volney's *Ruins*. John Thelwall, for instance, was particularly hostile to popular enthusiasm, as we shall see, regarding it as contrary to the true spirit of enlightenment. Important members of the leadership of the LCS may have been committed to infidelism of various kinds, but the radical movement in general was a loose and diverse one. Popular debating societies argued over whether Brothers should be 'received as a Prophet, or punished as an impostor'.[53] No doubt such clubs aspired to a place in the 'enlightened' public sphere, although polite commentators more often sniffed at their 'motley mixture of religious and prophane lectureship'.[54] Prophetic practice had no easily identifiable place in the polite public sphere, but for some involved in the radical movement, the illumination of the spirit could still be invoked as sufficient authority to participate in politics. Whatever the political affiliations of Brothers himself, some of those involved in circulating his work were performing the same function for the radical movement. George Riebau—who published the writings of Brothers—was a member of the LCS. Seale and Crosby were publishers who brought out volumes by Brothers and Joanna Southcott as well as the work of Paine and Thomas Spence.[55]

One important figure in the perpetuation of such an idea of politics was Lord George Gordon. Gordon is often dismissed by

[53] This question was advertised for debate at the Westminster Forum in the *Morning Chronicle*, 28 Oct. 1794. Brothers was debated again on 25 November and 26 December. See Donna T. Andrew (ed.), *London Debating Societies, 1776–1799* (London Record Society, 1994), 329 and 331.

[54] Thomas Dutton's *The Literary Census: A Satirical Poem with Notes* (1798) gives an account of these meetings as disrespectful and lewd gatherings, 107–8. Like W. H. Reid's, *The Rise and Dissolution of the Infidel Societies in this Metropolis: Including, the Origin of Modern Deism and Atheism; the Genius and Conduct of those Associations; their Lecture-Rooms, Field-Meetings, and Deputations* (1800), Dutton's view is that sceptically minded radicals and itinerant preachers ('Babel's workmen', 28) are equally subversive of the social order. Dutton was not opposed to reform, and attacked the reactionary Thomas J. Mathias's *The Pursuits of Literature* (1794), but he was against what he called 'anarchy and mob-government', p. xi, and a suspicion of the enthusiasm of the lower orders permeates his poem, as it does the writing of many other 'liberal' reformers in the period, Leigh Hunt's being the most obvious example in this book.

[55] See J. F. C. Harrison, *The Second Coming: Popular Millenarianism 1780–1850* (Routledge & Kegan Paul, 1979), 224.

historians as a crackpot Calvinist whose anti-Catholic prejudices sparked off the riots of 1780, but there were some strong links between Gordon and the LCS. Gordon's secretary, for instance, Robert Watson, was a member from as early as 1792.[56] Thomas Hardy, the Society's first secretary, was a deeply religious man and 'very intimate' with Gordon, although he later distanced himself from 'his wild schemes'.[57] Most of the literature on Hardy presents him as a sober and reasonable individual. He presented himself in this way too, but the prosecution at his trial for high treason was quick to see continuities in his behaviour with the sectarians of the seventeenth century: 'the idea that by the establishment of the rights of man, universal peace would be established throughout the world' was 'an enthusiasm dangerous in the highest degree . . . as dangerous as the enthusiasm of the Millenarians, or the fifth-monarchy-men, who in the last century occasioned some disturbances'. The judge pointedly made great play with the claim at the culmination of his summing up:

He is in his private character a sedate, moral, religious, good man, yet that his conduct in all these transactions marks strongly, that he is tinctured deeply with enthusiasm: and I recollect the Counsel in reply mentioned the famous case in which enthusiasm was worked up to its utmost height, in the fifth-monarchy-men, who might be perfectly good moral and religious characters, and it would be upon their religion that the act of high treason would be fixed, to give countenance to the charge. So if a man is an enthusiast, his being a moral and religious man is at least a neutral circumstance, because a moral, religious man, if he chooses to let his enthusiasm carry him beyond his judgement, is exposed to be drawn into the circumstances in which the prisoner now stands.[58]

---

[56] See *Selections from the Papers of the London Corresponding Society 1792–1799*, ed. Mary Thale (Cambridge: Cambridge University Press, 1983), 24 n. See also Iain McCalman's recent work on Gordon and Watson: 'New Jerusalems: Prophecy, Dissent and Radical Culture in England, 1786–1830', in Knud Haakonssen (ed), *Enlightenment and Religion: Rational Dissent in Eighteenth-Century Britain* (Cambridge: Cambridge University Press, 1996); 'Mad Lord George and Madame La Motte: Riot and Sexuality in the Genesis of Burke's *Reflections on the Revolution in France*', *Journal of British Studies*, 35 (1996), 343–67; and 'Newgate in Revolution: Enthusiasm and Romantic Counterculture', *Eighteenth-Century Life*, 22 (1998), 95–110.

[57] *Selections from the Papers of the LCS*, p. xxii, and Thomas Hardy, *Memoir of Thomas Hardy* (1832), in David Vincent (ed.), *Testaments of Radicalism: Memoirs of Working Class Politicians 1790–1885* (London: Europa Publications, 1977), 8.

[58] See Manoah Sibley, *The Genuine Trial of Thomas Hardy for High Treason*, 2 vols, (1795), ii. 430–1 and 589.

In the judge's eyes Hardy's religious beliefs do not mitigate his crime. Indeed they identify him as a historical type. The immediate response of the modern reader may well be to dismiss these remarks as a smear. Clearly the judge does want to take political advantage of the association of Presbyterianism with seventeenth-century republican fanaticism, but he can only do so because of the deeply enshrined logic of the discourse on enthusiasm. The judge's choice of this means of attack may have been made easier by the fact that Hardy did hold a fiercely millenarian view of contemporary history. He told David Bogue that he believed Ezekiel 21 to be a reference to events in France, and in another letter, written only a few weeks before his arrest for High Treason, he gave the opinion that the 'reign of the Beast of Civil and Ecclesiastical Power is almost at an end—Thanks to the Supreme Ruler of the Universe—for his great goodness hitherto—and the bright prospect before us'.[59] This language—not unlike that found in 'Citizen' Lee's poetry and prose discussed below—would have been regarded as enthusiasm by most observers at the time. It is hard to imagine that his co-defendants in 1794, most of whom believed that they were forwarding the work of a rational enlightenment, would have condoned it.

Although little work has been done on the relationship between Calvinism and popular radicalism, it is striking that several London radicals in the 1790s had these kinds of connections. Thomas Spence had been deeply influenced by another Scottish Calvinist minister James Murray when he was in the North-East. Thomas Hardy, J. S. Jordan, Richard 'Citizen' Lee, Garnet Terry and others active in the capital seem to have had contacts with the vibrant culture of popular Calvinism deplored by Bennett and Bogue. What defined this culture as 'calvinist' for contemporaries was not any kind of theological rigour, but its stress on what Leigh Hunt called 'THEIR DOCTRINE OF FAITH ALONE WITHOUT MORALS' (H 12). It was a belief that was attacked so often in the press and in fiction that it obviously spoke to the deepest anxieties of the elite about social insubordination. The large congregations to whom popular ministers such as William Huntington and others preached in the 1790s had always been and were to remain objects of suspicion for the polite. Field meetings that took place beyond places sanctioned by the polite idea of religious feeling were seen to promote hopes of

[59] See *Selections from the Papers of the LCS*, 307 n.

salvation that encouraged their listeners to think beyond polite ideas of obedience. In 1808 the *Satirist* gave a bitter description of the kind of theology with which it associated with such assemblies:

Though robbery, adultery, and murder are forbidden by the commandments, yet nevertheless, if you commit them, and still have faith to be saved, the greater your faith, and therefore the greater your merit.[60]

This was a culture—much to the disapproval of polite commentators—given to fire and brimstone sermons, theatrical performances in the pulpit, and emotional confessions of guilt and loud protestations of faith. For all Wesley's increasingly Arminian emphasis, his followers were no less suspect from this point of view. Their emphasis on inward persuasion brought Wesleyan Methodism close to 'the perilous ground' (*Life of Wesley*, ii. 180) of enthusiasm according to Robert Southey. Both wings of the Methodist movement as well as other denominations in London's popular religious culture (all often simply described as Methodist, where they seemed to be encouraging enthusiasm) continued to be suspected of eroding moral and social constraints. It may well be that they did encourage, intentionally or not, some to vault over political boundaries as well. My more general point is that Painite natural-rights thinking did not simply eradicate an older tradition of religiously oriented radicalism in the popular culture. It is all too easy to slip into assumptions about the demise of enthusiasm on the basis of a teleology derived in part from those radicals, like Thelwall, who had huge personal and political investments in presenting the popular movement as 'enlightened'.[61] Nor should it be assumed that religious radicalism was aligned with the more moderate political thinking. Quite the contrary, in fact, since there is evidence that the most incendiary radical republicanism, which went underground after the middle of the decade, was often fiercely religious in its millenarianism. One result was various kinds of tensions and fissures within the radical movement, as well as strange accommodations, a situation that can be illustrated by briefly returning to the career of Richard 'Citizen' Lee.

[60] *Satirist*, 2 (1808), 342.

[61] For a thoughtful discussion of the strategic nature of the stress on reasonableness and enlightenment in the writings and speeches of men such as Thelwall, and their 'insisting on their right to a full share in the blessings of the Enlightenment' (141), see Paul Keen, *The Crisis of Literature in the 1790s* (Cambridge: Cambridge University Press, 1999), esp. 135–70.

'THE DIVINE RIGHT OF REPUBLICS'

Although often mentioned in studies of popular radicalism, Richard Lee has received little detailed attention from historians. Yet in late 1795 Lee was to have a role at the centre of parliamentary debates on the so-called Two Acts, Pitt's attempt to proscribe large-scale political meetings and tighten the definition of seditious writing. In order to justify its repressive legislation, the government wanted to present Lee, who had been publishing pamphlets for the previous year under such incendiary titles as *King Killing* and *The Happy Reign of George the Last*, as the LCS's official printer. Lee seems to have been hawking *King Killing* along with his other wares at the huge LCS rally held in Copenhagen Fields on 26 October 1795. Three days later the King's coach was attacked, when either a stone or a bullet passed through the window, and someone in the crowd wrenched open a door. Pitt's government used the incident to move against the radical movement. Lee's pamphlets were the most flagrant examples of radical literature available to them. Consequently Lord Mornington brought his name before Parliament on 17 November. He was arrested a few days later, and indicted for publishing seditious pamphlets on 1 December. The alliance of Foxite-Whigs and the LCS campaigning against Pitt's legislation denied Lee had any connection with the Society. Evidence suggests that he had been driven out of or seceded from the LCS 'for refusing to sell Volney's *Ruins* and Paine's *Age of Reason*', but even after his secession he still associated with the radical movement. As Lord Mornington, the government spokesman in Parliament, gleefully noted, despite the disclaimers of the LCS and its Whig supporters, Lee's name continued to appear on the list of booksellers receiving petitions against the Two Acts for the LCS. Lee was clearly committed to the radical movement, but also resisting the attempts of sections of the leadership to replace his Bible with Paine's *Age of Reason*.[62]

When Lee published his first collection of poetry *Flowers from Sharon* (1794), including several of the poems he published in the *Evangelical Magazine*, among the booksellers listed on the book's

[62] For a more detailed account of Lee's arrest, the debate in the House, and his relations with the LCS, see Mee, 'The Strange Career of Richard "Citizen" Lee', 158–61.

title-page were J. S. Jordan and Garnet Terry, both of whom, and especially the former, appear as shadowy but persistent figures in the world of radical religious enthusiasm in the 1790s. Jordan took over the publication of the first edition of Paine's *Rights of Man* from Joseph Johnson, but also worked with Terry in republishing an old ranter text from the seventeenth century, Samuel How's *The Sufficiency of the Spirit's Teaching*, in 1792. W. H. Reid later claimed that it was by reading How that Thomas Paine came to his conclusion that God existed only in the human mind, itself suggestive of the ways in which Deism and enthusiasm could come together as well as diverge within radical culture.[63] Whatever was at the root of Lee's politicization, it needs to be stressed that his republicanism did not entail the abandonment of his religious enthusiasm. *Flowers from Sharon*, originally sponsored by the *Evangelical Magazine*, was still being advertised in 1795 with Lee's next volume of poetry, the explicitly political *Songs from the Rock*.[64] Lee's enthusiasm may even have made the extremism of his fervour for the guillotine possible. Certainly there is a powerful biblical and millenarian content in the cheap political material Lee published in 1795, including the infamous *King Killing* broadsheet, while in poems such as 'Rights of God', the wrath of God is called down on the head of monarchy in the register of an Old Testament prophet:

> SOLE KING of NATIONS, rise! assert thy Sway,
> THOU JEALOUS GOD! thy potent Arm display;
> Tumble the BLOOD-BUILT THRONES of *Despots* down
> Let Dust and Darkness be the *Tyrant's* Crown![65]

Few eighteenth-century observers would have hesitated about calling this enthusiasm. Ignoring what his sometime publisher Garnet Terry also disdained as 'framed studied speech', the violence of Lee's language; its taste for the imperative case; and even its

[63] See ibid. 154–6, for details.

[64] A handbill exists advertising *Songs from the Rock* and a de luxe edition of *Flowers from Sharon*. See *Proposals for publishing by subscription, sacred to truth, liberty, and peace, songs from the rock, to hail the approaching day, . . . by Richard Lee* [1795?]. The same puff for *Flowers* also appears on the verso of an unpaginated page of a reissued edition of *Songs* (at British Library Rb 23 a. 10133). See Mee, 'The Strange Career of Richard "Citizen" Lee', 162–3.

[65] See *Songs from the Rock, to hail the approaching day, sacred to truth, liberty and peace. To which is added, the tribute of civic gratitude; a congratulatory address to Thomas Hardy* [1795], 17–18.

typographical penchant for capitalization; all breathe what the
eighteenth century defined as the disputatious spirit of enthusiasm.
There is little restraint in Lee's adoption of the prophetic stance.
Indeed where the poetry, as it often does, adopts an anti-Catholic
rhetoric, then it seems almost deliberately to take on the Protestant
extremism of the Gordon rioters of 1780, a language far from being
obsolete in 1795, as the millenarian anthologies put out by Terry
and others demonstrate.[66]

The circulation of Lee's poetry helps illustrate the currency of the
language of enthusiasm in radical circles. Two of his poems, *Death
of Mrs Hardy* and 'Civic Gratitude' are very personal responses to
Thomas Hardy as a radical hero and prophet. The former is reproduced in Hardy's autobiography, where Lee is warmly praised as a
'patriot bard'. Although the autobiography implies that Hardy did
not know Lee personally, they seem to have moved in similar religious circles in the metropolis.[67] Other connections included
Thomas Spence, through whose influence a language of radical
millenarianism survived well into the next century. Lee's poems
'The Triumph of Liberty', 'The Rights of God', and 'Sonnet to
Freedom' all appeared in the second volume of Spence's *Pig's Meat*
some time before May 1794.[68] Although Spence was involved in
radical politics from the 1770s, initially under the influence of the
minister James Murray, his ideas took on a more millenarian
emphasis around the same time that Lee published *Flowers from
Sharon*. Malcolm Chase has suggested that the experience of moving to London with its seething sub-cultures of field preachers and
prophets may have sparked off a millenarianism that had remained
latent since Spence's intensely religious upbringing on Tyneside.
Strands of enlightenment scepticism and religious enthusiasm
are laced together in Spence's writing.[69] His journal *Pig's Meat*

[66] Much of Terry's output, for instance, was anti-Catholic material from the late
seventeenth century.
[67] *On the Death of Mrs. Hardy, Wife of Thomas Hardy, of Piccadilly;
Imprisoned in the Tower for High Treason* (n.d. [1794]), 4, and Hardy's *Memoir*,
ed. Vincent, 61. A Revd Mr Stevens whose chapel Hardy had attended appeared as
a witness at his trial for high treason. The advertisement for Lee's second book of
poems claims that a Revd Mr Stevens had recommended it. If they are the same man,
it suggests at least that Hardy and Lee may have moved in similar Calvinistic circles
in the capital.
[68] See Mee, 'The Strange Career of Richard "Citizen" Lee', 255 n. 15, for details.
[69] Chase, *'The People's Farm': English Radical Agrarianism 1775–1840* (Oxford:
Oxford University Press, 1988), 48. See also Iain McCalman, *Radical Underworld:*

published both Lee's poetry and translations from Volney: despite
tensions in the LCS, boundaries between religion and scepticism
could be porous ones. In their habitually hostile attitudes to clerical
institutions, for instance, enthusiasm and enlightenment are not
always easy to tell apart, giving a kind of credence to Burke's claim
that they were the both forms of *transparence*. 'Superstition' and
'priestcraft' were key negative terms in both lexicons. A confidence
in the sufficiency of power of the individual's spirit or mind could
excite both William Blake's belief that inspiration was open to all
and Paine's faith in the universality of rational judgement. While
distrusting Paine's deism, Blake could still praise him as a 'worker
of miracles' ('Anno. to Watson': E617). Committed though he was
to French scepticism of the kind associated with Volney, Daniel
Isaac Eaton republished John Cooke's seventeenth-century tract
Monarchy No Creature of God's Making (1794). The *Monthly
Review* was appalled by what it took to be this revisiting of seventeenth-century fanaticism: 'We see no end likely to be answered by
this republication; except it be to show that fanaticism is a useful
instrument, which may be employed at pleasure, in the service either
of monarchy or democracy.'[70] The 'divine right of republics' was no
basis for a political programme from its point of view. Eaton himself seems to have been more pragmatic. He published an article
under the heading 'The Reflexions of a True Briton' that put forward a radicalized version of the Whig truism (found in James
Mackintosh's rebuttal of Burke) that such paradigm-busting enthusiasm was necessary for any kind of fundamental change:

In revolutions, the sage Mably remarks, Enthusiasts are necessary, who in
transgressing all bounds, may enable the wise and temperate to attain their
ends. Had it not been for the Puritans, whose aim was equally to destroy
both Episcopacy and Royalty, the English would never have attained that
portion of civil and religious liberty which they enjoy.[71]

It was this kind of confluence that was anticipated and feared in
Burke's image of the popular politician as both rational system-
builder and enthusiastic prophet. When radicals refused to regu-

Prophets, Revolutionaries, and Pornographers in London, 1794–1840 (Cambridge:
Cambridge University Press, 1988), 66, and the discussion of such confluences in his
'Newgate in Revolution'.

[70] See the *Monthly Review*, 16 (1795), 208.
[71] *Politics for the People*, no. 11 [1793], 152.

late their ambitions, making public displays of their zeal, and reaching out to uneducated crowds at field meetings, then they were likely to be accused of enthusiasm whatever their intellectual affiliations.

Not that such confluences mean that the tensions between people like Lee and those who promoted the infidelity of Paine and Volney should be ignored. Lee's representation of Hardy as a 'CHRISTIAN HERO' is actually part of a explicit rejoinder to those in the LCS promoting religious scepticism:

Let the infidel candidly investigate (if Infidelity can possibly be candid) let him candidly investigate this illustrious Character, and then lift his audacious Front to the Heavens and tell the ALLMIGHTY, that pure Christianity is inimical to the Cause of Freedom—Rather let him yield to the Power of Conviction, and own with Admiration the Rationality of that sublime System which, while it gives GLORY TO GOD, inculcates PEACE ON EARTH, and GOOD WILL TOWARDS MEN.[72]

The violence of Lee's language throughout his volume; the appeal to the immediate power of grace; and the constant assertion of his ability to see God made him vulnerable to the charge of enthusiasm. Certainly this kind of defence of Hardy would hardly have helped to discredit the judge's summing up at the Treason Trials. Nor was Lee alone in the LCS in wanting to assert the importance of a specifically Christian politics. The spy James Powell reported to his masters that in September 1795 'a numerous meeting of the Methodists belonging to the Society request[ed] the Expulsion of Atheists and Deists'. The debate over this matter seems to have led to the secession of the Methodists themselves, possibly including Lee, a group that Powell calculated at six divisions with '*several hundred members from others*'.[73] Reid claimed that the secessions were the result of trying to force Paine and Volney on the membership.[74] Richard Hodgson, a leading member of the LCS from early on, seems to have been particularly zealous on this latter front. Methodism was an affront to his enlightenment principles. Possession of Paine's book was regarded 'as proof of civicism' for

---

[72] Lee, *Songs from the Rock*, 111.
[73] See letter 17 Sept. 1795, PC 1 23/38A [Public Records Office, Kew] and see 'Report of General Committee Sept 24 1795' in *Selections from the Papers of the LCS*, 308.
[74] *Selections from the Papers of the LCS*, 306 n. 40.

such men.[75] Certainly it was this kind of logic that two years earlier had encouraged the General Committee—on which Hodgson
sat—to reject the election of Lord George Gordon's attorney Robert
Watson as delegate for Division 12 of the society. At Hardy's trial
the spy Lynam explained that the Committee had been determined
to have nothing at all to do with Gordon as 'it would make them
disrespectful in the eyes of the public'.[76]Like Leigh Hunt a decade
later, the General Committee of the LCS seems to have subscribed
to the view that 'there are certain opinions of Deity, which the age
has grown too enlightened to endure in the way of dogmatism'
(H p. vi). Many leading members of the LCS wanted to present its
debating clubs and meetings as respectable and regulated forms of
sociability, an extension not abrogation of the polite public sphere.
Francis Place's retrospective account of the movement, for instance,
stressed its 'readings, conversation, and discussion'.[77] Taken as
neutral terms these activities were also important features of the
capital's popular religious culture, but there—whatever the actual
practice—they were usually described by polite commentators in
terms of violence, tastelessness, and even immorality. Rant rather
than polite conversation was widely assumed to be the *via media* of
the Methodist. The intellectual leadership of the LCS was under-
standably eager to affiliate itself to enlightenment notions of
progress and equally keen to shield itself from the charge of enthusiasm. This meant distancing the LCS from associates of Gordon;
Citizen Lee's faith in 'the divine rights of republics'; and even
Methodism, but the movement remained particularly vulnerable to
the charge of enthusiasm whatever it actually said or did. 'Readings,
conversation, and discussion', when carried on by the lower classes,
were always prone to being represented as laziness, rant, and disputation. When the Whig Henry Spencer contrasted the followers
of Fox, Sheridan, and Tooke with the vulgar followers of popular
preachers such as William Huntington, Rowland Hill, and Richard

---

[75] *Selections from the Papers of the LCS*, 306. Hodgson had refused to cooperate
with the Friends of Religious and Civil Liberty at a meeting of 15 Oct. 1795, because
the latter 'pledged themselves to believe in the scriptures', see Powell PC 1 23/38A.

[76] Ironically Watson himself was not sympathetic to the religious aspects of his
employer's beliefs, see McCalman, 'Newgate in Revolution', 102.

[77] Francis Place, *Autobiography of Francis Place*, ed. Mary Thale (Cambridge:
Cambridge University Press, 1972), 131; and see the discussion in Keen, *The Crisis
of Literature*, 155–70, of these self-representations by Hardy, Place, Thelwall, and
others.

Brothers, he was suggesting that anti-ministerial politics had nothing to do with the ignorance of vulgar religious enthusiasm, but his list of reformers, like Spencer himself, is decidedly genteel, and leaves open the question of where he would have placed Richard Hodgson, Francis Place, John Thelwall, and even William Godwin.[78] Did Spencer regard men such as these, for all their professed enlightenment principles, as any more capable of a rational politics than Brothers? My next section will examine in more detail why even such explicitly self-designated 'enlightened' figures as Thelwall and Godwin found themselves vulnerable to the charge of enthusiasm, and how their own understanding of the term structured their writing.

GODWIN'S 'ARDENT ENTHUSIASM'

To link William Godwin's 'dry page' with enthusiasm may seem perverse.[79] In literary studies especially, he is often represented as an archetypal cold fish, someone who inhabited that 'frozen zone' of enlightenment which W. H. Reid believed would never catch the interest of the masses.[80] This idea of Godwin has been compounded by the influence on Romantic studies of Wordsworth's account in *The Prelude*. Wordsworth represents Godwinianism as a metaphysical distraction, which lured him away from his real business of sounding the human heart. Or at least Romantic studies has often read Wordsworth's poem in that way. In fact I shall be arguing in Part II that Wordsworth adapts a Burkean treatment of revolutionary discourse to represent Godwinianism as the enthusiasm of enlightenment, a kind of false prophecy to be contrasted with his own more regulated intimations of eternity. What it was about Godwin's ideas and their reception that made this move possible, I shall be exploring in more detail here.

Contrary to what the modern reader might expect, Godwin's *Political Justice* was immediately understood by some of his contemporaries in terms of the discourse on enthusiasm. The politically

---

[78] Hunt described Hill as someone who 'plays about his pulpit with the uncouth vivacity of a shopkeeper' (H 31).

[79] Thomas Mathias, *The Pursuits of Literature: A Satirical Poem in Four Dialogues*, 8th edn. (1808), 216.

[80] Reid, *The Rise and Dissolution of the Infidel Societies in this Metropolis*, 89.

unsympathetic *British Critic,* for instance, described Godwin's ideas of the 'omnipotence of truth' and the 'perfectibility of man' both as forms of 'enthusiasm'. The *Monthly Mirror* found that '*wild theories,* and *mad-brained enthusiasms*' were 'liberally interspersed in that voluminous production'. Even the much more politically sympathetic *Analytical,* always on its guard against enthusiasm, could echo this approach, if with a more positive inflection:

If his ardent enthusiasm in favour of truth and liberty, have betrayed Mr G into a few extraordinary and chimerical positions, though we may be disposed to smile at their singularity and extravagance, we can scarce censure the principle in which they originate.[81]

Dr Samuel Parr was an old friend of Godwin's, but in 1801 he devastated the philosopher by publishing a sermon which presented the entire exercise of *Political Justice* as vitiated by enthusiasm. Parr built upon Burke's view of revolutionary ideology in his general condemnation of 'the progress of speculations, carried on with a glowing and impetuous spirit of enthusiasm'.[82] For Parr no less than Burke 'excessive zeal for religion' and 'a supposed proficiency in philosophy' were to be opposed to the sensible pragmatism of those who 'have sounded more skilfully the depth of the human heart'.[83] Parr made it clear that the latter comprised the whole tradition of regulated sociability embodied in eighteenth-century moral philosophy from Shaftesbury and Hutcheson through to Adam Smith and Thomas Reid. Ironically, as we shall see, this tradition of benevolence was one that Godwin claimed for himself, and one which he saw too as foregrounding a necessary discourse of regulation.

Before examining Godwin's ideas on benevolence more closely, some of the other grounds on which the charge of enthusiasm was brought against him need to be examined. Godwin himself gave a hostage to fortune perhaps when, sounding very much like Shaftesbury, he described the ability of visions of human progress to 'inspire to a sound mind such generous enthusiasm, such enlightened ardour, and such invincible perseverance' (*Godwin Works,* iii.

---

[81] See *The British Critic,* 1 (1793), 317; *Monthly Mirror,* 12 (Mar. 1801), 182–3; and *Analytical Review,* 16 (1793), 404.

[82] Samuel Parr, *A Spital Sermon, Preached at Christ Church, upon Easter Tuesday, April 15, 1800* (1801), 2.

[83] Ibid. 11.

9). This 'generous enthusiasm' sometimes inflects Godwin's prose with a millenarian fervour:

If there be such a thing as truth, it must infallibly be struck out by the collision of mind with mind. The restless activity of intellect will for a time be fertile in paradox and error; but these will only be diurnals, while the truths that occasionally spring up, like sturdy plants, will defy the rigour of season and climate. (iii. 15)

The passage climaxes with a call for 'unlimited speculation' (iii. 15). Such confidence sounds as if it is dispensing with any regulation in the search for truth. Its eagerness for 'the restless activity of intellect' could be taken by opponents to prove Burke's charge that opinion for opinion's sake was the guiding light of revolutionary ideology. From this perspective the 'collision of mind with mind' sounded less like the polite conversation of Shaftesbury and more like the acrimonious controversy associated with religious Dissent. Any notion of regulation taking place prior to the exchange of ideas seems to have disappeared: conflict between different opinions will winnow out the truth. As late as 1801, assailed on all sides for his enthusiasm, Godwin was still prepared to refuse any such regulation in his reply to Parr:

It is a serious thing to say, that men must neither argue nor write, till they have first subdued the free-born nature of their souls to the trammels of some fortunate and highly patronised creed, which is to be received as orthodox. (*Godwin Works*, ii. 206)

In *Political Justice* he had implied that all mediating authorities, especially the Church, were to be superseded in the interests of truth. Priests are condemned for their tendency to be 'imperious, dogmatical, and impatient of opposition' (iii. 37). 'Nothing is too sacred', wrote Godwin, sounding dogmatical to Parr, 'to be brought to the bar of the touchstone of examination' (iii. 15). Samuel Parr had no hesitation in seeing a dangerous enthusiasm behind the idea of 'unlimited speculation': 'We have a better security in common sense, which understands and obeys fixed rules, than in enthusiasm, which might violate them with good intentions, and very bad effects.'[84] Godwin's speculations at the end of *Political Justice* on a future when the human intellect might have control over its own mortality seems to have caused particular offence. The *British Critic*

---

[84] Ibid. 16.

was outraged by the idea that the 'mind may be omnipotent over matter'.[85] Burke's claim that men of letters privileged their own ideas over circumstance seemed to be corroborated by *Political Justice*. Godwin's conformity with the typology of fanaticism seemed particularly strong in those passages where he disparaged ties of kinship and affection as so many obstacles to properly disinterested moral behaviour.

Although the first edition of *Political Justice* presented abstract justice as the basis of his system, Godwin was coming to place a greater and greater stress on the idea of benevolence as an integral part of human nature, but Parr accused Godwin of sacrificing 'the real social affections' to the chimera of universal benevolence. Parr's attack on Godwin differentiated universal benevolence sharply from the eighteenth-century British tradition of moral philosophy. Parr's notes are full of praise for Adam Smith's idea that benevolence needs a 'proper limited object' if it is not to be 'dissipated and lost'. Reason is 'the moral power by which actions ought to be regulated'.[86] The irony is that Godwin was himself influenced by this same philosophical tradition. In the second edition of *Political Justice*, for instance, 'benevolence' tends to replace 'virtue' as the key term. Shaftesbury, Hutcheson, and even Hume are all cited in support of the possibility of 'disinterested benevolence'.[87] The difference between Parr and Godwin can be described in terms of a different understanding of regulation in relation to benevolence. Parr shared the belief of Hume and Smith that benevolence could degenerate into a passion, if it ignored normative ideas of the 'real social affections'. Although Parr seems to have been happy to overlook the differences between Shaftesbury and Smith on this score, he believed that Godwin's perfectibilarianism had thrown off the proper constraints on benevolence. Universal benevolence could be approved as 'an emotion of which general happiness is the cause, but not as a passion, of which, according to the usual order of human affairs, it could often be the object'.[88] What

[85]   *British Critic*, 1 (1793), 316. Godwin himself traced the phrase to Benjamin Franklin via Richard Price. See *Godwin Works*, iii. 460.

[86]   Parr, *A Spital Sermon*, 10, 49, and 54.

[87]   See Mark Philp, *Godwin's Political Justice* (Duckworth, 1986), 147 and 153. Jones, *Radical Sensibility*, 89–102, suggests that Godwin was influenced by this tradition rather earlier than Philp allows and finds it to be an important presence even in the 1st edition.

[88]   Parr, *A Spital Sermon*, 6.

Parr chose to ignore was that Godwin had his own concerns about regulation. Godwin was afraid that there were those who might debase his idea of benevolence even as they believed themselves to be expounding it.[89]

Godwin's ideas on benevolence and the spread of truth had even in *Political Justice* been tempered by a concern for regulation. His description of his perfectibilarian doctrines as a 'generous enthusiasm' may have owed more to Shaftesbury than, say, Hume, in its willingness to link enthusiasm and benevolence positively. Godwin even refers to the latter as a 'passion', but he was careful to stress that such positive effects were only likely to operate on those with a 'sound mind' (*Godwin Works*, iii. 9).[90] The kind of enthusiasm it might inspire in the unsound mind, and what defined such a mind were only implied in the pages which followed. There it emerges that Godwin had little faith in the ability of even the sound of mind to survive the tumults of the crowd. His own ideas might not even survive such a buffeting, and he was always concerned that he himself might be 'propagating blind zeal, where we meant to propagate reason' (iii. 118). The best-known example of this reflex in Godwin's thinking is his concern about political associations. Even where popular assemblies were discussing his own ideas, he was anxious about the infectious passions of the crowd overwhelming the light of individual judgement. Godwin feared that where 'the sympathy of opinion catches from man to man, especially in numerous meetings, and among persons whose passions have not been used to the curb of judgement, actions may be determined on, which

---

[89] Godwin seems to acknowledge that the perfectibilarian doctrines of *Political Justice* might be construed as enthusiasm in his reply to Parr, but sounding rather like Hume or Smith he argues that their influence was likely to be controlled by the everyday round of human sociability: 'The intercourse of the world has a powerful tendency to blunt in us the sentiments of enthusiasm, and the spirit of romance; and whatever truth we may suppose there is to be in the doctrine of the progressive nature of man, it is so far remote from the transactions of ordinary life, and the feelings which impel us in such transactions to bend to the routine of circumscribed and unspeculative men, that it can with difficulty preserve its authority in the midst of so much contagion' (*Godwin Works*, ii. 198). The difference from Hume is perhaps that it is worldliness which Godwin construes as the contagion here. Godwin seems prepared to entertain the notion that *Political Justice* is founded on the uncertain grounds of enthusiasm, perhaps somewhat ironically, but then implies the nobility of such conceptions in comparison to the compromises of everyday affairs. If worldliness is a regulating principle here, it is not unproblematically a positive one for Godwin.
[90] See Jones, *Radical Sensibility*, 90–2.

solitary reflection would have rejected' (iii. 118). Sentiments such as these almost echo Burke's on 'electrick communication'.[91] One difference is that Godwin seems to have allowed for a built-in regulatory principle when it came to reading. Whereas the presence of the crowd threatened to infect ideas with enthusiasm, reading for Godwin—unlike the Attorney-General at the trial of Paine—seems to act as its own guarantee of regulation, but the assumptions of the law officer are not entirely absent from Godwin's position on the dissemination of knowledge. Literature 'exists only as the portion of a few. The multitude, at least in the present state of society, cannot partake of its illumination' (iii. 16). Replying to Parr in 1801, Godwin affirmed that 'a truly virtuous character is the combined result of regulated affection' (ii. 183). *Political Justice* had implied that the multitude was all too inclined to be dominated by enthusiasm. Among such multitudes the 'universal exercise of private judgment', the freedom on which Godwin's whole edifice rests, is likely to be clouded and overwhelmed. Human improvement is not the product of 'the energies of the people at large', but of a 'degree of study and reflection' (iii. 117).

Godwin's supporters were apt to use his opinions on associations as proof of his philosophical temper against those who accused him of enthusiasm. William Burdon, for instance, argued that 'Mr Godwin's is not a noisy, tumultuous address to the passions of men . . . but a calm, rational system .. slow in its operation, and silent in its effects.'[92] Literature's role in human improvement for Godwin had nothing to do with large public gatherings; it was a completely separate matter from meetings in which the private identity of each individual might be obscured.[93] Even so, Godwin's commitment to

---

[91] See above, 59.
[92] William Burdon, *Various Thoughts on Politics, Morality, and Literature* (Newcastle upon Tyne, 1800), 35. See the discussion in Keen, *The Crisis of Literature in the 1790s*, 58–61, which led me to Burdon.
[93] See *Godwin Works*, ii. 132 and the discussion of his dispute with Thelwall, below 115–20. In the 1798 edition of *Political Justice*, Godwin wrote of the way that 'contentious dispute and long consultation about matters of the most trivial importance' corrupted 'the simple and inartificial scene of things, when each man speaks and writes his mind, in such eloquence as his sentiments dictate, and with unfettered energy; not anxious, while he gives vent to his enthusiasm of his conceptions' (iv. 145). Here, of course, enthusiasm means something like Shaftesbury's 'noble enthusiasm'; those larger principles that are only likely to be obstructed by the self-interested passions of assemblies, but when answering Parr he had suggested such enthusiasm might need such worldly ballast if it were not to dissolve into unworldly speculation (see above, n. 89).

'free and unrestricted discussion' remained in an often uneasy tension with his concern to 'carefully distinguish between informing the people and inflaming them' (*Godwin Works*, iii. 115). Mark Philp has stressed Godwin's own sociability. His diary shows that he was in constant touch with literary circles in the metropolis in the 1790s, and met regularly with leaders in the radical cause.[94] John Binns recalled Godwin was a member of a least one discussion group which he and other autodidacts attended, but even here the model was still one of 'unreserved communication in a smaller circle' (iii. 120).[95] The class composition of such a circle might be different from that imagined by Shaftesbury. Godwin had moved far beyond the genteel 'chat' (*Characteristics*, 381) described in Shaftesbury's dialogues, but a suspicion of the crowd remained. Godwin seems always to have suspected that the LCS—whether in the lecture room or at its outdoor monster meetings—was incapable of preserving the distinction between society and the mob. On the defensive after Parr's attack, Godwin contrasted his own philosophical discourse with a negative picture of the popular radical movement: 'revolutionary lectures were publicly read here and elsewhere with tumults of applause; almost every alehouse had its artisans haranguing in favour of republicanism and equality' (*Godwin Works*, ii. 169). The alehouse had always been represented as the antithesis of both the regulated public sphere and the proper sensibility of domestic ideology. It was widely regarded as the scenario of regressive passions. Godwin represents the debating clubs and lectures associated with the LCS as a spectacle of good intentions overwhelmed by the infectious enthusiasm of the vulgar, an example of 'the contagiousness of human passions when exposed in society' (ii. 176).

The most celebrated lecturer in the metropolis from 1793 to 1797 was John Thelwall, a veteran of tavern 'spouting clubs', but also a friend of Godwin's and a man who devoted a great deal of time in his lectures to disseminating the tenets of *Political Justice*. Despite these credentials, his popularity as a public lecturer earned him a stinging rebuke from Godwin. The latter's anonymous *Considerations on Lord Greville's and Mr Pitt's Bills* (1795) was written against the Two Acts, passed in the wake of the debates over

---

[94] See Philp, *Godwin's Political Justice*, 164, and Keen, *The Crisis of Literature in the 1790s*, 29.

[95] John Binns, *Recollections of the Life of John Binns* (Philadelphia, 1854), 45.

'Citizen' Lee in the House, but widely assumed to be directed specifically against Thelwall. Godwin's strategy was to present the acts as unnecessary measures against a radical movement that was essentially a matter of philosophical enquiry (from which Thelwall's lectures were an unfortunate deviation), but any purely strategic explanation for his attack on Thelwall must also account for the antipathy to popular assemblies expounded in *Political Justice*. In its development of that antipathy, *Considerations* can often sound rather Burkean. Burke's fear of the energy of ideas acting without the slowing effects of a proprietorial stake in the land surely informs its account of the 'abundance of impetuous and ardent activity, and very little of the ballast, the unwieldy dulness of property' (*Godwin Works*, ii. 130).[96] Godwin complains that the absence of men of 'eminence' from LCS meetings meant that there was no one to 'temper' (ii. 130) their excesses, and goes on to imply that Thelwall, a self-made man of letters of the sort feared by Burke, could neither control himself nor his audience. Godwin grants that Thelwall's career commenced with 'uncommon purity of intentions', but then implies that these intentions had become discomposed along the way:

The lecturer ought to have a mind calmed, and, if I may be allowed the expression, consecrated by the mild spirit of philosophy. He ought to come forth with no undisciplined passions, in the first instance; and he ought to have a temper unyielding to the corrupt influence of a noisy and admiring audience. (ii. 132)

This passage may leave us in some doubt as to whether Thelwall is himself guilty of 'undisciplined passions', but it goes on to suggest that whatever state the lecturer himself is in he is likely to become infected by the crowd he addresses. Animating the crowd, its interest kindles into enthusiasm, and the infection overwhelms the speaker himself. Here it is the audience, 'persons not much in the habit of regular thinking' (ii. 133), which transports the speaker out of his regulated selfhood. It seems that the speakers of the LCS—Thelwall chief among them—are either not capable of regulating their own enthusiasm, and so unable to distinguish inflaming from educating, or likely to be themselves overwhelmed by the sympa-

---

[96] Compare Burke's description of property as 'the sluggish principle' and 'the ballast in the vessel of the commonwealth' in *Reflections* (*The Writings and Speeches*, viii. 102).

thetic identification with their audience. Literature requires leisure to consume, and the process of reflection that Godwin imagines as integral to the reading process brings with it an in-built regulating process. Things are rather different when addressing crowds:

Sober inquiry may pass well enough with a man in his closet, or in the domestic tranquility of his own fire-side: but it will not suffice in theatres and halls of assembly. Here men require a due mixture of spices and sea-soning. All oratorical seasoning is an appeal to the passions. (ii. 133)

Unlike the conservative press writing after Burke, which was quick to condemn both print and platform radicalism, Godwin was willing to defend unlimited enquiry in literature and among small circles of thinking men, but once radical ideas moved on to a pop-ular platform, he perceived great danger from the enthusiasm of the crowd. Godwin even invoked the *locus classicus* of late eighteenth-century enthusiasm when he compared Thelwall's attempts to tem-per the passions of his audience to 'lord George Gordon preaching peace to the rioters in Westminster-Hall' (ii. 133). When it came to popular assemblies his views on the possibility of self-regulation were little different from the *British Critic*'s opinion that 'in vulgar minds the transition from contempt and dislike to acts of violence is but too easy'.[97]

THELWALL'S 'ENTHUSIASTIC VIRTUES'

Thelwall was furious at this representation of his lectures as pan-dering to the basest passions of his audiences. Much of his lecturing had been devoted to promoting Godwin's ideas. He had described *Political Justice* as 'the most extensive plan of freedom and innova-tion ever discussed by any writer in the English language'. Reflecting on the attack in Godwin's *Considerations*, he com-plained that 'the bitterest of my enemies has never used me so ill as this friend has done', but his anger came not just from a sense of personal betrayal.[98] It spoke to a fear he had expressed himself.

[97] *British Critic*, 7 (1796), 262.

[98] See B. Sprague Allen, 'Godwin's Influence upon John Thelwall', *PMLA* 37 (1922), 662–82. Thelwall praises *Political Justice* in *The Tribune: Consisting Chiefly of the Political Lectures of John Thelwall*, 3 vols. (1795–6), ii, p. vii. On his complaint against Godwin, see *The Politics of English Jacobinism: The Writings of John Thelwall*, ed. Gregory Claeys (University Park: Pennsylvania State University Press, 1995), 382b.

Thelwall constantly affirmed with Godwin that his ideas were predicated on 'Reason and the pure spirit of philosophy'.[99] He shared Godwin's belief that the philosopher-politician had to act with 'a caution bordering on reserve'. The danger was that 'by pouring acceptable truths too suddenly on the popular eye, instead of salutary light he should produce blindness and frenzy'.[100] Thelwall had a strong if complex sense of the irrationality of the mob, and usually represented popular religious feeling as its worst form, presumably because they were most obviously at odds with his idea of enlightenment. He believed his own Deism to be a more orderly and rational form of belief. In this spirit he pointedly contrasted the principles of the French Revolution with those of seventeenth-century Puritanism, rebutting Burke's attempt to run them together under the category of enthusiasm. In lectures given in 1795, Thelwall carefully distinguished events in France from the English Revolution of the 1640s:

They [the fanatics of the seventeenth century] had light indeed (inward light) which, though it came not through the optics of reason, produced a considerable ferment in their blood, and made them cry out for that liberty, the very meaning of which they did not comprehend. In fact, the mass of the people were quickened, not by the generous spirit of liberty, but by the active spirit of fanaticism.[101]

From a Burkean perspective, such distinctions hardly mattered. Popular enthusiasm could attach itself to Christianity, deism, or even atheism. In all cases it was dangerous. This extended logic was frequently applied to Thelwall. One unsympathetic eye-witness account of his lectures claimed that Thelwall 'raves like a mad Methodist parson: the most ranting Actor in the most ranting Character never made so much noise as Citizen Thelwall.'[102] What

[99] *Political Lectures, Volume the First—Part the First: Containing the Lecture on Spies and Informers and the First Lecture on Prosecutions for Political Opinion* (1795), 12.

[100] *The Politics of English Jacobinism*, 337.

[101] *The Tribune*, iii. 188. See also Peter Kitson, ' "Sages and patriots that being dead do yet to us speak": Readings of the English Revolution in the Late Eighteenth Century', in James Holstun (ed.), *Pamphlet Wars: Prose in the English Revolution* (Frank Cass, 1992), 205–30, and Michael Scrivener, 'John Thelwall and the Revolution of 1649', in Nigel Smith and Timothy Morton (eds.), *Radicalism in British Literary Culture: From Revolution to Revolution* (Cambridge: Cambridge University Press, 2002), 119–32.

[102] Thomas Amyot quoted in E. P. Thompson, *The Romantics: England in a Revolutionary Age* (New York: W. W. Norton, 1997), 154. The same identification

really mattered to such critics was that Thelwall's desire for what he called 'extensive circulation' led him to address audiences widely believed to be incapable of regulating their passions.[103] Here also was the key difference between Godwin and Thelwall. Thelwall believed in disseminating ideas as broadly as possible; put that belief into practice; and trusted his audience to regulate themselves:

There is also another—better motive than that of prudence, to prompt us to this moderation in our deportment—Benevolence!—the kind and candid feelings of the heart! without which a pure and enlightened freedom never can be enjoyed, never can be understood. Anarchy may rage where asperity of soul triumphs in all its bitterness, but where personal hatred, and the burning desire of vengeance usurp dominion over the hearts of men, genuine liberty, and the tranquil happiness which liberty ought to secure to us, never can be hoped.[104]

Thelwall's 'us' brings into being an idea of a 'benevolence' which is at once popular and noble. If the LCS proved incapable of 'Peaceful discussion and not tumultory violence', however, the whole basis of Thelwall's claims for the right of the populace to be directly involved in political affairs collapsed. They would have proved themselves incapable of such self-regulation.

John Binns remembered Thelwall as 'a timid alarmist in private', but one of the 'boldest political writers, speakers, and lecturers of his time'.[105] This double identity structures Thelwall's profound ambivalence towards enthusiasm. Thelwall's constant stress on the need for moderation may well betray an anxiety that his audience might not live up to his faith in their ability to regulate themselves, but there was another more personal reason why Thelwall needed to convince himself of this capability. Thelwall seems to have been well aware, and sometimes even proud—as we shall see below—of

operates in the depictions of Thelwall as 'Citizen Rant' in Isaac Disraeli's *Vaurien* (1797) and George Walker's *The Vagabond* (1799). See ibid. 186.

[103] John Thelwall, *Peaceful Discussion and not Tumultory Violence the Means of Redressing National Grievances* (1795), p. iv.

[104] *The Politics of English Jacobinism*, 57–8. Thelwall had done much to take Godwin's ideas to a popular audience, reading from *Political Justice* to LCS meetings in early 1794, and at the Three Kings Tavern in the Minories. Taking Godwin into the tavern looked like a deliberate transgression of the regulatory boundaries which *Political Justice* set up in its discussion of popular assemblies. Presumably those were not the chapters of Godwin's book which Thelwall discussed in the Three Kings Tavern.

[105] Binns, *Recollections*, 44.

a disposition within himself towards 'enthusiasm'. At Thelwall's trial for treason in 1794, his lawyer conceded that the orator could be 'warm tempered' and 'sometimes apt to speak his sentiments in stronger terms than his sober judgment could approve'.[106] As a man who had received only a basic education, who had once been an apprentice tailor, he was particularly vulnerable to accusations that he lacked the cultural capital necessary to curb such tendencies, but he was also willing to represent his warmth as a sympathetic power within himself that justified his pretensions to address the public. What he termed variously 'popular enthusiasm', 'generous sympathy' or *social ardor* provided the basis of his connection with his audience.[107] This 'sympathy' connected him, he claimed, 'with the whole intellectual universe' including 'our starving manufacturers' and 'widows and orphans'.[108] Thelwall's inclusive address to 'us' reflects his own rhetorical status as an autodidact, one who presumed to speak to a plebeian public, not on the basis of the authority of institutions, wealth, nor family, or even education, but on the basis of 'free-born energies of the soul', energies that he assumed his audience could share whatever its social origins.[109] Not only his political opponents thought him a speaker capable of stirring the passions. Hazlitt described Thelwall as the most dashing orator he had ever heard, a man capable of awakening sympathies dormant in the breasts of his audience.[110] Godwin's suggestion that Thelwall might be possessed by this audience response rather than influencing it towards virtue implied that neither the author nor his listeners were capable of translating this sympathetic power into a valid form of public intercourse.

In much of his early literary work, Thelwall does present himself quite explicitly as a child of 'sweet enthusiasm' and 'rapture' in the

---

[106] *The Trial at Large of John Thelwall, for High Treason*, ed. John Newton (1794), 39.

[107] *The Tribune*, ii, pp. xii, xiv, and xv.

[108] *Political Lectures (No. 1) on the Moral Tendency of a System of Spies and Informers, and the Conduct to be Observed by the Friends of Liberty during the Continuance of such a System*, 2nd edn. (1794), 11 and 13.

[109] Thelwall, *The Peripatetic, or Sketches of the heart, of nature, and society; in a series of politico-sentimental journals, in verse and prose, of the eccentric excursions of Sylvanus Theophrastus, supposed to be written by himself*, 3 vols. (1793), i. 123.

[110] Hazlitt, 'On the Difference between Writing and Speaking', in *Complete Works of William Hazlitt*, ed. P. P. Howe, 21 vols. (J. M. Dent, 1930–4), xii. 264–5.

mould of both Shaftesbury and Rousseau.[111] *The Peripatetic*
(1793), for instance, the engaging medley that Thelwall described as
a combination of 'the novel, the sentimental journal, and the miscellaneous collection of essays and poetical effusions', is a celebration of nature as the teacher of 'the glorious maxims of relative and
social duty'.[112] It might be argued that enthusiasm is only being
granted relative licence here because of the literariness of the context, but *The Peripatetic* is both a display of social feelings and a
work of politics and social criticism. It does not in any simple sense
imply an aesthetic sphere separate from the public world. In terms
of the distinctions between 'enthusiasm' and 'sensibility' set out in
my previous chapter, one might say that Thelwall disregards the
kind of regulation that separated polite sensibility, which aims to
'restore the momentary wanderer to himself', from a more expansive movement out of the self and towards the multitude associated
with enthusiasm.[113] Nor at this stage in his career is it only in quasi-
literary genres that Thelwall's 'enthusiasm' is presented as a noble
benevolence. For all the stress on reason and moderation in his
pamphlets and speeches of the 1790s, they often represent a vigorous and public enthusiasm as the basis of his radical politics. The
'free-born energies of the soul', which reveal that *'Reason is not sole
Arbiter in the human mind,'* also played an important part in his
political lectures.[114] Defending himself against charges that his public lecturing was inflammatory, Thelwall argued that French philosophy had suffered from being without 'that active energy—that
collected, unembarrassed, firmness and presence of mind, which

---

[111] On Thelwall's relation to Shaftesbury and Rousseau, see the 'Introduction' to
The Peripatetic, ed. Judith Thompson (Detroit: Wayne State University Press, 2001)
and see below for Coleridge's letter to Thelwall that links the two men.
[112] *Peripatetic*, pp. vi and 18.
[113] Andrew   McCann,   'Politico-Sentimentality: John   Thelwall,   Literary
Production and Critique of Capital in the 1790s', *Romanticism*, 3 (1997), 35–42,
has argued that it contains a critique of the privileging of literary sentimentalism over
social conscience. Thelwall's preface pointed out that 'the subject of our political
abuses is so interwoven with the scenes of distress so perpetually recurring to the feeling observer, that it were impossible to be silent in this respect, without suppressing
almost every reflection that ought to awaken the tender sympathies of the soul'
(p. viii).
[114] *Peripatetic*, iii. 120. Thelwall continues: 'Imagination has also a considerable
share in the enjoyment and perturbation of the soul: nor will her vivid impressions
always submit to the cool and regular deduction of Philosophy.' These sentiments
perhaps point to Thelwall's reading in the British 'moral sense' tradition after
Shaftesbury.

nothing but the actual enjoyment of liberty, and an unrestrained intercourse with a bold resolute bustling and disputatious race of men can possibly confer'.[115] He was directly rebutting Burke's claim that revolutionary energy was a rootless kind of enthusiasm. Instead he presents enthusiasm as a positive and liberating force. But where for Burke enthusiasm unsettles gendered identity, for Thelwall, as for Shaftesbury, it is essential to a true masculinity. He goes on a few pages later to imply that Godwin's fear of popular assemblies (described as a suspicion of 'energy') is emasculated; its 'cold abstraction and retirement' evinces *'a feebleness of spirit'*.[116] Properly regulated warmth is the basis of true masculine identity. While Thelwall continues to see 'intemperance' as 'British vice', he also sees the population as capable of regulating its native energies into a powerful liberating force. In his 'Preface' to *The Tribune* Thelwall defended the lecturing form against Godwin's assault precisely because it was capable of 'combining together the advantages of elaborate research and popular enthusiasm'. Without what Thelwall calls 'generous sympathy', 'a nation is but a populous wilderness, and the philosopher only a walking index of obsolete laws and dead-lettered institutes'.[117] In the 'Farewell Address' to the *Tribune* he explained that he had delayed publication of his best lectures 'till leisure and fit opportunity enable me to send them into the world in some more convenient form, and in a more correct state'.[118] He regards these lectures as his best because they were 'delivered on the spur of an awful and momentous crisis'. The result was 'more of that fire of expression, and that rapid energy of conception and arrangement which constitute the soul of oratory'. The decision to delay publication may seem to be an act of self-regulation prior to coming before the public, but he had already delivered the lectures spontaneously from notes, bringing his 'fire of expression' directly before a public that both Burke and Godwin believed incapable of regulating its response. Indeed it is precisely the sympathetic responsiveness of 'popular enthusiasm' that his lectures are designed to exploit, transmitting his own 'energy' to the eager antennae of the crowd.[119]

The Two Acts and more directly the attacks of Church and King thugs on his lectures had effectively forced Thelwall out of political

---

[115] *Sober Reflections* (1796) in *The Politics of English Jacobinism*, 376.
[116] Ibid. 382.   [117] See *The Tribune*, i, pp. xii and xiv–xv.
[118] Ibid. iii. 332.   [119] Ibid.

life by 1797. He attempted to live by farming in Wales, supplemented by his literary pursuits, before bad harvests forced him back to lecturing, now on elocution and speech therapy. The latter provided him with a relatively successful career for the rest of his life, although he briefly rekindled his radical activism for a few years after 1815. Looking back on the 1790s, Thelwall tended to point to 'enthusiasm' as a personal trait that had been responsible for many of his problems, but never entirely abandoned his pride in its sympathetic potential. In the retrospective of his early life published in *A Letter to Henry Cline Esq* (1810), Thelwall explained his turn from an early interest in medicine to politics as a dubious triumph for 'the more ardent rays of popular enthusiasm'.[120] He is in part apologizing for youthful impetuosity, except that enthusiasm is not in any simple sense represented as a fault. He continues to see a 'generous sympathy' as essential to human affairs. Even his successes as a speech therapist, he ascribes to 'the degree of feeling I have been fortunate enough to inspire'. This ability he continues to call 'enthusiasm'. Although towards the end of the pamphlet he expresses a hope that he will be credited with being 'actuated more by the zeal of science, than the presumption of enthusiasm', it seems that he is not entirely willing to regard his infectious powers in a negative light.[121] These issues had been treated in more detail but with a similar ambivalence in the third-person memoir prefacing his *Poems, Chiefly written in Retirement* (1801). Thelwall recalled how he had worked behind the counter in the family silk business; as a tailor; and as an articled clerk to the attorney John Impey, before seeking to earn his living in London's literary world. His background was in no way plebeian, but he had come from that world where the journeyman, small master, and shopkeeper often mixed. For all the mixing, however, Thelwall was quite capable of anticipating the pompous petit bourgeois prone to congratulating himself on his own superiority. In the 1800s when he sometimes distanced himself from his radical past, the tendency emerged very clearly. Thelwall could insist that 'Condition . . . does not, by the same scale, dispense intelligence', but then expresses 'disgust' for the habits of the shopworkers.[122] Thelwall creates the possibility in the free energies of the mind for his own successful rise, and at the same

---

[120] *Letter to Henry Cline, Esq.* (1810), 2.   [121] Ibid. 64–5 and 142.
[122] 'Prefatory Memoir' in *Poems, Chiefly Written in Retirement*, 2nd edn. (1801), pp. x and xii.

time distances himself from the rough passions of the crowd. The spouting clubs where he had learnt his oratorical skills are dismissed as 'ranting seminaries', but he prides himself on his own tendency 'to give unreserved utterances to the existing convictions of his heart'.[123] It is not simply that his sensibility is more refined than that of his fellows at these popular clubs, for he recognizes in his own feelings an enthusiasm that has sometimes undone his aspirations to gentility. Thelwall's emotional sincerity has been both his making and unmaking. 'The discussions on the subject of the Slave Trade into which he entered with an almost diseased enthusiasm,' he tells the reader, 'led the way to the very considerable changes in his public sentiments.'[124] Events in France compounded this predisposition. 'Hurried away by the enthusiasm of the French Revolution, he had plunged into the vortex of political conviction.' Finally his political destiny was fixed by his involvement in the Westminster election of 1790, where he canvassed for John Horne Tooke.[125] 'The enthusiasm of Thelwall caught fire from such approximation'. Infectious sympathy undoes him, but it is never simply condemned. It retains an association with Shaftesbury's noble enthusiasm, and the possibility, however unstable, of a disinterested moral sense. For the Westminster election Thelwall 'threw up his profitable situation', put aside self-interest, 'to indulge his ardour in a laborious canvas'.[126] Enthusiasm may be unpredictable, but it also provides a pointer towards Thelwall's best self.

Looking back on the previous decade, Thelwall sometimes represents himself as a hostage to the idea of distraction discussed in my previous chapter, but his retirement to Wales in 1797—preceded by the well-known visit with Coleridge and Wordsworth at Nether Stowey in July—is taken to be the beginning of a more dialectically structured relationship between reflection and sociability in which 'the agitations of political feeling might be cradled to forgetfulness' and replaced by 'the calm enthusiasm of poetic meditation'.[127] In poetry the best self is extracted and nurtured from the chaotic tumults of impulse. The difference between the view of enthusiasm in these later reminiscences and the one given in the political writing of the mid-1790s is that now only in the chamber of the aesthetic can his innate enthusiasm be brought into a harmoniously

---

[123] *Poems, Chiefly Written in Retirement*, 2nd edn. (1801), pp. viii and xvii.
[124] Ibid., p. xiii.   [125] Ibid., p. xiv.   [126] Ibid., pp. xxiv–xxv.
[127] Ibid., pp. xxxvi and xxxix.

regulated form. Yet even here he cannot quite bring himself to dis-
avow the reach of a more democratic idea of enthusiasm. Judith
Thompson suggests that Thelwall's conversation poems of this
period, when compared with Coleridge's, with which they were to
some extent in dialogue, keep open the notion of retirement as a
moment of regulation preparatory to returning before the public.[128]
Certainly even Thelwall's 1801 collection remains resistant to an
idea of the value of retirement for its own sake: 'Whatever may have
been said by visionary enthusiasts, continued solitude is the grave
rather than the nurse of mind.'[129] The question of whether this
aspect of retirement is kept alive in the poetry of Coleridge and
Wordsworth is one I shall be returning to in Part II. I want to close
this discussion of Thelwall by showing that, whatever Coleridge
and Wordsworth did with it, even the rhetoric of retirement and
regulation within the aesthetic was not easily granted by the polite
press to someone whom they regarded as an upstart plebeian.

Thelwall remained defined by the categories of 'the uneducated
poet' discussed in my previous chapter for most of his public life.
Francis Jeffrey writing in the *Edinburgh Review*, for instance, was
unable to imagine Thelwall's sense of achievement as anything other
than the mania of 'enthusiasm'. Jeffrey's review of the 1801 *Poems*
opened with a discussion of literature as 'a pleasant a way to distinction, to those who are without the advantages of birth or fortune, that we need not wonder if more are drawn into it, than are
qualified to reach the place of their destination'.[130] The review goes
on to mock the very idea that an uneducated poet was capable of
carrying out the kind of self-fashioning to which Thelwall laid claim.
Rather than creating a proper self through working on their enthusiasm, uneducated poets are losing their true selves to impossible
visions of improvement, 'shoemakers and tailors astonish the world
with plans for reforming the constitution, and with effusions of relative and social feeling.' Thelwall's 'enthusiastic virtues' are simply
'an impatience of honest industry'.[131] Thelwall wrote an angry reply
to Jeffrey claiming never to have despised 'regularity'.[132] He also

---

[128] 'An Autumnal Blast, A Killing Frost: Coleridge's Poetic Conversation with
John Thelwall', *Studies in Romanticism*, 36 (1997), 427–56.
[129] Thelwall, 'Prefatory Memoir', p. xlv.
[130] *Edinburgh Review*, 2 (1803), 197–201: 197.   [131] Ibid. 197 and 200.
[132] *A letter to Francis Jeffray [sic] . . . on certain calumnies . . . in the Edinburgh
Review* (Edinburgh, 1804), 28.

explicitly discusses his use of the term 'enthusiasm' in the memoir. Like Shaftesbury, he presents it not as the passion of a 'vulgar and illiterate being', as he claims the *Edinburgh* has represented him, but as the raw material for all that is noble; the origin of his 'firmness' during his imprisonment in the Tower in 1794; as well as his 'keenness of perception, and habits of *feeling*'. Unlike both Jeffrey and Shaftesbury, he sees the ability to shape this raw material as available to the tailor's apprentice as well as the 'self-appointed guardians of English Literature'.[133]

Godwin and Thelwall must have looked like two sides of the same coin of enthusiasm to the critic looking from a Burkean perspective. The former in his solitude conjured visions of an impractical perfection, the latter propagated them—despite Godwin's reservations—with a missionary zeal. The historical irony is that both Godwin and Thelwall in their different ways were also concerned to distinguish their ideas from vulgar enthusiasm, developing their own versions of a discourse of regulation. This would seem to confirm Isaac Kramnick's view that 'bourgeois radicalism . . . casts an ominous shadow of discipline, regimen, and authority'.[134] Godwin certainly retained an anxiety about the possibilities of the multitude being able to control their own enthusiasm. He defended against Burke the right to unlimited speculation, but in practice he thought this freedom ought to be circumscribed. With Thelwall, the case is different, and more complicated. Enthusiasm was more fully central to Thelwall's sense of self. The word for Thelwall always brings with it the idea of universally available powers of the mind that provide the basis for both his poetic and political interventions. This benevolent power is attractive precisely because it offers a way of circumventing the barriers of cultural capital (even if he is quite capable of exploiting this democratic potential to fashion a sense of superiority for himself). There remains for Thelwall an anxiety about the possibilities of 'generous sympathy' overwhelming the subjectivity it offers to construct. Certainly the later Thelwall implies that his enthusiasm almost destroyed the incipient man of letters it helped create, but even here it remains a potentially noble

---

[133] *A letter to Francis Jeffray [sic] . . . on certain calumnies . . . in the Edinburgh Review* (Edinburgh, 1804), 37–8, 66, and 34.

[134] Isaac Kramnick, *Republicanism and Bourgeois Radicalism: Political Ideology in Late Eighteenth-Century England and America* (Ithaca, NY: Cornell University Press, 1990), 97–8.

force, enabling a disinterestedness beyond mere careerism. During his radical years, Thelwall saw in this power the molten core of his abilities as an orator, as well as the underlying force behind a potentially unlimited public sphere of sympathy that required neither wealth nor even education to enter. Regulation was an issue for Thelwall, but he believed that tumultuous popular meetings could regulate themselves.

The question is not so much to regulate or not to regulate, but who regulates whom. Even Richard 'Citizen' Lee—as his title suggests—fashioned an identity from his enthusiasm, even if it was one that claimed to dispense with the regulations of 'cold' Reason. His language of religious and political unworlding was a rhetoric which had developed its own traditional forms too.[135] The irony is that it is the Methodist republican rather than his more Jacobinical allies who seems to comes closest to the rhetoric of *transparence* condemned by Burke. Certainly Lee's poetry proclaims an ability to see the face of God, a face which smiles on 'the divine right of republics'. Lee effectively abolishes the distinction between poetry and enthusiasm. Even in 1795, while he was publishing broadsheets celebrating 'Citizen Guillotine', Lee was echoing John Dennis's call to return poetry to its origins in the religious sublime:

It gives Pleasure to the ingenious Christian, when the Language of Poetry resumes its original Office of communicating Divine Truth, displaying the Excellence of Religion, and attempting to praise the great Author of being and the source of Happiness.[136]

Little of Kramnick's disciplinary shadow taints Lee's enthusiasm, whether religious or political, but for many both inside and outside the LCS, this kind of enthusiasm was regarded as synonymous with fanaticism. Perhaps more surprising is the extent to which the shadow of regulation casts itself across Romantic poetry. This poetry is often defined as poetry of affect that seized upon the unworlding power of enthusiasm. The problem was that 'mere enthusiasm', to use Blake's phrase, was identified with the delirium

---

[135] See Clement Hawes, *Mania and Literary Style: The Rhetoric of Enthusiasm from the Ranters to Christopher Smart* (Cambridge: Cambridge University Press, 1996) for a study of this tradition.
[136] Lee, *Songs from the Rock*, additional page, verso (and also on the verso of *Proposals*).

of the crowd, and raised the spectre of dissolving the very subjectivity it was meant to be authenticating. Few poets could agree with Blake that such zealous enthusiasm could be 'the All in All' ('Anno. to Reynolds': E645).

PART II

The Poetics of Enthusiasm

CHAPTER THREE

Coleridge, Prophecy, and Imagination

HIGH ROMANTICISM AS it developed in England in the writing of Coleridge and Wordsworth is often represented as a retreat from a radical political commitment. An influential restatement of this narrative by M. H. Abrams in the 1970s represented the process in terms of the transformation of one kind of prophetic enthusiasm into another: 'faith in an apocalypse by revolution . . . gave way to faith in an apocalypse by imagination or cognition'.[1] Although not directly addressing the question of enthusiasm as such, Abrams made much of Schiller's idea that 'in the realm of Aesthetic Semblance, we find that ideal of equality fulfilled which the Enthusiast would fain see realized in substance'.[2] The system-building of enlightenment thinking and for that matter the fanaticism of the plebeian *Schwärmer* are displaced by the idea of an aesthetic revelation involving what Abrams called an 'imaginative transformation of the self'.[3] This account falls in neatly with Irlam's narrative of the rehabilitation of enthusiasm in the eighteenth century. The poet freed from the spectre of a millenarian fanaticism that imagines it can change the world becomes the prophet of the imagination. Part I of this book has questioned the idea that the aesthetic was easily granted such autonomy from other kinds of enthusiasm. Schiller's 'realm of the Aesthetic' was a sphere whose boundaries seemed to be constantly in need of defence and definition. Part II examines in more detail the writing of four poets of the Romantic period to reveal just how

---

[1] M. H. Abrams, *Natural Supernaturalism: Tradition and Revolution in Romantic Literature* (New York: W. W. Norton & Co., 1971), 334.

[2] Schiller, 'On the Aesthetic Education of Man', quoted in Abrams, *Natural Supernaturalism*, 352.

[3] M. H. Abrams, 'Constructing and Deconstructing', in Morris Eaves and Michael Fischer (eds.), *Romanticism and Contemporary Criticism* (Ithaca, NY: Cornell University Press, 1986), 167.

tirelessly the need to distinguish pathological from noble enthusiasm remained at work. This reflex, it argues, was a structuring principle of Romantic-period poetics, although the structure played itself out in different ways.

COLERIDGE'S CAREER OF ENTHUSIASM

New Historicist critiques of Abrams have redefined Romantic poetics negatively as an evasion or displacement of History. Prophecy and the poetics of affect more generally operate to displace politics from this point of view. Appealing as such a dichotomy may be, it too readily assumes an opposition that pits history against prophecy and enthusiasm. The result reproduces the very axiom of Romanticism it is meant to be critiquing, that is, the opposition between enthusiasm and politics (even if it inverts the valency of the opposition in the process). Radical politics and prophecy were not in any simple sense opposed in the 1790s, although some leading figures in the LCS, such as John Thelwall, were keen to suggest that they were. The French Revolution was widely understood in terms of Apocalypse and Millennium by many of his contemporaries. Some saw in it the direct hand of God. A few believed themselves to be directly informed of his will in the matter. What is distinctive about Romantic prophecy is the way it splits off its affective language from an association with radical public utterance. Where prophecy did lay claim to a public role, of course, it had always been readily identified with the enthusiasm of the crowd and the sacrifice of the autonomous self to the welter of the passions. Deeply imbricated with the discourse on enthusiasm as it had developed over the previous century, Romantic prophecy aimed to present itself as a properly regulated species of enthusiasm. Coleridge's 'Destiny of Nations', for instance, ends with an invocation of God that draws a distinction between biblical prophecy and mere enthusiasm:

> Whether thy Love with unrefracted Ray
> Beam on the PROPHET's purged eye, or if
> Diseasing Realms the *Enthusiast*, wild of Thought,
> Scatter new Frenzies on the infected Throng,
> Thou Both inspiring and predooming Both,
> Fit INSTRUMENTS and best, of perfect end.

> (*CPW* i, Part 1, 298, ll. 456–61)

In fact, for Coleridge, paradoxically, as we shall see in relation to his great millenarian poem 'Religious Musings', 'true' poetic enthusiasm was defined by its disavowal of any claim to the 'PROPHET's . . . eye'. Only in the diseasing realms of plebeian prophets such as 'Citizen' Lee could the claim to the powers of prophecy in such an unmediated form be made. *The Fall of Robespierre* secularizes the same set of associations when it describes 'Th'enthusiast mob, confusion's lawless sons' (*CPW* iii, Part 1, 23, line 248).

Given the clerical training of university-educated writers such as Coleridge and Wordsworth, it can be no surprise to see the persistence of this Anglican discourse on enthusiasm, but the same education would have introduced them to the poetics of regulation derived from Shaftesbury. Of course, literature and taste did not simply remain the same throughout the long eighteenth century. Shaftesbury's own style seemed mannered by the end of the century even to many of those, including Godwin, Wordsworth, and Coleridge, who admired his doctrine of 'natural' enthusiasm. The experiential self may be given more latitude later in the century than it is in the earlier poetry discussed by Irlam, this latitude may express itself in a degree of formal iconoclasm, or what Irlam calls 'formlessness', culminating perhaps in the ideas of Coleridge on organic form, but these developments still remain conditioned by a discourse of regulation.[4] Such continuities are often overlooked in favour of ideas of a romantic break with the eighteenth century. If poetry as a form became more unregulated in terms of neoclassical rules of composition, it nonetheless remained deeply attached to the idea that it is generated from something more than a mere enthusiasm of feeling. 'Enthusiasm and feeling profound and vehement' in Coleridge's poetics always have to be reconciled with 'judgement ever awake and steady self-possession' (*BL* ii. 17). If the idea of autonomy of the imagination can be viewed as a distinctively romantic development, it too has to be understood as a response to a deeply held desire for a ground or 'fixed principles' on which distinctions between the infectious passions of the crowd and the

[4] On 'formlessness', see Shaun Irlam, *Elations: The Poetics of Enthusiasm in Eighteenth-Century Britain* (Stanford, Calif.: Stanford University Press, 1999), 3. Pat Rogers, 'Shaftesbury and the Aesthetics of Rhapsody', *British Journal of Aesthetics*, 12 (1972), 244–57, sees in Shaftesbury ideas on poetic enthusiasm as a 'realignment of taste', 244, and declares them 'among the first important upholders of an organicist approach to the world' (251).

nobler feelings of the gentleman of taste could continue to be defended.[5] Coleridge may have believed that the individual could only truly be realized through 'yearning after that full and perfect Sympathy with the *whole* of our Being' (*Notebooks*, iv. 4730), but his conviction remained haunted by the fear that the aspirations of this nobler enthusiasm might betray itself into a vulgar avatar:

I tremble, lest my own tenderness of Heart, my own disinterested Enthusiasm for others, and eager Spirit of Self-sacrifice, should be owing almost wholly to my being & ever having been an unfortunate unhappy Man! (*Notebooks*, iii. 3304)

Coleridge's notebooks betray a constant anxiety that his sense of 'something *great*—something *one* & *indivisible*' might be mired in the 'immense heap of *little* things' (Griggs, i. 349). 'My illustrations swallow up my thesis', he wrote in one entry, 'I feel too intensely the omnipresence of all in each' (*Notebooks*, ii. 2372). Such confusions spoke of the distraction of the crowd.

David Riede has given an account of Coleridge's career revolving around two significant shifts. The first involves a move from 'an initial trust in the iconoclastic authority of the experiential self', associated with Coleridge's Jacobin years, to an 'embrace of the authority of transcendent imagination'.[6] Another follows this relatively familiar first shift: Coleridge's 'ultimate elevation of the authority of the larger culture over the individual imagination'.[7] The final section of this chapter is concerned with this later development and the suspicion of enthusiasm that continues to underpin it, but I think there is serious doubt about whether Coleridge ever really trusted the authority of the experiential self: 'Have Mercy on me, O something *out* of me!' he confided in his notebooks, 'For there is no *power* . . . in aught *within* me' (*Notebooks*, ii. 2543). Riede himself starts out by acknowledging that 'from the beginning of his authorial career to the end, Coleridge was fond of pointing

[5] For two important discussions of the developments of such distinctions in the eighteenth century, see John Barrell, 'The Public Prospect and the Private View: The Politics of Taste in Eighteenth-Century Britain' and 'The Dangerous Goddess: Masculinity, Prestige and the Aesthetic in Early Eighteenth-Century Britain', in his *The Birth of Pandora and the Division of Knowledge* (Basingstoke: Macmillan, 1992).
[6] David G. Riede, *Oracles and Hierophants: Constructions of Romantic Authority* (Ithaca, NY: Cornell University Press, 1991), 166.
[7] Ibid.

out that the excess of fancy, the faculty founded in experience, was delirium, and that the excess of imagination was mania'.[8] 'Delirium' and 'mania' are among the forms of 'distraction' registered in the lexicon of the discourse on enthusiasm. If Coleridge continually sought 'the passion and the life whose fountains are within' that seemed to evade him in 'Dejection: An Ode' (*CPW* i. 699, l. 46), he was equally concerned with proving limits to the torrent of enthusiasm:

Does the sober Judgment previously measure out the banks between which the Stream of Enthusiasm shall rush with its torrent sound/For rather does the Stream itself plough up its own Channel, & find its banks in the adamant Rocks of Nature? (*Notebooks*, ii. 2553)

Words such as these might be read simply as the Romantic casting off of external restraints, the fulfilment of a developing poetics of affect narrated in their different ways by critics such as Abrams, Clark, and Irlam, but in fact Coleridge's sentiments here equally insist on the kind of operation of natural limits found in Shaftesbury's *Characteristics*. Enthusiasm creates 'its own Channel', but the process of creation insists on the discovery of limits always already there waiting in 'the adamant Rocks of Nature'.

Coleridge's interest in 'the pathology of the benevolent passions' followed eighteenth-century poetics in holding out a role for poets as the regulators of diseased enthusiasm, blessed with the ability to turn ranting into true feeling by acts of self-regulation:[9]

Idly talk they who speak of Poets as mere Indulgers of Fancy, Imagination, Superstition, &c—They are the Bridlers by Delight, the Purifiers, they that combine them with *reason* & order, the true Protoplasts, Gods of Love who tame the Chaos. (*Notebooks*, ii. 2355).

As a writer for whom religious feeling remained a priority throughout his career, Coleridge sought the power of the spirit, but this aspiration was tempered by the fear that inspiration could overwhelm the seer. To keep its value, inspiration for Coleridge had to be properly regulated. By the end of his life, in the second of the shifts detected by Riede, he had come to believe only the institutional authority of the Church could provide the security he sought

---

[8] Ibid. 165.
[9] See Chris Jones, *Radical Sensibility: Literature and Ideas in the 1790s* (New York: Routledge, 1993), 103; and see also 143, where he points out Coleridge's long interest in 'the pathology of the benevolent passions'.

from the vicissitudes of 'the low-born mind' ('Monody on the Death of Chatterton': *CPW* i, Part 1, 143, l. 87). The reliance on institutional authority as a restraint on the excess of enthusiasm is the classic Anglican position in the discourse on regulation (powerfully redefined by Burke in the 1790s). 'Nature' could not now be trusted by Coleridge to provide its own embankment. Here is not so much the fulfilment of but a retreat from the relative latitude of those Whig versions of regulation, such as Shaftesbury's, that rejected the authority of the Church to impose limits. Coleridge's clerisy is explicitly contrasted with the enthusiast who trusts his own inner light over learning and tradition. Religion is still valued most when it burns within, enthusiasm is rehabilitated to that degree for Coleridge, but the burning must take place safely with the brazier of the Church if the sparks are not to fly out and incinerate what they are meant to preserve. Not only religious but also poetic inspiration needed to be governed by a clerisy who could prevent the fountains within simply emptying themselves into the amorphous ocean of the crowd.

'MAD-HEADED ENTHUSIASTS'

Poetics for Coleridge was bound up with awkward problems of religious and political enthusiasm in his 'radical years'. Rational Dissent grounded in Hartley's philosophy as popularized by Priestley looked for a time to have answered some of the questions for him. Hartley's associationism provided a way of grounding sensations in an ultimate God. Priestley's eschatalogical politics extended Hartley's philosophy to derive an account of the progressive unfolding of history from the same divine source. For Burke, of course, these answers were merely fanatical wishful thinking, the substitution of wild speculations for practical politics and time-tested institutions. Only by demonstrating the properly regulated nature of their religious and political views could Rational Dissenters hope to persuade others (and perhaps themselves) that they were not mere throwbacks to the enthusiastic sectarians of the Commonwealth. The problem was particularly acute in relation to prophecy and politics for this combination was the one most relevant to those spectres of the Civil War. Nowhere is Coleridge's negotiation of these issues to be seen more clearly than in 'Religious

Musings'. First published in its entirety in his *Poems on various Subjects* in April, 1796, it is a poem that illustrates the dynamics of regulation at work even in Coleridge's most radically committed verse. Both politics and prophecy in the poem seem to proceed from the expansive selfhood Riede sees in the poetry of the 1790s:

> The whole ONE SELF! SELF that no alien knows!
> SELF, far diffus'd as Fancy's wing can travel!
> SELF, spreading still! Oblivious of its own,
> Yet all of all possessing!
>
> (*CPW* i. 181, ll. 154–7)

In fact this self is not autonomous, but founded on Hartley's apprehension of the divine order.[10] While 'the smooth Savage roars | Feeling himself, his own low Self the whole' (ll. 151–2), Coleridge presents his millenarian vision as a subordination of the self to divine discipline:

> GOD only to behold, and know, and feel,
> Till by exclusive Consciousness of God
> All self-annihilated it shall make
> GOD its Identity: God all in all!
> We and our Father ONE!
>
> (*CPW* i. 177–8, ll. 40–4)

'Self-annihilation' had a special role in Hartley's vocabulary, as Coleridge's own note to this passage acknowledges.[11] 'Annihilation' was the key to the process whereby a person's soul is absorbed into God. A few years after writing this passage, Coleridge had come to suspect the philosophy of Hartley and Priestley of effectively collapsing the Creator into the creature. Consciousness in their philosophy became mere 'light-headedness' (*BL* i. 112), because it seemed to leave no role for the reason and will in the generation of ideas: 'the will, the reason, the judgment, and the understanding, instead of being the determining causes of association, must needs be represented as its *creatures*, and among its mechanical *effects*' (i. 110). Accusing Hartley and Priestley of reducing consciousness to 'mechanical *effects*', of course, recalls the

[10] See Riede's excellent account of Coleridge's debt to Hartley, *Oracles and Hierophants*, 178–80.
[11] For a fuller discussion of Hartley and the idea of self-annihilation in relation to Blake, see below, Chapter 6.

vocabulary of the discourse on enthusiasm, and it is not difficult to see how passages such as the one just quoted from 'Religious Musings' could be represented in terms of Hume's definition of enthusiasm as a merging of the subject with God. The destruction of the proper self is also a form of egotism that fills the universe with the feelings of the individual. Anxieties about such matters in relation to Hartley's influence were to come later for Coleridge, although I shall suggest below that even 'Religious Musings' displays a disciplinary urge of sorts. In the mid-1790s Hartley still looked to Coleridge less like a conduit for enthusiasm than a bulwark against its excesses: tracing back sensations via the theory of association to God provided a limit for the expansiveness of the sympathetic soul. 'Religious Musings' is careful to distinguish self-annihilation in this self from the mere welter of the passions or the 'Anarchy of Spirits' (l. 146).

'Anarchy of spirits' was a concern at this time to the entire reform movement in its desire to represent itself as the harbinger of 'reform not riot'. Coleridge's pamphlet *A Moral and Political Lecture* stressed the importance of regulated sympathy to the radical movement:

It will therefore be our endeavour, not so much to excite the torpid, as to regulate the feelings of the ardent! and above all, to evince the necessity of *bottoming* on fixed Principles, that so we may not be the unstable Patriots of Passion or Accident. (*L1795* 5)

This regulated activism is contrasted by Coleridge in *Conciones ad Populum* with the 'ardor of undisciplined benevolence' (*L1795* 35), an ardour he specifically identifies with the 'mad-headed Enthusiast' (38). His primary example of the latter is Robespierre:

Enthusiasm, even in the gentlest temper, will frequently generate sensations of an unkindly order. If we clearly perceive any one thing to be of vast and infinite importance to ourselves and all mankind, our first feelings impel us to turn with angry contempt from those, who doubt and oppose it. The ardor of undisciplined benevolence seduces us into malignity: and whenever our hearts are warm, and our objects great and excellent, intolerance is the sin that does most easily beset us. But this enthusiasm in Robespierre was blended with gloom, and suspiciousness, and inordinate vanity. His dark imagination was still brooding over supposed plots against freedom—to prevent tyranny he became a Tyrant—and having realized the evils which he suspected, a wild and dreadful Tyrant.—Those loud-tongued adulators, the mob, overpowered the lone-whispered denunciations of conscience—he despotized in all the pomp of Patriotism, and masqueraded on the bloody stage of Revolution, a Caligula with the cap of Liberty on his head. (*L1795* 35)

Robespierre becomes the classic prophet seduced into 'intolerance' by images of 'vast and infinite importance' like the Puritans in Hume's *History*. More specifically he is also the man who loses himself to the adulation of the mob. Coleridge had floated similar concerns about whether his own sympathetic nature could provide a coherent and regulated identity to George Dyer: 'The finely-fibred Heart, that like the statue of Memnon, trembles into melody on the sun-beam touch of Benevolence, is most easily jarred into the dissonance of Misanthropy' (Griggs, i. 155). Revealingly in terms of the politics of retirement that I shall be discussing later, Coleridge sees the fact 'that the best of us are liable to be shaped & coloured by surrounding Objects' as 'a demonstrative proof, that Man was not made to live in Great Cities!' (Griggs, i. 154.) Coleridge registers a fear that his own imaginative sympathy may be a dangerous ally in this context, asking Dyer to help him find literary employment 'which does not require my Residence in Town'. Although he admits that the benevolent Dyer seems to have resisted these distinctively urban dangers, Coleridge implies that others sympathetic to reform had not been able to regulate their sympathies in the same way.

The criticism of Robespierre and the comments to Dyer are akin to Godwin's attack on Thelwall in their stress on the dangers of losing the self in the sympathies of the crowd. Ironically, in a letter written only a few months after Coleridge's exchange with Dyer, Thelwall was to recommend a career in metropolitan journalism precisely to provide an anchor against what he took to be Coleridge's solitary flights of enthusiasm (an idea echoed in Barbauld's poem 'To S. T. Coleridge').[12] Although they were not yet in correspondence, Coleridge may have had Thelwall in mind when in *Conciones ad Populum* he turns from Robespierre to discussing the British radical movement. There Coleridge contrasts 'the inflammatory harangues of some mad-headed Enthusiast' with a 'small but glorious band' of patriots who have disciplined themselves by moral exercises in the mode of Shaftesbury:

---

[12] Thelwall told Coleridge that London was his 'proper sphere', see below for a full discussion of their exchanges on this matter. For Barbauld's critique of Coleridge's inclination towards solitary enthusiasm, see Chapter 4.

These are the men who have encouraged the sympathetic passions till they have become irresistible habits, and made their duty a necessary part of their self-interest, by the long-committed cultivation of that moral taste which derives our most exquisite pleasures from the contemplation of possible perfection. (*L1795* 40)

Despite their religious differences, a key matter that I shall return to shortly, Coleridge's concern with the 'cultivation of the moral taste' seems to echo not only Shaftesbury, but also Godwin's emphasis on the importance of general intellectual and moral enlightenment to any prospects of political change. In 1811 Coleridge was prepared to give Godwin the credit for providing 'the first system in England that ever dared reveal at full that most important of all important Truths, that Morality might be built up on its own foundation, like a Castle built *from* the rock & *on* the rock, with religion for the ornaments & completion of it's roof & upper Stories' (Griggs, iii. 313–14). Not long after this letter was written, Coleridge was arguing that religious institutions would have to have a role rather less ornamental than the one suggested here. The final section of this chapter discusses the expanded role that Coleridge came to give the Church in the management of enthusiasm, but even in the 1790s Coleridge had little faith in the ability of those 'Unillumined by Philosophy' (*L1795* 38) to regulate themselves. Contrary to Thelwall, Coleridge argued in *Conciones ad Populum* that reformers 'should plead *for* the Oppressed, not *to* them' (43). Of course, despite the reference to religion as an 'ornament' in his letter to Godwin, Coleridge's main difference from the philosopher in the 1790s revolved around the fact that he regarded the Bible as above all else what the reformer should take to the poor. Scriptural authority functioned precisely as a touchstone that could provide an external validation for individual utterance and limit the anarchy of spirits. Only the Bible, he would argue in 1809, had prevented Luther from succumbing to a faith in the 'holy right of Insurrection' (*Friend*, ii. 116).

Coleridge's primary concern in this period was with the dangers of benevolence untethered by Christian principles and knowledge of the Bible. Rather than Godwin's 'private Societies' (*L1795* 43), which Coleridge felt relied on an uncertain trickle-down principle, he offers Methodism as a model for popular enlightenment:

He would appear to me to have adopted the best as well as the most benevolent mode of diffusing Truth, who uniting the zeal of the Methodist with the views of the Philosopher, should be *personally* among the Poor, and teach them their *Duties* in order that he may render them susceptible of their *Rights*. (*L1795* 43)

Methodism features here not as the religion of the crowd, but the more regulated and philosophical zeal of Wesley himself. Coleridge praised Wesley for introducing 'sobriety and domestic habits among the lower classes, it makes them susceptible of liberty, however absurd their enthusiasm may be' (*Watchman*, 13). Although he valued it as a religion of the heart, clearly Coleridge also recognized its disciplinary successes (as Southey was to do in his *Life of Wesley*). Where Godwinian notions of perfectibility offered prospects of improvement too distant for the poor to appreciate, religion is 'the only means universally *efficient*' (*L1795* 44). Coleridge deems the poor too transient in their passions to regulate themselves. They are incapable of the kind of rational judgement that Godwin supposed to be essential to progress: 'Possessing no *stock* of happiness they eagerly seize the gratifications of the moment, and snatch the froth from the wave as it passes by them' (45). By inculcating the idea of future rewards and punishments, religion ensures that the poor too consider a larger horizon than their own 'low-born mind': 'In a man so circumstanced the Tyranny of the *Present* can be overpowered only by the tenfold mightiness of the *Future*' (45). The poor lack, it seems, not only the ability to derive fixed principles from themselves, but even the domestic affections that provide an objective correlative to universal benevolence for the bourgeoisie: 'Nor is the desolate state of their families a restraining motive, unsoftened as they are by education, and benumbed into selfishness by the torpedo touch of extreme Want' (45). The poems Coleridge wrote over 1797–8 develop the idea of the domestic affections as a regulating mechanism for a benevolence that might otherwise break its banks and drown what it was meant to sustain, but such home-made autonomy was not available to the poor in his judgement.

Coleridge's disagreements with Godwin over this period return again and again to the question of domestic affections. Whereas Godwin saw a potential conflict between universal benevolence and more local attachments, although not perhaps to the extent that his opponents claimed, Coleridge tended to regard the former as properly growing out of the latter:

The ardour of private Attachments makes Philanthropy a necessary *habit* of the Soul. I love my *Friend*—such as *he* is, all mankind are or *might be*!

The deduction is evident—. Philanthropy (and indeed every other Virtue) is a thing of *Concretion*—Some home-born Feeling is the *center* of the Ball, that, rolling on thro' Life collects and assimilates every congenial Affection. (Griggs, i. 86)

Coleridge anticipates Parr's argument that 'the real social affections' were the only sure ground of universal benevolence. Somewhat unfairly, Coleridge, like Parr, believed that Godwin's 'proud Philosophy . . . denounces every home-born feeling, by which it is produced and nurtured' (*L1795* 46). Parr's praise for Adam Smith's idea that benevolence needs a 'proper limited object' if it is not to be 'dissipated and lost' finds a poetic if muted articulation in Coleridge's conversation poems.[13] If these poems articulate Coleridge's faith that universal benevolence was to be 'begotten and rendered permanent by social and domestic affections' (*L1795* 46), the latter seem to be inflated to the point that they obscure the possibility of benevolence operating on any wider public stage. Yet even this strangled theory of the affections is not made available to the poor in Coleridge's political writing of the 1790s. Their domestic feelings were too attenuated to be left to operate as the basis of moral action. They had to be restrained by a statute of limitation formed beyond themselves. In the present state of society, only the Bible, propagated with a combination of zeal and philosophy by leaders such as himself, could provide improvement in the moral condition of the poor, and this improvement had to precede any participation for them in politics. The alternative, Coleridge believed, was to see reform left to the delirium of the crowd.

Against the revolutionary *transparence* of Godwin and Robespierre, 'Religious Musings' advances a Christianized politics as the proper basis of radical reform. In keeping with its reservations about unmediated apprehensions, it represents this reform as the product of a long process of enlightenment comprising scientific and political advances corresponding to what Priestley had called 'the general Enlargement of Liberty' (Rutt, xxii. 236). 'Religious Musings' represents the fulfilment of prophecy as the product of a spirit of Necessity working through the agency of an elect which comprises the heroes of the English enlightenment generally and Rational Dissent in particular: Milton, Newton, Franklin, Hartley, and Priestley himself. For if Coleridge set Godwin at defiance, he

---

[13] See the discussion of Parr's critique of Godwin in the previous chapter.

could not afford to align himself with the kind of prophecy traditionally associated with vulgar enthusiasm and more recently manifested in the Brothers controversy. Such illapses of the spirit were merely another form of the doctrine of *transparence* if they pretended to an immediate apprehension of the divine will. Coleridge's poem represents its millenarianism as a regulated use of prophecy. Should all prophetic discourse give itself over to mere enthusiasm, then mocking unbelievers, the most obvious contemporary example being Thomas Paine in *The Age of Reason*, would treat 'all pretensions to Prophecy, or other supernatural powers, as effects of enthusiasm or imposture'.[14] Coleridge, like most rational Dissenters, was committed to the idea that 'prophecies are necessary to Revealed Religion as perpetual Testimonies' (*L1795* 151–2). This commitment produced a situation wherein Coleridge's Christian politics struggled to distance itself from both religious and secular enthusiasm.

This problem was one faced by Dissent in general, intensely so after Burke's attack in the *Reflections*. It was conditioned by both internal and external factors, pressures that could lead to fissures within the ranks of Dissent. Many educated Dissenters were committed to an idea of enlightenment that was bound to be wary of what were seen as the unenlightened passions of the mob. After all as recently as the Birmingham Riots of 1791 the political hierarchy had turned those passions against Dissenters. If High Church intolerance waned during the eighteenth century, it was powerfully reinvigorated by Burke, as we saw in the previous chapter, to the disappointment of those Dissenters who had looked to an eventual reunion of polite and rational believers across the denominations.[15] To identify Richard Price with the regicides of the 1640s was to claim to unmask the enlightened pretensions of Dissent as nothing more than a new species of an old disease. Both the rationalism of the Enlightenment and the inner light of the Puritans were simply deluded forms of *transparence* from a Burkean point of view. These hostile conditions combined to intensify the pressure on Dissenters

---

[14] Significantly this fear was articulated in a review of *An Enquiry into the Pretensions of Richard Brothers by a Freethinker* in *Analytical Review*, 21 (1795), 321. As an organ of Rational Dissent, the *Analytical* was consistently nervous that enthusiasm would bring Christianity per se into disrepute.

[15] See the discussion of the tensions that arose between Barbauld and Priestley over these issues in the next chapter.

to present their millenarian politics as an enlightened and regulated form of public discourse that could not be mistaken for either religious enthusiasm or revolutionary *transparence*. Contrary to the assumptions of critics such as Abrams and Irlam, even elite religious writers, such as Coleridge, were well aware of the continuing presence of popular enthusiasm around them, and distanced themselves from it.[16] Coleridge and his circle, for instance, followed the Brothers controversy carefully. One of his letters to Dyer ends with a joke at the expense of the Paddington Prophet a few days after the latter's arrest: 'Poor *Brothers*! They'll make him know the *Law* as well as the *Prophets*!' (Griggs, i. 156). The pun on the moral code reiterates Coleridge's position on the importance of moral teaching to the poor that takes up most of the letter. Most of Coleridge's scattered references to Brothers over this period, as Morton D. Paley has acutely noted, perform the same distancing function. The implication is always that Coleridge 'shared the norms of evidence with his [political] opponents and therefore is, though a millenarian, not a madman'.[17] Whatever his differences of political opinion, Coleridge perceived himself as sharing a conception of the public sphere with the government that necessarily excluded enthusiasts such as Brothers.

The acceptably regulated version of prophetic discourse that Coleridge articulates in 'Religious Musings' is one that presents itself as subjecting the ecstasies of inspiration to the authority of 'fixed principles'. In contrast to the unrestrained violence of Richard Brother's millenarianism or, to make a more strictly poetic comparison, Richard Lee's confident declaration of his ability to 'see' the divine plan working out directly before him, Coleridge's millenarianism aims to conform to more generally held assumptions about public discourse. His enthusiasm is ringed with caution. The French Revolution is not to be understood as the final fulfilment of biblical prophecy in itself. It is the opening only of the fifth of the seven seals. The poem itself is concerned with the ultimate descent of divine justice at the end of time, an event left to some uncertain future date:

---

[16] Irlam's account of the rehabilitation of 'enthusiasm' in literary culture is predicated in part on his confident sense of 'the gradual passing of religious fundamentalism'. See *Elations*, 52.

[17] Morton D. Paley, *Apocalypse and Millennium in English Romantic Poetry* (Oxford: Clarendon Press, 1999), 126.

And lo! the Throne of the redeeming God
Forth flashing unimaginable day
Wraps in one blaze earth, heaven, and deepest hell

(*CPW* i. 190, ll. 400–2)

The question remains open as to when that ultimate fulfilment will be. Coleridge reassures the 'Children of Wretchedness' (l. 301) that 'Yet is the day of Retribution nigh' (l. 303), but he also takes care to counsel them that 'More groans must rise, | More blood must steam, or ere your wrongs be full' (ll. 301–2). The poems collected by 'Citizen' Lee in *Songs from the Rock* call directly on God for an immediate display of his apocalyptic power and show little compunction in describing the tumultuous bloodletting involved. Lee conforms to Coleridge's notion of the 'mad-headed Enthusiast' who will make the altar of freedom steam with blood. The bloodiness of Coleridge's poem appears only as part of a poetics of deferral. 'Religious Musings' produces images of apocalyptic violence to control and contain them. Coleridge twice cautions those impatient for apocalyptic change to 'Rest awhile' (ll. 300 and 307). Discussing a similarly cautious invocation of the Millennium in Coleridge's *Moral and Political Lecture* of the previous year, Nicholas Roe comments that 'the emphasis is less on immediate fulfilment than aspiration'. The aspiration itself is being disciplined and defined against the exorbitance of enthusiasm.[18]

If the poem's ambivalent millenarianism is a nascent form of Romantic irony, contrasting it with the unashamed enthusiasm of Richard Lee's claim to have direct access to 'divine Truths . . . which . . . depraved Reason will always stumble at' allows us to see that Coleridge's irony is operating so as to reinforce certain kinds of cultural boundaries.[19] Coleridge is much more concerned than Lee to instantiate and develop a productive relationship between poetry and prophecy that still manages to keep them distinct from each other. Towards the close of 'Religious Musings', therefore, Coleridge swerves away from laying claim to the power of prophecy as such. His province is poetry, dealing with prophetic matter, to be

[18] Nicholas Roe, *Wordsworth and Coleridge: The Radical Years* (Oxford: Clarendon Press, 1988), 215.
[19] For a discussion of 'Romantic Irony' in the context of the period's millenarianism, see Greg Kucich, 'Ironic Apocalypse in Romanticism and the French Revolution', in Keith Hanley and Raman Selden (eds.), *Revolution and English Romanticism: Politics and Rhetoric* (Hemel Hempstead: Harvester, 1990), 67–88.

sure, inspired and sublime, but not itself claiming to be prophecy. As the poem approaches what could have been a climactic vision of the last days, Coleridge draws back. His 'Fancy falls' (l. 384). The apocalyptic moment invites representation, a desire on Coleridge's part is articulated, but it remains unimagined and unimaginable. The veil must ultimately remain unlifted. The poem concludes with the acceptance that mere mortals do not enjoy divine inspiration:

> I haply journeying my immortal course
> Shall sometime join your mystic choir! Till then
> I discipline my young noviciate thought
> In ministries of heart-stirring song.

(ll. 410–13)

Recognizing this disciplinary aspect to the poem's millenarianism may help explain the generally positive reviews his poem received, even though the Brothers affair was making the question of prophetic politics a particularly fraught one at the time.

One reviewer in particular, John Aikin, showed that he was only too well aware of the dangers with which Coleridge was flirting, but decided that the poet stopped short of enthusiasm:

Often obscure, uncouth, and verging to extravagance, but generally striking and impressive to a supreme degree, it exhibits that ungoverned career of fancy and feeling which equally belongs to the poet and the enthusiast. The book of Revelations may be a dangerous fount of prophecy, but it is no mean Helicon of poetic inspiration. Who will deny genius to such conceptions as the following.[20]

A Dissenter himself, brought up at the Warrington Academy, where his father had taught with Priestley, Aikin could well sympathize with Coleridge's attempt to articulate a variety of Christian politics distinct from the enthusiasm of those such as Brothers and Lee. Much of Aikin's writing was concerned with the rationality of his Unitarian principles, and their commensurability with the developing norms of the polite public sphere. For Aikin, Dissent had to be defended against the imputation that it still perpetuated the uncouth and gloomy enthusiasm of his Presbyterian forebears. His review of 'Religious Musings' effectively credits Coleridge with managing to handle this combustible matter with self-discipline. Recognizing elements of enthusiasm in the poem's obscurity and

[20] *Monthly Review*, 20 (June 1796), 194–9.

uncouthness, he ultimately decides that these have been safely brought into the aesthetic discourse of the sublime.

A rather less sympathetic response to Coleridge's poem came from John Thelwall who, as a deist, unlike Aikin, was inclined to conflate all kinds of Christian millenarianism with enthusiasm. Of course, as we have seen, Thelwall himself was vulnerable to charges of enthusiasm, but for reasons quite different from Dissenters such as Aikin and Coleridge. No less than they, he too wanted to claim an enlightened pedigree for his beliefs, one that distinguished them from the enthusiasm of the seventeenth century, but for him the difference was best defined by excluding all religious feelings from the public sphere. From this perspective, Coleridge's 'Religious Musings' was too much like the ranting enthusiasm of the seventeenth-century 'conventicle', and Thelwall was quick to condemn it, even though the poet had confided in him that he had built on it 'all my poetic pretentions'. Coleridge had urged him to read 'with a POET's Eye, with the same unprejudiceness, I wish, I could add, the same pleasure, with which the atheistic Poem of Lucretius' (Griggs, i. 205). By mentioning the atheism of Lucretius, Coleridge was provocatively raising for Thelwall what was to develop into an ongoing disagreement about 'Modern patriotism'. As Coleridge had made clear in the essay of that title in *The Watchman*, he believed that patriotism without Christian principles amounted to libertinism. Only the principles of 'Hope and Fear' found in Christianity could guarantee that the population would assent to the view that 'it is your *duty* to be just, because it is your *interest*' (*Watchman*, 99). Thelwall's reply to Coleridge denied this conclusion and asserted instead that any politics based on an appeal to revealed religion was no better than enthusiasm.[21] What praise he could muster for 'Religious Musings' related 'almost exclusively to those parts which are not at all religious'. Coleridge's millenarianism he condemned as 'the very acme of abstruse, metaphysical, mistical rant, & all ranting abstractions, metaphysic & mysticism are wider from true poetry than the equator from the poles'.[22] Thelwall's distinction between 'rant' and 'poetry' confirms Aikin's sense that there was a line to be drawn between prophecy and literature, but draws

[21] For the text of Thelwall's letter, see Warren E. Gibbs, 'An Unpublished Letter from John Thelwall to S. T. Coleridge', *Modern Language Review*, 25 (1930), 85–90.
[22] Ibid. 87.

it on different principles and at a different place. Ironically Thelwall the radical accepts something of Burke's terms, seeing in the Rational Dissenter of the 1790s the spectre of the 'nonsense of the conventicle'.[23] Later on in the letter, he urges Coleridge to drop his plans for the ministry, 'a miserable speculation even if your opinions were settled which, in spite of your enthusiasm, nay by your enthusiasm I am sure they are not'.[24] The double-take on the word 'enthusiasm' acknowledges two different senses: one related to the long-standing discourse on religion, the other to the sympathetic energies that Thelwall often used the word to describe in himself. The fact that he sees these energies in Coleridge too prompts him to suggest that he will be unable to bear the external disciplinary restrictions of the Church. Instead he advises 'London is your proper sphere.'[25] Thelwall here opens up the prospect of urban public opinion as a regulating context for Coleridge's talents. We have already seen that Coleridge distrusted such a career precisely because it privileged the infectious and unstable responses of the crowd over more fixed and certain principles. Retirement rather than engagement with the social life of the metropolis then became Coleridge's preferred model for the discovery of universal sympathy (even if in practice he did continue to engage in a career in journalism for much of his life).

Unsurprisingly Coleridge rejected Thelwall's analysis of 'Religious Musings' and, more particularly, he rejected the reading of his version of millenarianism as no better than unenlightened enthusiasm. For Coleridge believed himself to be as in touch with the true spirit of enlightenment as any classical republican. 'How are these opinions connected with the *Conventicle* more than with the Stoa, the Lyceum, or the grove of Academus?' he asks Thelwall in his reply (Griggs, i. 213). He insists to Thelwall that modern patriots had to be 'the disciples of Lord Shaftesbury & Ro[u]sseau, as well as of Jesus' (214).[26] Without the anchor of a philosophical Christianity, the trust of Shaftesbury and Rousseau in an innate moral sense left no certain means of distinguishing a noble enthusi-

---

[23] *Modern Language Review*, 25 (1930), 88.   [24] Ibid. 89.   [25] Ibid.
[26] Thelwall's dialectic of retirement and sociability remained in many ways much more indebted to Shaftesbury and the line of eighteenth-century retirement poetry connected with his name than to any relationship with Coleridge. *The Peripatetic* derived from the manner of *Characteristics*, both in content and in its miscellaneous style, not least in its effusive transports of 'sweet enthusiasm', although with a more democratic and open kind of 'Nature' in mind than Shaftesbury's patrician park.

asm from the panic of the mob for Coleridge. He was convinced that 'the man who suffers not his hopes to wander beyond the objects of sense will, in general, be *sensual*' (214). Although he defended his '*metaphysics*' to Thelwall by pointing to the example of Akenside (215), an eighteenth-century disciple of Shaftesbury's whom both men clearly admired, he also insisted that only fixed Christian principles could discipline the metaphysician's tendency to lose himself in the larger idea. Writing to Thelwall directly he could say 'on your *heart* I should rest for my safety' (213), but more often he was sceptical of the possibilities of anyone managing a practical universal benevolence without the disciplining effects of the Bible. Ten years later, for instance, he claimed only the Bible had stopped Luther from falling into Rousseau's enthusiasm before the fact.[27] Even so Coleridge's correspondence with Thelwall in the mid-1790s seems to have intensified the anxiety already discernible within 'Religious Musings' itself to present his millenarian politics within the standards of rational discourse. Whatever their religious differences, Coleridge was as sensitive as Thelwall to the question of where poetic enthusiasm ended and mere rant began. Both men feared the kind of radical political change that had more in common with the enthusiasm of the seventeenth century than the enlightened politics of their own time. Both men, for instance, represented Cromwell as the victim of 'an enthusiasm . . . blended with gloom, and suspiciousness, and inordinate vanity' (*L1795* 35).[28] Although they professed to different versions of enlightenment, both feared that the energies of the mob were more likely to bring a regression back to the enthusiasm of a previous age than herald an enlightened New Jerusalem. No wonder then that prophetic politics and poetics came to seem a hostage to fortune to Coleridge. Whereas religion had appeared to offer a means of regulating the passions of popular politics, soon it appeared that Coleridge wanted more protection for his sense of the fountains within from the more uncertain passions of the crowd.

[27] See the discussion of *The Friend*, below.
[28] See Peter Kitson, ' "Sages and patriots that being dead do yet speak to us": Readings of the English Revolution in the Late Eighteenth Century', in James Holstun (ed.), *Pamphlet Wars: Prose in the English Revolution* (Frank Cass, 1992), 205–30, and Michael Scrivener, 'John Thelwall and the Revolution of 1649', in Nigel Smith and Timothy Morton (eds.), *Radicalism in British Literary Culture: From Revolution to Revolution* (Cambridge: Cambridge University Press, 2002), 119–32.

RETIRING ENTHUSIASM

One feature of this development in Coleridge's thinking may be the uneven but gradual withdrawal from public issues into a more domestic world in the poetry after 'Religious Musings'. The attempt to offer a disciplined version of the language of apocalypse in 'Religious Musings' is effectively abandoned in favour of a much more quietist version of unworlding. The unsociability of enthusiasm, as we saw in Part I, was often defined by its disruption of the normative idea of the family, the bedrock of Parr's idea of real social relations. Closer to Coleridge, Robert Southey claimed to 'have seen the instances of the mischief Brothers did in making tradesmen leave their business and their families'.[29] Coleridge's poetic reinscription of the millenial moment within the domestic sphere in poems such as 'Frost at Midnight' represents a strategy for insulating poetry from more dangerous forms of enthusiasm. Whereas these threatened to splinter disciplined subjectivity through a violent eruption of revelation into the public world, Coleridge's poetic revelation increasingly affirmed the enlightenment notion of the modern public as a communion of autonomous readers, but grounded in the authority of an ultimate God. Private judgement—for Coleridge anchored in the principles of Christian faith—is the basis of public opinion in the bourgeois public sphere. Where the prophetic figure that threatens to speak directly to a public does appear in Coleridge's poetry of this period, it is as a figure of potential danger. Coleridge after 'Religious Musings' returns to the figure of prophetic power whose influence must be regulated; withdrawn from public controversy; effectively shown to be operating within safe limits, if it is to have a curative effect. To overextend the reach of the subject is to risk dissolution and distraction.

The Coleridgean need to distinguish the 'I myself I' from the delirious anarchy he came to see in Hartley's psychology; and to ground the subject in an ultimate 'Life' became recurrent concerns of his writing from the mid-1790s onwards.[30] Where Hartley and

---

[29] 'To James Grahame, 4 January 1808', in *New Letters of Robert Southey*, ed. Kenneth Curry, 2 vols. (New York: Columbia University Press, 1965), i. 468–9. See also the account of Brothers in Southey's *Letters from England*, ed. Jack Simmons (Cresset, 1951), 432–3.

[30] See Riede's account in *Oracles and Hierophants*, 185–6.

Priestley had once seemed to ground everything in God, now they seemed only to be reducing God to the 'heap of little things'. Although he by no means suddenly abandoned their ideas, Coleridge came to view Priestley and Hartley as little better than Godwin, because their associationist psychology offered no determinate bulwark against the distracted enthusiasm of the senses:

How is it that Dr. Priestley is not an atheist?—He asserts in three different Places, that God not only *does*, but *is*, every thing.—But if God *be* every Thing, every Thing is God—: which is all, the Atheists assert. (Griggs i. 192)

To identify Priestley with Godwin is to conflate religious and enlightenment enthusiasm in ways traceable back to Burke, Hume, and even earlier writers.[31] The more local point is that Coleridge began to suspect the prophetic perspectives opened up by rational Dissent of enthusiasm, a perception that would only have been exacerbated by his correspondence with Thelwall. Reviews of his poetry at this time would have reinforced his sense of the danger. The *Critical*'s review of 'Ode on the Departing Year', for instance, advised Coleridge that 'Poetical Enthusiasm should take Reason for her Companion'.[32] The result was a disavowal even of the regulated version of prophecy found in 'Religious Musings'. Again and again the poetry of this period conjures the figure of an inspiration that is powerfully attractive, but dangerous and uncertain. The free will became crucially important to Coleridge's distinction between a noble enthusiasm and a 'mechanic' philosophy, but this contrast is not reducible to a simple binary between religious affect and enlightenment rationalism. 'Mechanic' was a term with a long history in the discourse on enthusiasm as we have seen. Coleridge's use of the phrase implies that the materialist philosopher preached as psychology what the enthusiastic crowd practised as religion. Coleridge's war on materialism was also a struggle against excesses that betrayed spirituality to the instinctual and unreflective passions. The greatness of Shakespeare for Coleridge lay in his ability to be 'all things, yet for ever remaining himself' (*BL* ii. 28). If the individuated will was lost in the process of creative inspiration, the poet had been lost to the very enthusiasm that was meant to rescue

---

[31] For Coleridge's recommendation of Swift and other Anglican writers on enthusiasm to the clerisy, see the discussion of *Aids to Reflection* below.

[32] *Critical Review*, 20 (July 1797), 343.

an unspiritual world. Yet if Coleridge follows Shaftesbury's advice and practises control 'to gain him a will' (*BL* i. 28), the extent to which this willing agent re-emerges into the public sphere is severely circumscribed. The disciplining of enthusiasm in Coleridge's poetry comes close to disabling precisely the public practice of the moral sense that Shaftesbury and others intended it to validate.

Within conversation poems such as the 'Eolian Harp' even the limited kinds of visionary claims desired in 'Religious Musings' are disavowed by Coleridge. Although there is an expansive movement that attempts to comprehend 'the one life within us and abroad' (as Coleridge put it in a line added in 1828: *CPW* i. 233, l. 26), this aspect is carefully insulated from the start. The poem opens with the kind of domestic scene common to the conversation poems. Coleridge is with Sara and 'our cot o'er grown' (l. 3), around them is 'the world so hush'd' (l. 10). Retirement from the more hectic social world seems to be the precondition of an apprehension of a universal benevolence:

> Full many a thought uncalled and undetained
> And many idle flitting phantasies,
> Traverse my indolent and passive brain,
> As wild and various as the random gales
> That swell or flutter on this subject lute!
>
> And what if all of animated nature
> Be but organic harps diversely framed
> That tremble into thought, as o'er them sweeps
> Plastic and vast, one intellectual breeze,
> At once the Soul of each, and God of All?
>
> (ll. 39–48)

The first five lines of this famous passage hint at the kind of enthusiasm of the senses feared throughout the eighteenth century. The various negatives—'uncall'd', 'undetain'd', 'indolent', passive', 'wild', and 'random'—open up the possibility of consciousness descending into mere delirium. This possibility is halted by an act of self-division that tempers the impulse towards losing subjectivity in the sublime. Coleridge's poetry frequently seeks 'an outward confirmation of that *something* within us, which is our *very self*' (*BL* ii. 217). This confirmation provides a limit to the unmooring of subjectivity. The turn in the poem towards Hartley and Priestley's ideas attempts to retrieve Coleridge from a potential delirium with an affirmation of his participation in a higher order. His transport discovers the omnipresence of God in the sensational world, but in a presentiment of his later disenchantment with this philosophy it turns out something more is needed.

This additional bulwark is the intervention of Sara and her pious stress on the need for quiet devotion at the end of the poem. Sara calls him to focus his affections on the figure of Christ. He must abandon the utopian aspirations of 'Philosophy' (l. 57), with its aspiration to give a name to 'The Incomprehensible' (l. 59), a warning against the temptation to make the truth transparent; and instead return to the domestic ideal intimately tied to the idea of the family of the Church. Given Coleridge's often-repeated fear of being 'afloat on the wide sea unpiloted & unprovisioned' (Griggs, i. 273), it would be naive to read this rhetorical move as a biographical fact. Sara articulates a sentiment Coleridge frequently expressed in his notebooks. If anything the desire to find an anchor in Christ is given more rhetorical authority in the poem for seeming to come from outside the poet. Although he claims for himself the power of enthusiasm in the poem and opens up the possibility of an unworlding that accesses a higher truth, that process is anchored first in Hartleian philosophy, and then in the domesticated attachment to Christ. The second move perhaps implies the insufficiency (and even exorbitancy) of the first, foreshadowing his later doubts about Hartley and Priestley. Quietism becomes the key to the apprehension of its presence in these poems of the mid-1790s. Instead of the rapturous apprehension of the divine celebrated, even if in a qualified way, in 'Religious Musings', a controlled and mute perception of the divine presence is ultimately preferred here. Through this quietist emphasis, what Kelvin Everest has called 'the cumulative effect of a repeatedly arrested expansion', Coleridge's unworlding is defined against the enthusiasm of both 'flitting phantasies' and 'vain Philosophy'.[33] If these last are not quite the same thing for Coleridge in 1796, as they were for Burke, then they were soon to be so. His rejection of Hartley and Priestley's delirium placed their 'vain Philosophy' in the same category as the fantasies of enthusiasm.

Retirement could operate in this kind of poetic scenario as a necessary prelude to social action. Such, indeed, was the implication of

---

[33] Kelvin Everest, *Coleridge's Secret Ministry: The Context of the Conversation Poems 1795–1798* (Hassocks: Harvester, 1979), 220.

the whole tradition of retirement poetry that owed so much to Shaftesbury. Retirement in *Characteristics* is a necessary part of the make-up of the patrician gentleman who has a public role. 'Retirement', as Kelvin Everest has put it in relation to the poetry of the mid-century, 'conventionally pointed back to society'. Even so Shaftesbury and the poets who developed his ideas were often ambivalent about taking their benevolence out into proximity with the crowd.[34] Akenside played down, for instance, the relationship between his metaphysical enthusiasm and political liberty in the second edition of *Pleasures of Imagination*.[35] Even so Anna Letitia Barbauld still thought even the first insufficiently ardent.[36] Coming in 1795 her judgement was perhaps especially unusual in granting such latitude to poetic enthusiasm. For the 1790s, as we saw in the previous chapter, witnessed a critical juncture in the long-standing fear that the sympathetic passions might be a stalking horse for the crowd's indiscipline. Rational Dissenters known to both Barbauld and Coleridge, including her brother John Aikin, were increasingly careful to hold the two apart. Coleridge's desire to find Thelwall a rural retreat 'where his natural impetuosity had been disciplined into patience' (Griggs, i. 342) was not unusual in this respect. The development of Coleridge's own conversation poems in this direction owed something to his continuing dialogue with Thelwall about the limits of enthusiasm. Now the subject at issue between them was not the place of religion in politics however, but another set of related issues, defined by Judith Thompson as 'the forms and effects of political repression, the ideology of retirement and the relative values of private and public speaking'.[37] Thompson may be overly restrictive if she confines what was a very extensive debate over these issues in the 1790s to the private correspondence of these two men only, but there is no doubt that both deemed enthusiasm

[34] Ibid. 192. Everest notes that 'increasingly as the eighteenth century wore on, the poet in nature seems to embrace an exhausted tranquility that comforts the defeated moralist'. This theme is explored in detail in John Sitter's *Literary Loneliness in Mid Eighteenth-Century England* (Ithaca, NY: Cornell University Press, 1982). See Chapter 1 above on the need for polite culture to steer between the extremes of enthusiasm represented by the crowd and the isolated prophet.

[35] For details, see Michael Meehan, *Liberty and Poetics in Eighteenth Century England* (Beckenham: Croom Helm, 1986), 54–6.

[36] Barbauld's 'Preface' to her edition of *The Pleasures of Imagination* discussed below, Chapter 4.

[37] See her 'An Autumnal Blast, a Killing Frost: Coleridge's Poetic Conversation with John Thelwall', *Studies in Romanticism*, 36 (1997), 429.

a necessary but potentially dangerous ingredient in poetry and politics. This discipline operates in Coleridge's poetry, strange perhaps to say, much more tightly than even in Shaftesbury's writing, possibly even in the period of Coleridge's own greatest political activism. So tightly indeed does the disciplinary consideration wind itself around his poetic enthusiasm that it seems to disallow the possibility of retirement translating into action at all. Shaftesbury had considered retreat and meditation a necessary preparatory to the conversation of culture: it was a stage in the regulation of the unrulier passions. Coleridge exaggerated this stage in the process, stressing retirement over the subsequent re-entry into the conversation of culture, and offered a narrower and more personalized idea of that conversation for an age that he increasingly feared was becoming '*sore* from excess of stimulation' (Griggs, v. 24).

Critics such as Kelvin Everest have read this aspect of Coleridge's conversation poems in the context of the kinds of repressive government policies that forced other radical writers, including Thelwall, into exile. More specifically, Everest reads the trope of the reclusive rural idyll in these poems as a metonym for a broader and still fundamentally political sense of sociability and community, a reading that anticipates Morton D. Paley's sense of the poems as a 'millennium in microcosm'.[38] Yet I am not so sure that the 'persistent desire for the small community of kindred souls in nature' that emerges from the poetry of Wordsworth and Coleridge in this period can be so easily translated into the at least potentially broader notion of 'sociability'.[39] The latter could conceivably stretch as far as the boisterous conviviality of the crowd, but Coleridge's metonym would seem to displace the larger potential with a much smaller one. Placing Coleridge in the tradition of eighteenth-century retirement poetry, as Everest very usefully does, only serves, I believe, to reveal the extent to which its dialectic of retirement and sociability becomes stalled in his poetry. Whatever ardour Akenside's *Pleasures of Imagination* may have lacked in Barbauld's eyes, it did offer a relationship between its enthusiasm and political liberty that pointed outwards toward society. Nor is this stalling in Coleridge's poetry only represented as the negative effect of external political conditions (as it is in Thelwall's). More often regret is

[38] See Everest, *Coleridge's Secret Ministry*, 91, and Paley, *Apocalypse and Millennium*, 121.
[39] Everest, *Coleridge's Secret Ministry*, 91.

associated with the need to leave the retired life in the first place. The retired life in itself becomes the site of authentic being.

These issues are nowhere more directly addressed than in Coleridge's 'Reflections on Having Left a Place of Retirement'. Probably written in March 1796, while completing 'Religious Musings', the poem looks like a classic statement of the dialectic of retirement and social action in Akenside, a resemblance made all the stronger by the title the poem originally bore when it was published in the *Monthly Magazine* in October 1796.⁴⁰ The original title 'Reflections on Entering into Active Life' defines the ultimate aims of retirement from the outset in terms of the kind of social improvement practised by the prison reformer John Howard (the example given in the poem itself). Given the *Monthly*'s dissenting connections, these affiliations are what one would expect of a poem published there. The poem begins with the sort of 'ascent' to a vantage point in nature from which universal harmony could be apprehended. The strategy is a familiar part of the rhetoric that poets such as Akenside had derived from Shaftesbury's *Characteristics*. In what might be called the classic form of retirement literature, the rapture of the ascent has to be regulated in seclusion before it can be made the basis of social action.⁴¹ The moment of 'transport' comes in Coleridge's poem with the literal ascent of a 'stony Mount':

> *Here* the bleak Mount
> The bare bleak Mountain speckled thin with sheep;
> Grey Clouds, that shadowing spot the sunny fields;
> And River, now with bushy rocks o'er brow'd
> Now winding bright and full, with naked banks;
> And Seats and Lawns, the Abbey and the Wood,
> And Cots, and Hamlets, and faint City-spire:
> The Channel *there*, the Islands and white sails,
> Dim Coasts, and cloud-like Hills, and shoreless Ocean—

⁴⁰ The poem appeared originally in the *Monthly Magazine*, 2 (Oct. 1796), 732–3.
⁴¹ See Meehan, *Liberty and Poetics*, 54–6, on Akenside, and for a more general statement of the conception of retirement poetry in relation to social action, see Everest, *Coleridge's Secret Ministry*, esp. ch. 5. For a patrician Whig such as Shaftesbury, the landscape recommended for such ascents was implicitly owned by the viewer; Coleridge's poem shows the more democratic possibilities opened up in the century after Shaftesbury by the poetics of enthusiasm. See Barrell's 'The Public Prospect and the Private View' essay in *The Birth of Pandora*.

> It seem'd like Omnipresence! God, methought,
> Had built him there a Temple: the whole World
> Seem'd *imag'd* in its vast circumference.
> No *wish* profan'd my overwhelmed Heart.
> Blest hour! It was a Luxury—to be!
>
> (*CPW* i. 262, ll. 29–42)

This discovery of universal harmony is worked through in retirement until it takes a form that can provide the basis for a return to society. Coleridge's poem seems to reach a perfect moment of regulation prior to a movement back towards the social. Where the 'overwhelmed heart' seems momentarily as if it might burst from its experience of fullness, desire is brought into a stable union with Christ. The practical benevolence that succeeds this moment of harmony is a version of the Christian ideal Coleridge had identified in Methodism:

> I therefore go, and join head, heart, and hand,
> Active and firm, to fight the bloodless fight
> Of Science, Freedom, and the Truth in CHRIST.
>
> (ll. 60–2)

Such at least is the poem's 'plot', but the 'writing' contains currents that cut across and perhaps disable this course. For the final section of the poem, supposedly oriented towards following the example of practical benevolence provided by the prison reformer John Howard, is constantly being pulled back towards the solitary joy of simply dwelling with Christ:

> The sluggard Pity's vision-weaving Tribe!
> Who sigh for Wretchedness, yet shun the Wretched,
> Nursing in some delicious solitude
> Their slothful loves and dainty Sympathies!
>
> (ll. 56–9)

'Delicious solitude' is a phrase that only reminds the reader of the attractions of the isolated state of harmony that has concluded the 'ascent' in the poem. The poem cannot quite shake off the longings of the 'vision-weaving tribe' for qualities it has earlier presented in a more positive manner. For all the rallying cry that ends the passage, a cry echoed in much of the dissenting literature of the period (including Coleridge's own 'Religious Musings'), the poem ends with a regretful look back on the cottage that he has been 'constrain'd' (l. 44) to quit for the active life:

> Yet oft when after honourable toil
> Rests the tir'd mind, and waking loves to dream,
> My Spirit shall revisit thee, dear Cot!
> Thy Jasmin and thy window-peeping Rose,
> And Myrtles fearless of the mild sea-air.
> And I shall sigh fond wishes—sweet Abode!
> Ah!—had none greater! And that all had such!
> It might be so—but the time is not yet.
> Speed it, O FATHER! Let thy Kingdom come.

The change of title in 1797 reinforces this sense of regret. The emphasis in the retitled version is directed even more strongly to the 'place of retirement' that is left behind. What is equally striking about the close of the poem is that the previous verse paragraph, focusing on the example of John Howard, has a pre-millennial emphasis on human agency that is replaced by a more passive post-millennialism calling on Christ to intervene.[42] The public orientation of the former is displaced even as it seems to be reiterated, and any possibility that Christ might come suddenly to blow apart the private utopia of the cottage is put gently aside by that 'not yet'. The domestic space of the cottage becomes the New Jerusalem, and any apocalyptic interruption of everyday relations is folded into the continuation of ordinary life, a structural feature of the conversation poems that is related to the deployment of 'spots of time' in Wordsworth's *Prelude*.

Increasingly in the conversation poems that came after 'Reflections', Coleridge uses the domestic space to negotiate a route between the twin poles of enthusiasm, that is, the implosion of the unsociable self and its infectious dissemination into the crowd. Coleridge in these poems is neither a prophet raging in the wilderness nor one preaching to the masses: he becomes a hierophant of domesticity. Where Shaftesbury's dialectic of enthusiasm defined sociability as the outcome of the regulation of enthusiasm, the regulated self in Coleridge is one at home with itself. Only in a 'hush'd' domestic scene of retirement can an 'unearthly minstrelsy' (l. 24) now work its charms it seems. The scenario is repeated, for instance, in 'Frost at Midnight', where the second of these phrases was transformed into a 'secret ministry' (*CPW* i. 453, l. 1), a change

---

[42] See the discussion of these distinctions in J. F. C. Harrison, *The Second Coming: Popular Millenarianism 1780–1850* (Routledge & Kegan Paul, 1979), 3–10.

that brings religion into play more clearly as the agent of regulation. The metaphor has often been discussed, but the religious connotations of 'ministry' are worth dwelling on further. Coleridge was still considering a career as a minister while the poem was being written. Thelwall had advised against this 'miserable speculation'.[43] Coleridge's poem insists on the vocation, even if it is now privatized and taken away from any association with the 'enthusiasm' Thelwall despised in the pulpit. For Coleridge undergoes something like a conversion in the poem through an unworlding glimpse of a divine harmony, but abjures the noisy associations of conversion-experience associated with Methodism in favour of a quiet confidence in the nearness of God. He also abandons the idea of ministering to the poor, an aspect of the public discourse of the more disciplined versions of Methodism that he had been extolling in his letters. Of course, field preaching was associated with the less-disciplined aspects of Methodism, and pointedly Coleridge's version is discretely 'secret'. Thelwall might well have applauded the abandonment of the demonstrative religious feelings of 'Religious Musings', but he would have been less pleased by the evacuation of the political and social programme that had gone with it. Never mind the immediate vision of the divine plan that someone such as 'Citizen' Lee laid claim to as part of the experience of religious transformation, even the more guarded public declaration of 'Religious Musings' has been left behind in 'Frost at Midnight'. There a public vision of prophetic power is proclaimed even if it is also eventually disclaimed. Here a subtler process of disavowal is at work that never even lets the 'ministry' appear in public. From the start the more indirect faculties of overhearing and sensing are brought to the centre of the experience. Seeing is displaced by intimation.

Yet if 'Frost at Midnight' seems to repudiate the public millenarianism of 'Religious Musings' as too much like enthusiasm, it is also charting a course away from the quick sands of solitude that were routinely regarded as the other pole of the pathology. Disclaiming any broader sense of public intercourse, the musing self is anchored by the 'cradled infant' (l. 7), a metonym for what Parr called 'real social affections'. Out of this relationship between father and child

---

[43] See the discussion of Thelwall's advice above, and note Thompson on the political aspect of 'ministry', 'An Autumnal Blast, a Killing Frost', 437.

merges a broader sense of 'dim sympathies' (l. 18). The moment of sympathetic identification that begins with the infant and moves on to the dim flickering of the hearth is not a sudden apprehension of universal benevolence. Such jolts out of the self could, of course, represent the kind of illapses of the spirit that drown that autonomy of the subject according to the discourse on enthusiasm. Discovering 'every where | Echo or mirror seeking of itself' (ll. 21–2) sounds like the beginnings of the kind of delirium Coleridge came to identify with Hartley's psychology, but his apprehension turns out neither to be a sudden jolt nor a welter of impressions, but a dim perception consecrated at the altar of domestic life. Unlike even the ascent at the beginning of 'Reflections', Coleridge is not taken out of himself, but deeper into himself. He discovers a continuous aspiration for sympathy, a longing buried within for some larger connection. Typically of Coleridge's conversation poems, however, this discovery does not point out to a larger society, nor does it presage the implosion of the self into dreaming memories, but leads back instead to the domestic security of the 'Babe, that sleepest cradled by my side' (l. 44). This situation is presented as the natural fulfilment of a dream from Coleridge's childhood. A boundary has been drawn, a loop, that prescribes a limit to the possibilities of sympathy. Obviously the associationist doctrine that places 'home-born Feeling' at 'the centre of the Ball' allows for the possibility that such a relationship could be understood metonymically to stand for broader social sympathies, as Everest has suggested, but the ball never really gets rolling in the conversation poems. We are returned to the kind of cottage that opens and closes 'Reflections', but here John Howard's active ministering among the poor and sick has been completely displaced by 'the secret ministry of frost' (l. 72). Coleridge's past and his son's future are to be tied together in a comforting unity of time and place that never ventures out into the crowded social world.

At least one reviewer of the volume in which 'Frost at Midnight' first appeared appreciated the delicacy of Coleridge's attempt to write with a rehabilitated enthusiasm. Christopher Moody writing in the *Monthly Review* begins with an attack on poetry that might seem strangely to echo Lee's reproachful attack on secular poetics at the end of *Songs from the Rock*:

Had poetry always been guided by reason and consecrated to morality, it would have escaped the contemptuous reproach with which it has been loaded both by antient and modern philosophers. Had this divine art been appropriated with due effect to divine subjects, wisdom could not have withholden her admiration. It is a matter of regret, therefore, that its professors seem to have been solicitous rather to please by the coruscations of a wild frenzy, than by a mild and steady lamp of truth.[44]

The difference is that Moody's 'mild and steady lamp of truth' excludes the apocalypticism of popular prophecy along with non-Christian immorality. 'Fears in Solitude', the title-poem of the volume, is praised for its 'patriotic enthusiasm, and [exhortation] to virtue with a Christian ardour', meeting Moody's demand for a quiet enthusiasm of 'solitude and religious contemplation'. Contrast this impulse in Coleridge's conversation poems as a group with Thelwall's poems of the period 1795–8, as Judith Thompson has recently done to excellent effect, and one sees the latter's much stronger sense of 'the despair, isolation and persecution suffered by the reformer who refused to lie low'. Even in his 1801 collection, Thelwall asserted that 'solitude is the grave rather than the muse of mind'. Where Coleridge and Wordsworth go on to construct a new poetic from the stalling of the dialectic of retirement and the active life, Thelwall registers frustration and regret and continues to write a kind of retirement poetry that docs look out again towards society.[45]

Coleridge's poetry of the second half of the 1790s is not entirely defined by the conversation poems, and one might say that it is in the so-called supernatural poems that one sees an enthusiastic poet who puts the autonomy of the self much more into hazard. Here it could be said that the fountains within are allowed to play more freely, and the poet becomes the prophet without apology. Nevertheless it seems to me that no less than in the conversation poems 'transport' is produced only to be disavowed at the moment it comes to the centre of the unworlding experience. The prophet in the wilderness common to both 'Kubla Khan' and 'The Ancient Mariner', who seeks to bring his disorienting message back to the hungry crowd, is never completely identified with the authenticated secret ministry of the poet. Coleridge is no less the 'reluctant apocalypticist' here than in the conversation poems.[46] Let me develop this point further by looking at the first of these poems in more

---

[44] *Monthly Review*, 29 (May 1799), 43–7.

[45] Thompson, 'An Autumnal Blast, a Killing Frost', 435. Everest himself notes these differences, *Coleridge's Secret Ministry*, 129.

[46] Paley, *Apocalypse and Millennium*, 126, uses this phrase of Coleridge's 'Ode to the Departing Year'.

detail. The figure of Kubla Khan himself, of course, is rendered in the poem in terms of the kind of orientalist discourse that frequently defined the cultures of the East in terms of their enthusiasm. For the eighteenth century Muhammad figured as one of history's great enthusiasts, not least because he translated a religious vision into a political movement that spread among the people. Several pamphlets from the period compared his conquering armies with those of the French Republic precisely in terms of their 'enthusiasm'.[47] Not long after he wrote 'Kubla Khan', Coleridge was working with Southey on a poem on 'th'enthusiast Warrior of Mecca' (*CPW* i. 571, l. 7) perhaps prompted by such topical analogies.[48] Here is a 'Prophet and Priest' (l. 2) who, much like Coleridge's account of Robespierre's enthusiasm, 'scatter'd abroad both Evil and Blessing'. The fourteen-line fragment closes with a passage containing many echoes of 'Kubla Khan':

> Loud the Tumult in Mecca surrounding the Fane of the Idol;—
> Naked and Prostrate the Priesthood were laid—the People
>   with mad shouts
> Thundering now, and now with saddest Ululation
> Flew, as over the channel of rock-stone the ruinous River
> Shatters its waters abreast, and in mazy uproar bewilder'd,
> Rushes dividuous all—all rushing impetuous onwards.

(ll. 8–14)

One significant difference is that the 'tumult' in this poem is much more clearly identified with the infectious enthusiasm of the crowd, as it was in the analogies between the armies of Islam and the French Republic current at the time. 'Kubla Khan' is not directly associated with the politico-religious iconoclasm of Robespierre and Muhammad in this respect. That these associations were at least in the background to Coleridge's poem is suggested by one other description of modern enthusiasm with which Coleridge would have been familiar.

---

[47] See, for instance, *A Letter to the Rt. Hon Charles James Fox* (1793), 40–4, and John Thelwall, *Rights of Nature* (1796), in *The Politics of English Jacobinism: The Writings of John Thelwall*, ed. Gregory Claeys (University Park: Pennsylvania State University Press, 1995), 426–7.

[48] On the collaboration in the context of Coleridge's reading in the history of religion at the time, see E. S. Shaffer, *'Kubla Khan' and the Fall of Jerusalem: The Mythological School in Biblical Criticism and Secular Literature 1770–1880* (Cambridge: Cambridge University Press, 1975), 56–8.

Thomas Taylor's *Essay on the Beautiful* (1792) drew a contrast between the beauties of classical enthusiasm, of the sort praised by Shaftesbury, and modern enthusiasm, which he claimed was 'nothing more than a phantom raised by bewildered imaginations, floating on the unstable ocean of opinion, the sport of the waves of prejudice'.[49] Kubla Khan's phantom may not depend on the enthusiasm of popular opinion, for he is the very type of the oriental despot, but his 'bewildered imagination' (a phrase of Taylor's that Coleridge may have developed into the 'mazy uproar bewilder'd' of 'Mahomet') threatens to overrun itself and drown in its own power. Of course, what happens instead is that this enthusiasm—to revert to the description of poetic enthusiasm found in Coleridge's notebooks—seems to be the classical sort able to 'plough up its own Channel, & find its banks in the adamant Rocks of Nature' (*Notebooks*, ii. 2553):

> The shadow of the dome of pleasure
> Floated midway on the waves;
> Where was heard the mingled measure
> From the fountain and the caves.
> It was a miracle of rare device,
> A sunny pleasure-dome with caves of ice!
>
> (*CPW* i. 513–14, ll. 31–6)

'Tumult' is safely contained here, whereas in 'Mahomet', it has been disseminated to the crowd incapable of regulating its effects into 'symphony and song'. Where a crowd does implicitly appear at the end of 'Kubla Khan', it is to witness a visionary whose infectious enthusiasm, for all the potential danger, seems to have been safely insulated:

> . . . Beware! Beware!
> His flashing eyes, his floating hair!
> Weave a circle round him thrice,
> And close your eyes with holy dread:
> For he on honey-dew hath fed,
> And drank the milk of Paradise
>
> (ll. 49–54)

[49] Thomas Taylor, *An Essay on the Beautiful from the Greek of Plotinus* (1792), pp. xviii–xix. Taylor was one of Coleridge's 'darling studies' during this period and his influence on 'The Ancient Mariner' and 'Kubla Khan' has often been explored, see, for instance, Jonathan Livingston Lowes, *The Road to Xanadu: A Study in the Ways of the Imagination* (Constable, 1927; 2nd edn. 1951), 232 and 393–4.

This image may glamorize the figure of the poet-prophet, but it also isolates him, separating him from any public discourse of prophetic utterance, a fact only reinforced by the unfinished, fragmentary presentation of the poem. Unlike 'Religious Musings', where a process of regulation seems to operate in order to create a potential sphere of regulated prophetic utterance, even that possibility seems to be disallowed here. By the end of the 1790s prophecy is identified with the tumults of vulgar enthusiasm if it pretends to a public voice. Only in isolation from the crowd can it provide a spectacle of aesthetic pleasure. 'Kubla Khan' represents the prophetic stance as cut off from any public as effectively as the government cut Brothers (and Thelwall too) off from his. Beyond the 1790s, Coleridge continued to distinguish himself from the tradition of dangerous prophetic enthusiasm as he retreated from Rational Dissent and political radicalism towards trinitarianism in religion, conservatism in politics, and Romanticism in literature. The process is complicated by the fact that it was in this period that Coleridge made his most explicit attempt to rehabilitate the word 'enthusiasm' itself, identifying it with the kind of authenticating process of unworlding described by Shaun Irlam, but equally distinguishing it from the association with the passions of the crowd. The latter, he insisted, ought properly to be called 'fanaticism', but this process of desynonimization was far from stable and its difficulties had consequences for the later and better-known distinction between Fancy and the Imagination.

ENTHUSIASM, FANATICISM, AND THE IMAGINATION

Several attempts to distinguish a safe from an unsafe understanding of 'enthusiasm' have been discussed in this book. Often, as with both Shaftesbury and Thomas Taylor, this process involved distinguishing a noble from a degraded version. Coleridge's method eventually came to rest on a process of desynonimization, shifting the negative connotations of enthusiasm onto the word 'fanaticism' (contrary to more general usage in the period). The word 'enthusiasm' tends to appear both in his poetry and political prose of the 1790s as the signifier of an unruly energy, which can destroy even as it animates. His own politics are implicitly contrasted with the 'enthusiasm' of Robespierre as a regulated or 'manly' passion for liberty. In *The Friend* essays of the next decade, in full retreat from his earlier radical politics, Coleridge began the long process of rewriting his own radical past that received its most famous statement in the *Biographia*. 'Enthusiasm' is a word that bears a lot of the burden of this process. In the essays originally published in 1809, Coleridge still continues to use the term in a way that identifies it with the passions of the crowd, what he calls 'the contagion of animal enthusiasm' (*Friend*, ii. 46), but there is also a drift towards giving the term less serious political associations. His own earlier politics are described in terms of 'the gradually exhausted Balloon of youthful Enthusiasm' (*Friend*, ii. 147). Enthusiasm is being used here to suggest an evanescent and never really threatening emotional attachment. Its unworlding potential is increasingly rendered as unworldly. A passing aspect of youthful high spirits, 'enthusiasm' cannot be confused with serious political commitment. Only a decade before enthusiasm was what defined the danger of Robespierre; even in *The Friend* it binds Luther to Rousseau, but behind a dismissive façade, Coleridge also begins moving it towards the idea of an inspiration that is safely located in an autonomous sphere distinct from the practical world of politics.

By the time he was revising and supplementing his essays from *The Friend* for the three-volume edition of 1818, the damaging pejorative associations of 'enthusiasm' with religio-political passions were increasingly being loaded by Coleridge on to 'fanaticism'. 'Enthusiasm' starts to be reserved for use as a word indicating a quiet sense of the nearness of God's being, that is, for exactly the kind of religious experience that it had traditionally been seen as so scandalously exceeding. Coleridge's new essay on 'Spiritual Truths and Understanding' proposes the idea of a 'true Christian *enthusiasm*' (*Friend*, i. 432).[50] In the first of his *Lay Sermons* (1816), Coleridge had already suggested that this energy might be the basis of a transformation in public culture: 'nothing great was ever atchieved without enthusiasm' (*SM* 23). The definition and what follows it sounds like pure Shaftesbury: 'For what is enthusiasm but the oblivion and swallowing-up of self in an object dearer than self,

---

[50] Coleridge was recalling his readers, as Shaftesbury and Thomas Taylor had done before him, to the word's classical origins: 'the original meaning of the Greek, Enthousiasmos, is: the influence of the divinity such as was supposed to take possession of the priest during the performance of the services at the altar' (*Friend*, i. 432), but with a Christian emphasis their work refuses.

or in an idea more vivid?' (*SM* 23) Of course, as always, Coleridge's larger 'idea' is different from Shaftesbury's in its more explicitly Christian sense of the 'object dearer than the self', but he faces the same problem in giving this 'idea' sufficient definition to distinguish it from the undisciplined enthusiasms of the crowd. 'Everywhere in Coleridge's pronouncements on poetic agency', Steven Knapp notes, 'the process of desynonymization works simultaneously to establish the seriousness of poetry and to save it from the consequences of such seriousness . . . Just as enthusiasm must in a sense be quarantined, protected from the social contagion that would degrade it to mere fanaticism, so poetry must be insulated from the modes of literality it both imitates and inspires.'[51] Perhaps because he was aware that his distinction between enthusiasm and fanaticism was difficult to sustain, it never even achieved a settled place in Coleridge's own lexicon. Once Coleridge acknowledges the possibility of 'an enthusiasm of wickedness' (*SM* 23), as he does in his *Statesman's Manual*, the wall provided by desynonimization is being breached from within. Celebrating enthusiasm's 'endless power of semination' (*SM* 24), Coleridge avoids the question of the limit to this process. 'Semination' disguises what was usually described as 'contagion', the more negative word more commonly associated with the enthusiasm of the crowd. Coleridge kept the latter association in play when he left the phrase 'contagious nature of enthusiasm' in his discussion of Rousseau in the revised 1818 version of *The Friend*. There Coleridge doubts the possibility that mere opinion or 'publicity' can come to a sense of the general will (as Thelwall seemed to believe it might in the mid-1790s), precisely because opinion is always vulnerable to the unstable passions of the crowd defined precisely in terms of its restless contagiousness:

It is a mere *probability*, against which other probabilities may be weighed: as the lust of authority, the contagious nature of enthusiasm, and other of the acute or chronic diseases of deliberative assemblies. (*Friend* i. 193)

Coleridge echoes Shaftesbury's opinion that 'fancy and opinion stand pretty much upon the same bottom' (*Characteristics*, 83). In order to distinguish genuine enthusiasm from mere opinion, Coleridge, of course, looked to a Kantian philosophy very different from Shaftesbury's 'moral sense', but even so he could not stop anx-

---

[51] Knapp, *Personification and the Sublime: Milton to Coleridge* (Cambridge, Mass.: Harvard University Press, 1985), 42.

ieties about the degeneration of enthusiasm into its diseased variety from tripping up his prose.

To shore up his philosophical distinction between 'enthusiasm' and 'fanaticism', Coleridge made use of the set of norms and codes of social behaviour and utterance that had long been taken to distinguish the quiet virtues of piety from the disruptive or 'modern' enthusiasm of the crowd. Coleridge defends his interest in Boehme, for instance, in the *Biographia*, by distinguishing his quietism from the vulgar enthusiasm of the crowd:

A meek and shy quietist, his intellectual powers were never stimulated into fev'rous energy by crowds of proselytes or by the ambition of proselyting. JACOB BEHMEN was an enthusiast, in the strictest sense, as not merely distinguished, but as contra-distinguished from a fanatic. (*BL* i. 147)

Boehme's mysticism is distanced from the ranting crowds of illiterate preachers that were the standard type of enthusiasm. Such distinctions routinely depended on class-based assumptions about taste and education as much as upon patterns of behaviour as such. How can such an uneducated man have produced the vision of ultimate principles that Coleridge ascribed to Boehme? His answer begins with the claim that the educated classes had betrayed their roles as spiritual leaders in the pursuit of more worldly knowledge. Deeper issues were 'abandoned to the illiterate and the simple, whom unstilled yearning, and an original ebulliency of spirit, had urged to the investigation of the indwelling and living ground of all things' (*BL* i. 148). One might think that Coleridge was advancing a religious version of Wordsworth's common language of men argument, castigated in the *Biographia*, except that he makes it clear that such men remained apt to mistake 'the anomalous misgrowths of his own individuality for ideas, or truths of universal reason' (*CCS* 165). Coleridge's praise of Boehme is qualified by an acknowledgement of the latter's 'utter want of all intellectual discipline, and from his ignorance of rational psychology' (*BL* i. 147). The indiscipline includes a tendency towards pantheism that Coleridge cannot excuse (for pantheism collapses the individual into the material world no less than the psychology of Hartley and Priestley according to Coleridge).[52] Boehme may have kept away from the crowd, but his origins within it mean he cannot altogether

---

[52] See *LPhil* 485 and implicitly *BL* i. 152. In 1818 he dismissed Behmenism in a letter to C. A. Tulk as 'mere Pantheism'. See Griggs, iv. 883.

be trusted to regulate his own deepest insights. Coleridge as reader, one is led to assume, has been able to supply discipline to these wild seventeenth-century texts, to winnow a noble enthusiasm out of the mixed matter before him, just as Southey was able to mediate 'our uneducated poets' to the public.

Despite these and other equivocations, by the time he came to write his *Aids to Reflection* (1825), Coleridge was still stressing the importance of the inner light of enthusiasm for the clerisy he believed would protect the nation against infidelity and unbelief. Here is the second of Coleridge's career shifts identified by Riede. The very fact that Coleridge came to believe that the nation needed a clerisy marks the extent to which he now thought institutions were necessary to channel enthusiasm; it could not now be trusted to plough up its own banks. More substantial forms of institutional regulation out of the self were now required to make it clear what kind of enthusiasm was needed for the health of the nation to be restored.[53] The clerisy was advised to immerse themselves in 'all the passages scattered throughout the writings of Swift and Butler, that bear on Enthusiasm, Spiritual Operations, and pretences to Gifts of the Spirit, with the whole train of New Lights' (*Aids*, 82), that is, a course of reading in the discourse on enthusiasm outlined in Part I of this book. Armed with this awareness of the dangers of enthusiasm, they can be trusted to encourage, but also to provide regulation for new spiritual warmth in their flocks. Distinguishing 'fanaticism' from 'enthusiasm' was an attempt to quarantine the spirituality associated with the latter from the passions of the crowd. If the distinction operated with an implicit contrast between the coarse materialism of the latter and the unworldliness of enthusiasm such as Boehme's, it was complicated by the fact that 'pretences to the Gifts of the Spirit' were potentially as much of a problem as infidelity in the culture of the crowd. While supposedly defending revealed religion from the infidelity of the leaders of the radical movement, Coleridge's *A Lay Sermon* (1817) admits in an early note that the idea 'has been most strangely abused and perverted from the Millenarians of the primitive church to the religious Politicians of our own time' (*SM* 147). When he describes the radical leaders as 'false prophets' (145), it is as if he is tacitly

[53] For an account of Coleridge's religio-political thinking during this period, see John Morrow, *Coleridge's Political Thought: Property, Morality and the Limits of Traditional Discourse* (Basingstoke: Macmillan, 1990), chs. 4 and 5.

admitting that there is little difference between religious and secular enthusiasm when it comes to the crowd.

Personally for Coleridge, the problem was made even more acute by the fact that his radical years were not infidel years, that is, he could not simply contrast a period of youthful unbelief with a later ardent Christianity. Coleridge's radical politics had always been founded on a discourse that had displayed prophetic pretensions, however limited, of its own, and he needed now to separate his mature religious beliefs from this youthful politico-religious enthusiasm. Significantly for this process, the *Biographia Literaria* (1817) begins with a discussion of 'Religious Musings' and an attempt to define Coleridge's Romantic aesthetics against the errors he made in framing that poem: 'I forgot to enquire, whether the thoughts themselves did not demand a degree of attention unsuitable to the nature and objects of poetry' (*BL* i. 7). Implicit here is the distinction between poetry and prophecy discussed earlier in this chapter. Coleridge implies that he now sees a clear distinction between the former and the latter. He claims to have 'used my best efforts to tame the swell and glitter both of thought and diction' (*BL* i. 7) in later editions of the poem, but this taming is not simply a matter of choosing more appropriate poetic diction. John Thelwall had seen in the swell and glitter of Coleridge's poem the 'rant' of 'enthusiasm'. The attempt to tame that 'rant' was a reflex of Coleridge's writing from the very beginning of his poetic career. Even the millenarian fervour of 'Religious Musings' itself participates in the attempt of Rational Dissent to validate its interest in prophecy as rational. By the time he was writing the *Biographia*, Coleridge felt more inclined to define his youthful commitments as 'enthusiasm', but now with a specialised sense that separated the term from any possibility of practical politics. Retailing the famous story of his encounter with a 'rigid Calvinist' (an archetype from over a hundred years of Anglican attacks on enthusiasm as much as a real person), Coleridge comments that 'in the expansion of my enthusiasm I did not think of *myself* at all' (*BL* i. 180). Such transports could point towards heroic self-sacrifice, but could also raise the spectre of losing the coherent self entirely. Given the political context, and the encounter with the archetypally grubby Presbyterian, one would think the spectre of the loss of the self in the crowd would haunt this passage, but now for Coleridge enthusiasm is the sign of a self-transcendence that can have no practical political effects (as contrasted with fanaticism). It is a label that he wants to use to allow himself to treat his own radical past as a harmless joke:

> I argued, I described, I promised, I prophecied; and beginning with the captivity of nations I ended with the near approach of the millenium, finishing the whole with some of my own verses describing that glorious state out of *the Religious Musings.* (*BL* i. 181)

All the energy expended in the previous decade to distance his poetry from 'rant' is now of no interest it seems. What allows this move to take place is the fact that Coleridge's idea of enthusiasm has been harnessed to the autonomy of the aesthetic that means it has no serious claims as a political category. As he says in *The Friend*, although he was 'a sharer in the general vortex . . . my little world described the path of its revolution in an orbit of its own' (*Friend* i. 223). Like Boehme, although with the addition of resources of education and taste that are taken to ensure the process against failure, Coleridge's youthful enthusiasm is kept clear of the more dangerous infection of the crowd through its idiosyncrasy. Pantisocracy is safely defined now not as a political experiment, but a preference for 'Religion and a small company of chosen individuals' (i. 224) over public politics and prophetic ardour. These 'Enthusiasts of kindliest temperament' (i. 225) were indebted to philosophical principles that kept them safer than had they 'been travelling with the crowd of less imaginative malcontents, through the dark lanes and foul bye roads of ordinary fanaticism' (224). Enthusiasm is now extraordinary in its unworldliness, and the possibility of such a refusal of things-as-they-are having a threatening dimension is hidden away.

The organicist theories of literature outlined in the pages that follow the discussion of poetic diction in the *Biographia* can be seen as Coleridge's distinctive contribution to the regulatory discourse of enthusiastic poetics that I outlined in my two opening chapters. His account of the growth of the work in obedience to inner laws till it achieves a complex 'Multëity in Unity' represents inspiration in terms of the kind of natural harmony promoted by Shaftesbury.[54] The distinction between such noble enthusiasm and the spasming of its vulgar variant perpetuated by the discourse of regulation,

[54] See 'Essays on the Principles of Genial Criticism' (1814), in *Shorter Works and Fragments*, ed. H. J. Jackson and J. R. de J. Jackson, 2 vols. (Princeton: Princeton University Press, 1995), i. 372.

presaged by the contrast between himself and the tallow manufacturer, is at the centre of Coleridge's theory of the Imagination. The Imagination has a unifying power that Coleridge contrasted with Fancy's 'anarchic flux of outward circumstance'.[55] His account of Fancy is close to the long eighteenth-century understanding of enthusiasm as a form of 'distraction'; insofar as the latter was defined as a flux of sensation and associations unmoored from any reality principle. Coleridge attempts to found the self in a universal subject that would reclaim 'a sense of wholeness or integrity in the face of incoherence'.[56] Without such a ground 'our whole life would be divided between the despotism of outward impressions, and that of senseless and passive memory' (*BL* i. 111). Throughout the *Biographia*, associationist theories are translated into the terms of the discourse on enthusiasm. The distracted collapsing of the Creator into his creation is central to Hume's definition of enthusiasm. Coleridge's Imagination, in contrast, is ultimately grounded in a God whose authorizing presence and distinct personality affirms the objectivity of his creatures. This distance retains what Coleridge sees as a proper role for volition, 'the free will, our only absolute *self*' (*BL* i. 114). Whereas enthusiasm involves annihilation of the subject, the loss of the autonomous self either in the amorphous identity of the crowd or through the imploding mania of the solitary, the poetic imagination is an act of free will whereby inspiration remains under the control of and ultimately affirms the self.

Coleridge continually denied that the lower classes were capable of wielding the regulatory powers of this free will. He rejected absolutely, for instance, any suggestion that someone such as Wordsworth's pedlar could possess the genuine enthusiasm of the poet himself. Chapter 5 will deal in more detail with Wordsworth's own ambivalence towards the powers of enthusiasm imputed to lower-class figures in his poetry. In relation to Coleridge what needs to be stressed is the way that these figures come to represent the invalidity of popular enthusiasm. They lack the 'TASTE' necessary to the poet who can 'regulate his own style' (*BL* ii. 81). They are closer to Boehme than Wordsworth. Here the *Biographia* provides a Coleridgean variant of the discourse of regulation, and its disenfranchisement of the peasant poet. The question is not so much one of internal or external regulation, but who is capable of regulating

---

[55] Riede, *Oracles and Hierophants*, 26.   [56] Ibid.

whom. 'Taste' remains the limit of the relative democratization of culture implicit in Shaftesbury's vision of the moral sense. Without an innate taste the moral sense cannot be free or distinguish itself from vulgar enthusiasm. Of course, taste turns out not to be innate in Shaftesbury, but to be the product of a (classical) education available to gentlemen. The democratization of Shaftesbury's ideas over the eighteenth century is evident in Coleridge's substitution of a classical tradition of the gentleman by the vernacular tradition represented by writers such as Shakespeare, Milton, and Wordsworth himself. This tradition, however, still operates exclusively, that is, it provides a 'grammar, logic, psychology' not available to those whose schoolroom has been the 'market, wake, high-road, or plough-field' (*BL* ii. 81).

For those who have access to this canon, the study of Milton and Shakespeare will 'secure in due time the formation of a second nature,' that is, the second nature which constitutes Shaftesbury's natural enthusiasm as opposed to the enthusiasm of the 'half-instructed Many' (*Friend*, i. 126). The true self once again is a constructed self, but it is a construction that reveals our true (second) nature to us. Freedom is found in regulation. Increasingly as his writing career went on, however, Nature could not be left to discover the limits of this enthusiasm itself; 'true Christian *enthusiasm*', as he put it in *The Friend*, depended upon not only the development of a literary taste, but, especially for those who had no access to a literary education, also 'the altar, the censer, and the sacrifice' (*Friend*, i. 433). In Hume's terms Coleridge's enthusiasm was increasingly given over to a form of superstition.

CHAPTER FOUR

Barbauld, Devotion, and the Woman Prophet

RECENT SCHOLARLY INTEREST in Anna Letitia Barbauld has been primarily concerned with the relationship between issues of gender and the question of women's participation in the public sphere.[1] My aim in this chapter is to show how an understanding of the discourse on enthusiasm helps explain some of the choices facing Barbauld in her 'very sophisticated negotiation of the intermediate terrain between the public and private'.[2] Part of the usefulness of focusing on enthusiasm is that it takes us beyond arid contraries of feeling versus reason that still often define much of the writing on Barbauld (not to mention many of the other writers discussed in this book). Barbauld was brought up in a centre of Rational Dissent at the Warrington Academy, and her early writing, especially, has been represented as an attempt to introduce an emergent language

---

[1] See, for instance, William McCarthy, '"We Hoped the *Woman* was Going to Appear": Repression, Desire, and Gender in Anna Letitia Barbauld's Early Poems', in Paula R. Feldman and Theresa M. Kelley (eds.), *Romantic Woman Writers: Voices and Countervoices* (Hanover, NH: University Press of New England, 1995), 113–37; William Keach, 'Barbauld, Romanticism and the Survival of Dissent', *Essays and Studies*, 51 (1998), 44–61; Maggie Favretti, 'The Politics of Vision, Anna Barbauld's "Eighteen Hundred and Eleven"', in Isobel Armstrong and Virginia Blain (eds.), *Women's Poetry in the Enlightenment: The Making of a Canon, 1730–1820* (Basingstoke: Macmillan, 1999), 99–110; Daniel E. White, 'The "Joineriana": Anna Barbauld, the Aikin Family Circle, and the Dissenting Public Sphere', *Eighteenth-Century Studies*, 32 (1999), 511–33; Lucy Newlyn, *Reading, Writing, and Romanticism: The Anxiety of Reception* (Oxford: Oxford University Press, 2000); Anne Janowitz, 'Amiable and Radical Sociability: Anna Barbauld's "Free Familiar Conversation"', in Gillian Russell and Clara Tuite (eds.), *Romantic Sociability: Social Networks and Literary Culture in Britain, 1770–1840* (Cambridge: Cambridge University Press, 2002), 62–81; and Deirdre Coleman, 'Firebrands, Letters and Flowers: Mrs. Barbauld and the Priestleys', in Russell and Tuite (eds.), *Romantic Sociability*, 82–103.

[2] Newlyn, *Reading, Writing and Romanticism*, 137.

of sensibility into its severe masculine culture of free enquiry.[3] Leaving aside the question of the gender politics of this move for the moment, her specific intervention in the culture of Dissent could be seen as part of the broader cultural development that included Henry Mackenzie's writing on the importance of good taste in matters of religion.[4] Both Barbauld and Mackenzie were attempting to create a space for a religion of the heart distinct from the unrulier versions of religious enthusiasm. Feeling and its various cognates were contested terms throughout the period. For Barbauld, as we shall see, the word 'devotion' carried much of the weight of this burden of defining authentic religious feeling. It was a word that she took to negotiate the treacherous ground between enthusiasm and cold formalism.

Quite early in her career as a writer, Barbauld was involved in several friendly disputes with Joseph Priestley, the most visible and one might say notorious Dissenter of this period. Understanding their relationship only in terms of feminine-gendered sensibility versus masculine-gendered reason obscures both the nuances and vicissitudes of their exchanges. Her ambivalence about Priestley, for instance, is travestied if it is regarded simply as a protest against Dissent's 'self-denial, rationalism, and emotional low temperature'.[5] Nor is it entirely a matter of dissenting culture's 'continuing relegation of women to the realm of nurturing domesticity', although there is no doubt that Barbauld's writing does push against this relegation.[6] Such accounts may be in danger of underestimating both her ability to intervene directly in a public culture beyond the private and domestic, and her proximity to the mainstream of the culture of Dissent. Priestley cannot simply be regarded as a representative of Dissent. If anything, Barbauld's position in her disagreement with Priestley seems to have been closer to the consensus at Warrington than his. For Barbauld, early on in her

[3] See, for instance, McCarthy, 'We Hoped the *Woman* was Going to Appear', 127. My view is that Barbauld was closer to the mainstream of opinion at the Academy than McCarthy allows and that Priestley's controversial nature often placed him beyond the pale of the ecumenical idea of politeness Barbauld usually respected in the 1770s and 1780s.

[4] Barbauld reproduced Mackenzie's La Roche story from *The Mirror* (see Chapter 1, for a discussion of the story) in her *Female Speaker; or, Miscellaneous Pieces, in Prose and Verse, Selected from the Best Writers, and Adapted to the Use of Young Women* (1811), 120–32.

[5] McCarthy, 'We Hoped the *Woman* was Going to Appear', 123.

[6] Keach, 'Barbauld, Romanticism and the Survival of Dissent', 50.

writing career at least, the extreme 'candour' of Priestley's writing brings it too close to the vehemence of enthusiasm that the polite culture of Warrington always reprobated. If she is concerned about the intellectualization of religion in her responses to Priestley, that is not the same thing as suggesting that she thought him cold. Quite the contrary was the case in fact: what she seems to have found daunting was his 'wild cascade' (*BP* 38, l. 30). What he lacks in Barbauld's estimation is not feeling, but the regulatory manners of sensibility as she understood them in the 1770s. For Priestley, on the other hand, her ideas on the proper relationship between religion and taste threatened to make religion too much a matter of aesthetic feeling, that is, something divorced in its artificiality from his ideal of candour. Sometimes he does seem to see in this tendency a confusion of the body and spirit that was a commonplace of the discourse on enthusiasm, as we have seen, but more often for Priestley feeling in this negative aesthetic sense is defined in terms of empty formality or mere manners as against the sublime of free enquiry. If Priestley sometimes by his own admission could fly close to the wind of enthusiasm, he seems more willing to take that risk than cling to what he sees as the mere superstition of 'taste'. 'Taste' for Priestley is too close to a Catholic infatuation with ceremonies and ritual traditionally despised by Dissenters.

This summary account of Barbauld's dispute with Priestley obscures the elasticity of her own sense of the relationship between sensibility and enthusiasm, and the fact that it was granted more latitude at different times in her writing career. The rest of this chapter will provide a more detailed topography for understanding this terrain, but I shall begin by sketching its outline further, before beginning with a more precise account of Barbauld's idea of 'devotion'. Some of the things that alarmed Barbauld most about Priestley's candour in the 1770s were publicly defended by her in the radical years of the 1790s. On one level, as I have argued throughout this study, merely by being a Dissenter one was liable to the charge of enthusiasm for some members of the establishment. The campaign for the repeal of the Test and Corporation Acts and expressions of support for the revolution in France made it even easier to make them seem throwbacks to the sectarians of the Civil War. As a woman actively involved in religious and political reform during this later period, Barbauld was easily caricaturable by political opponents as a hysterical prophetess, a victim of the impossibility of the female mind regulating its impulses. Barbauld was sharply aware from very early on in her career of the ways in which women writing on matters of political and religious importance were likely to be characterized. Her anthology *The Female Speaker* (1811) promotes the idea that 'it is pleasant to command our appetites and passions, and to keep them in due order within the bounds of reason and religion,' and importantly implies that her readers were capable of such control.[7] This emphasis on regulation is ubiquitous in Barbauld's work, but it would be wrong to see her simply as an unqualified proponent of moderation. For one thing, as Foucault's later work has suggested, self-governance may sometimes operate as a form of resistance.[8] For another, Barbauld was quite capable of practising less obviously moderate forms of public utterance, that is, resetting the gauge on her regulation for herself. 'Corsica', for instance, the best known and most popular poem of her first collection, was an attempt at the 'patriot enthusiasm' that she and many of her contemporaries associated with Mark Akenside (a poet she edited in 1795).[9] Regulation is always in a complex relationship with a desire to promote intensity of religious and political feeling in her work. 'Sympathy' is a key word in her lexicon in this respect. As in Shaftesbury's writing, whose passionate apostrophes to the 'animating and inspiring Power' appear in *The Female Speaker*, a matter that I shall return to later, regulation is the other side of a pronounced desire to reach beyond the self and things-as-they-are.[10] Precisely at the time that Dissenters were particularly open to the charge of enthusiasm then, perhaps encouraged by the prospect of reform at home and abroad, Barbauld seems to grant her own self more latitude in this respect. If Barbauld defended an idea of religious feeling grounded in manners and tradition early on in her career, one that Priestley believed too far

---

[7] See *The Female Speaker*, 12.

[8] I take, for instance, Foucault's discussion of self-mastery in *The Care of the Self*, trans. Robert Hurley (Harmondsworth: Penguin, [1984] 1986), to allow for the possibility of self-determination and, potentially, defiance of the totalizing networks of power that have been seen by critics such as Edward Said as dominating his earlier works and disallowing resistance. See Said's 'Foucault and the Imagination of Power', in D. C. Hoy (ed.), *Foucault: A Critical Reader* (Oxford: Blackwell, 1986), 149–55.

[9] See Michael Meehan, *Liberty and Poetics in Eighteenth Century England* (Beckenham: Croom Helm, 1986), 53, on Akenside as a poet of liberty.

[10] Several of Shaftesbury's apostrophes appear at the end of Book 4, 'Descriptive and Pathetic', of *The Female Speaker*, 300–4.

reduced the gap between the culture of Dissent and the broader culture of the national Church, she did not always have so sanguine a
view of the softening influence of Anglicanism. What had seemed to
her to be well mannered in the 1770s could seem like mystification
to her in the 1790s. From the late 1780s Barbauld showed herself
ready to take on the prophetic mantle for herself (as well as defend
the enthusiasm of Priestley's candour) and in the process her version
of Blake's 'honest indignation' attracted the charge of enthusiasm.
Her militant voice seems more muted from the middle of the 1790s,
as the prospects for political and religious reform seemed to evaporate. Dissenters at this time were debating questions of retirement
and domesticity that appear in Coleridge's conversation poems, but
even here retirement in Barbauld's writing—as in the poetry of
Thelwall—seems to be represented in terms of a necessary evil in
times of trouble rather than the higher state of being that it can
appear in the poetry of Coleridge and Wordsworth. Certainly her
writing continued to address the question of women's participation
in the public sphere, even if the enthusiasm of the 1789–95 period
becomes relatively muted again. Her great late poem *Eighteen
Hundred and Eleven* is prophetic in content but not really in style;
it regulates its enthusiasm for liberty into a more detached manner,
one that puts less store in sympathetic power than the disinterested
'prospect' of classical republicanism, but even this was felt by many
critics to represent a transgressive 'mismatch of gender and
genre'.[11]

BARBAULD, PRIESTLEY, AND THE QUESTION OF 'TASTE'

As it is defined in her essay 'Thoughts on the Devotional Taste'
(1775), Barbauld saw the term 'devotion' as a bridgehead between
the narrow sectarian interests of Dissent and the idea of a more
catholic Anglican culture. Initially Barbauld does admit that there
are dangers that feeling left to itself may be a conduit of enthusiasm:

If directed by a melancholy or enthusiastic faith, their workings are often
too strong for a weak head, or a delicate frame: and for this reason they

---

[11] Julie Ellison, 'The Politics of Fancy in the Age of Sensibility', in Joel Haefner
and Carol Shiner Wilson (eds.), *Re-visioning Romanticism: British Women Writers,
1776–1837* (Philadelphia: University of Pennsylvania Press, 1994), 241.

[that is, the religious affections] have been almost excluded from religious worship by many persons of real piety.[12]

Her attitude to the popular enthusiasm associated with Methodism is entirely negative. For Barbauld that kind of religious feeling represents a degenerate form of sensibility. She imagines with disdain 'some florid declaimer who professes to work upon the passions of the lower class, where they are so debased by noise and nonsense, that it is no wonder if they move disgust in those of elegant and better-informed minds'. Having made this admission, however, the main thrust of her essay turns in a quite different direction and against a quite different aspect of enthusiasm. The work of self-regulation that she imagines as beyond the Methodist crowd, she believes can be provided by the 'taste' of the person of sensibility. Animating Barbauld's essay is a fear that Dissenters were in danger of recreating what she sees as the 'critical and disputatious spirit' of their seventeenth-century Presbyterian forebears.[13] From this perspective, Dissent was falling into a vulgar enthusiasm, when it was tasteless enough to *insist* on its differences even from a liberal Anglicanism. For Barbauld it was an over-reliance on the self-sufficiency of human reason and an accompanying sectarian disputatiousness that had earned Dissent a reputation for enthusiasm: 'An establishment leads to superstition, a sect to enthusiasm; the one is a more dangerous and violent excess, the other more fatally debilitates the powers of the mind.'[14] If at the beginning of her 'Thoughts on the Devotional Taste' she is willing to acknowledge the dangers of an over-wrought emotionalism, her main concern is with excessive claims to the candour of free enquiry: 'a sect is never stationary, as it depends entirely on passions, and opinions.'[15] 'Opinion', as we saw in Chapter 2, was to become central to Burke's redefinition of enthusiasm in the 1790s. Among those whom Burke regarded as dangerous enthusiasts for 'opinion' were the best-known Dissenters in the country Richard Price and Joseph Priestley. No one's interventions in the public arena had been thought to recall the enthusiasm of the 1640s more than Priestley's; especially after the campaign for the repeal of the Test Acts intensified, he was constantly represented as an avatar of Oliver's preachers (one of the

---

[12] 'Thoughts on the Devotional Taste, on Sects, and on Establishments', in *Devotional Pieces, Compiled from the Psalms and the Book of Job* (1775), 3.
[13] Ibid. 29.   [14] Ibid. 35.   [15] Ibid.

associations Burke used to tarnish the image of Richard Price). Barbauld had known Priestley well for some time before this period. Her family had moved to Warrington in 1758, when her father John accepted the position of tutor in languages and belles lettres. Promoted to tutor in divinity in 1761, Aikin was succeeded as tutor in languages and belles lettres by Priestley. Priestley and his wife left Warrington for Leeds in June 1767, an event described in what may be Barbauld's earliest poem (she was 24 at the time). Priestley later claimed that Barbauld's interest in poetry had been inspired by reading his efforts. Yet for all their affinities, and they should not be underestimated, it seems Barbauld's essay is directed against what she perceived as the militancy of Priestley's brand of Dissent. A tendency towards abstruse speculation and a 'disputatious spirit, and fondness for controversy' that had given the mind 'a sceptical turn with an aptness to call in question the most established truths': these were qualities strongly associated with Priestley.[16] Instead of doctrinal (and political) differences, Barbauld seeks to stress the importance of praise and prayer in the Christian life, aspects that she believed for Dissenters 'hastens their re-union with the common reservoir from which they were separated'.[17] 'Devotion' is defined precisely in terms of this aesthetic and sentimental relationship with God:

Its seat is in the imagination and the passions, and it has its source in that relish for the sublime, the vast, and the beautiful, by which we taste the charms of poetry and other compositions that address our fine feelings.[18]

Although she is alert to the dangers of confusing agape and eros, she goes so far as to insist that the language of love with its 'exaggerated expressions' could provide a model for religious devotion if treated with taste.[19] The proposition would seem designed to set off all the trip wires surrounding 'sensuous incarnation' that writers from Mackenzie to Wordsworth were keen to guard against in their recommendations of affective religion.[20] Barbauld herself is alert to the danger of the self being lost in adoration, the recurrent eighteenth-century fear of transport without a return ticket, but for her that fear seems more to do with intellectual intensity than emotions as such.

[16] Ibid. 6.　　[17] Ibid. 44.　　[18] Ibid. 2.　　[19] Ibid. 23.
[20] See the discussion Mackenzie in Chapter 1. Wordsworth's anxieties over 'sensuous incarnation' are discussed at length in Chapter 5.

Barbauld's essay then is not primarily oriented against a dryness or coldness perceived in Priestley's brand of Dissent, but against its lack of regulation, its extended version of candour, its enthusiasm. For Barbauld's account of Priestley implied that the sublimity of his idea of God was too strong for human capabilities to comprehend, and that this overwhelming power put the idea of a coherent self-hood in danger. Priestley raised God 'too high for our imaginations to take hold of'. The consequence was that we 'grow giddy with the prospect, the mind is astonished and confounded at its own insignif-icance . . . and the only feeling the soul is capable of in such a moment is a deep and painful sense of its own abasement'.[21] Indeed perhaps sensitive to Priestley's knowledge of Hartley's vocabulary, and anticipating Coleridge's fear of the delirious consequences of their theory of consciousness, she warned a friend against 'such an annihilation of ourselves as is nearly painful'. She contrasted Priestley's *'sublime'* with the less arduous *'pathetic* of Religion'.[22] Although written in a friendly spirit, her poetic 'Character' of Priestley described him in terms that anticipated both Burke's attack on Price's enthusiasm 'kindling as it advances' and Wordsworth's idea that Godwin confused reason with his own pas-sions. In the poem she acknowledges the debt of her own poetic inspiration to the 'wild cascade' (*BP* 38, l. 30) of Priestley's think-ing, an 'impetuous river' (l. 19) whose dangers she imagines taming by returning it to what Barbauld's essay described as the 'ocean' of the Church. Clearly she saw in Priestley's theology the kind of unworlding sublimity that threatened to sweep away the subjectiv-ity (and the domestic affections) it was meant to be authenticating.

Priestley's account of the development of Christianity, on the other hand, had always been wary of the dangers of allegory cloud-ing with 'sensuous incarnation' (*WP* iii. 72)—the phrase is Wordsworth's—what he saw as an essentially rational religion of Christ. His *Institutes of Natural and Revealed Religion* (1772), for instance, contrasted the superstition of the heathens with the enthu-siasm of the Jewish poets. The former tended 'to debase their facul-ties', confusing exalted religious feelings with the passions, but the

---

[21] Barbauld, 'Thoughts on the Devotional Taste', 10–11.
[22] Mrs Barbauld to Nicholas Clayton, 21 Feb. [1776], Nicholson Collection, Liverpool Public Library, quoted in R. K. Webb, 'Rational Piety', in Knud Haakonssen (ed.), *Enlightenment and Religion: Rational Dissent in Eighteenth-Century Britain* (Cambridge: Cambridge University Press, 1996), 299.

latter displayed 'a noble enthusiasm' (Rutt, ii. 246). These are exactly the terms Wordsworth used to praise the 'enthusiasm' of the Old Testament prophets over the 'superstition' of the classical tradition. Wordsworth was aware that the latter could produce a state of superstitious abjection before the idol, but he was also alert to dangerous errors that could proceed even from the noblest enthusiasm. If Barbauld seems less concerned about distracting dangers of sensuous incarnation than either Wordsworth or Priestley, her security is predicated on the category of taste that operates to ensure the language of love in a religious context degenerates neither into enthusiasm nor superstition. In fact, Wordsworth had a faith in 'taste' of his own as a bulwark against enthusiasm, as we will see in the next chapter, but for Priestley it was a category that itself remained too close to the pleasures of imagination and worldly ambition. For Priestley 'taste' often seems little better than a fashionable superstition. Her essay's title he regarded as 'a debasing of the subject' (Rutt, i. 280).

Before turning to look at Priestley's response to Barbauld's criticism in detail, more needs to be said about the relationship between enthusiasm and sensibility illuminated by her essay. A useful paradigm was set out some time ago in Donald Davie's *A Gathered Church* (1978). Correcting the continuing Arnoldian association of Dissent with philistinism and iconoclasm, Davie brings to light a more liberal tradition of 'accommodation' with the cultural mainstream that he identifies in its earliest stages with Isaac Watts and Philip Doddridge (who taught Barbauld's father at his Northampton Academy). Although he is rather dismissive of Barbauld herself, Davie's account of a dissenting culture that could claim Arnoldian virtues is anticipated in her validation of 'a devotion generous, liberal, and humane, the child of more exalted feelings than base minds can enter into, which assimilates man to higher nature'.[23] For Barbauld the common culture and traditions of what R. K. Webb calls *practical* piety are more important than differences of theology.[24] Looking back to the militancy of the seventeenth-century Puritans, she defines the disputatious spirit in the

[23] Barbauld, 'Thoughts on the Devotional Taste', 4. See Donald Davie, *A Gathered Church: The Literature of the English Dissenting Interest, 1700–1930* (Routledge & Kegan Paul, 1978), 10–12. He dismisses Barbauld's 'superciliousness', 134, although he does take this fault to be representative of Unitarianism more generally rather than simply hers.
[24] Webb, 'Rational Piety', 288.

writing of Priestley in terms of the 'enthusiasm' of the sects, that is, precisely in the terms that Geoffrey Hartman uses to distinguish eighteenth-century literariness from the ranting of hacks and enthusiasts. Daniel E. White and Anne Janowitz have both suggested that the accommodating tone of Barbauld's poetry and prose was typical of the 'tempered' manners and values of Dissent.[25] White believes that Dissent was not so much a counter-public, as 'a sub-category of the classical public sphere, a fragment that exerted critical pressure from within'.[26] Janowitz takes a slightly different view, identifying this formation more specifically with the Warrington Academy, and contrasting it with the spirit of public engagement that Barbauld found among the intellectual Dissenters that surrounded the publisher Joseph Johnson in the 1780s and 1790s. Janowitz acutely describes Barbauld's career in terms of a journey from the ideal of social intercourse at the academy conceived of as 'informal, familiar, and amiable' to 'a more urban and militant notion of sociability linked to political activism'.[27] Obviously the urgency of much of the writing of this later period, including pamphlets such as *Sins of Government, Sins of the Nation* (1793), brings it closer to the myriad heterotopic counterpublics that 'contested the exclusionary norms of the bourgeois public sphere, elaborating alternative styles of political behaviour and alternative norms of public speech'.[28] Among these might even be included the counter-public of enthusiasm that she had earlier disparaged in Methodism and other popular religious movements, but I will be returning to this point later. For now I want to concentrate on Barbauld's more familiar and 'amiable' persona. The only caveat that could be entered against Janowitz and White's account of this persona at this stage in my argument is against making the culture of the Warrington Academy seem too cosy and homogeneous. Clearly the Aikins, the Priestleys, and others, such as William Enfield, were very close, but important differences between them should not be overlooked. Barbauld obviously found Priestley's manner challenged the politeness of the public sphere too directly. Instead of negotiating with the classical public sphere

---

[25] White, ' "Joineriana" ', 518, and Janowitz, 'Amiable and Radical Sociability'.

[26] White, ' "Joineriana" ', 513.

[27] Janowitz, 'Amiable and Radical Sociability', 62.

[28] Nancy Fraser, 'Rethinking the Public Sphere: A Contribution to the Critique of Actually Existing Democracy', in Craig Calhoun (ed.), *Habermas and the Public Sphere* (Cambridge, Mass.: MIT Press, 1993), 116.

'from within', as White describes it, Priestley often seemed to be defiantly outside, blowing the trumpets of Joshua to bring down the walls entirely. At this stage in her career at least, Barbauld wanted sharply to separate the culture of Dissent from any taint of the counter-public of enthusiasm. Rather than the chapels and field meetings of Methodism or even the more 'rational' language of Priestley's controversialism, she wanted to align Dissent with the good taste that she saw as part of the Anglican tradition. In her concern with politeness and regulation we might understand her not just as a product of a mid-eighteenth century phenomenon of sensibility, but as part of the line of dissenting 'accommodation' that reacted against the association of Presbyterianism with uncouth iconoclasm by stressing ecumenical good taste. Both Watts and Doddridge were influenced by and transmitted to others Shaftesbury's ideas on politeness, but ironically both were accused of enthusiasm for expounding an affective religion.[29] Little wonder then that Barbauld and others were keen to stress the amiability and politeness of the culture at Warrington.

With regard to her concern with politeness and regulation it is instructive to compare Barbauld's attitude to Priestley with her responses to William Enfield.[30] Barbauld wrote a poem, for instance, praising Enfield's 'candid manners' and 'active mind' (*BP* 68, l. 11). Barbauld's 'Character' of Enfield contrasts with her sense of Priestley's as 'eccentric, piercing, bold' (*BP* 37, l. 3):

> Goodness by happy sympathy impart,
> And with thy own sweet morals charm the heart.
>
> ('William Enfield': *BP* 68, ll. 13–14)

---

[29] See Isabel Rivers, *Reason, Grace, and Sentiment: A Study of the Language of Religion and Ethics in England, 1660–1780*, Cambridge Studies in Eighteenth-Century English Literature and Thought, 2 vols. (Cambridge: Cambridge University Press, 1991–2000), i. 192–5; and see Lucy Aikin's comment that 'Long before my time . . . my kindred—the Jennings' [*sic*], the Belshams, my excellent grandfather Aikin, and his friend and tutor Doddridge—had begun to break forth out of the chains and darkness of Calvinism, and their manners softened with the system. My youth was spent among the disciples or fellow-labourers of Price and Priestley, the descendants of Dr John Taylor, the Arian, or in the society of that most amiable of men, Dr Enfield. Amongst these there was no rigorism . . . in *manners*, the Free Dissenters, as they were called, came much nearer to the Church than to their own strict brethren, yet in *doctrine* no sect departed so far from the Establishment.' Quoted in White, ' "Joineriana" ', 515.

[30] Enfield came to Warrington as tutor in belles-lettres in June 1770.

Enfield was regarded as much less disputatious than Priestley. His strengths, according to Barbauld's brother John Aikin, were 'amiable endowments that conciliate affection'. Aikin described Enfield's religion as 'despising superstition, and fearing enthusiasm'. Throughout Aikin's account of Enfield there is a stress on his liberal sentiments and his opposition to what Barbauld thought of as the gloominess of Presbyterianism. Enfield was much more tolerant of the Church of England than Priestley. Apparently he shared Barbauld's sense that the 'broader' culture of the national Church could provide a softening of the disputatious enthusiasm of sectarianism: 'To *dissent* was by no means part of his natural disposition; on the contrary, he could not without a struggle differ from those whom he saw dignified by station, respectable for learning and morals, and amiable in the intercourse of society.'[31] Doctrinal differences were less important to him than the prospect of a shared culture embodied in the more liberal wing of the Church of England. However, Aikin makes it clear that Enfield's hopes for a reunion with the national Church did not survive the reassertion of orthodoxy after the defeat of the campaign for the repeal of the Test and Corporation Acts. Faced with an illiberal Church of England, Aikin claims, Enfield asserted the political and religious rights of Dissent with 'courage and zeal'.[32] Barbauld's career contains a similar transformation, but earlier on, at least, had more affinity with Enfield's amiability than Priestley's zeal. To some extent she seems to have seen herself as collaborating with Enfield throughout her career (even after his death). Five of her hymns were published in Enfield's anthology *Hymns for Public Worship* (1772). She later made it clear that *The Female Speaker* was conceived of as a companion volume for Enfield's *The Speaker* (1774): both volumes were involved in a project of cultivating readers of restrained feelings and good taste.[33] While Barbauld admired Priestley's power and remained on friendly terms with him, she clearly felt in the 1770s that his iconoclasm and penchant for controversy were regressive. Enfield's example should allow us to see that this response cannot only be considered as a function of gender differ-

---

[31] Aikin, 'Biographical Account of the Author of these Volumes', in William Enfield's *Sermons on Practical Subjects* (1798), pp. vii, xiv, and xvi.

[32] Ibid., p. xviii.

[33] See 'Preface' to *The Female Speaker*: 'The pieces in Dr. Enfield's Speaker have been rather avoided, as that excellent collection is well known', pp. v–vi.

ence. She is defending what White calls the 'tempered' manner and values of Dissent.[34] Barbauld was not the only Dissenter alarmed by Priestley's militancy. Another of his close friends, Theophilus Lindsey, took him to task for the way he staggered 'his readers by the harshness of his expressions . . . with a fearless conviction of the truth, [he] never uses any softening'.[35] Priestley always pushed the idea of candour towards a Godwinian collision of minds rather than Shaftesbury's idea of conversation taught by Doddridge and his followers at Warrington. This mental warfare could be too much for those Dissenters, including Barbauld, who saw themselves as inhabiting a portion of the same public sphere as the Church of England.

Priestley certainly took her essay to be impugning his behaviour, and wrote to her directly in protest, asking her to make changes to future editions.[36] His letter is quick to point out that the dangers of confusing sentiment with religion were much greater than those threatening his more rational discourse. Her comparison of the language of religion and the language of love, he declares 'a profanation of the subject' (Rutt, i. 280). Yet once again it is important to see that Priestley does not reduce the differences between them simply to one between feeling and reason. He argues for a view of religion not simply as a matter of reason but as 'an elevated passion, or affection' (Rutt, i. 280). It is the word 'taste' that he most objects to in her essay. If the metaphor of 'taste' suggested something too grossly physical to Priestley, another aspect to his objection soon emerges. 'Taste' is too attenuated a faculty to be given a serious role in religious matters. An aversion to the specifically aesthetic associations of the term seems to be in play for Priestley. 'Taste' is dampening of religious 'passion' in its artificiality, and this concern with mere politeness is what makes an accommodation with the Church possible by turning a blind eye to theological differences. Priestley expresses particular surprise at Barbauld's positive attitude towards religious establishments, especially her view that 'an establishment will preserve devotion from ever sinking into contempt' (Rutt, i. 282). Priestley believed that what Barbauld saw as the disputatious enthusiasm of sects was the astringent means of keeping the road to

[34] White, ' "Joineriana" ', 518.
[35] Lindsey to William Tayleur, 3 Dec. 1778, quoted in *BP* 247.
[36] See 'To Mrs Barbauld, Dec 20, 1775', in Rutt, i. 278–86, discussed in Webb, 'Rational Piety', 299–300, and Coleman, 'Firebrands, Letters and Flowers', 84–5.

religious and civic truth open. Her conciliatory language of taste
and sensibility, he believed, was a means of making defections from
Dissent to the Church of England easier.

The sense of surprise and hurt in Priestley's letter no doubt stems
from the fact that he and Barbauld had sometimes seemed very close
in their understanding of religion. The Preface to his *Two
Discourses* (1782), for instance, is proud to announce that one of
Barbauld's best-known poems, 'Address to the Deity', had been
inspired by the sermon on 'Habitual Devotion' included in the pamphlet (Rutt, xv. 101). Later in the Preface he comments: 'If my theological publications have been more of a *speculative* than of a
practical nature, it is merely because circumstances have led me to
it, and by no means because the former are more pleasing to me'
(102). One might find a hint of defensiveness here about Barbauld's
charge that there was a species of unworlding at work in his
theological and other researches distracting believers from the prac-
ticalities of their religion. Interestingly the sermon on 'Habitual
devotion', originally given (1764) before his dispute with Barbauld,
has quite a lot to say about enthusiasm. Like Hartley and like the
Barbauld poem his sermon inspired (and to which I will return
shortly), Priestley recommends a Christianity that sees God as
immanent and pervasive: 'He sees God in every thing, and he sees
every thing in God' (105). Here is the radical Unitarianism of
Coleridge's 'Religious Musings'. For Priestley, the everyday world
and its commercial and temporal requirements militates against the
practice of such religion: 'the more imperfect of the middle classes
of mankind will have their minds too much engrossed by this world
. . . they will be apt to be overborne by the superior power of things
seen and temporal' (106). Where Adam Smith (and later Samuel
Parr) saw such worldly concerns as a necessary bulwark against
enthusiasm, Priestley sees them as diluting the fervour proper to
religion: 'the more perfect of the middle classes . . . will produce a
kind of *religious fervour*, which rousing the mind to a greater exertion of its powers, will produce good resolutions with considerable
strength and vigour, and thereby break their growing attachment to
the world' (106). Not that Priestley is in any sense recommending
enthusiasm in his sermon. Habitual devotion of the sort that tends
towards meditation is favoured over 'tumultuous and excessive joy'
(116). Having discussed the deadening effects of superstition and
merely formal religion, he goes on to directly address the question

of enthusiasm: 'another inconvenience we are apt to be betrayed into, by imperfect and unworthy conceptions of God. It is that kind of enthusiasm which arises from an excess of religious joy, as the superstition I have just described arises from an excess of religious fear' (119). Obviously Priestley is operating with something like Hume's distinction between superstition and enthusiasm, but (as Hume might well have predicted of the militant Dissenter) he is much more tolerant of the latter than the former tendency as the second sermon of the *Two Discourses*, 'On the Duty of Not Living to Ourselves', makes clear. This sermon is devoted to the power of human sympathy and sociability:

I may add, that not only are the highest and the worthiest principles of human conduct either truly social, or a reinforcement of the social principle, but even the lowest appetites and passions of our nature are far from being indifferent to social connexions, considerations, and influences. (128)

No less than Shaftesbury, Priestley sees a continuity between the higher instinct 'whereby we are continually led out of ourselves' and the passions of the crowd. Although he is careful to state that 'our happiness depends upon our keeping their proper objects in view', he is equally certain that 'it has pleased our Divine Author to appoint, that all our appetites and desires, to whatever sense, external or internal, they be referred, should point to something beyond ourselves for their gratification; so that the idea of *self* is not in the least necessary to a state of the highest enjoyment' (129). He goes on to quote Matthew 22: 37, 39, commenting:

This is the Christian *self-annihilation*, and a state of the most complete happiness to which our natures can attain; when, without the least idea of being in pursuit of our own happiness, our faculties are wholly absorbed in those noble and exalted pursuits in which we are sure not to be finally disappointed, and in the course of which we enjoy all the consistent pleasures of our whole nature. (135)

Here Priestley seems to be advocating precisely that degree of religious fervour that Barbauld's 'Essay' had suggested was too overpowering. Not that Priestley does not see dangers in this regard himself. His sermon ends by warning his reader:

I would be no advocate for enthusiasm. The fervour of devotion cannot always be kept up. That is inconsistent with the condition of our nature, and far from being necessary in our present state: but that cheerful serenity and composure in which moderate acts of devotion leave the mind, is an excellent temper for entering upon, and persevering with spirit and alacrity, in any useful and honourable undertaking. (142)

This comment at least acknowledges the possibility that his earlier remarks could be taken as encouraging enthusiasm. These caveats notwithstanding, Priestley had a strong sense of the role of sympathetic identification in arousing a commitment to truth. Priestley's *Course of Lectures on Oratory and Criticism* (1777) delivered when he was a tutor at Warrington broached topics such as 'Of the Tendency of strong Emotions to produce Belief, and the transferring of passions from one Object to Another' (Rutt, xxiii. 320). Wary of any usurpation of the role of reason, he was also clear that sympathy was essential to all forms of human communication and implicitly preferred to court the danger of enthusiasm rather than get lost in the desert of conformity.

Barbauld's 'Address to the Deity' offers an interesting commentary in respect of Priestley's ideas, both on the first sermon that inspired it and the second of Priestley's *Two Discourses* that she probably knew too. A fervent sense of the pervasive presence of God in the universe is an important part of the poem's attempt to awaken its readers:

> Nor less the mystic characters I see
> Wrought in every flower, inscrib'd in every tree;
> In every leaf that trembles to the breeze
> I hear the voice of GOD among the trees.
>
> *(BP* 5, ll. 59–62)

Yet throughout the poem Barbauld also demonstrates the kind of modesty contemporaries associated with female sensibility. Indeed the poem opens on precisely such a note:

> Permit my feeble voice to lisp thy praise;
> And trembling, take upon a mortal tongue
> That hallow'd name to harps of Seraphs sung.
>
> *(BP* 4, ll. 2–4)

For all her poem's emphasis on the affective nature of religious experience, her representation of devotion coincides with the sort of tastefully restrained scenario imagined in Mackenzie's story of La Roche from *The Mirror*. Barbauld actually republished Mackenzie's story in her *Female Speaker* anthology, presumably as an example of the regulation of passion that the preface to her book recommended to female readers.[37] Depth and stillness as in La Roche's grief at the death of his daughter are the defining features of the religion of sensibility explored in Barbauld's 'Address':

> As by a charm, the waves of grief subside;
> Impetuous passion stops her headlong tide;
> At thy presence all emotions cease,
> And my hush'd spirit finds a sudden peace,
> Till every wordly thought within me dies.
>
> *(BP* 4, ll. 13–17)

However, the moment of unworlding hinted at in the last line here does open out towards something like Priestley's idea of religious fervour:

> Till all my sense is lost in infinite,
> And one vast object fills my aching sight.
>
> (ll. 19–20)

If this experience seems to bring her close to the kind of 'annihilation of ourselves' that she sometimes feared, it is quickly disavowed as unsustainable:

> But soon, alas! This holy calm is broke;
> My soul submits to wear her wonted yoke;
> With shackled pinions strives to soar in vain,
> And mingles with the dross of earth again.
>
> (ll. 21–4)

Priestley had also suggested such heights of transport could not be long sustained, but this did not disqualify them as a variety of genuinely religious experience for him.

The parallels between Barbauld's poem and Priestley's two sermons are close enough to explain the surprise and hurt of his response to her 'Essay'. All of them represent religion as a matter of affect. Both Barbauld and Priestley were alert to the dangers of this power degenerating into enthusiasm on the one hand and empty formalism on the other. Barbauld's poem more than her essay allows the differences between them on where to draw these lines to remain hazy, but where Priestley's sermons seem to prefer to risk the dangers of enthusiasm than fall into the pit of superstition, Barbauld's essay is drawn more to the culture of the establishment

---

[37] See n. 4 above.

as the source of the 'liberal' manners that prevent sensibility becoming an unruly enthusiasm. This emphasis on sensibility over and against more violent religious passions is a pervasive feature of her poetry. Her hymns, for instance, regularly stress the importance of a sense of the quiet nearness of God over the flights of transport associated with the excesses of religious enthusiasm:

> Cease, cease your songs, the daring flight controul,
> Revere him in the stillness of the soul:
> With silent duty meekly bend before him,
> And deep within your inmost hearts adore him.
>
> ('Hymn I': *BP* 55, ll. 57–60)

Yet it would be wrong to suggest that the differences between Barbauld and Priestley were absolute and unchanging on these matters. What seemed dangerous to her about Priestley's candour in the 'Essay' at other times in her career seemed a necessary commitment to the pursuit of truth regardless of infringements against taste.

THE RELIGIOUS SUBLIME

Commenting on the earlier period of Barbauld's career, Janowitz claims that 'the sense of freedom within propriety structures many of Anna Letitia Barbauld's images: demonstrating the elasticity of a necessary boundary'.[38] Barbauld's essay on devotional taste acknowledged the importance of candour, a central tenet of the culture of Dissent that surrounded her, but also registered a concern that too much freedom of enquiry in religious matters could render its object contemptible. This kind of excess of opinion was behind her preference for a deep and silent devotion not too quick to enter into the lists of controversy. If there is a valorization of a feminized discourse in this preference, as several critics have suggested, then the gendering of amiability over strong enthusiasm should not be essentialized. The amiable candour that Barbauld contrasted with Priestley's militancy was also practised and preached by men such as her brother John Aikin and William Enfield. Nor, perhaps most importantly of all, should we overlook the fact that Barbauld herself sometimes stretched the elasticity of affect into regions that

---

[38] Janowitz, 'Amiable and Radical Sociability', 67.

were close to Priestley's 'fervour'. From the 1780s Barbauld often practised a less politely amiable idea of public discourse, one which sometimes made frequent use of prophetic language to break through 'plausive argument, the daring lye | The artful gloss' ('Epistle to Wilberforce': *BP* 116, ll. 28–9). Barbauld's writing from this period insists that 'Truth is of a very intolerant spirit. She will not make any compromise with Error.'[39] Whereas candour had to make its compromise with Anglican manners in some of the earlier writing, now there is a much less conciliatory attitude. Barbauld's 'mental mode is that of intervention now rather than meditation'.[40]

Before looking at her writing from this period in more detail, however, we need to acknowledge that even in her first volume this strain had been a feature of her poetry. Any narrative of linear development from the amiability of the Warrington years to the radicalism of London threatens to blind us to the diversity of her poetry and the pressure that she continually put on the limits of sensibility. If there are hints of an extreme of unworlding in 'An Address to the Deity', these are more pronounced in another of the poems in her 1773 volume 'A Summer Evening's Meditation'. Her intentions in this respect are indicated to the reader by the epigraph from Young's *Night Thoughts*: '*One sun by day, by night ten thousand shine*' (*BP* 81). The epigraph effectively announces that the poem will 'launch into the trackless deeps of space' (*BP* 83, l. 82), and in doing so signals Barbauld's sense of equality with the male canon of poetic enthusiasm.[41] An even more obvious poetic influence on Barbauld's poem in this respect would have been Mark Akenside's *The Pleasures of Imagination*, edited by Barbauld two decades later, but published in a revised edition just before Barbauld's *Poems*.[42] Her critical essay on Akenside contrasted 'the deepest gloom' of Young's Calvinism with the more liberal sentiment to be found in *The Pleasures of Imagination*:

---

[39] *An Address to the Opposers of the Repeal of the Corporation and Test Acts*, 4th edn. (1790), 15.

[40] Janowitz, 'Amiable and Radical Sociability', 73.

[41] On Young and enthusiasm, see Shaun Irlam, *Elations: The Poetics of Enthusiasm in Eighteenth-Century Britain* (Stanford, Calif.: Stanford University Press, 1999), chs. 6 and 7.

[42] Mark Akenside, *The Pleasures of Imagination*, ed. with a critical essay by Anna Letitia Barbauld (1795). *Pleasures* had been published before her first volume of poems in *The Poems of Mark Akenside, M.D.* (1772).

The religion of the other, all at least that appears of it, and all indeed that could with propriety appear in such a Poem, is the purest Theism; liberal, cheerful, and sublime; or, if admitting any mixture, he seems inclined to tincture it with the mysticism of PLATO, and the gay fables of ancient mythology.[43]

Her own 'A Summer Evening's Meditation' is full of Shaftesburian rapture—the rapture that Barbauld's essay on Akenside identified as a direct source for *Pleasures of Imagination*—at the limitlessness of creation, but in the process Barbauld discovers the God within:

> At this still hour the self-collected soul
> Turns inward, and beholds a stranger there
> Of high descent, and more than mortal rank;
> An embryo GOD; a spark of fire divine.
>
> (*BP* 82, ll. 53–6)

Again this would seem to echo Akenside's poeticization of Shaftesbury:

> . . . we feel within ourselves
> His energy divine: he tells the heart,
> He meant, he made us to behold and love
> What he beholds and loves, the general orb
> Of life and being; to be great like him,
> beneficent and active.[44]

The end of the Barbauld's poem does provide the standard disclaimer that acknowledges the impossibility of her encompassing the infinite perspective to which she aspires:

> . . . Let me here
> Content and grateful, wait th'appointed time
> And ripen for the skies: the hour will come
> When all these splendours bursting on my sight
> Shall stand unveil'd, and to my ravish'd sense
> Unlock the glories of the world unknown.
>
> (*BP* 84, ll. 117–22)

But any understanding of these lines purely in terms of female modesty needs also to take into account the kinds of disavowal endemic in eighteenth-century poetic enthusiasm per se. Those found in

---

[43] 'Essay on Akenside's Poem on the Pleasures of Imagination', in Akenside, *Pleasures of Imagination*, pp. i–xxxvi.

[44] Akenside, *Pleasures of Imagination*, 119: iii. 624–9.

Coleridge's 'Religious Musings' are a late example of this reflex in
the elite poetics of unworlding. Male poets were thought to have the
ability to express their enthusiasm without dissolving their selves,
but had to demonstrate their discipline. The review of 'Religious
Musings' written by Barbauld's brother credited Coleridge with
managing this feat, but also reveals that such judgements were not
unconditional. Given this disciplinary context, the sustained
exploration of the imagination's yearning for 'solitudes of vast
unpeopled space' (*BP* 83, l. 94) in Barbauld's poem is perhaps all
the more remarkable, the concluding disavowal notwithstanding.
However much the poetics of amiable sociability defines her poetry
of this period, Barbauld did not forswear the attempt at the sublime
of poetic enthusiasm. Indeed she was later bold enough to suggest
that at least one male precursor had not always been sufficiently
able to practise the ardour of enthusiasm that he preached.
Barbauld claimed that most of Akenside's poem had the appearance
'of being laboured into excellence'. She preferred poetry that
savoured more of 'being thrown off at once amidst the swell and
fervency of a kindled imagination':[45]

IF the genius of AKENSIDE be to be estimated from this Poem, . . . it will be
found to be lofty and elegant, chaste, classical, and correct: not marked
with strong traits of originality, not ardent nor exuberant. His enthusiasm
was rather of that kind which is kindled by reading and imbibing the spirit
of authors, than by contemplating at first hand the works of nature.[46]

Whether she would have pressed this judgement in 1773 is a moot
point, but poems such as 'A Summer Evening's Meditation' are
effectively an assertion of her ability to a stretch beyond Akenside
and others in the school of Shaftesbury without annihilating the
self. The *Westminster Magazine* similarly detected 'a masculine
force in them which the most vigorous of our [male] poets has not
excelled'. The judgement does not present her as a poet of delicate
sensibility, but as someone capable of stretching the religious sublime to invigorating lengths.[47]

These matters are questions of degree. How far could enthusiasm
be pushed before it came to be regarded as too vehement and entangled in the passions? Did self-annihilation offer an invigorating

[45] Barbauld, 'Essay on Akenside's Poem', p. xi. [46] Ibid., p. xxix.
[47] See 'Observations on Female Literature', *Westminster Magazine*, 4 (1776),
283–5: 285.

vision of Eternity or a terrifying prospect of dissolution? How far did the gender of the writers and the readers concerned influence these judgements? Barbauld affiliated herself in 'An Address to the Deity' and 'A Summer Evening's Meditation' with a poetics of unworlding that Akenside, Young, and others had learnt in part from Shaftesbury, but she granted her own enthusiasm more latitude than some of these male precursors, whom she judged neither sufficiently 'ardent nor exuberant'. Judgements by writers and critics about how far such enthusiasm could be taken varied according to a reading context that changed over the eighteenth century as well as in relation to the social and gendered identities of writers and readers. Possibly the rehabilitation of enthusiasm charted by Irlam had developed further towards a freedom about 'form-lessness' in the 1770s than it had for Akenside in the 1740s.[48] Even so there remained in play questions about how such enthusiasm could be regulated into properly aesthetic forms. Relatively speaking, religious reveries such as 'A Summer Evening's Meditation' were capable of being conceived of as private, and so insulated from the infectious enthusiasm of the crowd. Self-annihilation could be risked in a sphere that limited the dispersal of the self. 'Meditation' could be seen as a key word in this respect, bringing Barbauld close to the Anglican perception that proper religious warmth was a matter of quiet devotion that shunned the crowd. The morals and manners movement that has been seen as comprising Dissenters such as Barbauld as well as Church of England evangelicals such as her sometime friend Hannah More always defined the difference between its religious feelings and the less regulated passions of the Methodists in terms of this kind of distinction.[49] Neither, for all their unworlding of experience, do 'An Address to the Deity' or 'A Summer Evening's Meditation' display the public disputatiousness that Barbauld found alarming in much of Priestley's religious writing. Nothing in them pushes Barbauld's affective religion close to the crowd. Yet even in her early poetry Barbauld sometimes did carry her enthusiasm over into public and

[48] See Irlam, *Elations*, 3, on formlessness, and Pat Rogers, 'Shaftesbury and the Aesthetics of Rhapsody', *British Journal of Aesthetics*, 12 (1972), 244–57, on Shaftesbury's influence on eighteenth-century ideas of organic form.

[49] On More's admiration for Barbauld, see G. J. Barker-Benfield, *The Culture of Sensibility: Sex and Society in Eighteenth-Century Britain* (Chicago: University of Chicago Press, 1992), 264.

political matters that pushed against the insulating walls of the private sphere.

'PATRIOT ENTHUSIASM'

If she was a follower of Akenside, his example was not limited to 'ideas of the fair and beautiful in morals and in taste, gathered from the writings of SHAFTESBURY, HUTCHINSON', but also what she saw as the poet's 'high sense of liberty'.[50] Akenside was a poet strongly identified with the patriot enthusiasm of the Whig tradition despised by Hume and Samuel Johnson. Johnson condemned Akenside's 'unnecessary and outrageous zeal for what he called and thought liberty'. Dissenters such as Andrew Kippis, another product of Doddridge's at Northampton, were much more likely to be attracted to what they saw as his 'most ardent spirit of liberty'.[51] Barbauld's poem 'Corsica', the poem that leads off her 1773 collection, articulates some of that spirit for the radical opposition of the 1760 and 1770s. The late 1760s saw a growing campaign of opposition to the government for its failure to live up to what were represented as the true Whig principles of liberty. The letters of 'Junius' in the *Public Advertiser* attacked the government for its use of bribery and corruption to manipulate Parliament, extolled the cause of John Wilkes, and took the part of the American colonies in their campaign against taxation without representation. Patriot opinion was also calling on the government to intervene on the side of the Corsicans, under General Pasquale Paoli, who were preparing to resist the invasion plans of their French overlords. Barbauld's poem is a contribution to this campaign written in the style of Akenside's patriot enthusiasm:

> What then should BRITONS feel? should they not catch
> The warm contagion of heroic ardour,
> And kindle at a fire so like their own?
>
> (*BP* 21, ll. 15–17)

No less than Akenside, Barbauld here makes 'raptur'd fancy' the basis of a poetics of liberty. Akenside understood his *Pleasures of Imagination* to work 'by exhibiting the most engaging prospects of

---

[50] 'Essay on Akenside's Poem', pp. viii and xvi.
[51] Both quoted in Meehan, *Liberty and Poetics*, 53.

nature, to enlarge and harmonize the imagination, and by that
means insensibly dispose the minds of men to a similar taste and
habit of thinking in religion, morals, and civil life'.[52] Barbauld
encouraged a similar enthusiasm for virtue. Deeds such as Paoli's
'. . . give mankind | A glimpse of higher natures' (*BP* 24, ll. 108–9).
Such glimpses, Barbauld suggests, can encourage Britain to live up
to its reputation as the home of liberty.

Her poem 'The Invitation' is quite explicit about the role of
enthusiasm in drawing the individual out of the private into the
public sphere through the power of sympathetic identification:

> And fond enthusiastic thought, that feeds
> On pictur'd tales of vast heroic deeds;
> And quick affections, kindling into flame
> At virtue's, or their country's honour'd name.
>
> (*BP* 13, ll. 121–4)

Lucy Newlyn is surely right to suggest that from early on Barbauld
proceeded on the assumption that 'few can reason, but all can
feel'.[53] I do not wish to exaggerate the extent to which Barbauld
stretched her idea of sympathy towards what her contemporaries
would have regarded as a dangerous enthusiasm. Much of what she
wrote even in this strain stays within the bounds of what was
regarded as the poetics of the sublime, however open to contesta-
tion such boundaries were. Her poetic enthusiasm needs to be
placed side by side with her strictures on Priestley's 'vigour'. One
should also note that there are disavowals even in poems such as
'The Invitation' when it comes to the specific possibility of a woman
either sustaining 'patriot passion' (l. 167) or 'launch[ing] our souls
into the bright unknown' (l. 182):

> Here cease my song, Such arduous themes require
> A master's pencil, and a poet's fire:
> Unequal far such bright designs to paint,
> Too weak her colours, and her lines too faint,
> My drooping Muse folds up her fluttering wing,
> And hides her head in the green lap of spring.
>
> (*BP* 15, ll. 83–8)

Even so, what Lucy Newlyn calls Barbauld's 'lively experimentation with contemporary male forms' often does push at the limits taken to regulate the poetics of enthusiasm, even for her male precursors such as Akenside, never mind what was thought to be possible for a woman writer to do in the genre.[54] The practice of her enthusiasm in such poems, as the *Westminster Magazine* saw it, exceeded her professions of female modesty.

Even those who admired the achievement of her 1773 volume sometimes registered a concern at the stretch and power of her imagination in such poems. The positive review she received for *Poems* from William Woodfall in the *Monthly* illustrates the gendered ambivalence towards her success. Woodfall was impressed with 'the smoothness and harmony' of her poetry; but the 'justness of thought, and vigour of imagination' he found 'extraordinary'.[55] His remarks pertain particularly to 'Corsica'; a poem written in a strain of patriot enthusiasm that the second part of the review implied was more properly a masculine province. After the praise that takes up most of the first part of the review, Woodfall reveals the disappointment of his expectation that 'the *Woman* was going to appear':

If she, as well as others of our female writers, has, in pursuing the road to fame, trod too much in the footsteps of the men, it has been owing, not to a want of education, but to a want of *proper* genius. If the amiable Writer of these poems had been educated more under the direction of a mother, than of a father: if she had taken her views of human life from among her female companions, and not altogether under the direction of men, either living or dead, we should have been as much enchanted with her feminine beauties, as we are now pleased and astonished by the strength of her imagination, the variety of her knowledge, and the goodness of her heart.[56]

Woodfall praises the volume as a whole, but admits his disappointment that there is not more of feminine softness in it. His opinion is not, however, reducible to a complaint at the lack of feeling as such. He is disappointed at the absence of *softer* emotions and the language of love associated with what he thinks of as female sensibility. What he finds extraordinarily present in their stead is the vigorous patriotism of 'Corsica' and the religious sublime of poems

---

[54] Newlyn, *Reading, Writing, and Romanticism*, 157.
[55] *Monthly Review*, 48 (1773), 54–9 and 133–7 (the review appeared in two sections): 54.
[56] Ibid. 137.

such as 'An Address to the Deity': both genres that he assumes to be masculine. For all that he admires 'the variety of her knowledge, and the goodness of her heart', his comments on the 'proper genius' of women suggests a doubt over whether a woman writer is ever going to be truly capable of regulating such poetic enthusiasm. There are hints in this direction in the muted negative comments on 'Corsica' in the first part of the review. Woodfall implies that ardour has overtaken judgement in the portrait of Paoli. He also registers pleasure bordering on relief at Barbauld's acknowledgement of disappointment ('the error of her zeal') in the additional lines added after Paoli's defeat at the Battle of Pontenuovo in June 1769:

> . . . Forgive the zeal
> That, too presumptuous, whisper'd better things
> And read the book of destiny amiss.
> Not with the purple colouring of success
> Is virtue best adorn'd: th'attempt is praise.
> There yet remains a freedom, nobler far
> Than kings or senates can destroy or give;
> Beyond the proud oppressor's cruel grasp
> Seated secure; uninjur'd; undestroy'd;
> Worthy of Gods: The freedom of the mind.
>
> (*BP* 26, ll. 192–201)

Written some time after the main part of the poem, these lines may simply express Barbauld's dismay at Paoli's eventual fate. She continues to zealously assert 'the freedom of the mind'. Yet Woodfall eagerly seizes on the lines as a welcome disavowal of public intentions and proof that her patriot enthusiasm was not taking her too far beyond the boundaries that circumscribed women writers.

Let me return now to Anne Janowitz's suggestion that Barbauld took on a new language of political intervention when she moved to London in the 1780s and mixed with the intellectual activists of the Joseph Johnson circle. Janowitz thinks of this transformation in terms of its use of a language of 'analysis' rather than of the 'manners' prized in the discourse of sensibility.[57] Barbauld's writing in pamphlets such as *An Address to the Opposers of the Repeal of the Corporation and Test Acts* (1790) and *Sins of Government, Sins of the Nation* (1793) certainly represents a direct intervention in

---

[57] Janowitz, 'Amiable and Radical Sociability', 62.

politics, but whether or not this shift represents a movement to a language of 'analysis' is another matter. Not that I am suggesting that Barbauld was not perfectly capable of offering a cool analysis of the political situation in the early 1790s. Her intellectual acuity is beyond question; and plenty of it is on display in these pamphlets. What I want to guard against is any possibility of Janowitz's careful opposition between 'analysis' and 'manners' being reduced to one between 'reason' and 'feeling'. Barbauld's political writing of this period is nothing if not impassioned, and often takes on a tone of unapologetic patriot enthusiasm. Indeed, now this language seems more unbridled in its readiness to adopt a fully prophetic register and put aside the regulatory caution of much of her earlier writing. Whereas her 1775 essay had cautioned against excessive candour, now it seems Barbauld is unwilling to admit of any limit to the pursuit of truth: 'The spirit of Enquiry, like a severe and searching wind, penetrates every part of the great body politic; and whatever is unsound, whatever is infirm, shrinks at the visitation.'[58] *An Address to the Opposers* displays the millenarian confidence in the 'sure operation of increasing light and knowledge' that brought Burke's charge of enthusiasm down on the head of Richard Price.[59] The caution of Barbauld's earlier writing is thrown aside in favour of directly prophetic exhortation:

Can ye not discern the signs of the times? The minds of men are in movement from the Borysthenes to the Atlantic. Agitated with new and strong emotions, they swell and heave beneath oppression, as the seas within the Polar Circle, when, at the approach of Spring, they grow impatient to burst their icy chains; when what, but an instant before, seemed so firm, spread for many a dreary league like a floor of solid marble, at once with a tremendous noise gives way . . . and the air resounds with the clash of floating fragments.[60]

If the 'floating fragments' of this passage were picked up in Coleridge's 'Kubla Khan', as they may well have been, it seems significant that he was to equivocate about taking the prophetic mantle that Barbauld seems to seize so confidently here. One of her opponents, William Keate, described the style of the pamphlet as 'very animated . . . ; but as the author did not allow himself time to cool, with great intemperance'. A sentence added to his critique

---

[58] Barbauld, *Address to the Opposers*, 33.   [59] Ibid. 31.
[60] Ibid. 31–2.

recorded his shock to discover that language of such extravagance could have come from 'a female pen'.[61] *Sins of the Government, Sins of the Nation* for its part casts itself as a kind of jeremiad against the government's proclamation of a day of fasting in support of the war effort. Quite specifically Barbauld takes on the role of the prophet at the city gate who castigates God's people for backsliding after the example of their rulers, and prophesies doom to the nation as a consequence. Such a confrontationally prophetic mode, especially when it was discovered that it came from the pen of a woman, was immediately seized on as proof of the enthusiasm of which Dissenters were always suspected. Barbauld's political writing of this period was easily satirized as the voice of the hysterical prophetess. Women, as I pointed out in my first chapter, were felt to have a biological disposition towards this species of enthusiasm. Barbauld's opponents quickly availed themselves of the association. Horace Walpole, for instance, who had been an admirer of her poetry, began to refer to her as 'Deborah Barbauld' in his letters, and identified her with the sectarian extremism of 'Presbytyrants'.[62] Soon afterwards he was refusing to read her work. Later he dismissed Barbauld and Helen Maria Williams as 'two prophetesses'.[63] *Sins of Government, Sins of the Nation* is written in a vigorous and prophetic style. When Barbauld translated Rousseau's idea of the general will into the language of the Bible in her pamphlet, the *British Critic* made the predictable reply in terms of Burke's over-determined redefinition of enthusiasm: 'The glorious effects of it are however displayed in a style of enthusiasm, which is rather forgetful of facts.'[64]

In her writing of this period, Barbauld often seems willing to grant an extended licence to the politics and poetics of affect that made it almost impossible for political opponents such as the *British Critic* to refrain from accusing her of enthusiasm. In poems such as 'To a Great Nation' and 'Epistle to Wilberforce' no less than the political pamphlets of this period, her own style is concerned

[61] William Keate, *A Free Examination of Dr. Price's and Dr. Priestley's Sermons* (1790), 55 and 64. See the discussion of Keate's response in Janowitz, 'Amiable and Radical Sociability', 72–3.

[62] 'To Hannah More, 29 September 1791', in *The Yale Edition of Horace Walpole's Correspondence*, ed. W. S. Lewis, 48 vols. (New Haven: Yale University Press, 1937–83), xxxi. 361–2.

[63] 'To Mary Berry, 26 July 1791', ibid. xi. 320.

[64] *British Critic*, 2 (1794), 81–5: 84.

not so much with control as provoking her readers into action. As with a great deal of other political writing from the first few years of the 1790s, the emphasis is a Blakean 'rouz[ing of] the faculties to act' ('To Dr Trusler, August 1799': E 702). Of course, not all those in favour of political change agreed where the line between raising political consciousness and encouraging a dangerous enthusiasm was to be found. Barbauld's exchange with Gilbert Wakefield over the propriety of public worship, for instance, in some respects seems to mirror the disagreement between Godwin and Thelwall discussed in Chapter 2. Although writing in a religious rather than political context, Barbauld and Wakefield were equally as exercised as Godwin and Thelwall over the dividing line between democratic sympathies and the delirium of enthusiasm.[65] Wakefield had resigned from a position as an Anglican clergyman and taken up the post of Classics tutor at the Warrington Academy in 1779, but he refused to participate in the public forms of worship practised by the Dissenters there. Although it was dedicated to John Aikin, his *Enquiry into the Expediency and Propriety of Public or Social Worship* (1792) made it clear that he thought even liberal Dissenters still too prone to the enthusiasm of their seventeenth-century forebears. The *Enquiry* contrasted the simplicity of Christ's worship with the 'fervour' of 'all *methodists,* and most *dissenters*'.[66] At certain points in his argument Wakefield simply sounds like a radical Protestant bewailing the continuation of popish superstition in the reformed churches: '*Christians,* who pretend to a love of enquiry and a regard for the scriptures, might be ashamed to defend practices, which rest on no better authority, than the *Popish* trumpery of *traditionary* superstitions.' But he goes beyond this position in his fear that any kind of 'social worship' will infect the purity of prayer with the multitude's 'tumultuous murmurs'.[67] Barbauld's reply was predicated on a contrary view of the necessity and desirability of human sociability: 'prone as men are in

---

[65] In fact both Barbauld and Wakefield were deeply involved in political matters at this time. See Janowitz, 'Amiable and Radical Sociability', 75–6. Her reply to Wakefield explicitly drew analogies between social worship and political meetings. She described forms of religious worship as 'a virtual declaration of the rights of man', because 'invidious distinctions of wealth and titles are not admitted'. See Barbauld, *Works,* ii. 448 and 446.

[66] Wakefield, *An Enquiry into the Expediency and Propriety of Public or Social Worship* rev. edn. (1792), 15 and 14.

[67] Ibid. 18–19.

every other circumstance to associate together, and communicate the electric fire of correspondent feelings', she found it strange that Wakefield should recommend 'unsocial reserve only where those interests are concerned which are confessedly the most important'.[68]

Her pamphlet is not unconcerned about the infectious nature of human sympathy running out of control. Indeed, her idea of public worship sometimes sounds as if its primary concern is containment: 'Public worship has this further advantage over private, that it is better secured against langour on one side, and enthusiasm on the other.' Public worship both encourages the ardour proper to such important matters and provides a crucible for it to be regulated into its proper shape. But at other points in her pamphlet, she seems willing to grant an almost limitless expansion to the ability of human beings to be moved by one another's feelings:

The flame indeed may be kindled by silent musing; but when kindled it must infallibly spread. The devout heart, penetrated with large and affecting views of the immensity of the works of God, the harmony of his laws, and the extent of his beneficence, bursts into loud and vocal expressions of praise and adoration; and from a full and overflowing sensibility, seeks to expand itself to the utmost limits of creation. The mind is forcibly carried out of itself; and, embracing the whole circle of animated existence, calls on all above, around, below, to help to bear the burden of its gratitude. Joy is too brilliant a thing to be confined within our own bosoms; it burnishes all nature, and with its vivid colouring gives a kind of factitious life to objects without sense or motion.[69]

My next chapter will argue that Wordsworth's ability to impart such 'factitious life' was both a source of joy and anxiety to the poet. Here the concern about regulating such enthusiasm into appropriate limits present elsewhere in Barbauld's pamphlet and much of her other work seems to fall away. We have much more of Priestley's sense that excess of fervour is a better risk to take than indifference. To Wakefield passages of this tone and style only confirmed his sense that Dissent had not progressed beyond the enthusiasm of the seventeenth century. He was particularly sharp on Barbauld. Rounding impatiently on the idea of 'devotional taste,' as Priestley had done, Wakefield attacks her for promoting ideas of religion 'that savour of all that is visionary, fanatical, and supersti-

---

[68] Barbauld, *Works*, ii. 419.   [69] Ibid. 421 and 428.

tious'. Her attempts to distinguish between the feeling of sensibility and the passions of the crowd are dismissed. She is indicted among those who have 'transferred religion . . . from the *intellect* and *heart* to *fancy* and the *senses*'.[70] Her plea that the social affections be allowed into religious observance is dismissed as 'extravagant enthusiasm'. No less than the *British Critic*, whose politics he was deeply opposed to, Wakefield sees Barbauld's doctrines as undermining the rational basis of religion and playing to the unstable and evanescent emotions of the crowd: 'The flame of enthusiasm crackles loud, and blazes bright; but soon vanishes into air.'[71] Unlike Priestley, however, Wakefield seems not just opposed to Barbauld's aestheticization of religious feeling, but to the idea of any kind of affect being allowed a place in the context of religious worship. Wakefield may have been particularly dismissive of a female opponent, but in the next section of his pamphlet Priestley is accused of the same lapse:

The *Doctor* like *Mrs. Barbauld*, entertains certain conceits of habitual devotion, which are, to my apprehension at least, romantic and mysterious; intoxicating vapours from the chasm of puritanical fanaticism.[72]

Wakefield admired Priestley's political and philosophical principles, but as with Godwin's commentary on Thelwall, where those principles were being promulgated on the basis of affect, they were deemed to be liable to transmutation into the mere enthusiasm of the crowd. Both Barbauld and Priestley, if in different ways and at different times, no less than Thelwall, were acutely aware of the dangers of ardour developing into enthusiasm, but their faith in sympathy meant that they could see enthusiasm as a lesser evil than the empty formality of superstition, whether of the Church or State. Wakefield was much less sure that there was any difference: they were both simply forms of unreason.

RETIRING FROM ENTHUSIASM?

The relative latitude that Barbauld gives the affections in the early 1790s might be seen as a specific product of the optimism of the

---

[70] A *General Reply to the Arguments against the Enquiry into Public Worship* (1792), 20–1.
[71] Ibid. 21.   [72] Ibid. 26.

early years of the revolutionary decade. By the mid-1790s many Dissenters had retreated from this confidence in the liberating potential of the social sympathies. Anne Janowitz has noted that some relaxed 'passionate radical and internationalist aim of *fraternité* . . . into a more local and familiar idea of friendship'.[73] Keach offers an even more negative account of a 'movement from enthusiastic assertiveness to pessimistic resignation'.[74] The parallel movement in Coleridge's poetry published in dissenting periodicals at the time has already been discussed, but the movement was neither universal nor unequivocal in those circles. Janowitz, for instance, usefully contrasts the responses of John Aikin and Gilbert Wakefield. Aikin wrote to Wakefield just after his release from prison in 1798 inviting him to abandon his political militancy in favour of a more restricted idea of sociability: 'Cease then, my Friend, thy generous hopeless aim . . . And in the soothing voice of friendship drown | The groans and shouts, and triumphs of the world.' Wakefield's reply refuses to back down from his defiance of 'the grim visage of despotic power, | lawless, self-will'd, fierce, merciless, corrupt'.[75] One might be reminded of Judith Thompson's contrast between Coleridge and Thelwall. Certainly the discourse of retirement in the latter remains regretful and still oriented towards an eventual return to the public arena.[76] Barbauld herself comes close to the position of Thelwall. Her 'To Mr. S. T. Coleridge' offers a direct reflection on the dangers of retirement in the context of the disillusionment of the late 1790s. Indeed we might see the poem as entering into a dialogue with Coleridge's 'Reflections on Having Left a Place of Retirement'.

Both Barbauld and Coleridge's poems were originally published in the *Monthly Magazine*, edited by Barbauld's brother John Aikin. Coleridge's poem, as we have seen, extols the engaged virtues of the prison reformer John Howard, but between its two early versions becomes increasingly equivocal about 'Entering into Active Life' (to use the phrase from the original title). Barbauld had praised Howard herself in 'Hymn: Ye are the Salt of the Earth,' another

---

[73] Janowitz, 'Amiable and Radical Sociability', 77.
[74] Keach, 'Barbauld, Romanticism and the Survival of Dissent', 56.
[75] Quoted in Janowitz, 'Amiable and Radical Sociability', 77.
[76] See the discussion of Thelwall and Coleridge's attitudes to retirement in the previous chapter.

poem originally published in the *Monthly*. The hymn represents the political activists of her time as latter-day prophets:

> Your's is the writing on the wall,
> That turns the tyrant pale.
>
> (*BP* 128, ll. 35–6)

Taken together these poems by Barbauld and Coleridge published in the *Monthly* ought to be seen as part of a debate within the dissenting community about the limits of their patriotic enthusiasm. Even several decades later, Barbauld's poetry could still be regarded by a relatively sympathetic reviewer as going too far in its ardour. Her poem 'To the Poor' (129–30), for instance, inflected like her hymn with the language of biblical prophecy was chastised for precisely this failing in the *Literary Gazette*:

Mrs. Barbauld's fiery democracy sometimes carried her almost the length of profanation; witness the following passage in Lines 'To the Poor' which we do not quote, however, without giving their author credit for the utmost benevolence of heart and excellence of intention, though her patriotic enthusiasm ran away with her understanding and disqualified her judgment.[77]

Barbauld's poem to Coleridge administers a gentle chastisement of its own, but for quite different reasons. In place of the idea of enthusiasm as a paradigm-busting force that Barbauld came increasingly to share with Priestley, Coleridge is represented as someone whose imagination is tempted towards conformity and withdrawal.[78]

One might contrast Barbauld's attitude towards Coleridge with the changing nature of her view of Priestley during this period. What in the 1770s seem to have represented a rough and unmannerly enthusiasm in Priestley's zeal, by the 1790s is more often looked upon as a laudable commitment. Her sonnet 'To Dr. Priestley. Dec. 29, 1792', for instance, praises Priestley's 'ample stretch of thought' (*BP* 125, l. 15) that seems able to grasp 'future periods' (l. 16), whereas earlier she had represented such 'stretch' as threatening to snap even her elastic notion of sociability. A review

---

[77] *Literary Gazette*, 24 Sept. 1825, 611. The poem had been written in 1795, but was not published until 1825.

[78] Lisa Vargo usefully situates Barbauld's poem as part of a debate about activism in Unitarian circles, but does not notice the background of the issue in Barbauld's relationship to Priestley. See 'The Case of Anna Laetitia Barbauld's "To Mr C(olerid)ge"', *Charles Lamb Bulletin*, 102 (1998), 55–63.

of Priestley's character in 1803 suggested that she was weighing up the vicissitudes in her own response to the philosopher:

One person . . . may be disposed to laugh at the Birmingham philosopher for the precipitous and unguarded manner in which he has thrown his opinions before the public; for the hearty good will with which he enters into the arena of controversy; for the amusing egotism of a heart that has nothing to hide; for the frankness with which he pours himself out before his readers . . . but there are others who will view with affectionate reverence, the child-like simplicity of an ingenuous. Penetrating, and philosophical spirit, the generous imprudence of an eager champion for truth, who follows her, regardless of consequences, in every track where he entertains the least hope of finding her; and the comparative indifference for personal considerations . . . which has made him neglect those guards and fences within which a more wary combatant would have intrenched himself.[79]

As the tone of the paragraph suggests, Barbauld's response at the time of writing, when Priestley was exiled in the United States, was more inclined to an 'affectionate reverence' for what she could forgive as a form of 'generous imprudence'. Faced with a political and religious establishment that seemed to be asserting the old hierarchies, to the point that they had driven Priestley from his home, Barbauld stresses the heroism of his enthusiasm. Writing in the 1770s, she had been able to imagine an accommodation of Dissent with the Church of England under the rubric of 'liberal sentiments', in 1803 the establishment was looking more and more like a tyranny that had to be opposed with honest indignation.

If Barbauld was forced more and more into retirement by the practical position of Dissenters in a hostile print culture (and, more specifically, the breaking up through death and imprisonment of the circle that surrounded the publisher Joseph Johnson), there is little sign that she either passively accepted this situation or transmuted it into a Romantic idea of a 'higher' freedom. *The Female Speaker* anthology brought out in 1811 may have stressed the importance of regulating the passions, but its inclusion of Shaftesbury's apostrophes kept alive the flame of patriot enthusiasm. One of her selections from Isaac Watts illustrates her continuing commitment to the politics of sympathy and society rather than any idea of retirement as a good in itself:

[79] Barbauld's account was published in the *Norwich Iris*, 24 Dec. 1803. See *BP* 246.

Our souls may be serene in solitude, but not sparkling, though perhaps we are employed in reading the works of the brightest writers. Often has it happened, in free discourse, that new truths are strangely struck out, and the seeds of truth sparkle and blaze through the company, which in calm and silent reading would never have been excited.[80]

The year after she published *The Female Speaker*, Barbauld came before the public for one last time as a poet and patriot, but one adopting a more detached and disinterested voice than the 'sparkle and blaze' of patriot enthusiasm.

Barbauld's *Eighteen Hundred and Eleven* is a very slippery poem. Lucy Newlyn has spoken, for instance, of its 'generic unclassifiabil-ity'.[81] In terms of content, it offers a prophetic vision of the decline of the British Empire and the emigration of the spirit of liberty to America (an idea that had been current at least since the American War of Independence). Yet descriptions of the poem both now and in the responses of Barbauld's contemporaries often seem undecided as to whether it ought to be regarded as a prophecy or a satire. Croker's infamous attack on the poem, for instance, barely mentions its generic relation to prophecy, or, perhaps even more strangely, the known history of Barbauld's prophetic interventions in public debates in the 1790s. The more sympathetic *Monthly Review* did begin by noting its prophetic content: 'By long prescrip-tive right, poets are prophets as well as satirists, and, while they lash the vices and follies of the present generation, can take a glance at futurity and announce things that will be "hereafter" '; but it is a comment about the casting of satire in terms of a prediction of the future, rather than the poem's style as such, and the review has little to say about the specific form of Barbauld's 'prophetic warn-ings'.[82] Perhaps one should not be surprised about the lack of seri-ous comment on Barbauld's career as prophet, since the poem certainly has less of the spirit or style of Old Testament prophecies than her poetry or prose works of the early 1790s. Although at cer-tain key points it personifies and addresses Britain and London as the Book of Jeremiah does Jerusalem, one could only very loosely

[80] See 'On Conversation from Watts', in *The Female Speaker*, 79–80.

[81] Newlyn, *Reading, Writing, and Romanticism*, 168.

[82] See *Monthly Review*, 67 (1812), 428–9. The more hostile *Anti-Jacobin Review*, 42 (1812), 209 also mentioned Barbauld's role as prophet, but only as a dismissive aside: 'Mrs B. is a prophet; and to prophets it is given to penetrate the veil of futu-rity'; it comments on her 'prediction of the decline of British commercial power'.

describe the poem as a 'jeremiad'.[83] Most critics usually start by thinking of the poem in terms of Juvenalian satire. Reviews by Barbauld's contemporaries pointed out the parallels with Samuel Johnson's imitation of Juvenal's third satire in 'London'.[84] Certainly what Maggie Favretti calls the 'skilfully phrased heroic couplets' of Barbauld's poem do not suggest the irregularity and metaphorical obscurity strongly associated with biblical style (Blake's 'London' rather than Johnson's is a more obvious translation of Lowth's theories on prophetic poetry into contemporary poetic form).[85] Coleridge's 'Religious Musings' moves further in this direction than Barbauld's poem, although not without equivocations of its own. Both Coleridge and Barbauld offer an account of the progress of liberty and enlightenment in Britain. Both were oriented towards a politically reformist view of history, foregrounding names such as Milton and Priestley, a point that Barbauld's reviewers were quick to make. For the pre-millenialist vision of Coleridge's poem, these men appear as agents of a divine will working itself out in history (in 1795–6, of course, when 'Religious Musings' was written, it was easier to see history as the positive expression of divine will for a reform-minded Dissenter). No less than John Howard in Barbauld's hymn, they are latter-day prophets, but *Eighteen Hundred and Eleven* is much less biblical in its treatment of these heroes of reform than Coleridge's poem or Barbauld's own work from the 1790s. Barbauld stresses their 'Roman virtue' (*BP* 156, l. 148) rather than their patriot enthusiasm, that is, their disinterested concern for their country rather than their zeal. Patriot enthusiasm was strongly associated with Akenside's name when it came to poetry, and if her stately couplets do not call to mind a biblical style, nor do they seem influenced by the flexible blank verse of his 'heady blend of patriot zeal and poetic enthusiasm'.[86] Blank verse was associated with the poetics of religious and political liberty, liberated as it was, in Blake's words, from 'the modern bondage of Rhyming', and Barbauld had exploited the connection herself to considerable effect in poems such as 'Corsica' and 'A Summer Evening's Meditation'.

---

[83] The description is Anne K. Mellor's, see her 'The Female Poet and the Poetess: Two Traditions of British Women's Poetry, 1780–1830', in Armstrong and Blain (eds.), *Women's Poetry in the Enlightenment*, 91.

[84] Mellor makes this point, ibid. Comparison between Barbauld's poem was also made by contemporaries, see *Universal Magazine*, 17 (1812), 217.

[85] Favretti, 'The Politics of Vision', 99.   [86] Meehan, *Poetics of Liberty*, 54.

For all that it is a vision of futurity, *Eighteen Hundred and Eleven* attempts little of the zeal of the former or the 'unworlding' effects of the latter. Its description of London in ruins does not attempt a vision from Eternity. There is a restraint and even a certain detachment for most of the poem that helps explain why some reviewers described it as a satire and stressed its coldness.

This point should not be exaggerated. Her poetry and prose over the previous decades had demonstrated that both the righteous indignation of prophetic register and the ardour of patriot enthusiasm were well within her grasp as a writer when she chose. There are points in *Eighteen Hundred and Eleven* where the rhythm does intensify and a more apocalyptic tone emerges:

> There walks a Spirit[87] o'er the peopled earth,
> Secret his progress is, unknown his birth;
> Moody and viewless as the changing wind,
> No force arrests his foot, no chains can bind.
>
> (*BP* 158, ll. 215–18)

Yet I am not sure that much else in the poem represents Barbauld 'assuming the mantle of an Old Testament prophet'.[88] The powerful apostrophes and exhortations of her poetry and prose of the early 1790s quickly, as we have seen, provoked politically hostile reviewers to ridicule her as the histrionic figure of female prophecy. *Eighteen Hundred and Eleven* is more cautious in this regard than the prose of the 1790s. If Barbauld eschewed the rhetorical possibilities of prophecy and patriotic enthusiasm for the most part in her poem, however, she was not to escape censure for what was her most widely reviewed poem. Not surprisingly, the conservative press attacked Barbauld's poem as an act of literary treason at a time of war, but for the most part these reviewers did not chastise her as a 'Deborah', nor even as someone whose 'patriotic enthusiasm ran away with her understanding and disqualified her judgment'. Croker's infamous attack in the *Quarterly* stressed instead the coldness and regularity of her poem rather than its ardour.[89]

---

[87] One might compare this line to Barbauld's description of a time when 'the genius of Philosophy begins walking abroad' in *Sins of the Government, Sins of the Nation*. The difference is the unequivocal prophetic mode of the latter passage (it comes directly after the exhortation of her readers to look at 'the signs of the times') compared to the more 'disinterested' mode of *Eighteen Hundred and Eleven*.

[88] Mellor, 'The Female Poet', 92.

[89] See the *Quarterly Review*, 7 (1812), 309–13.

The *Eclectic* suggested there was something unfeeling and 'unfilial' about such a poem at a time of war: 'It seems hardly possible that such a poem as this could have been produced, without the concurrence of a peculiarly frigid temperament,—with a system of speculative opinions which seem contrived to damp every glowing sentiment,—and the spirit of that political party, which cherishes no sympathy with the honour and happiness of England.'[90] These reviews perpetuate Burke's language in their representation of Unitarianism as a frozen zone. He had been able to conflate ideas of Dissent as simultaneously overly warm and too frigid. Although Barbauld was accused of too much warmth by political opponents both before and after 1812, it is the charge of frigidity that is the dominant target in the reviews of *Eighteen Hundred and Eleven*. In relation to Barbauld here the strategy suggests that she is unwomanly in her lack of specifically domestic feeling. The poem displayed a species of grandeur, suggested the *Eclectic*; 'it has a vigour and majesty', that potentially places it in the line of Akenside's patriotic enthusiasm, but uses the designation to reinforce its perception of the lack of feminine softness in the poem.[91] The criticism recalls Woodfall's discussion of 'Corsica' and his concern that her poetry did not display the softer emotions. Croker's review deploys similar assumptions to more damagingly hostile effect.

One might say that *Eighteen Hundred and Eleven* was caught in the same discourse of sensibility—now turned to an explicitly conservative political agenda, as it had been in the hands of Burke—that she herself had sometimes expounded. Burke had suggested the self-sufficiency of dissenting controversialism was unfeeling in its disregard for tradition, manners, and the domestic ties. Reviewers of *Eighteen Hundred and Eleven* similarly disapprobated Barbauld for her privileging of speculative opinions and stoical disinterestedness over the ties of hearth and home at a time of war, and made it clear that this crime was particularly heinous for one of her sex. Yet they could scarcely attack this controlled and measured poem for what could be considered an unworldly ardour either of passion or speculation. Barbauld had eschewed the enthusiasm that she had shown herself capable of articulating in favour of a more subdued political intervention at a time of national despair. Righteous indignation, she may have judged, would have been inappropriate at such a juncture, and anyway would have enabled reviewers to parody her as the hysterical prophetess. As it was, Barbauld's very detachment seems to have been understood as a violation of the assumptions of gender in relation to genre. Maggie Favretti has put the matter adroitly: 'The very "distinterested" composure and vision necessary in a gentleman who could claim to interpret the "interests of Europe" was somehow threatening, emerging as it was from the pen of an old woman.'[92] Barbauld's detachment suggested that she had the elevated prospect that was seen to be the particular domain of the gentleman, and in the discourse of civic humanism the basis of his claim to be able to judge the best interests of his society. If during the eighteenth century there was a great deal of confusion about exactly who in a commercial society could claim this sort of disinterestedness, it was unlikely to be granted to a woman. Hannah More, as Favretti notes, had quite specifically pointed out that women did not have access to 'that wider range of distant prospects which he who stands on a loftier eminence commands'. Shaftesbury's great apostrophes to freedom are predicated on an access to this kind of prospect.[93] The supposed distinterestedness given concrete form by his position as an aristocratic landowner is the social guarantee that stands behind his enthusiasm; Shaftesbury's 'ascent' takes off from a prospect that he literally owns. His apostrophes were included in the *Female Speaker* anthology that was published just a year before *Eighteen Hundred and Eleven*. Barbauld's taste for them is reflected in her love of Akenside, but *Eighteen Hundred and Eleven* generally eschews such enthusiasm to emphasize instead the 'equal wide survey' that must precede it in classical republican thought. Even so, for Croker and Barbauld's other critics this measure of control was itself unnatural. It is as if Croker would have been happier to have encountered the more predictable stereotype of the hysterical prophetess. Joanna Southcott would have made an easy contemporary parallel for

[92] Favretti, 'The Politics of Vision', 108.
[93] More's *Strictures on the Modern System of Education*, quoted ibid. 102. See John Barrell's work for the best exploration of how the aristocratic idea of disinterestedness evolved to meet the situation of a commercial society; for instance, *English Literature in History 1730–1780: 'An Equal Wide Survey'* (Hutchinson, 1983) and 'The Public Prospect and the Private View: The Politics of Taste in Eighteenth-Century Britain' in his *The Birth of Pandora and the Division of Knowledge* (Basingstoke: Macmillan, 1992). Favretti reads Barbauld's poem as a critique of the lack of genuine disinterested public spiritedness in such a society.

satire. Woodfall had suggested that the more rapturous poetry of 'Corsica' ignored the fact that 'there is a sex in minds as well as in bodies . . . A woman is as perfect in her kind as a man: she appears inferior only when she quits her station, and aims at excellence out of her province.'[94] Whatever register such a political intervention adopted, enthusiastic or disinterested, it was going to be viewed as a crime against the sexed nature of writing.

Most contemporary criticism dealing with Barbauld has represented her as an advocate of female sensibility. Some critics have argued that this advocacy often pushes against ideas that excluded the affections from the public sphere. Judgements about these matters need to acknowledge that she was more than capable of the patriot zeal associated with Akenside, the religious sublime of Young, and the righteous indignation of biblical prophecy. All three kinds of writing were and perhaps still are associated with masculine 'vigour', but there is a danger that we essentialize such judgements if we persist in seeing Barbauld as primarily a creature of sensibility rather than someone also closely involved with the developing poetics of enthusiasm. Male writers could not simply assume their rights to the religious or political sublime; it was always haunted with the spectre of a degeneration into another kind of enthusiasm altogether. Barbauld's friend and colleague Joseph Priestley's prose was always subject to this criticism, but so also were poets such as Akenside when they were deemed not to have sufficiently regulated their ardour into proper poetic form. Such judgements about boundaries depended in part on who was doing the judging. Patriot zeal was always going to look like mere enthusiasm to someone such as Samuel Johnson, especially when expressed in the language of affect that Shaftesbury passed to Akenside. If the person being judged were a Dissenter, he was likely to be granted even less latitude; if the writer were a Dissenter and a woman, even less; but the catch for Barbauld was that regulation itself was often felt to be largely beyond a woman writer. Reviewers expected from women neither the vigour of enthusiasm nor the coolness of detachment, but a response that was feeling but submissive and 'melting'. 'Softness' rather than vigour or control were expected. One may praise Barbauld's ability to work within and challenge these expectations over a long and productive career,

94 *Monthly Review*, 48 (1773), 137.

but ultimately she was caught in this trap. Even her own niece ended up having to present her as a champion of domestic virtues and children's literature. What the *Westminster Magazine* had once believed to be a genius exceeding 'the most vigorous of our poets' became 'a legacy for young ladies'. The latter was conceived of as a safe and innocuous haven from the kind of religious and political controversy that Barbauld had excelled at for several decades.[95]

---

[95] William Keach points out that the title of Lucy Aikin's anthology of Barbauld's writing, *A Legacy for Young Ladies*, had already become 'the most familiar way of representing her to early nineteenth-century readers', 'Barbauld, Romanticism and the Survival of Dissent', 45.

CHAPTER FIVE

Wordsworth's Chastened Enthusiasm

SHAUN IRLAM REPRESENTS Wordsworth Preface to *Lyrical Ballads* as the terminal point in the eighteenth century's rehabilitation of enthusiasm:

Today, most readers still associate poetry with the expression of emotion. The continued currency of Wordsworth's phrase 'spontaneous overflow of powerful feeling' indicates how much we continue to inhabit a post-Romantic ethos of sentiment. But the position of sentiment in poetry hasn't always been secure.[1]

The cultural significance of Wordsworth's role in the process can hardly be overestimated, but his own enthusiasm was far from secure, despite the century of rehabilitation Irlam charts in its earlier stages. If within the aesthetic sphere enthusiasm was desired as the basis of poetic inspiration, it was also disavowed where it seemed to lead to the 'distraction' associated with Methodism and other popular forms of religion. Francis Jeffrey could still see in Wordsworth's *Excursion* (1814) too much of 'the mystical verbiage of the methodist pulpit'.[2] Nor was Wordsworth himself without anxieties on this score. His disavowal of 'extraordinary calls' in *The Prelude* (XIII. 101) should remind us of the role of this phrase in Wesley's conflict with the Bishop of Exeter. No less than Wesley, Wordsworth was beset with the problem of distinguishing his transports from the illapses of vulgar enthusiasm. His poetry frequently raises the spectre of himself as 'A solitary, who with vain conceits | Had been inspired, and walked about in dreams' (*Prelude 1805*,

---

[1] Shaun Irlam, *Elations: The Poetics of Enthusiasm in Eighteenth-Century Britain* (Stanford, Calif.: Stanford University Press, 1999), 239.

[2] See Jeffrey's review of *The Excursion* in *Edinburgh Review*, 24 (Nov. 1814), 1–30: 3, and also Richard E. Brantley, *Wordsworth's 'Natural Methodism'* (New Haven: Yale University Press, 1975), 8.

VIII. 809–10). The ability to grant a 'factitious life', as Barbauld put it, to external nature is constantly being subjected to disciplinary regulation within Wordsworth's writing.

No doubt Wordsworth does view enthusiasm as a healing influx of passion in his writing, but this therapeutic sense of the word and its associations is always haunted by a pathological other. My account of the development of a poetics of enthusiasm is closer to the double-bind described by David Riede:

> Wordsworth seeks to anchor the imagination in actualities outside the self—in nature and in human society—but ultimately he wants the imagination to transcend both nature and society, though he must struggle with the fear that the unanchored imagination may be akin to madness.[3]

Part of the purpose of this chapter is to suggest that terms such as Riede's 'madness' might productively be replaced with the more nuanced idea of 'enthusiasm' to give us a greater understanding of the tensions in Wordsworth's poetry. Riede's double bind is a familiar aspect of the discourse of regulation outlined in Part I. Enthusiasm's unworlding power was widely regarded as having a restorative potential. Shaftesbury and a long line of thinkers identified it with the ability to reach beyond or even annihilate (in Hartley's vocabulary) the baser self, but the still dominant pejorative sense of the term conjured the pathological loss of the self in the object of sympathy. Wordsworth's need for 'the imagination to transcend both nature and society' articulates a desire for the imagination to be more than the enthusiasm of the senses. Coleridge came to believe that the philosophy of Hartley and Priestley was only a latter-day variant of such enthusiasm, but he also feared that Wordsworth was particularly inclined towards this error. In his 1803 notebook Coleridge denounced Wordsworth's tendency 'always to look at the superficies of Objects for the purpose of taking Delight in their Beauty, & sympathy with their real or imagined Life' (*Notebooks*, i. 1616). Later still Coleridge wanted to distance Wordsworth's poetic mission from 'compounding a mind out of the senses' (21 July 1832: *TT* i. 307). Anchoring the Imagination in a

---

[3] David G. Riede, *Oracles and Hierophants: Constructions of Romantic Authority* (Ithaca, NY: Cornell University Press, 1991), 96. See also the excellent discussion of Wordsworth's ambivalent relationship to poetic enthusiasm and its proximity to features of crowd psychology in Timothy Clark, *The Theory of Inspiration: Composition as a Crisis of Subjectivity in Romantic and Post-Romantic Writing* (Manchester: Manchester University Press, 1997), 92–114.

distinct spiritual order or 'mind' was one kind of disciplinary solution to this danger:

> And so the deep enthusiastic joy.
> The rapture of the hallelujah sent
> From all that breathes and is, was chastened, stemmed,
> And balanced by a reason which indeed
> Is reason, duty and pathetic truth
>
> (*Prelude 1805*, XIII. 261–5)

Where 'mind' became abstracted from 'reason' and 'duty', however, it too could seem to be leading into a dangerous unworlding neglectful of what Parr called 'real social affections'. Seeing 'into the life of things' ('Tintern Abbey': *LB*, l. 49) had to be distinguished from what both Burke and Parr thought of as the *transparence* of revolutionary ideology. They took the latter to be a species of 'enthusiasm' in this respect, and Wordsworth used the word and its associated vocabulary to describe his own revolutionary youth in *The Prelude*. The prophetic impulse retrieved from this youthful excess had to present itself as properly regulated if it were to be mistaken for a latter-day variant of 'the mystical verbiage of the methodist pulpit'.

The Prelude is an extended attempt to demonstrate that a continuity of subjectivity could survive and benefit from the transports of enthusiasm and remain grounded in the world without dissolving into it. Wordsworth's qualifications as a writer are advanced on the basis of his having negotiated or worked a way through these dangerous waters.[4] In this respect the emphasis on work and preparation in Wordsworth is commensurate with his privileging of the visionary over the visible (to use William Galperin's distinction) after the example of Coleridge. The visible world of the senses pulled the unworldliness of enthusiasm back down to earth, providing it with the ballast of things as they are; on the other hand, the unworlding visionary ideal prevented genuine poetic enthusiasm becoming confused with the bodily passions: both together they served to emphasize the disciplined nature of Wordsworth's visionary gleam. Nevertheless, if Wordsworth strives to present himself in this mediated light in *The Prelude* and elsewhere, he is also always

---

[4] See Clifford Siskin, *The Work of Writing: Literature and Social Change in Britain 1700–1830* (Baltimore: Johns Hopkins University Press, 1998), especially 109–18.

involved in the production of the alternative that he consciously works upon in order to distinguish his true self. 'Sensible impressions' (*Prelude 1805*, XIII. 103), for instance, become what Wordsworth constantly produces in order to identify his own more mindful enthusiasm that works upon them, but the process continually raises the question scouted by the philosophers of the moral sense in the eighteenth century, that is, whether the moral sense could be isolated from what Shaftesbury called 'the combustible matters . . . within' (*Characteristics*, 23).

ENTHUSIASM AND TASTE IN WORDSWORTH'S PROSE

That Wordsworth was involved in the rehabilitation of enthusiasm discussed by Irlam and others is not seriously in doubt. My emphasis on the disciplinary aspect of Wordsworth's poetry is not meant to obscure its commitment to a poetics of affect. The 1802 version of the 'Preface' to the *Lyrical Ballads* makes it quite clear that for Wordsworth enthusiasm was a necessary condition of poetic composition:

What is a Poet? To whom does he address himself? And what language is to be expected from him?—He is a man speaking to men: a man, it is true, endowed with more lively sensibility, more enthusiasm and tenderness, who has greater knowledge of human nature, and a more comprehensive soul . . . whence, and from practice, he has acquired a greater readiness and power in expressing what he thinks and feels, and especially those thoughts and feelings which, by his own choice, or from the structure of his own mind, arise in him without immediate external excitement. (*WP* i. 138)

Reading this passage in isolation one might be forgiven for thinking with Irlam that a Romantic aesthetic has emerged fully formed here and entirely comfortable about a poetic 'enthusiasm' derived from self-generated thoughts and feelings. Those thoughts and feelings, however, we are assured have been made safe by 'practice'. Just as for Shaftesbury the combustible matter of enthusiasm could be made safe by practices of tasteful self-division, so too in Wordsworth poetic enthusiasm is the product of a process of regulation. Wordsworth's 'Essay, Supplementary to the Preface' of 1815 described Shaftesbury as 'at present unjustly depreciated' (*WP* iii. 72). Both the idea of poetry as an enthusiasm that could perceive the

218 The Poetics of Enthusiasm

higher harmony of nature and the discourse of regulation-within that permeates the Preface would have been familiar to Wordsworth either directly from *Characteristics*, which he had almost certainly read by 1785, or from the 'Shaftesbury school of poets', such as Mark Akenside and James Thomson, whom he also greatly admired.[5] Shaftesbury and Akenside share a sense that contemplating the harmony of nature was a direct route to the perception of a higher order in the universe. In this respect Coleridge's fears about Wordsworth's sensuous enthusiasm should be considered in tandem with his belief that Thelwall's admiration for Shaftesbury needed to be supplemented with a love of Christ. For Coleridge without the intervention of Christianity the tradition of Shaftesbury offered no guide to the difference between the senses and the spirit. Wordsworth's poetry, like Shaftesbury's philosophy, has relatively speaking more faith in the ability of 'the Spirits of the Mind' (*PB* [MS 1 and 2] 135, l. 1166) to perceive a higher order in nature without the aid of supernatural intervention. If there is an emphasis on regulation in Wordsworth, it is even quite late in his career an internal process rather than the Christian power out of the self that both Burke and Coleridge considered necessary.

Meditation on enthusiasm, a process of self-division, was as fundamental to Wordsworth's idea of poetic enthusiasm as it was to Shaftesbury and his followers:

For all good poetry is the spontaneous overflow of powerful feelings; but though this be true, Poems to which any value can be attached, were never produced on any variety of subjects but by a man who being possessed of more than usual organic sensibility had also thought long and deeply. For our continued influxes of feeling are modified and directed by our thoughts, which are indeed the representatives of all our past feelings; and as by contemplating the relation of these general representatives to each other, we discover what is really important to men, so by the repetition and continuance of this act feelings connected with important subjects will be nourished, till at length, if we be originally possessed of much organic sensibility, such habits of mind will be produced that by obeying blindly

---

[5] See *WP* iii. 72–3, but the 'Essay' strangely does not mention Akenside. For the debt to Akenside, see Mary Jacobus, *Tradition and Experiment in Wordsworth's Lyrical Ballads (1798)* (Oxford: Oxford University Press, 1976), especially 51–8 and 111–12; and Duncan Wu, *Wordsworth's Reading 1770–99* (Cambridge: Cambridge University Press, 1993), 1–2. Wu finds 'borrowings throughout Wordsworth's juvenile verse', and notes that he would have had a copy of Barbauld's edition of *The Pleasures of Imagination* to hand after August 1795 when Dorothy was given one.

and mechanically the impulses of those habits we shall describe objects and utter sentiments of such a nature and in such connection with each other, that the understanding of the being to whom we address ourselves, if he be in a healthful state of association, must necessarily be in some degree enlightened, his taste exalted, and his affections ameliorated. (*WP* i. 126)

Later on in the Preface, of course, Wordsworth returns to the idea of spontaneous outpourings of feeling: 'I have said that Poetry is the spontaneous overflow of powerful feelings: it takes its origin from emotion recollected in tranquility' (i. 148). The idea of recollection suggests not just remembering, but also the bringing together of what has been broken up, that is, the kind of gathering together of the self implied in Shaftesbury's soliloquies.[6] The ecstasies of enthusiasm implied by the spontaneous overthrow of powerful feeling have to invigorate a reconstituted subjectivity if they are to have any value for Wordsworth. The origin of poetic composition is in the restorative bringing together of what passion has momentarily threatened to blow asunder. Elevation is both a necessary condition and a desired effect of poetry for Wordsworth, but if the invigoration of the subject by passion leads to its dissolution what was meant to restore has destroyed the patient. Wordsworth's restorative enthusiasm is always in tension with a fear of the consequences of the loss of the self. Book XIII of *The Prelude* invokes 'mind' as a prior ordering principle of identity that must control and survive the ecstasies of the poet. This need to regulate what transports and restores becomes a structural principle in *The Prelude* in the relations between the spots of time and the ongoing sense of Wordsworth's organic personality.

---

[6] For a detailed examination of Shaftesbury's soliloquy as a poetics, see Robert Marsh, 'Shaftesbury's Theory of Poetry: The Importance of the "Inward Colloquy" ', *ELH* 28 (1961), 54–69. Wu, *Wordsworth's Reading*, 36–7, suggests that Wordsworth had almost certainly encountered Shaftesbury by 1785. There is a great deal of literature on Shaftesbury and Wordsworth. Two relatively recent studies are Michael Meehan, *Liberty and Poetics in Eighteenth Century England* (Beckenham: Croom Helm, 1986) and Chris Jones, *Radical Sensibility: Literature and Ideas in the 1790s* (Routledge, 1993). Meehan, 151, takes the view that although 'cultivation of ideas on the relationship between political freedom and creative power had been assiduous in the century following the publication of Shaftesbury's *Characteristics*, . . . it was only really in Wordsworth's writings that an adequate response is to be found to the fullest range of his investigations'. For Jones on Shaftesbury's influence, see n. 8 below, but he has little to say about the mature poetry in relation to this matter. The view taken in this chapter is that Wordsworth's mature poetry perpetuates and even intensifies some of Shaftesbury's anxieties about granting too much liberty to enthusiasm.

Returning to the account of this process given in the Preface, Barbara Johnson has pointed out that one of the strange features of the long passage quoted above is its 'use of the word "mechanical"— which has been the name of a negative value everywhere else in the preface—as the height of poeticity'.[7] She sees this as a sign of the struggle and ultimate failure of the Preface to produce the distinction it needs between natural and unnatural passion. 'Mechanical' was a word strongly associated with both the enthusiasm of the tub preacher and increasingly for Coleridge with the associationism of Hartley. For Swift the mechanical operation of the spirit had been part of the instinctual spasming of unregulated enthusiasm that could not differentiate the senses from divine inspiration. For Coleridge it became the mindless 'delirium' of consciousness proposed by Hartley's model of the mind. Here in this passage from Wordsworth's Preface, however, the word is provided with a positive sense by the proximity of 'habit'. Rather than the distracted or mindless response to external stimuli or internal passions, 'mechanically' here denotes a practice of working upon one's emotions that has become 'habitual' and so a second nature in Shaftesbury's sense. The confusion identified by Johnson speaks to a troubling question at the heart of the regulatory discourse on enthusiasm: how far is the regulatory principle different from the combustible matter that it is meant to be disciplining? Wordsworth, like Shaftesbury, gives 'taste' a key role in determining this question.

Chris Jones points out that in Wordsworth's hands these disciplinary practices are 'expanded beyond Shaftesbury's limited formulations into the egalitarian sympathy of radical sensibility'.[8] Comparatively speaking there is a democratic aspect to Wordsworth's Preface that later frustrated Coleridge in the implication that these regulatory habits are open to anyone 'of much organic sensibility' to acquire, but these egalitarian inflections quickly become entangled in the thornier issue of 'taste'. No less than Shaftesbury, Wordsworth believed '*accurate* taste in Poetry and in all the other arts, as Sir Joshua Reynolds has observed, is an

---

[7] Barbara Johnson, *A World of Difference* (Baltimore: Johns Hopkins University Press, 1987), 94.

[8] Jones, *Radical Sensibility*, 199. Jones goes on to admit that Shaftesbury may only be an ultimate source of these aspects of Wordsworth's writing. Among possible mediators, of course, are Akenside (see n. 5 above). See n. 6 above for more detail on Wordsworth and Shaftesbury.

acquired talent, which can only be produced by thought and a long continued intercourse with the best models of composition' (*WP* i. 157). Of course, reflecting the developments of almost a century, Wordsworth's version of taste *is* relatively democratic compared to the aristocratic Shaftesbury's. Where the latter is committed to a narrow classical canon, Wordsworth sees a reading in the '*elder* writers' of the vernacular tradition as a proper education. This development, however, should not obscure the fact that for both writers only a certain kind of cultural capital can form a basis for the regulation of enthusiasm. Indeed Wordsworth's 'Essay, Supplementary to the Preface' seems to suggest that Shaftesbury was correct to set little store in the English tradition at the beginning of the eighteenth century, as if the vernacular muse had not yet developed the regulatory mechanisms for dealing with enthusiasm Shaftesbury found in the ancients (*WP* iii. 72). The implication is that only later has a properly regulated tradition of poetic enthusiasm slowly emerged (to find its fulfilment in Wordsworth himself, who will pass it on to his readers). True, Wordsworth does there champion an idea of taste as active rather than passive, but his comments also imply that few readers can manage 'the exertion of a co-operating *power*' (*WP* iii. 81). The difficulty facing the poet is invigorating and inspiriting the reader through language, 'a thing subject to endless fluctuations and arbitrary associations' (*WP* iii. 82). Earlier in the supplementary essay, Wordsworth had identified the similarity between religion and poetry and their shared problems in their reliance of 'sensuous incarnation' (iii. 65). This sensuous form, he implies, obscures and confuses the grand conceptions of poetry even as it gives them life. To find a way through these associations requires a reader with the energy of mind to perceive there is 'an enthusiastic, as well as an ordinary, sorrow' (82). 'Enthusiastic' here seems to refer to the deeper kind of sensitivity that Coleridge came to associate with the word in the early 1810s; it is precisely not an openness to the diversity of associations available to any reader, as the attack on popular responses to poetry that follows makes clear. Indeed the essay as a whole recommends itself to those 'who, being enthusiastic, are, at the same time, modest and ingenious' (*WP* iii. 63). Popular taste, Wordsworth suggests, is too readily won over by works 'such as startle the world into attention by their audacity and extravagance' (83). As in Coleridge's idea of fanaticism, the enthusiasm of the crowd, Wordsworth implies, neither modest nor ingenious, simply swarms around what is vivid. This enthusiasm does not have the mental discipline, the true 'corresponding energy' (*WP* iii. 82), to find sympathy in the deepest conceptions of an author. These last he claims 'are most naturally and most fitly conceived in solitude, so can they not be brought forth in the midst of plaudits, without some violation of their sanctity' (83). The solitary poet requires the solitary reader if the grandeur of his conceptions are to survive. Strangely enough, what had seemed like a statement of liberty for the reader, a validation of 'energy of mind' in the reception of poetry, turns out to be a form of disciplining that requires a direct but carefully regulated contact between the writer and reader insulated from the crowded social space of the reading public.

'FACTITIOUS LIFE' AND MORAL ENTHUSIASM

The poems that were gathered together in *Lyrical Ballads* are to some extent a collection of case studies of characters unable to regulate their enthusiasm fully for themselves. Although their passions allow them to animate the universe with what Barbauld called 'factitious life' and experience the dim awakenings of the genuine moral sense, they cannot bring off the meditative discipline that Wordsworth himself lays full claim to in poems such as 'Tintern Abbey' and later *The Prelude*. The ballads seem to know more than the characters that inhabit them, even if the polite observer or narrator who appears in some of them (not to be confused with Wordsworth himself) is often educated by the raw enthusiasm he encounters there. One of the most detailed accounts of the awakening of enthusiasm in such a character comes in *Peter Bell*, a poem written for but not actually included in the collection, and not published finally until 1819. Alan Bewell suggests that the poem does show Peter finally providing a regulated form for his enthusiasm: 'Wordsworth attempts to show how, through a discipline of imagination, Peter (and, by extension, his class) can be made a useful member of society, one who does "that which is lawful and is right".'[9] Explicitly written against the supernaturalism of Coleridge, Wordsworth's purpose is to show that 'the Spirits of the mind' could themselves provide the basis of a moral universe with-

[9] Alan Bewell, *Wordsworth and the Enlightenment: Nature, Man, and Society in the Experimental Poetry* (New Haven: Yale University Press, 1989), 118.

out the aid of any external spiritual agencies.[10] Yet there is more hesitancy about the poem than Bewell's description allows, perhaps partly because its materials were drawn from the kind of Methodist conversion narrative that was strongly associated with the pathology of religious enthusiasm. There is a satirical aspect to the poem that sits uneasily with the idea of the poem as a serious study in the psychology of conversion. Moreover, Peter does not exactly regulate the spirits of his mind himself; he does not have the talents of the poet described in Wordsworth's Preface to the *Lyrical Ballads*, and at a key point a mind in danger of descending into delirium is rescued by the indirect intervention of a Methodist minister:

> 'Repent! repent,' he cries aloud,
> 'God is a God of mercy,—strive
> To love him then with all your might;
> Do that which lawful is and right
> And save your souls alive.
>
> My friends! My brethren, though you've gone
> Through paths of wickedness and woe
> After the Babylonian harlot,
> And though your sins be red as scarlet
> They shall be white as snow.'
>
> Just as he pass'd the door these words
> Did plainly come to Peter's ears,
> And they such joyful tidings were
> The joy was more than he could bear;
> He melted into tears.—

> (*PB* [MS 2 and 3] 1196–210)

Wordsworth's attitude to Methodism was as ambivalent as Southey's. He was quite capable of seeing it as a dangerous encouragement to religious enthusiasm among those who could not control their passions once they were enflamed: 'With the Methodists on one side, and the Catholics on the other, what is to become of the poor Church and people of England, to both of which I am most tenderly attached' (*MY* i. 313). At other times, such as in his remarks about *Peter Bell* made to Isabella Fenwick, he seems to have seen the movement as both awakening and regulating the moral sense of the lower classes:

[10] See 'To Robert Southey' in *PB* 41 and note Bewell's discussion in *Wordsworth and the Enlightenment*, 115–19.

The worship of the Methodists or Ranters is often heard during the stillness of the summer evening in the country with affecting accompaniments of rural beauty. In both the psalmody of the voice of the preacher there is, not unfrequently, much solemnity likely to impress the feelings of the rudest characters under favourable circumstances.[11]

'Impress' is an interesting word in this context. For it brings with it a sense of arousal, but also containment. Rude characters such as Peter Bell need to have their moral sense aroused, but it must also be impressed upon them (lest it run into a form of indulgence or religious enthusiasm in its most negative sense). The need for the passions to be involved in the moral life is something that seems to escape the purview of the solid Anglicans—squire and clergyman— who provide the poem's narrator with his audience in the frame narrative. Wordsworth would have agreed with Wilberforce, to whom he sent a gift of the 1800 *Lyrical Ballads*, on the need for 'a considerable degree of fervour and animation' in any religion designed to appeal to the lower classes. For both men, however, these religious passions no less than other kinds had to be restrained 'within due bounds'.[12] That Peter does not actually join the Methodists may be significant in this respect. The minister rouses his moral imagination, but his company is not seen as appropriate for the final form of Peter's new consciousness, perhaps because Wordsworth still had doubts about its disciplinary effectiveness. What is left unclear by the poem is where the limits to Peter's enthusiasm lie given that he has neither the leisure nor education to exercise 'taste' in the terms set out by Wordsworth's prose. The light satire on the Anglican establishment in the frame narrative should not distract us from the poem's concerns about such bounds. For not only are the stolid local worthies parodied, but also the poet himself is treated as an object of mild satire:

> Sure in the breast of full-grown poet
> So faint a heart was ne'er before.
> Come to the poets' wild delights;
> I have ten thousand lovely sights,
> Ten thousand sights in store.

(PB [MS 2 and 3] 76–80)

[11] Quoted in *The Poetical Works of William Wordsworth*, ed. E. de Selincourt, 2nd edn. (Oxford: Oxford University Press, 1952), ii. 527.
[12] Wilberforce, *A Practical View*, quoted Bewell, *Wordsworth and the Enlightenment*, 117.

No less than for Peter, there is a question of exactly how these 'wild delights' are translated into an appropriately regulated form by a poem that seems deeply uncertain about itself. It is a question that haunts *The Prelude* in terms of the relationship between the poet's enthusiasm for nature and the more Coleridgean perception of the philosophical mind. The troubling parallel between the poet and Peter in terms of 'extraordinary calls' may be one reason why Wordsworth delayed publishing the poem for so long. They opened the possibility of readers missing the distinction between Wordsworth's sense of the poet's vocation and 'the mystical verbiage of the methodist pulpit'. As late as 1831 Wordsworth himself confessed 'I am as much Peter Bell as ever' (*LY* ii. 439).

When he did finally publish *Peter Bell*, critics such as Jeffrey were all too ready to see in Wordsworth himself an over-excited sensibility that was no better than the vulgarity of the Methodists.[13] In the Preface to the *Lyrical Ballads*, Wordsworth claims to make these passions into objects of pleasure precisely by bringing his own practised and educated taste to bear on them. Jeffrey later claimed to be relatively tolerant of the *Lyrical Ballads* as an experiment in taste in this respect. By the time of *The Excursion* his tolerance has evaporated. Jeffrey suspects that Wordsworth's taste is being infected itself by the rawer enthusiasm that he is proposing to work upon: 'the inward transport and vigour by which they are inspired, should be tempered by an occassional [*sic*] reference to what will be thought of them by those ultimate dispensers of glory [that is, men of good taste].'[14] In 1814 Jeffrey believed that Wordsworth had come to be swallowed up by the vulgar passions of 'dalesmen and cottagers'. Without the twin supports of good taste (defined by deference to traditional canons of judgement) and polite society, he had become 'a sincere convert to his own system'.[15] Yet these dangers had already been anticipated by Wordsworth himself, and came to provide a fundamental reflex of his writing. The 1802 Preface to the *Lyrical Ballads* itself had already acknowledged the danger that when handling the unstable passions of his lower-class characters the poet might give way to 'an entire delusion, and even confound and identify his own feelings with theirs' (*WP* i. 138). If Wordsworth extended the reach of poetry beyond the limits insisted

---

[13] The same attitudes were at work in the responses to the poem of Leigh Hunt and associates such as Hazlitt.

[14] See Jeffrey's review in the *Edinburgh*, 24 (1814), 3.   [15] Ibid. 4.

upon by critics such as Jeffrey (and Shaftesbury), he was far from suggesting that taste did not need to have a regulatory relationship with enthusiasm. In the Preface the discipline and techniques of the poetic profession itself are brought forward against poetry becoming mere enthusiasm. Whereas Shaftesbury suggested the formal structures of dialogue were one way of bringing the combustible power of enthusiasm into conformity, Wordsworth places his emphasis on metre as a prior structure outside of the self 'to which the Poet and Reader both willingly submit' (*WP* i. 144). The external discipline of metre ensures against the danger that 'the excitement may be carried beyond its proper bounds' (*WP* i. 144). Nor did he suggest that characters such as Peter Bell could exercise this taste derived from the disciplinary practise of poetry in the same way as a poet such as Wordsworth himself. Indeed taste is represented in the Preface as operating precisely to stop the enthusiasm of characters of Peter's ilk infecting the poet who wished to write about them.

Well versed in the political pamphlets of the day as he was, Wordsworth may have been aware of the exchanges between Godwin and Thelwall on the dangers of those who address the crowd being carried away by the power of sympathetic identification. Bewell claims that 'since Wordsworth's fragmentary "[Essay on Morals]" indicates that *The Recluse* was initially conceived as a project that would counter an abstract "system of ethics" with a politically effective moral rhetoric, it should not surprise us that he would be so interested in these highly charged debates concerning the role that impassioned language plays in governing the lower classes or inciting them to violence'.[16] He would also probably have been aware of Burke's redefinition of enthusiasm in terms of the pathology of public opinion, that is, the rapid 'electrick' communication that overwhelmed individual judgement in the infectious communication of ideas. Although it does not use the word 'enthusiasm' in this context, the Preface itself seeks to carefully distinguish Wordsworth's healthful enthusiasm from those distracted by 'the rapid communication of intelligence':

For a multitude of causes unknown to former times are now acting with a combined force to blunt the discriminating power of the mind, and unfitting it for all voluntary exertion to reduce it to a state of almost savage

---

[16] Bewell, *Wordsworth and the Enlightenment*, 117.

torpor . . . The most effective of these causes are the great national events which are daily taking place, and the encreasing accumulation of men in cities, where the uniformity of their occupations produces a craving for extraordinary incident which the rapid communication of intelligence hourly gratifies. (*WP* i. 128)

Whereas earlier in the eighteenth century 'opinion' may have been a relatively innocuous pairing with 'enlightenment', for Wordsworth in 1798, possibly already under the influence of Burke, it suggests the feckless and unruly enthusiasm of the crowd. Jon Klancher has described the effect of circulation feared by Burke and Wordsworth as 'dissemination' to distinguish it from what was regarded as the healthful circulation of knowledge more often identified with public enlightenment.[17] Wordsworth's Preface suggests that literature is the means by which the enthusiasm of print can be regulated into healthful form, but the prospects are dimmed for him by the current state of public taste: 'our elder writers . . . driven into neglect by frantic novels, sickly and stupid German tragedies, and deluges of idle and extravagent stories in verse' (*WP* i. 128). Literariness in itself then is no guarantee of a healthy enthusiasm, or, to put it another way, not all poetic enthusiasm is properly literary.

J. J. McGann has specifically invoked the phenomenon of Della Cruscanism as the object of Wordsworth's opprobrium when it came to the contemporary desire for 'outrageous stimulation'.[18] McGann's contrast between Wordsworth's aesthetics and those of the Della Cruscans can be explored further to open up the question of the different kinds of poetic enthusiasm available when Wordsworth wrote. Della Cruscanism took its name from the pseudonym of its chief practitioner Robert 'Della Crusca' Merry.[19] No less than Wordsworth, Merry took part in the eighteenth century's appropriation of enthusiasm to poetic purposes, but few commentators seem to have regarded his practice as a rehabilitation. As I

[17] See Jon Klancher, *The Making of English Reading Audiences, 1790–1832* (Madison: University of Wisconsin Press, 1987), 34–6.

[18] Jerome McGann, *The Poetics of Sensibility: A Revolution in Literary Style* (Oxford: Clarendon Press, 1996), 75.

[19] For a more extended account account of Robert Merry's career in contrast with Wordsworth's, see Mee, ' "Reciprocal Expressions of Kindness": Robert Merry, Della Cruscanism and the Limits of Sociability', in Gillian Russell and Clara Tuite (eds.), *Romantic Sociability: Social Networks and Literary Culture in Britain 1770–1840* (Cambridge: Cambridge University Press, 2002), 104–22.

pointed out in my first chapter, Edward Jerningham, who was associated with Merry, was taken to task for assuming too readily that
poetic enthusiasm could be easily differentiated from its pathological other.[20] Merry was regarded as even more dangerous than
Jerningham by the guardians of culture. Rather than regulation,
Merry seemed deliberately to practise a poetics of distraction. He
made few efforts, certainly less than Wordsworth in his Preface, to
present his poetic enthusiasm as a safely regulated affair. Merry
wrote to Hester Lynch Piozzi, for instance, to say that his long poem
Diversity (1788) was written under a 'poetical mania'. Whereas the
fear that sociability might abandon itself to mere sensation structures Shaftesbury's definitions of enthusiasm, Merry's 'Extatic
poetry' flaunts his emotional vicissitudes as proof of his sympathetically porous relationship to sensation.[21] The world of the poem is
one in motion; its universe is fluxile and in-perception:

> To naught confin'd I ever range
> In wild propensity of change.[22]

Wordsworth's early poem *An Evening Walk* has a not dissimilar
sense of the active energies of the universe:

> A heart that vibrates evermore, awake
> To feeling for all forms that Life can take,
> That wider still its sympathy extends,
> And sees not any line where being ends;
> Sees sense, through Nature's rudest forms betrayed,
> Tremble obscure in fountain rock and shade;
> And while a secret power whose form endears
> Their social accent never vainly hears.[23]

Both poems seem to be attempts to render Hartley's language of
vibrations into a poetic vision of universal harmony. Of course, one
might read this impulse as not much different from that of the
Pedlar who is able to sympathetically identify even with the 'loose

[20] Jerningham only really became involved in the original newspaper project once
Robert Merry was withdrawing, see W. N. Hargreaves-Mawdsley, *The English
Della Cruscans and their Time, 1783–1828* (The Hague: Martinus Nijhoff, 1967),
182–3.
[21] See ibid. 188, and Robert Merry, *Diversity: A Poem* (1788), 11.
[22] Merry, *Diversity*, 34.
[23] *An Evening Walk*, ed. James Averill (Ithaca, NY: Cornell University Press),
135: ll. 125–32. See Jones on the influence of Shaftesbury on Wordsworth's early
poetry, nn. 6 and 8 above.

stones that cover the highway' in 'The Ruined Cottage'. Exactly the same power is claimed by Wordsworth himself in Book III of *The Prelude*:

> Even the loose stones that cover the highway,
> I gave a moral life, I saw them feel,
> Or linked them to some feeling.
>
> (*Prelude 1805*, III. 125–7)

Later on, Wordsworth names these responses in terms of the 'enthusiastic joy' (XIII. 261) that Coleridge's philosophy must discipline. In the reworking of 'The Ruined Cottage' at the end of the 1790s, Wordsworth seemed increasingly concerned to maintain a distinction between the philosophical discipline of his Pedlar, who is more and more represented as a meditative thinker much like Wordsworth himself, and the kind of 'distraction' that simply responds to external sensations.[24] Merry's poetry in comparison seems relatively relaxed about allowing any coherent sense of selfhood to be annihilated in the interests of garnering a diversity of responses to a universe of energy.

Simon Jarvis has suggested that we understand the distinction Wordsworth seems to want to draw between these different versions of poetical enthusiasm in terms of 'superstition' and 'idolatry'.[25] Jarvis's stimulating discussion takes its cue from the manuscript fragment associated with the reworking of 'The Ruined Cottage' now known as 'The Baker's Cart'. There a starving woman projects what Barbauld calls 'factitious life' on to the wagon which has failed to bring her family relief from famine:

> . . . by misery and rumination deep
> Tied to dead things and seeking sympathy
> In stocks and stones.[26]

Jarvis acutely links the latter phrase to the denunciation of the idolatrous Hebrews in Jeremiah 2: 26–7. He goes on to make a connection with a key passage from the Preface to Wordsworth's 1815 collection:

---

[24] Wordsworth, *The Ruined Cottage and The Pedlar*, ed. James Butler (Ithaca, NY: Cornell University Press, 1979).

[25] Simon Jarvis, 'Wordsworth and Idolatry', *Studies in Romanticism* 38 (1999), 1–27.

[26] Ibid. 3. Wordsworth, *The Ruined Cottage*, 467.

The grand store-houses of enthusiastic and meditative Imagination, of poetical, as contradistinguished from human and dramatical Imagination, are the prophetic and lyrical parts of the Holy Scriptures, and the works of Milton; to which I cannot forbear to add those of Spenser. I select these writers in preference to those of ancient Greece and Rome because the anthropomorphitism of the Pagan religion subjected the minds of the greatest poets in those countries too much to the bondage of definite form; from which the Hebrews were preserved by their abhorence of idolatry. (WP iii. 34)

From this point onwards, Jarvis thoughtfully develops his argument in terms of Wordsworth's attitude to 'idolatry' as the term that distinguishes the pathology of the woman's response in 'The Baker's Cart' fragment from the healthy moral vision of the Pedlar. The productive distinctions raised by Jarvis's discussion could be taken further if the passage was considered in relation to the discourse on enthusiasm.

The Hebrew prophets were routinely identified with genuine enthusiasm. Priestley among others had defined their opposition to idolatry in terms of the distinction between 'enthusiasm' and 'superstition' (of the pagan poets) essential to eighteenth-century theories of religion.[27] In David Hume's classic statement of the distinction, superstition is defined in terms of fear:

In such a state of mind, infinite unknown evils are dreaded from unknown agents; and where real objects of terror are wanting, the soul, active to its own prejudice and fostering its predominant inclination, finds imaginary ones, to whose power and malevolence it sets no limits.[28]

Such a fear of imaginary agents, I would suggest, is much like the despair and terror of the woman in 'The Baker's Cart', who attributes her situation to the malevolence of 'stocks and stones'. Her situation is not dissimilar from that of the Hebrews when they turn to the worship of stocks and stones in Jeremiah. The Pedlar's is a rather different response, one that lies much closer to Hume's contrary definition of enthusiasm:

In such a state of mind, the imagination swells with great, but confused conceptions, to which no sublunary beauties or enjoyments can correspond. . . . In a little time, the inspired person comes to regard himself as a

---

[27] See the discussion in the previous chapter.

[28] 'Of Superstition and Enthusiasm', in *Essays Moral, Political, and Literary*, ed. T. H. Green and T. H. Grose, 2 vols. (Longmans, Green & Co., 1875), i. 144.

distinguished favourite of the Divinity; and when this phrensy once takes place, which is the summit of enthusiasm, every whimsy is consecrated: Human reason, and even morality, are rejected as fallacious guides; and the fanatic madman delivers himself over, blindly and without reserve, to the supposed illapses of the Spirit, and to inspiration from above.[29]

Hume is talking about enthusiasm here in relation to religious pathology, but for Priestley and many others in the eighteenth century these same expansive impulses were present in a healthful form in the biblical prophecies, and could even be recreated more modestly in poetry. As long as the poet disciplines himself, so as not to 'regard himself as the distinguished favourite of the Divinity', or, in Jeffrey's terms, so as not to privilege his own passions over conventional good taste, these raptures and transports could be refreshing (as Hume himself sometimes allowed them to be in terms of politics and culture).

At this point, I would like to rejoin Jarvis's discussion of Wordsworth and idolatry. Jarvis's view is that Wordsworth comes to evolve an idea of *a priori* moral systems such as Godwin's as a form of superstition. His point takes off from the description of the distinctly Godwinian character of Rivers in the Preface to his play *The Borderers*: 'He looks at society through an optical glass of a peculiar tint: something of the forms of objects he takes from objects, but their colour is exclusively what he gives them, it is one, and it is his own.'[30] The problem, as Jarvis perceives it, 'is not that Rivers is insufficiently willing to endow social objects with imaginative meaning of his own but that he is too willing so to do . . . Once again we have a pejorative counterpart to the laudable bestowal of moral meaning'.[31] It should be apparent that in terms of Hume's definition this presumption is closer to enthusiasm than superstition or idolatry. Jarvis may be right to understand Margaret's abject response to the Baker's cart in terms of superstition, but the case of Rivers seems different. His response is not one of abjection, but more like the egotism and self-projection of Hume's definition of enthusiasm. Rivers has no sense of immediate inspiration, but his 'confidence and presumption' is exactly of the sort that led Burke to describe the rational projectors of the

[29] Ibid. 145.
[30] William Wordsworth, *The Borderers*, ed. Robert Osborn (Ithaca, NY: Cornell University Press, 1982), 65.
[31] Jarvis, 'Wordsworth and Idolatry', 15.

Revolution in terms of enthusiasm. For Hume enthusiasm was always associated with an expansion of the self of the sort Wordsworth identifies in Rivers: 'The fanatic consecrates himself, and bestows on his own person a sacred character, much superior to what forms and ceremonies institutions can confer on any other.'[32] For Burke, this self-sufficiency or faith in *transparence* was what linked religious and radical enthusiasm.[33] Although he does use the word 'superstition' to describe Rivers, the qualities Wordsworth associates with him are much closer to Hume and Burke's ideas on 'enthusiasm': 'Having shaken off the obligations of religion and morality in a dark and tempestuous age, it is probable that such a character will be infected with a tinge of superstition.'[34] Rivers may be confused by the situation, but he is not afraid. His enthusiasm is projected into the void left by what escapes his under-standing. When the superstition associated with tradition falls away, Rivers simply projects his own desires onto the moral order of the universe. Much of what Wordsworth says of Rivers resonates with Coleridge's account of Robespierre and the later contrast between the enthusiasm of Luther and Rousseau. To use Pocock's terms, the world-as-it-is simply falls away as a 'context' that might delimit the reasoning mind.

Jarvis wants to praise Wordsworth's critique, because it sees beyond Rivers's illusory sense of 'the sufficiency of the independent intellect' to a truer sense of the complex relationship of humanity to its world. To me, this view seems to grant rather too much too quickly to Wordsworth, and ignores the contexts that help us understand the nuances of his position. A critique of 'the sufficiency of the independent intellect' was precisely what Burke, in almost exactly these words, advanced against radical ideology. I do not simply want to make the crude historicist move of identifying Jarvis's position with Burkean conservatism. That is obviously far from being what his work is about, but attention to this context can illuminate some of the limitations of Wordsworth's enthusiasm in Jarvis's own terms. Although Wordsworth may present himself as developing a fuller and more open relationship to the world around him, his reaction against radical *transparence* and the distractions of enthusiasm, as he saw them, included some important exclusions

---

[32] Hume, 'Of Superstition and Enthusiasm', i. 148.
[33] See Chapter 2 for a discussion of Burke's attitude.
[34] Wordsworth, *The Borderers*, 66.

that ought to qualify any account of his relations with otherness. Recall John Mullan's comment on the eighteenth century's belief in 'the necessary separation of polite society from society at large'.[35] Jarvis sees in Wordsworth a belief that 'real social exchange could only happen if we could understand the material world, even down to the stick which we whittle, as composed of more than "idle objects" and our dependence upon it as more than humiliating servitude'.[36] This Adornian understanding of Wordsworth begs a number of questions in terms of Mullan's distinction. Wordsworth's construction of Rivers after all, and it is a *construction* of the revolutionary sensibility, deliberately suggests that to break with habit and tradition is to render oneself immediately open to delusive sympathies. To be fair, as I have already suggested, Wordsworth does recognize something of this danger in his own situation, but for the most part it is only those who lie outside the boundaries of polite society who are reckoned to be in danger. Whatever 'real social exchange' might be, it is hard to see that the various regulatory mechanisms that Wordsworth puts in place around his own enthusiasm could constitute an open and reciprocal relationship between himself and the world.

These issues might be better illustrated by returning to the Della Cruscan example with which I began this discussion. Whereas Wordworth's enthusiasm is constantly harried by the Coleridgean nightmare of a subjectivity simply made up of sensation without a governing free will, Merry's poetry appears willing to risk self-annihilation in its imagining of its relations with the world. The perceiving consciousness is not a fixed viewing position but constituted and indeed reinvented out of its reciprocal relationship with a fluxile universe. Perhaps this is why Hester Lynch Piozzi judged Merry's *Diversity* to be 'all so about nothing'.[37] Compared to Wordsworth's mature poetry, it seems unconcerned about preserving a fixed moral centre for its relations with the universe. Coleridge's journey away from the materialism of Joseph Priestley expressed itself in terms of a concern to preserve the unity of self against the 'delirium' of mere sensation.[38] When Coleridge made

---

[35] See Chapter 1 for a fuller discussion of Mullan's point.

[36] Jarvis, 'Wordsworth and Idolatry', 19.

[37] Quoted in Hargreaves-Mawdsley, *The English Della Cruscans*, 52.

[38] See Riede, *Oracles and Hierophants*, 175–91. Coleridge asked: 'But what is the height, & ideal of mere association?—Delirium.' See *Notebooks*, i. 1771.

his distinction between 'Imagination' and 'Fancy' in the *Biographia*, he stressed the role of the controlling will in the former. Coleridge, as we have seen, believed that associationism denied free will and left the individual 'divided between the despotism of outward impressions, and that of senseless and passive memory'. From the later Coleridgean perspective, Merry is a poet of 'Fancy' in danger of dissolving the self into the object of perception. Literary history is disposed to judge the poetry of Merry and his like in Coleridge's negative terms, but perhaps we should see it as a serious attempt to write a poetry of association under Hartley's influence. Horace Walpole was in no doubt that Merry's ideas could be traced back to 'the new Birmingham warehouse of the original Maker', that is, the philosophy that Priestley had derived from Hartley.[39] The kind of open-ended imaginative sympathy represented in his poetry was associated with the idea of universal benevolence, an idea that both Coleridge and Wordsworth increasingly came to perceive both as a threat to 'practical' benevolence and to the sovereignty of the subject. This threat was vilified as a form of *transparence* insofar as it denied the mediating power of traditional authority.

Wordsworth was no less interested than Merry in 'the manner in which we associate ideas in a state of excitement' (*WP* i. 123–4), but his poetics increasingly had a countervailing interest in regulation that is deliberately flaunted in Merry's poetry. Walpole's sneering reference to a Birmingham warehouse is oriented not only against Merry's ideas, but also his descent down the social scale into the world of middle-class manufacturers and Rational Dissenters.[40] Merry believed that melting down the social bond was in the interests of expanding and redefining what benevolence might be. What is striking about his writing after 1789 is his willingness to use with a positive spin the vocabulary that Burke activated to represent the Revolution in terms of a dangerous enthusiasm. The Preface to his *Laurel of Liberty* (1790) asserts that 'the progress of Opinion, like a rapid stream, though it may be checked, cannot be controuled'. The poem describes itself as 'enthusiastic verse'. A visit to revolutionary Paris is explained in terms of 'extatic fervour in the soul'

---

[39] See Walpole's letter (10 Nov. 1790) to Edward Jerningham, in *Edward Jerningham and his Friends: A Series of Eighteenth-Century Letters*, ed. Lewis Bettany (Chatto & Windus, 1919), 50.

[40] For the details of this 'descent', see Mee, ' "Reciprocal Expressions" ', 110–18.

and 'dear delirium'.[41] Whereas for Burke (and Coleridge) such language is often used to suggest the frightening destruction of determinate identities, for Merry it seems to imply a joyous giving up (and enriching) of subjectivity to the spirit of liberty. In terms of his own circulation in person and in print, Merry was moving increasingly beyond the polite circles of his upbringing. The chorus of the ode performed at the meeting of the 'Friends of Liberty' in 1791 celebrated the idea of a rapid and limitless communication of energy:

> Fill high the animating glass,
> And let the electric ruby pass
> From hand to hand, from soul to soul;
> Who shall the energy controul.
> Exalted, pure, refin'd,
> The Health of Humankind![42]

What Burke saw as the scandal of 'electrick communication everywhere', Merry saw as the possibility of an infinitely expanding social energy. 'The point is not to bring order to variety', McGann says of Della Cruscanism more generally, 'but to stimulate and provoke'.[43] Merry's version of patriot eloquence, its celebration of Genius's 'wild propensity of change', had moved far beyond the regulatory tradition of sociability associated with Shaftesbury's Whiggism.[44] Wordsworth's Preface to the *Lyrical Ballads*, I would suggest, could be seen as part of a cultural and historical reaction that moved it back the other way. Poetic enthusiasm in this reaction elevates the poet beyond himself, it may take him or her into the hearts of others, it provides an idea of authentic being, but this rapture is shadowed by a contrary disciplinary agenda that was socially exclusive and protective of a regulated idea of selfhood. Both Merry and Wordsworth were dedicatees of a poetics of 'enthusiasm', both ought to be thought of as heirs of Shaftesbury in this respect, but with very different ideas of what that might mean.

---

[41] See Merry, *The Laurel of Liberty* (1790), pp. vi, 9, 7, and 23.
[42] *Ode for the Fourteenth of July, 1791, the Day Consecrated to Freedom: Being the Anniversary of the Revolution in France* (1791), 6–7.
[43] McGann, *The Poetics of Sensibility*, 90.   [44] Merry, *Diversity*, 34.

'EXTRAORDINARY CALLS'

By the time Wordsworth wrote his Preface to the *Lyrical Ballads*, Merry was dead, having been driven into exile in the United States.[45] Thelwall, who provides another kind of contrast with Wordsworth's poetic enthusiasm, had been driven into internal exile.[46] Both Merry and Thelwall's poetic and political enthusiasm had in Burke's terms been very directly regulated by *'a power out of themselves'*.[47] Wordsworth, of course, by this time, was involved in an uneasy and uneven journey away from his own earlier radicalism, and away from the less regulated idea of poetic enthusiasm to be found in *An Evening Walk*. The version of *The Prelude* completed in 1805 was in part an attempt to make sense of this journey, and to present his qualifications as the kind of regulated poet outlined in the Preface to the *Lyrical Ballads*. The rest of this chapter is concerned with the ways that the discourse of enthusiasm structured Wordsworth's representation of his poetic development. Earlier I suggested that Wordsworth's idea of poetic enthusiasm was closer to Shaftesbury and Akenside's than Coleridge's because of the omission of an explicitly religious context for the word. For Coleridge, as for John Dennis at the beginning of the century and Richard 'Citizen' Lee at the end of it, the highest raptures of enthusiasm were always to be reserved for religious matters, dangerous though they might be in themselves. For Wordsworth, in 1798 at least, as for Shaftesbury, Nature and the 'Spirits of the Mind' are sufficient both as sources of enthusiasm itself and of its regulation. The situation is rather different in *The Prelude*, perhaps reflecting the growing influence of Coleridge, and his concern that Wordsworth was too prone to construct a sense of mind out of the combustible matter it was meant to be regulating. Not that the 1805 version of *The Prelude* allows much of an explicit role either for the institutions of the Church or for a particularly Christianized language. What does emerge is a language powerfully inflected with

---

[45] See Mee, ' "Reciprocal Expressions" ', 115–16.

[46] See E. P. Thompson, 'Hunting the Jacobin Fox', in his *The Romantics* (New York: Norton, 1997) for an extended account of Thelwall's fate. The specific way his career affected his understanding of his radical 'enthusiasm' is discussed in Chapter 2.

[47] *The Writings and Speeches of Edmund Burke*, viii: *The French Revolution 1790–94*, ed. G. Mitchell (Oxford: Oxford University Press, 1989), 111.

the strains of biblical prophecy. Obviously identifying the poet as strongly with the prophet as Wordsworth's poem does is an attempt to claim a certain kind of cultural authority.[48] Yet the claims made on prophecy brought with them a deficit that Wordsworth had to respect. Especially where this language seemed relatively free of the direct controlling influence of the Church, as it was in *The Prelude*, it was likely to seem a sort of presumption that threatened to confound poetic with unrulier forms of enthusiasm. After all, even *The Excursion*, a poem more explicitly Christian than *The Prelude* of 1805, was for Francis Jeffrey too much like the enthusiasm of the Methodist in this respect.[49] Wordsworth himself, as we have seen, was no less conscious than Jeffrey of the dangers of

> ... false imagination, placed beyond
> The limits of experience and of truth
>
> (*Prelude* 1805, x. 845–7)

Indeed as a poem of apprenticeship (Clifford Siskin calls it the longest résumé in literary history) *The Prelude* is constantly attempting to show that its prophetic pretensions are properly disciplined, that is, assuring his readers that his enthusiasm is meant 'not in a mystical and idle sense' (ii. 235). Such reminders are attempts at confirming the status of his writing as poetry and so as qualitatively different from 'mystical verbiage'.

The language of prophecy is a particularly unstable element in this process, because of the long-standing historical memory of its role in stirring up religious enthusiasm, and there were plenty of contemporary examples, as we have seen, of the continuation of this aspect of the popular imagination. Thus, contrary to the suggestions of critics such as Riede, for Wordsworth to create an 'oracular self' is not in itself a guarantee of poetic authority. Undisciplined prophetic pretensions invited at best ridicule and at worst contempt. Looking at the language of prophecy from this point of view means that we have to reconsider the widely accepted but recently

---

[48] Riede, *Oracles and Hierophants*, 97, is aware of a tension between 'the poetics of prophecy' and a 'poetics of error' in Wordsworth, but his opposition still rather obscures the cultural history of anxieties surrounding the former (the phrase is originally Geoffrey Hartman's).

[49] See Robert Ryan's excellent discussion of the complex attitude to the Church of England in *The Excursion: The Romantic Reformation: Religious Politics in English Literature 1789–1824* (Cambridge: Cambridge University Press, 1997), esp. 100–18.

much-contested claim that Romanticism in general and
Wordsworth in particular were involved with a process of displacing public history onto private apocalypse. For critics such as
M. H. Abrams, this 'imaginative transformation of the self' is to be
celebrated as the basis of a great poetic achievement.[50] For New
Historicist critics such as Alan Liu, the same movement is an evasion of history. I would argue that the dichotomy between History
and Apocalypse accepted by both sides of the argument is itself a
Romantic construction. Perhaps its currency even indicates the
eventual success of Coleridge and Wordsworth in rewriting these
terms for literary criticism. Yet this success in terms of our understanding of Romantic enthusiasm should not be allowed to obscure
either their own anxieties nor the immediate reservations of critics
such as Jeffrey. The process of rehabilitation, as we have seen, was
a long and uneven one. It neither began nor ended with Coleridge
and Wordsworth. Alongside their rewriting of the poetics of enthusiasm there still existed a troubling other in the enthusiastic public
sphere, associated with Methodism and popular excesses of all
kinds. The continuing presence of this unregulated species of enthusiasm made possible attacks such as Jeffrey's. Whether it took a
religious guise (as in Methodist preaching) or secular form (as
Jeffrey thought it did in Thelwall's poetry), the *Edinburgh* was
always on the look out for its encroachment.[51]

Wordsworth does not simply assume a language of prophecy. No
such stable language was available to be assumed in poetry.
Wordsworth had to participate in an uneasy process of rehabilitation that had much to do with the fear of the dangerous nature of
enthusiasm, a response which was itself part of a broader unease
about public spaces becoming infected by 'the discomforting proximity of the lower orders'.[52] In this context then, the Romantic
Apocalypse of the Imagination represents not so much a displace-

---

[50] See Abrams, 'Constructing and Deconstucting', in Morris Eaves and Michael
Fischer (eds.), *Romanticism and Contemporary Criticism* (Ithaca. NY: Cornell
University Press, 1986), 167.

[51] See above Chapters 1 and 2 for these aspects of the *Edinburgh*'s writing against
popular enthusiasm both religious and secular.

[52] See Gillian Russell, *The Theatres of War: Performance, Politics, and Society
1793–1815* (Oxford, Clarendon Press, 1995), 123. Russell's claim is made specifically in relation to the theatrical space and relates to the retreat of the elite into the
domestic space of private theatricals, but it is a feature of the development of the
public sphere more generally in the period. See the attitudes to debating clubs such
as the Westminster Forum, discussed above in Chapter 2.

ment of History as the rewriting of prophecy. *The Prelude* is the key text in the rehabilitation of enthusiasm in the Wordsworthian canon, for it is here that the language of prophecy is most clearly subjected to reworking. The 'spots of time' that recur through the poem are the laboratories of this process. M. H. Abrams argued that these spots of time transform 'the Christian paradigm of right-angled change into something radically new'.[53] The outcome is 'a pattern . . . in which development consists of a gradual curve back to an earlier stage, but on a higher level incorporating that which has intervened'.[54] What Abrams rather casually ignores is that such 'right-angled irruptions' were widely identified in Wordsworth's time with the delirium of enthusiasm. Ideas of 'instantaneous regeneration, assurance, and sinless perfection' (*Life of Wesley*, ii. 23) were what Southey disapprobated most about Wesley's teaching, even after he had decided that the general effects of the Methodist movement had been towards disciplining the lower classes, but Wesley himself tried to lay down the role of such ideas in the movement. Distancing oneself from such sudden irruptions of the unworldly was essential to most definitions of true piety at the time in both Anglican and dissenting traditions.[55] Southey decried the tendency to make religion 'a thing of sensation and passion, craving perpetually for sympathy and stimulants, instead of bringing with it peace and contentment' (*Life of Wesley*, ii. 217). He was not seeking to distance the spiritual life from feeling as such, only—as Barbauld had done in the 1770s—attempting to distinguish 'the quiet regularity of domestic devotion' from the tastelessness of 'public performances' (ii. 218). Any appeal to the authenticating power of enthusiasm in the period always had to distance itself from such right-angled disruptions of coherent subjectivity.

Wordsworth's case is no different in these general terms from the ongoing requirements of the rehabilitation of enthusiasm. Affective appeals to the influx of the spirit had to distance themselves from any claim to *immediate* intercourse with the divine presence. Whereas prophetic enthusiasm was traditionally identified with the distracted subject, Wordsworth exploits the process of unworlding

---

[53] M. H. Abrams, *Natural Supernaturalism: Tradition and Revolution in Romantic Literature* (New York: W. W. Norton & Co., 1971), 113.

[54] Ibid. 114.

[55] For Wesley's attempt to regulate the enthusiasm of his own movement, see Chapter 1.

in the interests of discovering an abiding self beyond the fluctuations of the world as it is, but the allied process of folding spots of
time back into a continuous sense of self-identity is part of a long
English tradition of making sure that the transports of the sublime
come with a return ticket back to a coherent subjectivity. His situation was in some respects not very different from Wesley's.[56]
Although *The Prelude* seems consciously to avoid making its interest in spiritual agency too explicitly Christian, both Wesley and
Wordsworth were faced with the problem of representing their
prophetic faith as more than a dangerous enthusiasm. Wordsworth
was careful to present his spiritual ecstasies as the product of a serious preparation as Siskin and other critics have pointed out
recently.[57] Moreover both men laid a stress on the productiveness
of spirituality against the dangers of revelling in the intoxication of
the moment of conversion. The fruits of conversion and notions of
steady stages of spiritual growth are privileged over the sudden
ecstasies of the spirit in their writing as a means of distinguishing
themselves from those who laid too ready a claim to spiritual
enlightenment:

> Them the enduring and the transient both
> Serve to exalt. They build up greatest things
> From least suggestions, ever on the watch,
> Willing to work and to be wrought upon,
> They need not extraordinary calls
> To rouse them: in a world of life they live
> By sensible impressions not enthralled,
> But quickened, rouzed, and made thereby more fit
> To hold communion with the invisible world
>
> (*Prelude 1805*, XIII. 97–105)

'Extraordinary calls'—a phrase at the very centre of disputes about
the 'enthusiasm' of Methodism—implied a sudden and perfect
apprehension of truth.[58] Spiritual transports were disavowed

---

[56] The parallels between Wesley and Wordsworth have been extensively documented in Brantley, *Wordsworth's 'Natural Methodism'*, but my approach here is
more focused on their anxieties about excess, and the disciplinary nature of their
responses.

[57] See, for example, Siskin, *The Work of Writing*, and Brian Goldberg,
'"Ministry More Palpable": William Wordsworth and the Making of Romantic
Professionalism', *Studies in Romanticism*, 36 (1997), 327–47.

[58] The phrase was at the centre, for instance, of the exchanges between the Bishop
of Exeter and Wesley discussed in Chapter 1.

absolutely by neither Wordsworth or Wesley, but their effects are worked out gradually. Ecstasies of conversion, for both Wesley and Wordsworth, are the beginning not the end of a disciplinary process. Unworlding is a necessary component of the ideas of regeneration promoted in the writing of both men, but its benefits are lost if they are not reinscribed into a continuous sense of the productive subject.[59]

To return to the double bind identified by Riede set out at the beginning of this chapter, this disavowal of 'extraordinary calls' is not simply a matter of distancing the language of prophecy from supernatural agency. Wordsworth's 'spots of time' are also distanced from the sensuousness that Wordsworth routinely identified with the 'soulless eye'. Part of the scandal of vulgar enthusiasm, as we saw in Chapter 1, was the perception that it was too eager to claim to be able to comprehend (and in turn represent) the spiritual world. Distinctions between the spiritual and carnal eye were routine in popular religious writing, but to commentators such as Leigh Hunt these distinctions were not properly observed by those who drew them. The heat and passion of Methodist discourse suggested to observers such as Hunt and Southey that popular religious feeling remained in the thrall of 'sensible impressions'. *The Prelude* may affirm the possibility of 'communion with the invisible world', but not immediately. Nor does it claim to be able to represent directly that world with any particularity. Those who claimed too easy a communication with the world of spirits (as Hunt's brother Robert believed Blake to do) were making the barriers between sensible and spiritual impressions too porous to observe the distinction properly. For Hunt and other elite commentators on popular religious experience, the spiritual world was to be approached only through various strategies of indirection if it were not to be travestied and sullied with the grossness of the eye.

The discourse of regulation that Wordsworth would have found in Shaftesbury and poets such as Akenside offered one route through which prophecy could be disciplined into poetry. *The Prelude* certainly exploits the techniques of self-division outlined in *Characteristics*. The spots of time are opportunities for self-division

---

[59] See Brantley, *Wordsworth's 'Natural Methodism'*, 68–9. For a discussion of Wesley's ideas of limit and extent in relation to religious feelings and the role of reason as a mediating power, see Brantley, *Locke, Wesley, and the Method of English Romanticism* (Gainesville: University of Florida Press, 1984), 68.

in which the mature self looks back on a previous version and sees a deeper continuity in the development of an organic subjectivity beneath the surface of the world as it is. The natural self that is actually created or 'discovered' in these moments is a paradox of artifice, the product of a 'rigorous inquisition' (1. 159) through the self that had also been essential to Shaftesbury's ideas of natural self-fashioning. Wordsworth throughout his poem seeks to demonstrate his own ability to move beyond 'present joy' (1. 109) into a narrative of personal development that qualifies him as a poet. Ironically enough, true authenticity of being in Wordsworth, as in Shaftesbury, is predicated on the ability to divide the self. One cannot be authentic without enthusiasm, but only enthusiasm that has been worked upon can provide a durable basis to identity. *The Prelude* begins with just such a moment of 'unworlding' that it proceeds to refine and discipline:

> Trances of thought and mountings of the mind
> Come fast upon me. It is shaken off—
> As by miraculous gift 'tis shaken off—
> That burden of my own unnatural self,
> The heavy weight of many a weary day,
> Not mine, and such as were not made for me.

> (*1805 Prelude*, 1. 20–5)

Certain parts of Book 1 may seem unapologetically to identify the poet with the prophet in this ability to see beyond the world as it is:

> . . . To the open fields I told
> A prophecy: poetic numbers came
> Spontaneously, and clothed in priestley robe
> My spirit, thus singled out, as it might seem,
> For holy services.

> (1. 59–63)

Yet the reader is quickly made aware of a potential error even in the moment of release: 'Or shall a twig, or any floating thing | Upon the river, point me out my course?' (1. 31–2) Poetry such as Robert Merry's, I suggested earlier in this chapter, building perhaps on the idea of self-annihilation found in Hartley and Priestley, seems more willing to abandon the self upon the stream of experience and consciousness in order to harvest new associations and emotional responses. Wordsworth figures such abandonment as a serious diminution of possibility, becoming a mere 'twig or any floating thing'. Unworlding is the sign of a healthy return to nature in the poem, but also brings with it the spectre of a mindless play of sensation. There is a voice that tempts the prophet to think only of 'present joy':

> So, like a peasant, I pursued my road
> Beneath the evening sun; nor had one wish
> Again to bend the sabbath of that time
> To a servile yoke.
>
> (1. 110–13)

The figure of the peasant here is ambiguous, and one that is ultimately disavowed in *The Prelude* in favour of a more regulated (and by implication professional) self-image. The comparison with the simplicity of the peasant may function as the sign of an authentic and uncomplicated relationship to nature in these lines, but it is haunted by the idea of a weak surrender to the temptation of 'present joy'. Ultimately, the model of the carefree peasant is disavowed. Such joys are subsumed in Wordsworth's poem to a process of development in which the poet incorporates but also transcends the knowledge of the peasant. *The Prelude*, no less than the *Lyrical Ballads*, will distinguish Wordsworth from the peasants with whom he seems to consort. He marks himself by his ability to bend 'present joy' towards higher purposes. He will not shirk from the 'service' outlined in the earlier reference to the prophetic task, that is, he must 'brace [himself] to some determined aim' (1. 124). The unworlding experience cannot simply stand as a spontaneous event, important though the recovery of the power to feel is to the poem, but has to be written into a narrative of improvement that sets him apart from those who can *only* feel. Wordsworth, like Shaftesbury, will do productive work on his enthusiasm, and 'through myself | Make rigorous inquisition' (1. 158–9). What might be a mere matter of 'animal delight'—as such experiences among peasants and Methodists alike were usually deemed to be—turns into a process of 'sanctifying by . . . discipline' (1. 439). 'Extraordinary calls' are valuable only if they are worked into a true faith by those with the cultural capital to undertake such work.

Francis Jeffrey was hard on those he thought abandoned their true social station to follow such calls, whether in religion, poetry, or politics, throughout his reviewing career. John Thelwall he dismissed as someone incapable of regulating his enthusiasm into a productive form. Indeed his 'enthusiastic virtues' are simply to be dismissed as 'an impatience of honest industry'.[60] Not only is Thelwall's poetry useless, but it has distracted him from the sphere of life where he could be useful. Jeffrey's attacks on Wordsworth are part of the *Edinburgh*'s more general campaign against popular enthusiasm. Wordsworth seemed both to be encouraging delusions of grandeur among the lower classes of the sort enjoyed by Thelwall and in the process abandoning the regulatory traditions of his society and education that protected Wordsworth himself from infection. Wordsworth would sympathize with Thelwall when the latter was attacked by Jeffrey, but he was not free from the same assumptions as the *Edinburgh* reviewer. Peasants and other uneducated people were frequently presumed not to have the mental powers to undertake the kind of disciplinary work that could distinguish the wheat from the chaff of enthusiasm. Their responses to reading, for instance, as Paul Keen has shown, were often assumed to be too immediate and literal to become the storehouse for future acts of mental development.[61] They were too likely to show the effects immediately in rash action or the involuntary ('mechanical') responses of their bodies. Methodist conversion narratives were regarded as a rich source of evidence of this kind of behaviour.

One of the ways in which *The Prelude* seeks to distinguish itself from this kind of vulgar enthusiasm, for all its involvement with the language of prophecy and conversion, is by de-corporealizing the senses, that is, by uncoupling the visionary from the visible.[62] Wordsworthian calm betokens a meditative frame of mind that is able to separate the bodily passions from the nobler kinds of enthusiasm:

> Oft in those moments such a holy calm
> Did overspread my soul that I forgot
> That I had bodily eyes, and what I saw
> Appear'd like something in myself, a dream,
> A prospect in my mind.

(II. 368–71)

[60] See the discussion of Jeffrey's attack on Thelwall at the end of Chapter 2.

[61] See Paul Keen, *The Crisis of Literature in the 1790s: Print Culture and the Public Sphere* (Cambridge: Cambridge University Press, 1999), esp. 57–8. This issue is discussed in relation to anxieties about literal and figurative agents in Steven Knapp's excellent *Personification and the Sublime: Milton to Coleridge* (Cambridge, Mass.: Harvard University Press, 1985), 99–100 and *passim*.

[62] See William H. Galperin, *The Return of the Visible in British Romanticism* (Baltimore: Johns Hopkins University Press, 1993), esp. in relation to Wordsworth, ch. 7.

Nature, on the one hand, offers a guarantee that Wordsworth's enthusiasm is a response to permanent and substantial forms, not the ideal dreaming of the fanatic, but, on the other, a process of rhetorical de-corporealization also functions in *The Prelude* as a way of distancing Wordsworth's feel for stocks and stones from the 'electrick' energy of the senses that critics regularly deprecated in poets such as Thelwall and Merry (not to mention the enthusiasm of Methodism). There are parallels here with Wesley's analogical empiricism when accounting for the reality of spiritual experience. The spiritual leaves an impression like any other sensation, both have their origins in God, but the former has to be understood in such a way that it is distanced from the grossness of the passions.[63] The experiences that Wordsworth feels in 'solitude' are not the delusions of enthusiasm. They do not 'Speak to my eye' (IV. 391); they have not become fouled with the sensual, but they really were, he insists, at the same time, 'heard and felt' (ibid.). The attempt is to separate the instinctual or the 'mechanical' from spiritual experience marked as genuine, but it is one that is constantly circling round its own terms, anxious to rescue them from associations with the twin polarities of enthusiasm, that is, on the one hand, an unworlding that abandons the world too completely, or, on the other, a sensuousness that mires the spiritual with the passions. The intercourse with nature is only the worthless spasming of the enthusiast if it is not disciplined with an idea of the regulating mind that the poem identifies with Coleridge's philosophy, but cut free from the world of nature entirely such ideas represent an unworlding without any anchor in the world as it is.

Because of the infectious nature of enthusiasm, liable to intensify the passions and even overwhelm its own source, solitude itself is one form of regulation, as it was for Shaftesbury, insofar as it creates the conditions for quiet meditation. The product of habitual acts of self-regulation in solitude in his childhood, Wordsworth represents himself as able to sift the beneficent from dangerous enthusiasm. At the beginning of Book VII, for instance, journeying to London, Wordsworth describes himself as 'self-willed, | Yet temperate and reserved, and wholly free | From dangerous passions' (VII. 70–2). Solitude was not without dangers of its own when it came to enthusiasm, as poems such as Wordsworth's 'Lines written

---

[63] See the discussion of Wesley in Chapter 1.

246 The Poetics of Enthusiasm

on a Yew Tree' suggest, but the infectious conditions found in
urban centres seem more threatening to Wordsworth's sense of
wholeness. Book VII of *The Prelude* tells of the dangers facing even
a well-regulated subjectivity when confronted with the infectious
proximity of the crowd. Just as Godwin's account of Thelwall's
oratory represented him as a well-intentioned man liable to be swallowed up by the enthusiasm he had stirred in those around him, so
Wordsworth represents himself as deeply troubled and almost
undone by the 'colours, lights, and forms; the Babel din' (VII. 157).
Only a deep training in a version of Shaftesbury's techniques of regulation, above all, an ability gained through habitual practice in
solitude to relate the confusion of the senses to a larger harmonious
whole, ultimately preserves Wordsworth from the 'endless stream
of men and moving things' (VII. 158):

> But though the picture weary out the eye,
> By nature an unmanageable sight,
> It is not wholly so to him who looks
> In steadiness, who hath among least things
> An under-sense of greatest—sees the parts
> As parts, but with a feeling of the whole.
>
> (vii. 707–12)

Whereas a poet such as Merry continually throws the self into
hazard in relation to the social in order to reap 'a feeling of the
whole', Wordsworth's habitual stance is one of self-preservation in
the face of such external dangers. Both positions owe something to
Shaftesbury. Merry's is related to but much extends Shaftesbury's
notion of 'amicable collision' (*Characteristics*, 31) as a means of
developing the self towards benevolence. Wordsworth, of course,
follows more closely Shaftesbury's warnings about not exposing
one's transports to the public before they are regulated into a relatively safe form. Merry seems to risk more than either Shaftesbury
or Wordsworth. 'The combustible matters' that 'lie prepared within
and ready to take fire at a spark' (*Characteristics*, 23) are not
brought into harmonious form before they appear in public.
Although Merry proposes a universe bound together by universal
benevolence, there is a paradigmatic difference of emphasis: 'diversity' of experience rather than 'a feeling of the whole' is Merry's
signature theme. Wordsworth operates with a narrower idea of the
conversation of culture, even perhaps narrower in some ways than

Shaftesbury, in order to ensure that 'the shapes | Of wilful fancy' are not 'grafted upon feelings | Of the imagination' (VIII. 583–5). The sociability of conversation imagined by Shaftesbury has little part in Wordsworth's experiences in London, and in the poem as a whole sociability seems reduced to a close-knit circle of friends, primarily Dorothy and Coleridge, who can be relied upon to echo the poet's sentiments. Here is a 'superstitious' limit that Simon Jarvis's account of Wordsworth's relations with otherness overlooks. Preserving 'a feeling of the whole' is predicated on the exclusion of vast swathes of affective human experience, and it seems any possibility of regulation for those whose enthusiasm discovers itself in an urban context is denied. Wordsworth's prophetic ardour is regulated in solitude far from the urban centres that Southey and others believed to be the forcing houses of the most dangerous strains of enthusiasm. These solitary acts of 'mental discipline', as James Chandler accurately describes them, are the spots of time disposed throughout the poem.[64] They are essentially apostrophes to Nature as the emblem of a higher harmony of the sort strewn through Shaftesbury's *Characteristics*. The subject is elevated and then reintegrated into an authentic self by the process. The right-angled turn is folded back into a continuous sense of identity progressing through time in a coherent manner. Frequently these moments of elation are described in the grand prophetic manner, but the potential folly of an over-reaching enthusiasm is qualified by a rhetoric of workmanship and professionalism that separates Wordsworth's transports from the extraordinary calls of the Methodist.

TRANSPARENCE AND REVOLUTIONARY ENTHUSIASM

The language of prophecy also appears as a political discourse in the poem, that is, as a means of representing Wordsworth's youthful responses to the Revolution in France. Given that the coincidence of prophetic language and political discourse was strongly marked as a sign of dangerous enthusiasm in Wordsworth's culture, *The Prelude* sets itself a difficult task in distinguishing his own healthful prophesying from the diseased *transparence* of political zealotry.

[64] James K. Chandler, *Wordsworth's Second Nature: A Study of the Poetry and Politics* (Chicago: University of Chicago Press, 1984), 199.

The crossing of the Alps episode in Book VI of Wordsworth's *The Prelude* is widely regarded as 'the major piece of English apocalyptic poetry in the Romantic period'.[65] It is a passage described by Alan Liu as 'a sustained effort to deny history by asserting nature as the separating mark constitutive of the egotistical self'.[66] Written in 1804, the passage narrates the crossing of the Simplon Pass which Wordsworth had made after having been caught up in the revolutionary enthusiasm of France in 1790. Having looked forward to the crossing as a moment of sublime revelation, the poet meets a peasant who tells him that he is already on his way down the mountain. At this point, the narrative is interrupted as the narrator breaks in with a hymn to the creative power that had anticipated the crossing with such intensity:

> . . . In such strength
> Of usurpation, in such visitings
> Of awful promise, when the light of sense
> Goes out in flashes that have shown to us
> The invisible world, doth greatness make abode,
> There harbours whether we be young or old.
> Our destiny, our nature, and our home
> Is with infinitude, and only there—
> With hope it is, hope that can never die,
> Effort, and expectation, and desire,
> And something evermore about to be
>
> (VI. 532–42).

For Elinor Shaffer, who objects to the New Historicist emphasis on the evasions of Wordsworth's imagination, there remains in such a passage the possibility of a transformative utopia.[67] She is right, I think, to claim that the language of Apocalypse is not *necessarily* to be thought of as operating in a simple binary against history and politics, but she underestimates the extent to which this possibility is cordoned off in Wordsworth's passage. Wordsworth's evasion is not one of displacing History onto the Imagination, but rather one of reconfiguring or rewriting the Apocalyptic moment in quite specific ways:

---

[65] Elinor Shaffer, 'Secular Apocalypse: Prophets and Apocalyptics at the End of the Eighteenth Century', in Malcolm Bull (ed.), *Apocalypse Theory and the Ends of the World* (Oxford: Blackwell, 1995), 150.

[66] Alan Liu, *Wordsworth: The Sense of History* (Stanford, Calif.: Stanford University Press, 1989), 13.

[67] Shaffer, 'Secular Apocalypse', 150.

> . . . the sick sight
> And giddy prospect of the raving stream,
> The unfettered clouds and region of the heavens,
> Tumult and peace, the darkness and the light,—
> Were all like workings of one mind, the features
> Of the same face, blossoms upon one tree;
> Characters of the great apocalypse,
> The types and symbols of eternity,
> Of first, and last, and midst and without end
>
> (VII. 564–72).

'The theory of denial is Imagination,' says Alan Liu; but what is denied here is not History alone, not only the events of the French Revolution or Napoleon's crossing of the Alps, but also the possibility of a different kind of apocalyptic thinking identified by Wordsworth and his contemporaries with the counter-public of enthusiasm.[68] Strictly speaking, the rhetorical swerve made by Wordsworth is not one of denial at all, for the apocalyptic does not necessarily deny the historical and political, but one of disciplinary regulation that distances his poetic enthusiasm from its more political forms (whether inflected with religion or not). The Apocalypse is closed off from the public space inhabited by someone such as Richard Lee's radical imagining of the Last Days. The problem faced by Coleridge in 'Religious Musings' of laying claim to the prophetic experience is addressed in *The Prelude* by a process of internalization that reinforces the process of de-corporealization described in the previous section. Wordsworth's Apocalypse privileges an act of mental discipline over the immediacy of seeing found in Lee's poetry. The latter was paradigmatically enthusiastic in its translation of spiritual experience into an immediate visual act that could function as the basis of political intervention. In *The Prelude*, no less than in Coleridge's conversation poems, the language of prophecy came to be safely separated from public political utterance by the poetic reconstruction of apocalyptic unveiling as an intensely private experience. The spots of time are incorporated into Wordsworth's development in another sense too. They are precisely sublimated into a higher realm by the act of recollection that pulls them into a narrative of the organic development of the self beyond the exigencies of historical experience. The mind that feels

[68] Liu, *Wordsworth*, 5.

sympathy with the rocks and stones of the Alps, to reconfigure Simon Jarvis's example, is not denied as such, but it is reconstituted in terms of a 'higher' level of experience: one that defines Wordsworth's enthusiasm less in terms of the material experiences of crossing the mountain, but as a de-corporealized mental apocalypse. Such experiences are moments of enthusiasm that Wordsworth builds into himself in order to move beyond them into maturity.

If Wordsworth's disciplining of the prophetic keeps alive any utopian possibility, his Apocalypse of the Imagination is what Ernst Bloch called an 'abstract utopia', that is, one that does not provide 'an historical alternative—a utopia to be translated into reality'.[69] Wordsworth's millennium is always already, it seems, achieved in 'the invisible world' (l. 536), it wants only to be rediscovered as a fixed quantity by the work of the poet (and his reader). Historically Wordsworth's transformation of the apocalyptic moment would seem to stand at the head of a peculiarly English brand of conservative thinking defined by Patrick Wright:

> It stages utopia not as a vision of possibilities which reside in the real—nor even a prophetic if counterfactual perspective on the real but as a dichotomous realm existing alongside the everyday . . . what much utopianism has alluded to or postulated as the challenge of history . . . ends up behind us already accomplished.[70]

Here is another important difference from the apocalypticism of a plebeian prophet such as Richard Lee, and even, I will argue in my next chapter, from Blake's claim that Jerusalem was in Oxford Street (the claim that Southey took to be a proof of Blake's madness or enthusiasm). Although there are important differences between Lee's poetry and Blake's prophetic books, both in their different ways lay claim to 'a vision of possibilities which reside in the real'. In *The Prelude*, the Simplon Pass has an important proleptic role in preparing the reader for the necessary disappointment of such possibilities in the realm of the political.

When it comes to describing his own political enthusiasm of the 1790s in Book x, Wordsworth uses specifically prophetic terms:

---

[69] See Ernst Bloch, *The Principle of Hope*, trans. Neville Plaice et al. (Oxford: Blackwell, 1986), 12.

[70] Patrick Wright, *On Living in an Old Country* (Verso, 1985), 78.

> But as the ancient prophets were inflamed,
> Nor wanted consolations of their own
> And majesty of mind when they denounced
> On towns and cities, wallowing in the abyss
> Of their offences, punishment to come;
> Or saw like other men, with bodily eyes,
> Before them, in some desolated place,
> The consummation of the wrath of Heaven;
> So did some portions of that spirit fall
> On me, to uphold me through those evil times,
> And in their rage and dog-day heat I found
> Something to glory in, as just and fit
> And in the order of sublimest laws.
> And, even if that were not, amid the awe
> Of unintelligible chastisement
> I felt a kind of sympathy with power—
> Motions raised up within me, nevertheless
> Which had relationship to highest things . . .
>
> (X. 401–18)

The treatment of prophecy in this passage is far from straightforward. While the validity of the republican enthusiasm represented here is ultimately disavowed in the poem, the idea of a specific prophetic insight dwelling within Wordsworth's radicalism is not cast away, but now transferred to an intimation of 'higher things'. Wordsworth's youthful enthusiasm is no bad thing in itself, one might say, but its validity depends on a work of regulation of which the French revolutionaries are not capable. Coleridge explored a parallel understanding of his own youthful 'enthusiasm' in the essays he wrote in *The Friend* after reading Wordsworth's long poem. Wordsworth's youthful revolutionary zeal is represented as the anticipation of another, more disciplined and mediated kind of prophetic insight, the kind of Apocalypse that bursts into the narration of the Simplon Pass episode from the mature present as a hymn to the Imagination.[71] Although there is much that is positive about the representation of Wordsworth's pro-revolutionary friend Michel Beaupuy, there is a structural significance to the emphasis on his early death. For Beaupuy, who is 'enthusiastic to the height | Of highest expectation' (IX. 300–1), is not able to provide a

---

[71] Compare the fate of radical 'enthusiasm' in Coleridge's *The Friend*, written after he had read Wordsworth's poem; see above 164–7.

sustainable form of regulation that will preserve his sense of self from the dangers of his own enthusiasm. His feverishness is the disease that kills him rather than a symptom of it. He is almost too good for this world in the immediate strength of his enthusiasm. Wordsworth's own youthful enthusiasm, in contrast, is incorporated and transcended by the older poet.

A similarly complex strategy of desire and discipline is evident later in Book X, when Wordsworth discusses his youthful response to French military expansion:

> And now, become oppressors in their turn,
> Frenchmen had changed a war of self-defence
> For one of conquest, losing sight of all
> Which they had struggled for—and mounted up,
> Openly in the view of earth and heaven,
> The scale of liberty. I read her doom,
> Vexed inly somewhat, it is true, and sore,
> But not dismayed, nor taking to the shame
> Of a false prophet; but, roused up, I stuck
> More firmly to old tenets, and, to prove
> Their temper strained them more. And thus in heat
> Of contest, did opinions every day
> Grow into consequence, till round my mind
> They clung, as if they were the life of it.

(X. 791–804)

The 'false prophet' in this passage is one who would foretell the doom of France and proclaim failure to fulfil millenarian hopes, while the true prophet holds 'firmly to old tenets'. Needless to say that at the perspective from which these events are being related, that is, from the narrator's position looking back from 1804, these old political tenets have already been discarded, but Wordsworth credits himself with a resolution to be contrasted with what Coleridge had called 'dough-baked patriots' (*L1795* 8). Ultimately this resolution allows him to discover a more permanent kind of insight within his earlier political enthusiasm, Wordsworth implies, even if he discards its transient political content. The dim sense of a higher unity becomes the kernel of the experience even as, paradoxically, its political content is put aside. This discovery itself is not a sudden conversion. Other stages of apprehension form a prelude to this higher knowledge, and these too he represents in terms of a prophetic power that Wordsworth disavows in its specific political form, even as he builds it into his sense of his higher poetic enthusiasm:

> This was the time, when, all things tended fast
> To depravation; the philosophy
> That promised to abstract the hopes of man
> Out of his feelings, to be fixed thenceforth
> For ever in a purer element,
> Found ready welcome. Tempting region that
> For zeal to enter and refresh herself,
> Where passions had the privilege to work,
> And never hear the sound of their own names!
>
> (x. 805–13)

Nicholas Roe has argued that these lines specifically allude to the 'tempting region' of Godwin's ideas, but prior to ascribing a particular referent to them it is worth dwelling on the language that Wordsworth uses here.[72] For he names his attraction to Godwin's ideas in terms of prophetic 'Zeal'. Implicitly, he is pouring petrol on the flames of his revolutionary enthusiasm. One does not normally associate Godwinianism with 'zeal' and the 'passions', but I have already described the post-Burkean logic whereby a philosophy of abstract reasoning could be construed as a version of prophetic enthusiasm. Wordsworth seems to make exactly this Burkean move in *The Prelude*, and very explicitly echoes its apprehension of the danger that an unmediated Reason can act with the vehemence of passion by another name.[73] From this perspective, Godwinianism is a species of revolutionary *transparence* that shares with religious enthusiasm a refusal to accommodate itself with what Wordsworth calls 'the familiar face of life' (XII. 67). In contrast to the 'abstract hopes' of such philosophy, the evolutionary narrative of progress that provides the larger picture of his development in *The Prelude*

---

[72] Nicholas Roe, *Wordsworth and Coleridge: The Radical Years* (Oxford: Clarendon Press, 1988), 6–7.

[73] See Chapter 2 and also the excellent discussion in Jones, *Radical Sensibility*, 96. Both Godwin and Hutcheson tend to conflate the passions that impel men to benevolent actions with the power that regulates and directs them: Hutcheson more directly using a language of affection, Godwin using a language of reason and understanding, although the latter seems almost to anticipate Wordsworth's critiques when he asserts: 'Passion is so far from being incompatible with reason, that it is inseparable from it. Virtue, sincerity, justice and all those principles which are begotten and cherished in us by a due exercise of the reason will never be very strenuously espoused till they are ardently loved' (*Godwin Works*, i. 81).

appears as a properly regulated use of enthusiasm. In its enthusiasm
for casting off the familiar in a radical unworlding, Godwinianism
is simply:

> . . . a work
> Of false imagination, placed beyond
> The limits of experience and of truth.

> (x. 846–8)

For all they may describe a difference from the arrogance of the doctrine of *transparence*, the limits accepted by Wordsworth prescribe
a distance, their own distance from the social relations identified
with the crowd in London. 'Social freedom' finds its 'only basis' in
the 'freedom of the individual mind' (x. 824–5). Paradoxically
echoing Godwin, who also feared that private judgement was vulnerable to the dangerous enthusiasm of the crowd, only the practice
of regulation in solitary relations with nature guarantees a true
sense of benevolence. Simon Jarvis sees Wordsworth's critique of
Godwinianism as preserving a space for a fuller engagement with
otherness than revolutionary *transparence* allows. Leaving aside the
issue of whether Wordsworth's representation of Godwinianism as
a form of *transparence* is valid, I would suggest that Wordsworth
himself hardly offers an expansive sense of the possibilities of relating to the world. Of course Wordsworth is not valorizing private
judgement in Godwin's sense. 'Freedom of the individual mind' for
Wordsworth consists of a carefully mediated apprehension of a universal harmony roughly parallel to those glimpsed in Shaftesbury's
apostrophes to Nature, yet the emphasis on the sanctity of the individual mind does recall Godwin's own anxieties about enthusiasm.

Chris Jones has pointed out that Shaftesbury often spoke of the
moral sense 'in terms of the heart and affections'.[74] He might have
added 'enthusiasm'. Hutcheson's development of Shaftesbury's
work, Jones goes on, located the moral sense more firmly in reflective faculties, that is, in a kind of intuitive appreciation of moral
qualities brought closer to ideas of conscience in order to distance
it from the pejorative associations of 'enthusiasm' with the passions
of the crowd. Even so, for all Hutcheson's relative caution, the over-
tones of sense in the term still gave rise to suspicion that the 'moral
sense' was nothing better than enthusiasm. Wordsworth struggles

---

[74] Jones, *Radical Sensibility*, 62.

to distinguish his own sympathy for stocks and stones from enthusiasm precisely by stressing the mental discipline of his poetry. Jerome McGann has suggested that Wordsworth's poetics displaces the 'conversational' mode of Della Cruscanism with a 'meditative' poetics.[75] One might say Wordsworth privileges one aspect of the poetic tradition that stemmed from Shaftesbury over another. If the poetics of retirement routinely pointed back to society, as Kelvin Everest has suggested, the social in Wordsworth takes an extremely attenuated and restricted form. Shaftesbury's writing has faith in, as Michael Meehan calls it, 'patterns of untrammelled growth in the natural world, under conditions of freedom'.[76] This free play under liberty in Shaftesbury could be allowed because of a faith in nature's essential and self-righting harmony. If *The Prelude* reassures its readers of the latter, it is cautious over the extent to which the self can be put into play to discover it.

Prophecy in Wordsworth becomes a relatively unsocialized and private discourse. When he represents himself as a true prophet adhering to his 'old tenets', Wordsworth inscribes an idea of prophecy entirely different from the practice of radical prophecy in the 1790s (whether in its religious or Godwinian guise). Thus in terms of the chronology of *The Prelude*, the loyalty of the true prophet seems valued within the chronology of the past being narrated, even while its content is disavowed at the level of the narration, that is, the particular form of Wordsworth's enthusiasm in the 1790s may be disavowed, but the potential for a deeper enthusiasm, produced by disciplinary work on his youthful zeal, is affirmed. In terms of the temporality of the poem as experienced by the reader, the true prophet has already been revealed in Book VI to be the prophet of Imagination, the prophet who has been able to re-collect his transports into a developing subjectivity that is insulated from the violent sympathies of the crowd.[77] Where the latter are all too vulnerable to 'a transport of the outward sense' (XI. 187), as Book VII makes clear, 'vivid but not profound' (188), Wordsworth claims for himself an enthusiasm sanctified by the anchor 'of mind'. The discipline of 'mind' gives 'a substance and a life to what I feel' (XI. 340). 'The spirit of the past' becomes available as part of a continuity for 'future restoration' (XI. 341–2). Rather than the violent

[75] McGann, *The Poetics of Sensibility*, 79.
[76] See Meehan, *Liberty and Poetics*, 26.
[77] See Roe, *Wordsworth and Coleridge*, 6–7.

unworlding of 'extraordinary calls' Wordsworth offers a vision of 'discipline | And consummation' (XIII. 270–1).

To read *The Prelude* in this way, however, perhaps underestimates the work of writing that has to be done in the poem. For Wordsworth constantly produces the possibility of other unregulated enthusiasm in order to work upon it, and something of this combustible matter always seems to remain in excess of its disciplinary plot. 'Enthusiastic joy' and prophetic *transparence* may appear in the poem only to be subsumed into Wordsworth's higher development of 'mind', but their appearance alerts the reader to the relationship between this higher knowledge and what Wordsworth and many of his contemporaries regarded as its dangerous avatars. No less than Shaftesbury, Hutcheson, and even Coleridge, he faces the problem of defining the limit to enthusiasm's 'endless power of semination' (*SM* 24). Wordsworth's failure to publish the poem may have had something to do with a fear that the combustible matter within had not been fully brought inside the pale of the philosophical poem Coleridge imagined him writing. Placing Wordsworth as the culminating example in a narrative of rehabilitation overlooks his own attraction to the kind of enthusiasm that the poem he was writing claimed to be disciplining. *The Prelude* implies that there is always work for the poet to do in order to validate his enthusiasm.

CHAPTER SIX

Energy and Enthusiasm in Blake

IN 1769 SIR JOSHUA REYNOLDS warned aspiring painters that 'mere enthusiasm will carry you but a little way'.[1] In his annotations to Reynolds's lectures, William Blake responded with characteristic bluntness: 'Meer Enthusiasm is the All in All!' (E 645) Blake's attitude defiantly kicks away the discourse of regulation that defined most literary attitudes to enthusiasm in the period. Whereas these attitudes usually assumed the necessity but not the sufficiency of enthusiasm, Blake insisted that 'Enthusiastic Admiration is the first Principle of Knowledge & its last' ('Anno. Reynolds', E 647). Both Wordsworth and Coleridge were closer to Reynolds than Blake on this matter. None of those three thought that enthusiasm could be the 'last word' on anything; Blake seems to have been much more open to the currents of dangerous secular and religious enthusiasms swirling around the London of his time.[2] Not that he ought to be regarded as someone who simply asserted the value of religious enthusiasm over enlightenment scepticism. For Blake was influenced by the questioning spirit of writers like Paine and Volney as much as the spirituality he found in Swedenborg and the Bible. He did believe that the enlightenment cult of Reason could develop a diseased form, but his opinions on this matter do not represent a critique of revolutionary *transparence* as such. He does not deny the possibility of sudden and unmediated apprehensions of truth.

Blake ought to be understood as one of 'the free Enquirers on both political and religious topicks' who, according to John Aikin,

---

[1] Sir Joshua Reynolds, *Discourses on Art*, ed. Robert R. Wark, 3rd edn. (New Haven: Yale University Press, 1997), 31.

[2] These matters are explored in Jon Mee, *Dangerous Enthusiasm: William Blake and the Culture of Radicalism in the 1790s* (Oxford: Clarendon Press, 1992). The point is not that Blake's work *reflects* any single variant of enthusiasm, religious or otherwise, but that like many autodidact 'seekers' he was responsive to the possibility of interrelating the currents around them. The apparent eclecticism of this kind of popular discourse was part of what alarmed polite commentators.

surrounded the enlightened publisher Joseph Johnson in the 1790s.[3] Unlike Burke, for Blake the danger was not that these men and women would make their enquiries unlimited. Precisely the contrary is the case in fact. Reason is dubious for Blake when it limits these enquiries to its own narrow horizons. One might say that Blake attacked the evolution of a superstitious reverence for Reason rather than enthusiasm for rational enquiry as such. Blake's critique of the cult of Reason is part of a larger hostility towards 'Mystery' that insisted on the visibility of the visionary world. He denied the disembodied nature of spirituality routinely affirmed by hegemonic religious discourse: 'A Spirit and a Vision are not, as the modern philosophy supposes, a cloudy vapour or a nothing: they are organized and minutely articulated beyond all that the mortal and perishing nature can produce' (*DC*: E 541). Enlightenment historians such as Hume, Gibbon, and Voltaire, Blake argued, refused 'to see spiritual agency' (E 544). Such blindness rendered their histories 'not worth any man's reading; he who rejects a fact because it is improbable, must reject all History and retain doubts only' (E 544). 'Modern philosophy', from this point of view, was too quick to relegate certain kinds of experience from its consideration. It was too quick to assert that some things could not or ought not to be seen.

If one lets the matter rest there, however, Blake might still seem to be simply defending traditional religious values against the rise of secularism; whereas, he continually aligned the two in their blindness to spiritual agency. All kinds of elite thinking in the period, whether religious or otherwise, were hostile to sudden 'illapses of the spirit': an anxiety that was part of the problem of 'imaging the unseen' that Barbara Stafford's work has explored.[4] The integrity of individual identity was threatened by sudden interventions of 'spiritual agency' in temporal affairs. 'Enthusiasm' was a word still strongly associated with such dangerous right-angled turns. Significantly at around the same time that the word 'enthusiasm' and its cognates start to appear in Blake's writing, so too do the calls to 'Self-Annihilation' in *Milton* and *Jerusalem*. The Blakean enlightenment required the constant casting off of 'Selfhood'. For Blake developed a critique of the dialectic of enlightenment that saw

[3] The phrase is taken from John Aikin's obituary for Johnson in the *Gentleman's Magazine*, 79 (1809), 1179.

[4] See Barbara Maria Stafford, *Body Criticism: Imaging the Unseen in Enlightenment Art and Medicine* (Cambridge, Mass.: MIT Press, 1991; repr. 1997).

the liberating potential of its bold enquiry after truth as frozen into the form of Reason. Subjectivity had to be put into hazard for Blake if this enquiry was to be carried forward. Knowledge depended on enthusiasm as the paradigm-busting impulse that allows us to see beyond 'the same dull round' (*There is No Natural Religion*: E 2). Too great a concern for the continuity of the self could only limit the opportunity of enthusiasm to harvest new forms of knowledge and identity. The Blakean idea of 'Mental Fight' (*M* 1. 13: E 95) carries forward the Godwinian idea of 'the collision of minds' in a way that seems much less defensive about the autonomy of private judgement.

BLAKE AND THE BODY OF ENERGY

Despite its commitment to ocular proof, what Locke called 'demonstration', certain forms of seeing were routinely excluded in the eighteenth century as manifestations of the pathology of a dangerous enthusiasm. The aversion could be regarded as part of a more general philosophical commitment to dualism articulated in Bishop Butler's dictum that 'our gross organized Bodies, with which we perceive the Objects of the Sense, and with which we act, are no Part of our selves'.[5] Whether identified in terms of mind or spirit, identity existed beyond the combustible matter of the senses, however much in the Lockean paradigm it also depended on them. Certainly popular religious enthusiasm, as we have seen, was often regarded as the tainting of the spirit by the senses. Both Wesley and Southey, for instance, were equally uneasy at the presence in Methodist hymnody and other forms of writing 'of expressions which strongly savour of "knowing Christ after the flesh" '.[6] Coleridge and Wordsworth shared with them an anxiety about fleshly vision as a threat to the purity of the Imagination. This chapter argues that Blake is much less concerned about such contamination. When he writes of the 'Spiritual Body', the first term does not cancel the second; far from it, in fact, because 'the notion that man has a body distinct from his soul, is to be expunged' (*MHH* 14:

[5] Butler, *Analogy of Religion, Natural and Revealed, to the Constitution and Cause of Nature* (Dublin, 1736), 17.
[6] See Donald Davie, *A Gathered Church: The Literature of the English Dissenting Interest, 1700–1930* (Routledge & Kegan Paul, 1978), 32.

E 39). 'Energy' is what defines the spiritual body for Blake, not the vaporous idea of the 'soul'. The same priority, I am going to argue in this chapter, is as much at work in Blake's later poetry as it is in *The Marriage of Heaven and Hell*. Although Blake did sometimes operate with a distinction between 'spiritual' and 'vegetable' sight in the later illuminated books, these terms do not map on to a conventional distinction between the body and the soul as distinct essences. The emphasis on 'Self-Annihilation' in *Jerusalem*, for instance, is not a form of the mortification of the flesh. Rather it is an enlargement of the senses beyond a constricted sense of selfhood described most gloriously in *Jerusalem*'s final vision of Eternity:

> . . . regenerations terrific or complacent varying
> According to the subject of discourse & every Word & Every Character
> Was Human according to the Expansion or Contraction, the
>   Translucence or
> Opakeness of Nervous fibres such was the variation of Time & Space
> Which vary according as the Organs of Perception vary & they walked
> To & fro in Eternity as One Man reflecting each in each & clearly Seen
> And seeing.

$$(J \ 98. \ 34\text{--}40\text{: E } 258)$$

Wordsworth worried about the role of material signs in the communication of poetic and religious truths in his 'Essay, Supplementary to the Preface', because he thought that they threatened to obscure the purity of the Imagination with the grossness of embodiment. Blake agreed with Wordsworth that 'it is impossible to think without images of somewhat on earth' ('Anno. to Lavater': E 600). Yet whereas Wordsworth feared that the necessity of 'sensuous incarnation' bred 'kindred errors', Blake took a quite different view. Not that Blake is unaware of the dangers of reifying the sign over its significations. His work is constantly describing situations wherein what is a means to spiritual insight becomes mistaken for an end in itself. The fate of Reason as a liberating energy that becomes frozen is a case in point. So too is the vegetating body, but this problem is not primarily to do with sensuality.

'Abstract' rather than 'sensuous' incarnation is what lies at the heart of reification for Blake:

> We are led to Believe a Lie
> When we see not Thro the Eye

('Auguries of Innocence', 125–6: E 492)

Seeing is believing in Blake. The emergence of the delusive high-priest of both Reason and Religion in Blake's mythology is associated precisely with the urge to keep things 'unseen'. The word 'unseen' recurs three times on a single plate in the account of the beginning of Urizen's regime of mystification in *The Book of Urizen*. What pretends to transcend visibility for Blake is always suspect. Coleridge backed away from his early intellectual mentors Hartley and Priestley because he believed their theology threatened to lose God in his Creation. Later on in the chapter I shall be exploring the possibility that Blake had rather more sympathy in this respect for Hartley and Priestley than is usually imagined. In *Jerusalem* Los insists that one cannot expect to see divinity anywhere else than in created forms:

> Go, tell them that the Worship of God, is honouring his gifts
> In other men: & loving the greatest men best, each according
> To his Genius: which is the Holy Ghost in Man; there is no other
> God, than that God who is the intellectual fountain of Humanity
>
> (*J* 91. 7–10: E 251)

The whole Blakean enterprise remains committed to the 'improvement of sensual enjoyment' (*MHH* 14: E 39). 'Look', 'see', 'behold' the viewer-readers of his illuminated books are constantly enjoined. The form of the illuminated books, moreover, means that Blake is constantly making vision visible to his readers. Wordsworth's impulse, on the contrary, is to privilege *intimation* over seeing. The difference is not just between their chosen media. Rather, one ought to say, the choice of media expresses the difference.

The constant presentation of spiritual life to the viewer in Blake's words and images helps explain why so sensitive a critic as Donald Davie could assent to a view of his work as comparable to Methodist hymnody in its 'arrogance, vulgarity, and excess'.[7] Davie shares the eighteenth-century judgement that nothing could be so certain an index of vulgarity as to find spiritual agency everywhere. For Davie no less than for Coleridge or numerous eighteenth-century churchmen, even those of an evangelical persuasion, such readiness is inflationary and cheapens spiritual value. John Wesley distanced himself from 'extraordinary calls' for this reason. Davie believed that Charles Wesley's hymns smacked less of enthusiasm

---

[7] Davie, *A Gathered Church*, 50, is assenting to Martha W. England's words in *Hymns Unbidden* (1966).

than Blake's poetry, because they showed him more of the spirit of accommodation to eighteenth-century ideas of politeness and manners.[8] In my terms, Wesley was more ready to accept the discipline of regulation. The spiritual fervour of his hymns is more veiled and so more tasteful by the Arnoldian standards Davie sets himself. The class assumptions that underpin these judgements are made apparent when Davie pronounces Blake 'not a hero of the democratizing of Scripture, but a martyr to it'.[9] Only those with access to a wider culture through privileges of leisure and education can avoid 'sociopolitical resentment and aspiration thinly cloaked in religious terminology'.[10] His views here echo Barbauld's concern that Joseph Priestley's disputatiousness was confirming a view of Dissent as vulgar and uncouth.

Needless to say most professional Blake criticism departs from this condescending view, but its energies have tended to be invested in distinguishing Blake from the culture of enthusiasm despised by Davie, rather than questioning the grounds of his condescension. Where Davie sees only philistinism in Blake's iconoclasm, however, Clement Hawes and others have begun the work of looking at such enthusiasm as a language with a grammar of its own.[11] For Hawes, as I pointed out in my first chapter, enthusiasm provides those excluded from the polite world with a means of expressing themselves. If this rather ignores the existence of an elite poetics of enthusiasm, it does enable us to see why Blake continually defined his own poetics against those of the 'Classical Learned' ('Anno. Thornton', E 667). Even so, the popular culture of enthusiasm was a complex phenomenon, and by no means did it provide an unequivocal discourse of liberation. Many of those Methodists charged with enthusiasm, for instance, would have been appalled at the idea that they were confusing agape and eros. They would have insisted on the spirituality of their intentions whatever critics read into their linguistic practice. The constant references to the 'carnal' and 'spiritual' eyes in Methodist literature was meant to reinforce not collapse precisely this distinction. There were some enthusiasts, such as some Moravians or those on the fringes of Sweden-

---

[8] Davie, *A Gathered Church*, 50–2, again agreeing with England.
[9] Ibid. 54.   [10] Ibid. 52.
[11] See Clement Hawes, *Mania and Literary Style: The Rhetoric of Enthusiasm from the Ranters to Christopher Smart* (Cambridge: Cambridge University Press, 1996).

borgianism in the 1780s and 1790s, who did explicitly embrace ideas about the spirituality of sex. Blake's illuminated books, perhaps influenced by these aspects of Swedenborgianism, or perhaps attracted to Swedenborg because of this inflection in the Swedish prophet's writings, do seem to celebrate the divinity of desire. Recent Blake scholarship has made serious advances in documenting these similarities, which my own earlier work on Blake rather overlooked. My present concerns in this chapter lie elsewhere however, and are less concerned with sources than understanding the cultural logic of Blakean enthusiasm and its derogation of the call to be 'Passive & Polite & a Virtuous Ass' ('Anno. to Reynolds': E 642).

The idea that at some time soon after 1800 Blake became much more quietist remains firmly entrenched in some critical quarters. It was around this same time that the word 'enthusiasm' and its derivatives also started to appear more often in his writing. Could this coincidence represent a parallel to Coleridge's attempt to clear a space for a pious enthusiasm after 1800? Several of Blake's letters from the 1800 to 1804 period ask the recipients to forgive him for his 'enthusiasm', although any sense of repentance is undercut by insisting that it is 'a Source of Immortal Joy even in this world' ('To William Hayley, May 6 1800': E 705).[12] Of course, if one understands enthusiasm simply in terms of ardour of religious belief, so that it operates in a binary contrast, say, with freethinking religious scepticism, this might seem a retreat, but such an understanding would run counter to the account of enthusiasm that I have been advancing in this study. Piously regulated 'enthusiasm' for someone such as Coleridge was understood, at least in his later work, as a bulwark against the two-headed beast of radicalism and infidelity, but even he continued to fear the tendency of religious enthusiasm to transform itself into an ally of the dangerous passions associated with the crowd. Blake's emphasis on the sufficiency of enthusiasm and the possibility of it acting as 'a Source of Immortal Joy even in this world' should alert us to the fact that he used the word rather differently from the later Coleridge. Exploring Blake's use of the word 'enthusiasm' after 1800 reveals a new self-consciousness on

---

[12] See also the letters to Thomas Butts, 25 Apr. 1803 (E 728), and again to William Hayley, 23 Oct. 1804 (E 757). He was much less apologetic to Thomas Butts in November 1802, when he wrote: 'My Enthusiasm is still what it was only Enlargd and confirmd' (E 720).

his part about the way the discourse surrounding the term operated in his culture.

This self-consciousness includes a new sympathy for those routinely condemned for their enthusiasm, such as Wesley and Whitefield, but not as figures whose discipline was later appreciated by Southey. They appear in *Jerusalem* rather as martyrs to the elite fear of enthusiasm expressed both in Southey's *Life of Wesley* and Hunt's *Folly and Dangers of Methodism*. They are men who far from protecting their Selfhood cast it off with little fear that they put their identities into hazard. The roles given to Wesley and Whitefield in the later prophecies, minor as it may be, should alert us to the fact that Blake's valorization of 'enthusiasm' after 1800 is not the rehabilitation of a more purely poetic form of transport. Obviously Blake had a taste for poets such as Young, but he does not distinguish this poetic strain of enthusiasm from the power displayed by the Methodists.[13] When he equates his enthusiasm with 'being drunk with intellectual vision', as he does in his October 1804 letter to Hayley (E 757), the figure of bodily intoxication precisely refuses the kind of regulation that was the usual precondition of this rehabilitation in eighteenth-century poetics. My next section explores the possibility that Blake's self-conscious promotion of enthusiasm in *Jerusalem* may have been intensified by encountering the sustained attacks on popular religious enthusiasm in the early issues of the *Examiner*. For Leigh Hunt and his brother Robert there was an absolute difference between the aesthetic sphere and the vulgarity of popular enthusiasm that Blake's validation of Whitefield and Wesley refuses.

HUNTING ENTHUSIASM

I have already made copious use of Leigh Hunt's *Folly and Danger of Methodism* to illustrate the durability of elite attitudes to religious enthusiasm right into the early nineteenth century. What makes the pamphlet particularly interesting for our purposes here is the fact that at the same time as it was originally being published as

---

[13] See the discussion in Jon Mee, ' "As portentous as the written wall": Blake's Illustrations to *Night Thoughts*', in Sandy Gourlay (ed.), *Prophetic Character: Essays on William Blake in Honor of John E. Grant* (West Cornwall, Conn.: Locust Hill Press, 2002), 171–203.

a series of letters in the *Examiner*, Blake was being attacked on similar grounds in the same place by Hunt's brother Robert. From the perspectives of the Hunt brothers and their concern with good taste, Blake was someone who failed to regulate his enthusiasm into acceptable form. Blake's reaction to this judgement, I shall be suggesting, may have made its way into *Jerusalem* in the form of a contrary assertion of the legitimacy of 'enthusiasm' as a basis for participation in the public sphere. Hunt's personal position on religious matters was broadly latitudinarian, close to what Blake pilloried as 'Natural Religion'. He later claimed that the *Examiner* 'advocated the mild spirit of religious government, as exercised by the Church of England, in opposition to the bigoted part of dissent'.[14] Perhaps in the early decades of the century he was less patient of the Church itself as an institution than his recollections suggest, but what is unquestionable is that he was inclined to a tastefully felt but rational religion rather than the enthusiasm he saw in Methodism. *The Folly and Danger of Methodism* is directed against 'the bigoted part of dissent', that is, those sects who attack the Church of England for its lack of spiritual zeal. No less than for Barbauld and other Unitarians in the 1770s, such zealous disputatiousness had no place in Hunt's idea of religious devotion. Hunt also shared their hope that the national Church would be reformed into a union of Anglicanism with 'the most learned and liberal of the Dissenters, the Unitarians and Universalists' (H 71). Hunt anticipated Donald Davie's desire for Anglicans and Dissenters to share in Arnold's sweetness and light. Methodism in Hunt's attack is functioning not as the name of a particular movement, but—as it often did in the eighteenth and early nineteenth centuries—as a synonym for 'all that enthusiastic multitude who in the spirit of Christian modesty call themselves the *Godly*, whether Arminian or Calvinists, or the innumerable divisions of these sects who all claim the miracles of the Apostolic age, the immediate interference of the Deity, and the holy ecstasies of the blessed' (H 2). Methodism for Hunt represents all those qualities of Dissent that Davie identifies with philistinism. Identified as a religion of gloominess and intolerance by Hunt, the removal of its influence is part of his enlightenment vision of progress (as it was for Thelwall in the previous decade). Hunt explicitly describes the Methodists as a throwback to

---

[14] Hunt, *Autobiography of Leigh Hunt*, ed. J. E. Marpurgo (Cresset, 1949), 178.

'the fanatics of the Commonwealth' (H p. ix). His liberalism perpetuates the dialect of enlightenment that casts popular forms of
knowledge and experience as a threat to right reason and cultural
value. In order to safeguard manners, its philistinism must be barred
from the public sphere. Hunt notes with disgust that 'among the
inspired teachers, who applied at Clerkenwell a few months ago for
licences, were a footman, a cobler, and a sheeps head seller' (81).
Those 'whose education has enabled them to search into the original languages of the scriptures and the antiquities of the church . . .
are therefore the only men competent to search into the truth of
what they teach' (3). Only 'the Classical Learned', to use Blake's
terms, have a right to judge of matters relating to their own salvation. The uneducated masses had to be weaned away from despotism and priestcraft, but they were not to be entirely trusted with
seeing the truth for themselves. For left to themselves, as Hume
before him had suggested, they would run into the slough of enthusiasm. Any claim to 'immediate inspiration' is suspect to Hunt in its
circumvention of the barriers of cultural capital and education that
protected his enlightenment values. George Whitefield emerges as
the villain of Hunt's pamphlet, more so than Wesley, perhaps
because he was easier to represent as the begetter of this vulgarity.
His Calvinism was closer to Hunt's idea of gloomy intolerance than
Wesley's Arminianism. His language was routinely described as
more violent and intemperate than Wesley's, and he was also generally identified with instituting the practice of field preaching.[15]
Whitefield is blamed for the dangerous step of taking the religious
message outside the walls of accredited institutions of knowledge
and spirituality. Liberal reservations about State Religion, it seems,
were outweighed for Hunt by a fear that outside its institutions the
masses would be unable to regulate their own enthusiasm.

Doctrinally Hunt associates enthusiasm with predestination and
election, that is, what he conceives of as Calvinism. His optimistic
view of God finds the exclusivity of election repellent, and predestination suggests to Hunt a barbaric idea of God as an arbitrary
tyrant. There is another side to this enlightenment coin, however.
Bennett and Bogue, who fall within Hunt's category of 'liberal
and learned' Dissenters, decried, at around the same time as the
Examiner, 'the popular poison, a bastard zeal for the doctrine of sal-

---

[15] See the account given in Southey, *Life of Wesley*, i. 229.

vation by grace'.[16] Hunt is no less hostile than they to the idea of imputed righteousness, not only because it is associated with the determinism of election, but also because he sees it as an encouragement to vice and, especially, sexual incontinence. The popularity of the doctrine of salvation by grace was taken to lie in the perception that it offered unconditional forgiveness. Although recent criticism on Hunt's relations with the Cockney School has taught us to think of him as an opponent of Christian moralism, the second of his *Examiner* essays was devoted to what he saw as the Methodist hatred of moral teaching. Demonstrating the alliance between free-thinking and the Church on such matters, Hunt even went to the Anglican prelate Bishop Stillingfleet for a classic statement of the dangers of the doctrine of salvation by faith alone: ' "Tis an easy way of salvation", says Bishop STILLINGFLEET, "if no more were required to mens' happiness by a fancy and strong opinion, which they will easily call believing" ' (H 83). In what follows Hunt readily trots out several case histories suggesting that immorality has been excused and even encouraged by the too-ready forgiveness of sins. Such practises throw 'down the last barrier between human frailty and human presumption . . . the greatest scoundrel has nothing to do but to believe, in order to enter at once upon the privileges of an Archangel' (H 33). The fact that Hunt's enlightenment discourse opposes the bright day of Reason to the gloominess of the Methodist who 'closes his eyes to the light of reason and of nature' (H 6) should not blind *us* to the equally disciplinary moralism behind his perspective. However different their politics were, Hunt agreed with Robert Southey, for instance, that the Methodist stress on imputed right-eousness encouraged moral laxity.

Hunt may condemn what he sees as Methodism's unworldly disdain for the joys of this world, but he is also more than willing to condemn the crowd for seeking to justify their own embodied pleasures as spiritual ecstasy. Methodist singing, love feasts, and numerous other means by which historians have shown us that popular religious groups provided experiences of pleasure and community—what I have been calling the counter-public of enthusiasm—are condemned by Hunt for a moral laxity that he believed encouraged over-familiarity between the sexes. Methodist hymnody he

---

[16] David Bogue and James Bennett, *History of the Dissenters, from the Revolution in 1688, to the Year 1808*, 4 vols. (1808–12), iv. 39.

dismissed as a 'disgrace'—'much of it very obscene' (H 58). The enlightenment critique of enthusiasm was obsessed with what it took to be a failure of the uneducated properly to distinguish the passions—associated with the body—from intellectual or spiritual matters. What Hunt quoting Wesley called '*inward impressions* on the soul' (H 83) had to be distinguished from the ecstasies of the body. Perpetuating traditional Anglican definitions of piety, the contained inwardness of these impressions is taken by Hunt as a sign that they have been regulated into harmony with the individual, unlike the bodily ecstasies of enthusiasm. The latter are the shocking exteriorized signs of 'distraction', to revert to Walter Benjamin's term, a form of seeing in which the autonomy of the beholder is overwhelmed by the sensations. For the distracted viewer in the modern city, the cushion of consciousness does not order the impressions of the senses into articulate form. Although Benjamin's ideas about distraction were conceived of in relation to the crowds of the nineteenth century, the phenomenon of urbanization in the eighteenth century had encouraged commentators to see the familiar sign of enthusiasm in the behaviour of its earlier counterpart (and frequently use the word chosen by Benjamin's English translators to describe it).[17] Southey defined religious enthusiasm as a primarily urban pathology. Limits to the freedom of enquiry have to be imposed on the masses, therefore, even for a liberal such as Hunt, because the people seem incapable of making a proper distinction between the autonomous viewing subject and the visible object. Although obviously much less concerned to defend the objective reality of the supernatural against the welter of mere impressions, Hunt seems almost as alarmed as Coleridge by the idea that the mind might be constructed out of the senses.

Hunt comments that the 'sensual reveries' of the Methodists reveal 'what influence the body has on this kind of devotion' (H 55). Women in particular are identified as vulnerable to this kind of confusion:

The Methodist magazines abound in the dying raptures of the godly, and it is curious to observe what an infinite number of rapturous females there are in comparison with the men . . . The language of these women is so entirely earthly, that in general if you change the name of the object, you might

---

[17] Benjamin, 'The Work of Art in the Age of Mechanical Reproduction', in *Illuminations*, ed. Hannah Arendt (Fontana, repr. 1982), 241.

think their devotion addressed to a mere lover. The Deity is personified in the grossest of images; the soul talks just as the body might be supposed to talk without a soul; and instead of the soul, GOD is adored with the senses. (H 55–6)

We have already seen that this idea is a traditional feature of attacks on enthusiasm. Swift—to whom Hunt makes constant reference in his notes—identified the female genitalia as the main oracle of enthusiasm.[18] Women were not deemed to have the rational powers necessary to regulate their own passionate natures. They could not be trusted to sublimate the ecstasies of the body into a truly spiritual rapture. Where men succumbed to enthusiasm, they were regularly regarded as effeminized, and Hunt has some striking passages on the confusion of the sexes as a dominant aspect of the literature of enthusiasm.

More generally the confusion of the passions of the body with spiritual agency remain at the core of Hunt's anxieties about 'imaging the unseen'. What he calls the 'aberration of eye' (H 62) recalls Wordsworth's phrasing of his own anxieties on this score. At the heart of the grossness which Hunt identifies with enthusiasm is its desire to collapse the visionary into the visible:

The dying Saints in the Godly Magazine are continually seeing things in Heaven, though the Scripture expressly says that the eye hath not seen, nor ear heard, nor the heart of man conceived what heaven is. (H 94)

He goes on to give a comically rendered account of the deathbed scene of a Miss Barker from the *Methodist Magazine* of April 1807:

> O what has Jesus brought for me:
> Before my ravished eyes!
> Rivers of life divine I see,
> And trees of Paradise!

'I see, I see, I see—I want to be filled with love'—Mrs Barker replied. 'You seem already so'—'Oh' she added, 'but I want to be filled.' (H 94)

Although played for comedy here, the spectacle of the enthusiastic body reappears so often in Hunt's pamphlet that it seems to betray a genuine anxiety. In fact it marks the point at which the older discourse surrounding religious enthusiasm coincides with the enlightenment fear that ocular proof might be an uncertain basis for

---

[18] See the discussion in Chapter 1.

knowledge. The fear that haunted the Enlightenment, from this point of view, one that Locke himself explicitly anticipated and attempted to allay, was that sensations were mired in the impurity and uncertainty of the passions, perhaps even to the extent that knowledge might be no more than enthusiasm. The rhetoric of seeing at the very heart of the trope of enlightenment was continually caught up in distinguishing false from true vision, but the most extreme case of this confusion, defined as the pathology against which the true seeing of the Enlightenment could be defined, remained the claim to be able to see God through and in the flesh. Hunt's essays may mock the evangelical distinction between 'carnal' and 'spiritual', but he effectively reinstates the opposition on another level as the difference between seeing with the senses and knowing with Reason.[19] Indeed the whole point of his jokes at the expense of believers such as Mrs Baker is that they are incapable of maintaining the distinction between carnal and spiritual they themselves seem to insist upon.

This question of the relationship between the carnal and spiritual eye brings me to Blake, and his encounter with the Hunts. On Sunday, 7 August 1808 a fiercely critical review of Blake's illustrations to Robert Cromek's edition of Robert Blair's *The Grave* appeared in the *Examiner*. Just over a year later it was followed by an equally hostile account of Blake's 1809 exhibition of paintings.[20] If one consults the volume of the *Examiner* that contains the first review, and looks at the next number of the weekly, there one finds Leigh Hunt's 'On the Indecencies and Profane Raptures of Methodism'.[21] G. E. Bentley Jr has suggested that the ferocity of Robert Hunt's attack on Blake may have originated in the perception that the engraver was a Methodist precisely of the sort concurrently being attacked in the pages of the *Examiner* by his brother.[22] Bentley's is an important insight, but not one that has not been pursued very far by critics. This comparative quiet might be explained as an embarrassment at the idea of Blake being mistaken for a vulgar enthusiast. Shuddering perhaps at the possibility that Blake

---

[19] See the discussion of such terms in H 5–7.

[20] The reviews are helpfully reproduced in G. E. Bentley, Jr., *Blake Records* (Oxford: Oxford University Press, 1969), 195–7 and 215–18.

[21] The review of Blake appeared in *Examiner*, 32, 7 Aug., 509–10 and the sixth of Hunt's essays began to appear in *Examiner*, 33, 14 Aug., 524–5.

[22] Bentley, *Blake Records*, 197.

could be identified with the kind of vulgarity ascribed to him by Davie, most critics prefer the idea that the Hunts misunderstood what they were attacking; but many other features of what Hunt's *Folly and Danger of Methodism* disdains as enthusiasm are vigorously present in Blake's illuminated books. 'Imaging the unseen' provides one useful axis around which to describe the differences between Blake and the Hunts. Robert Hunt protested loudly at the grotesque attempt to *'connect the visible and invisible world'* in Blake's designs for the 1807 edition of *The Grave*.[23] He was convinced of 'the utter impossibility of representing the *Spirit* to the eye'.[24] Only two other contemporary reviews of the Blair edition are known, and, although written from very different political perspectives, both of them reiterate Hunt's point of view. The *Anti-Jacobin Review and Magazine* found 'the same defect of giving substantial form to incorporeal substance'. Even the more generally favourable *Monthly Magazine* agreed.[25] According to Hunt the result of such representational strategies was a mixing of the sensual and spiritual of the sort his brother found to be the defining feature of Methodism. Of course, these reviewers all realised with Wordsworth that 'sensuous incarnation' was unavoidable if matters of religious significance were to be represented at all, but like him they felt steps had to be taken to prevent 'the lurking incitement of kindred error'.[26] 'An appearance of libidinousness intrudes itself upon the holiness of our thoughts,' lamented Robert Hunt of Blake's designs.[27] He was particularly upset about the concupiscence of the plate known as 'A Family meeting in Heaven', because it suggested that sexual relations might continue in the afterlife (an idea also found in Swedenborg, as it happens). The idea that eros and agape might be confused in this way was outrageous to Hunt. His attitudes to imaging the unseen correspond to the anti-pictorialism that W. J. T. Mitchell has found in most canonical Romantic poetry apart from Blake.[28] When Coleridge dismissed allegory as 'picture-language' (*SM* 30), he was displaying the same attitudes

[23] Ibid. 195. Robert Hunt is quoting from Fuseli's puff for the Blair volume.
[24] Ibid.
[25] Reproduced in Bentley, *Blake Records*, 199–208 and 209–10 respectively.
[26] See the discussion of this point in Chapter 5.
[27] Bentley, *Blake Records*, 197.
[28] See W. J. T. Mitchell, 'Visible Language: Blake's Wond'rous Art of Writing', in Morris Eaves and Michael Fischer (eds.), *Romanticism and Contemporary Criticism* (Ithaca, NY: Cornell University Press, 1986), 46–95.

that structure Robert Hunt's sense of the dangers courted by Blake in *The Grave* designs:

That work, [Robert reminded his readers in his review of the 1809 exhibition], was a futile endeavour by bad drawings to represent immaterially by bodily personifications of the soul, while it's partner the body was depicted in company with it, so that the soul was confounded with the body, as the personifying figure had none of the distinguishing characteristics of allegory, presenting only substantial flesh and bones.[29]

Coleridge, more generally, of course, shared the tendency of Burke and others to think of the sublime as resistant to the minute particularity of the body. Where the visible world intrudes in too much detail, it is likely to be an impediment to the visionary nature of the sublime: 'a soulless image on the eye' as Wordsworth put it, 'Which had usurped upon a living thought' (*Prelude 1805*, VI. 454–5). While there are distinctions between different kinds of seeing in Blake's work, a point that I will return to later, he always insisted that the sublime could be seen in its 'minute particulars': 'Obscurity is Neither the Source of the Sublime nor of any Thing Else' ('Anno. to Reynolds': E 658). Blake was convinced that the sublime could only be seen and represented via the fleshly particularity of the body. He complained at the disembodied nature of the 'Mathematical Diagram' ('Laocoon': E 274) used by Thomas Taylor to illustrate his edition of Plato.[30] The engravings to William Law's edition of Boehme, on the other hand, he praised for representing the spiritual world in a particularized corporeal form (right down to the internal organs).[31]

Barbara Stafford insists that both neoclassical and Romantic art should be regarded as different styles based on the same attitude to the body: 'Invisible Ideas or noumenal reality—which could be touched or grazed by the disembodied understanding—resided on

---

[29] Bentley, *Blake Records*, 216.

[30] Interestingly, in the early prose piece *An Island in the Moon*, Blake has the Pythagorean character Sipsop, who is often thought to be based on Thomas Taylor, complain that the philosopher Inflammable Gas is 'endeavoring to incorporate their souls with their bodies' (E 450). Inflammable Gas is often associated with Priestley, who as a follower of Hartley was indeed regularly attacked for tracing psychology to physiology. Blake's attitudes, I argue below, may owe more to Hartley than is often allowed, and certainly he is not hostile to the idea of the mutuality of the soul and body.

[31] See the discussion in Paley, *The Continuing City: William Blake's Jerusalem* (Oxford: Oxford University Press, 1983), 98–9.

the far side of appearances'.[32] For Wordsworth and Coleridge, as we have seen, this ultimate idea was usually *intimated*, glimpsed, or overheard rather than seen in any particularized or embodied form. Both were perpetuating an Anglican idea of true spirituality that had always been defined against the bodily excesses of enthusiasm. Both also participated in the late enlightenment anxiety that writing and books themselves in the wrong hands might provide a sensual distraction from the ultimate goal of truth. The feared consequence of such distraction was that the sublime would become debased into mere writing or image; just as in Leigh Hunt's *Folly and Danger of Methodism*, there is a fear that the matters of the spirit might be mired and devalued in the passions of the crowd. Whereas Wordsworth was concerned that 'sensuous incarnation' could lead to 'error', Blake's enthusiasm is committed to the expansion of sensual enjoyment. Blake's engraving style in the illuminated books implies quite a different perspective on the materiality of the sign from Wordsworth's. Words on the plates of Blake's illuminate books literally blossom into things. Their thinginess is not gross, but, potentially at least, a source of delight. Mitchell regards Blake's illuminated books as 'asking us to see his alphabetic forms with our senses, not just to read through or past them to the signified speech or "concept" behind them, but to pause at the sensuous surface of calligraphic and typographic forms'.[33] Robert Hunt's attack on Blake correctly identified a cardinal point of Blake's artistic practice (even if he devalued it).

'THAT ENTHUSIASM AND LIFE MAY NOT CEASE'

For the rest of this chapter, I shall pursue this aspect of Blake's practice specifically in relation to *Jerusalem*, in order to suggest that the book systematically links the possibility of the New Jerusalem to the improvement of sensual enjoyment, and deliberately contradicts the fears of the Hunts on this score. Criticism long ago recognized

[32] Stafford, *Body Criticism*, 11. See also Jean-François Lyotard's discussion of the 'negative presentation' of the sublime in *Lessons on the Analytic of the Sublime*, trans. Elizabeth Rottenberg (Stanford, Calif.: Stanford University Press, 1994), 153–6. Blake's definition of the sublime strikes me as deeply opposed to the Kantian version.

[33] Mitchell, 'Visible Language', 83.

that his encounter with the *Examiner* became woven into the fabric of *Jerusalem* by Blake. The poem claims to have been printed in 1804 on its title-page, but in the summer of 1807 George Cumberland's notebook recorded that 'Blake has engd. 60 Plates of a new Prophecy'.[34] Plates completed or altered after that date (there are at least twenty-five of them) seem to have incorporated the Hunts as enemies of Blake's in the three-headed figure of Hand (he also appears in *Milton*, but only on Plates 19 and 23). A hand was the editorial symbol of the three Hunt brothers. Each of the essays attacking the Methodists has one at the end. Critics have warned against identifying Hand too closely with the Hunts, lest we substitute biographical detail for the loose mythological logic of Blake's books.[35] Yet the clash with the Hunts may have influenced the logic of *Jerusalem* by allowing Blake to define his own enthusiasm more precisely. Throughout the poem, Blake associates Hand with the fear that enthusiasm was a cover for immorality. 'Natural Religion', as it is called in the poem, paradoxically privileges abstract ideas over sensual enjoyment. There are more specific aspects of the poem too that may have been derived from the clash with the Hunts. The defence of Methodism on Plate 22 of *Milton* and Plate 52 of *Jerusalem* may have its origins there. Paley believes that what attracted Blake to Methodism was its stress on the necessity of spiritual regeneration, a theme that is a constant presence in *Jerusalem*, but we should be wary of thinking in simple terms of these plates as defences of Methodism. There were many different aspects to Methodism and Blake's newfound respect for its founders is very different, for instance, from the respect that Southey eventually granted Wesley. Although Blake mentions Wesley [Westley] in the *Milton* plate, only Whitefield appears (on two separate plates, 52 and 72) in *Jerusalem*. Whitefield looms larger in Blake's defence of Methodism, in fact, just as he looms larger than Wesley in Hunt's essays. Wesley was an ambiguous, but often more palatable character for polite commentators at the time. Whitefield was another kettle of fish for reasons outlined earlier in this chapter. He is described by Hunt as 'a great sensualist' (H 90). Hunt had earlier made a sneering joke about Whitefield's struggles with the Holy Spirit:

---

[34] Bentley, *Blake Records*, 187.
[35] See Northrop Frye, *Fearful Symmetry: A Study of William Blake* (Princeton: Princeton University Press, 1947), 375–7, and also David V. Erdman, *Blake: Prophet against Empire*, 3rd edn. (Princeton: Princeton University Press, 1977), 457.

I need not expatiate here upon the different kinds of Spirit, though MR. WHITFIELD, who says that for twenty years after his conversion he was frequently relapsing into sin, gives us no small inuendo [*sic*] about some Spirit that used to have a very peculiar effect upon himself. (H 36)

Hunt's attitude to Whitefield, I believe, helps us understand the critique of the Natural Religion associated with the character of Hand in *Jerusalem*.[36]

Among the best known of these attacks is the Plate dedicated 'To the Deists' in *Jerusalem*. Blake's address condemns 'Natural Morality or Natural Religion' (*J* 52: E 200) precisely for moralism of the sort displayed by Hunt towards Whitefield:

We are Men of like passions with others & pretend not to be holier than others: therefore, when a Religious Man falls into Sin, he ought not to be calld a Hypocrite: . . . Foote in calling Whitefield Hypocrite: was himself one: for Whitefield, pretended not to be holier than others: but confessed his Sins before all the World. (*J* 52: E 201)

'To the Deists' could almost be read as a direct response to the way Hunt condemns Whitefield for his sensuality while professing an enlightenment faith in the natural world:

You cannot escape my charge that you are Pharisees & Hypocrites, for you are constantly talking of the Virtues of the Human Heart, and particularly of your own, that you may accuse others & especially the Religious, whose errors, you by this display of pretended Virtue, chiefly design to expose. (*J* 52: E 201)

Hunt's attack on Whitefield provides an excellent example of the proponent of natural religion acting as a pharisee. Throughout *Jerusalem* the character of Hand is associated with the Moral Law that Hunt effectively defends in his pamphlet even as he condemns the gloomy puritanism of Methodism. Plate 70, for instance, describes 'the form of mighty Hand sitting on Albions cliffs'. 'Imputing Sin & Righteousness', he is 'Plotting to devour Albions Body of Humanity & Love' (*J* 70. 17: E 224). The association made through the character of Hand between Natural Religion and the

---

[36] Morton D. Paley has placed the positive recuperation of Whitefield and Wesley in the context of the work that Blake was doing with William Hayley for the latter's projected biography of William Cowper. Given the fact that Leigh Hunt includes the example of Cowper as an illustration of the pernicious effects of enthusiasm, even if softened by the poet's gentility, this need not conflict with my reading. On Hunt and Cowper, see Chapter 1 and also Morton D. Paley, 'Cowper as Blake's Spectre', *Eighteenth-Century Studies*, 1 (1968), 236–52.

Moral Law should give us pause; it is scarcely an intuitive one. Natural Religion is usually associated with disgust for ideas of original sin rather than the defence of the Moral Law. One tends to think of Hunt, for example, as a freethinker rather than a pharisee, but Blake's presentation of Hand uncovers a logic to be found in *The Folly and Danger of Methodism*.

Nature is identified with virtue in Hunt's essays, but Nature is also an abstraction contradistinguished from the energies of the body. The latter are constantly presented there as gross and sinful. Blake's annotations on Wordsworth suggest that he detected something of the same logic in the writing of the Lake Poet. He saw 'in Wordsworth the Natural Man rising up against the Spiritual Man' ('Anno. to Wordsworth': E 665). The point is not so much that he fears Wordsworth is attributing sensual life to stocks and stones. It is not a fear of enthusiasm in that sense, rather the opposite. 'Natural Objects always did & now do Weaken deaden & obliterate Imagination in Me' (E 665) is a response not to the animation but the reification or abstraction of nature in Wordsworth's poetry. He sees both in the Hunts and Wordsworth, one might say, a superstitious reverence for Nature elevated as a fixed object over the viewing subject. Blake did recognize a contrary movement in Wordsworth's poetry. One might think of this countervailing tendency as the Wordsworth of 'deep enthusiastic joy' (*Prelude 1805*, XIII. 261) rather than the one who submitted to being 'chasten'd' by a Coleridgean idea of mind. This is the Wordsworth of sensual enjoyment rather than the one who Blake thought had descended into 'the Abstract Void' ('Anno. to *Excursion*': E 666). Those who took this last route Blake regarded as the pharisees of Natural Religion. *Jerusalem* represents them as the agents of a monstrous conspiracy to reify nature as an abstract idea of moral virtue over sensual enjoyment:

> And this the form of mighty Hand sitting on Albions cliffs
> Before the face of Albion, a mighty threatning Form.
> His bosom wide & shoulders huge overspreading wondrous
> Bear Three strong sinewy Necks & Three awful & terrible Heads
> Three Brains in contradictory council brooding incessantly.
> Neither daring to put in act its councils, fearing each-other,
> Therefore rejecting Ideas as nothing & holding all Wisdom
> To consist. In agreements & disagree[me]nts of Ideas.
> Plotting to devour Albions Body of Humanity & Love.

> (*J* 70. 1–9: E 224)

The Hunt brothers reduce 'Ideas' to 'nothing' insofar as they deny them physical form. Having made ideas into 'nothing' (like Wordsworth's 'Abstract Void'), they then reify them over embodied humanity as a moral law representing the totality of 'all Wisdom'. 'Humanity & Love' in the form of 'Albions body' are cast aside. A parallel can be found on Plate 30 where Hand produces 'a vaporous Shadow in a Void' (*J* 30. 37: E 177). If the spiritual and the sensual are to be kept apart, then the sensual becomes only vegetable matter, and the spiritual becomes a mere vapour.

Hunt's essay 'On Methodistical Inspiration' mocks Whitefield for his readiness to imagine the interpenetration of the physical and the spiritual worlds: 'Mr WHITFIELD insisted at one time, that JESUS Christ used to sit manifestly at the head of the table during the love-feasts' (H 32). If he read Hunt's account of Whitefield's love feasts, as he may well have done, it surely would have reminded Blake of his own account of a supper with Isaiah and Ezekiel in *The Marriage of Heaven and Hell*:

> The Prophets Isaiah and Ezekiel dined with me, and I asked them how they dared so roundly to assert. that God spake to them; and whether they did not think at the time, that they would be misunderstood, & so be the cause of imposition.
>
> Isaiah answer'd. I saw no God. nor heard any, in a finite organical perception; but my senses discover'd the infinite in every thing, and as I was then perswaded. & remain confirm'd; that the voice of honest indignation is the voice of God, I cared not for consequences but wrote.
>
> Then I asked: does a firm perswasion that a thing is so, make it so?
>
> He replied: All poets believe that it does, & in ages of imagination this firm perswasion removed mountains; but many are not capable of a firm perswasion of any thing. (*MHH* 12: E 38–9)

John Locke had defined enthusiasm precisely in terms of such 'perswasion'.[37] Rather than 'perswasion', Locke offered 'demonstration' as the foundation for knowledge, that is, the appeal to what Isaiah calls 'finite organical perception'. Blake offered a quite different idea of 'demonstration' in his annotations to Swedenborg: 'Who shall dare to say after this that all elevation is of self & is Enthusiasm & Madness & is it not plain that self derived intelligence is worldly demonstration' (E 606). Swedenborg had suggested that 'the natural man can elevate his Understanding to

---

[37] See the discussion of enthusiastic 'perswasion' in my Introduction.

superior Light as far as he desires it, but he who is principled in Evils and thence in Things false, does not elevate it higher than to the superior Region of his natural Mind'. Blake's annotation complains that Locke's idea of demonstration is fundamentally attached to a 'natural' or fixed idea of Self-hood that it cannot get beyond. Any perception that threatens to disrupt the unity of this bounded subjectivity is merely distraction to Locke: 'Simple country Hinds' who are 'Indignant against Knavery' are dismissed as 'Enthusiasts' when they rely on 'Native Honesty untaught' rather than what Blake condemned as an abstract 'Moral criterion' ('Anno. to Boyd' E 635). Hunt dismissed Whitefield and his 'simple' followers for just such enthusiasm. For all its purported attachment to a sunlit world of nature, Blake sees this position as an abstraction of the natural (and the self) that refuses to see it as a body of energy that can not only be apprehended in different ways but also radically transformed. What from a Lockean perspective is mere 'perswasion' or 'Enthusiasm', Blake celebrates in *Jerusalem* for offering the possibility of seeing beyond the dull rounds of 'the God of this world'. Later on I want to return to the theme of 'Self-Annihilation' in relation to this issue of casting off Self-hood, but what needs stressing here is that Isaiah is not in any simple sense appealing to the spiritual rather than the carnal eyes. He insists that 'the senses' can discover 'the infinite in every thing'. Similarly in *Jerusalem* Los insists that his raptures participate in the profane world around him, that is, the visionary in Blake is part of the visible world of the senses:

> . . . I heard in Lambeths shades:
> In Felpham I heard and saw the Visions of Albion
> I write in South Molton Street, what I both see and hear
> In regions of Humanity, in Londons opening streets.

> (*J* 34. 40–3: E 180)

Jerusalem may be a poem about transcendence, but the body for all that it may be radically transformed is not what is transcended. The vegetable body can be reconceived as a regenerate body of energy.

  Jerusalem contains several spirited assertions of the palpable reality of what Blake saw in vision. The repetition of the phrase 'I see . . .', usually insisting that the visionary narrative of the poem is going on in the world around Blake, provides the structural principle behind several important plates.[38] The poem more pervasively

---

[38] The phrase occurs at least thirty times in *Jerusalem* alone.

insists on 'the sensible presentation of what cannot be seen by the naked eye'.[39] It begins indeed with the assertion of the visible presence of Christ in the world around Blake:

> This theme calls me in sleep night after night, & ev'ry morn
> Awakes me at sun-rise, then I see the Saviour over me
> Spreading his beams of love.
>
> (*J* 4. 2–5: E 146)

The style of anatomical drawings comes to the fore in *Jerusalem*, as Marilyn Butler puts it, 'where blood pulses through Albion's veins, and fibres representing the nerve-system not only come to view but merge with the tendrils of plants to suggest the oneness of life'.[40] This oneness refuses any qualitative distinction between the spiritual and the embodied. *Jerusalem*'s insistence that its visions are going on 'in Londons opening streets' is worth considering in relation to Patrick Wright's discussion of different kinds of utopianism touched on in my previous chapter. Wright draws a distinction between utopias that are a 'vision of possibilities which reside in the real', others that are 'a prophetic if counterfactual perspective on the real', and a third variety that exist 'as a dichotomous realm existing alongside the every day'. Wright suggests that in the last of these categories 'what much utopianism has alluded to or postulated as the challenge of history . . . ends up behind us already accomplished'.[41] Wordsworth's visionary poetics participate in this last tendency. In contrast, Blake's enthusiasm insists on a counterfactual perspective on contemporary society that places Oxford Street in Jerusalem (if Albion's children would only see it). Jerusalem does not exist in a dichotomous realm. It is not alongside, but potentially the substance of the everyday itself. The New Jerusalem has to be realized in the world of the senses if it is to exist anywhere at all. What may seem 'meer possibilities', as Blake puts it in *Jerusalem*, 'to those who enter into them they seem the only substances' (*J* 13. 64–5: E 158). When he saw *Jerusalem* in 1811, it seems to have been precisely this interpenetration of the eternal and temporal that decided Southey the poem was 'perfectly mad'.[42]

[39] Marilyn Butler, 'Blake in his Time', in Robin Hamlyn and Michael Phillips (eds.), *William Blake* (Tate Publishing, 2000), 25.

[40] Ibid. 24.

[41] See Patrick Wright, *On Living in an Old Country* (Verso, 1985), 78, discussed in relation to Wordsworth in Chapter 5.

[42] Reported by Henry Crabb Robinson, see Bentley, *Blake Records*, 229.

Hunt's definition of Whitefield's enthusiasm is predicated on the same criterion. Significantly, antipathy to the idea that the spiritual world is available to the senses is strongly identified in *Jerusalem* with the figure of Hand.

Of course, it would be a gross simplification to suggest that Blake's texts themselves never register any anxiety about different ways of seeing the world. A distinction between the 'Vegetative Man & his Immortal Imagination' (*J* 32. 24: E 178) runs throughout *Jerusalem*. The key point is that in Blake's vocabulary bodies are not simply a priori 'vegetable.' Bodies can be perceived, he suggests, in different ways:

I see Every thing I paint In This World, but Every body does not see alike. To the Eyes of a Miser a Guinea is more beautiful than the Sun & a bag worn with the use of Money has more beautiful proportions than a Vine filled with Grapes. The tree which moves some to tears of joy is in the Eyes of others only a Green thing that stands in the way. Some See Nature all Ridicule & Deformity & by these I shall not regulate my proportions, & Some Scarce see Nature at all But to the Eyes of the Man of imagination Nature is Imagination itself. As a man is So he Sees. As the Eye is formed such are its Powers You certainly Mistake when you say that the Visions of Fancy are not be found in This World . . . ('To Dr. Trusler, Aug 23 1799': E 702)

These sentiments are given added piquancy because they were written to an Anglican clergyman who seems to have effectively accused Blake of enthusiasm. Where the clergyman takes the classic Anglican position that the visionary cannot be visible, Blake insists on the possibility that the vegetative world can be made visionary by 'rouz[ing] the faculties to act' (E 702). The fleshly world is always capable of regeneration or reconception in *Jerusalem*. Even where Blake seems to be most explicitly privileging the spirit over the senses, closer inspection reveals fleshiness to be far from identified with sinfulness. 'To the Christians' begins, for instance, with the doctrinal statement that 'we are told to abstain from fleshly desires that we may lose no time from the Work of the Lord' (*J* 77: E 231). We seem to discover a Blake close to conservative understandings of Pauline doctrine here. Before the main text of 'To the Christians', Blake quotes Acts 9: 4: 'Saul, Saul, why persecutest thou me?' If it is by Paul that 'we are told to abstain from fleshly desires that we may lose no time from the Work of the Lord', however, his doctrine turns out to be a form of persecution itself. 'The

Work of the Lord', it emerges later in the address, is not the morti-fication of the sinful body, but 'the liberty both of body & mind to exercise the Divine Arts of Imagination'. From this perspective, con-trary to the dualist reading that the first line of the Plate seems to invite, the body *is* 'more than Raiment' (E 232). Blake insisted as much in the response to Robert Hunt printed in the *Descriptive Catalogue* of his 1809 Exhibition:

A Spirit and a Vision are not, as the modern philosophy supposes, a cloudy vapour or a nothing: they are organized and minutely articulated beyond all that mortal and perishing nature can produce. He who does not imag-ine in stronger and better lineaments, and in stronger and better light than his perishing and mortal eye can see does not imagine at all. The painter of this work asserts that all his imaginations appear to him to be infinitely more perfect and more minutely organized than any seen by his mortal eye. (*DC*: E 541-2)

Romantic readings of Blake tend to read this comment on the 'per-ishing and mortal eye' as a faith in vision parallel to Wordsworth's condemnation of the 'soulless eye'. Placed in the context of his disputes with the *Examiner*, however, Blake's primary target seems rather to be Robert Hunt's desire to distinguish absolutely between the visible and the visionary. The 'cloudy vapour' echoes or antici-pates the description of Hand in Plate 30 of *Jerusalem* as 'a Vaporous shadow'. Two plates later Hand is described as 'the Reasoning Spectre' who 'Stands between the Vegetative Man & his Immortal Imagination'. Understanding spiritual life as a 'cloudy vapour' is the corollary of restricting the body to a vegetable form. Blake's idea of regenerated vision seems to abrogate the distinction between the things of the sense and the things of the spirit that is essential to the *Examiner*. *Milton* offers the possibility of 'Resurrection & Judgment in the Vegetable Body' (*J* 41. 28: E 143). Part of the temptation of Jerusalem earlier in the book is precisely to succumb to an idea of the 'Divine Body' as 'a delusive shadow, a thought that liveth not' (*J* 60. 55: E 212). 'Man in the Resurrection changes his Sexual Garments at will,' a voice tells her on the next plate (*J* 61. 51: E 212), as she struggles with her own feelings of sex-ual guilt, but changing the garments is rather different from dis-pensing with them entirely. One may transcend a particular bodily form without transcending embodiment itself. Indeed the Lamb of God convinces her that 'in my flesh I shall see God' (*J* 62. 16: E 213). Whereas 'enthusiasm' in the culture of the time was usually tied to a fear of the distraction of the crowd, the loss of the determinate self in the welter of sensory impressions, *'sore'* as Coleridge put it, 'from excess of stimulation' (Griggs, v. 24), Blake valorizes 'enthusiasm' precisely in the interests of an expansion of the sensual. Rather than in the state of retirement favoured by Coleridge and Wordsworth, Blake finds the New Jerusalem in the opening streets of London. His antipathy towards the 'vegetable body' is not an antipathy to the play of the senses, or the body as such, but to their reduction into a fixity of observer and observed. For Blake the vegetable is identified with abstraction: the spiritual life with the expanding and contracting energies of the body.

BLAKE'S 'RIGHT-ANGLED TURNS'

I began this chapter by commenting on the relatively late appearance of the word 'enthusiasm' and its cognates in Blake's writing. In fact only in *Jerusalem* of Blake's illuminated books do the words appear at all. Los labours in Plate 9 so that 'Enthusiasm and Life may not cease' (*J* 9. 31: E 152). The other two occurrences are on the famously problematic Plate 3 with its gouged out lines left as open wounds even on the printed version:

The Enthusiasm of the following Poem, the Author hopes [no Reader *will think presumptuousness or arroganc[e] when he is reminded that the Ancients acknowledge their love to their Deities, to the full as Enthusiastically as I have who Acknowledge mine for my Saviour and Lord, for they were wholly absorb'd in their Gods.*] I also hope the Reader will be with me, wholly One in Jesus our Lord, who is the God [*of Fire*] and Lord [*of Love*] to who the Ancients look'd and saw his day afar off, with trembling & amazement. (*J* 3: E 145)

The gouging of Plate 3 may represent Blake's bitter recognition of the limits that were imposed on enthusiasm within the aesthetic and religious spheres. It could possibly even be a specific response to his encounter with the Hunts over 1808–9. Regardless of whether or not they have their origins in this damaging exchange, these are perhaps the most extreme signs of Blake's refusal to recuperate his transports into a unified form. Blake's enthusiasm lies unregulated on the surface of the published book that is 'a broken text'.[43] M. H.

---

[43] On *Jerusalem* as a deliberately 'broken text', see Jerome McGann, *Towards a Literature of Knowledge* (Oxford: Oxford University Press, 1989), 12.

Abrams defined Wordsworth's smoothing over of the right-angled turns of prophetic inspiration into a coherent sense of personal and textual identity as a defining feature of Romanticism.[44] Blake's prophetic form was based on a much more literal and interruptive sense of inspiration made manifest in its most extreme form by Plate 3. Rather than a product of recollection in tranquillity, Joseph Viscomi has shown that the poem seems to have been composed and printed in spates as inspiration came to Blake.[45] Not that the text was unrevised, rather Blake chose to dispense with the appearance of unified form through the revisions he made. The result is a lack of continuity, a continual annihilation of determinate identity in the self and the text, that would have been the sign of enthusiasm to most readers of Blake's time. To play down the disorientation readers still experience when reading *Jerusalem* is posthumously to regulate Blake's enthusiasm into a more acceptably poetic form. Poets from Joseph Warton and Mark Akenside to Coleridge and Wordsworth all in different ways practised a poetics of enthusiasm in the eighteenth century. For all their differences, the common tendency was to be much more cautious in the treatment of enthusiasm than this opening plate of *Jerusalem* is. To declare one's complete absorption into the divine was to open up the fear of a transport which left one unhooked from a determinate self. Poetic celebrations of enthusiasm most often sought to be invigorated not distracted by enthusiasm. Blake's poetics of distraction puts the self into hazard in a way that I think would have alarmed most practitioners of this poetics.

The abrogation of such regulation in textual form was generally taken to be a sign that authors had been swallowed up by the combustible matter within them. *Jerusalem*'s reassessment of textual distraction should perhaps be seen as the corollary of the thematics of self-annihilation within the poem. For the latter brings forward

---

[44] See the discussion of right-angled turns in Chapter 5.

[45] Joseph Viscomi, *Blake and the Idea of the Book* (Princeton: Princeton University Press, 1993), 313, notes that even the sixty-plate version Cumberland saw in 1807 'seems to have been printed in various sessions and not systematically'. The rest, Viscomi suggests (339), was 'written and rewritten no doubt as inspiration struck . . . not laboured on year in and year out'. Paley, *Continuing City*, 27, advises against reading *Jerusalem* as rhapsodic, pointing out that there are signs of frequent revision, but rhapsody and revision are not necessarily incommensurable, especially, as Viscomi comments suggest, in a long poem written over many years. Certainly Blake did not erase all signs that the poem was written in bouts of inspiration. Paley himself, it ought to be said, provides a useful critique of Frye's stress on unity, 27.

as a positive principle the kind of distraction of the self often feared as a consequence of enthusiasm. One source of this principle of 'Self-Annihilation' for Blake may have been David Hartley's *Observations on Man* (1749). In Hartley's work, as Richard C. Allen has recently shown, the word 'annihilation' bore 'a distinctive meaning' specifically tied to the abrogation of rigid distinctions between spiritual and sensory experience.[46] Blake engraved a portrait for the 1791 edition of Hartley's *Observations*, but without the benefit of Allen's pathbreaking work scholars usually assume that he would have found the principles of the book unattractive. Robert Essick puts the standard view that it 'would seem to epitomize everything Blake most strongly criticized in eighteenth-century rational materialism'.[47] Annotations made in his copy of Richard Watson's *Apology for the Bible* support this assessment: 'Hartley a Man of Judgment then Judgment was a Fool what Nonsense' (E 619). Watson had been quoting an opinion of Hartley's on the authorship of the Bible, with which Blake obviously disagreed; but he may have found other parts of *Observations* more palatable. Certainly Allen's recent work on Hartley's philosophy presents it as more complex than Essick's summation allows.

Hartley's fame was mostly owed to the abridgement of *Observations* published by Joseph Priestley in 1775. This book fired an immediate controversy that focused on two main issues: first, the claim, as Priestley put it, 'that, though the subject is beyond our comprehension at present, man does not consist of two principles, so essentially different from one another as *matter* and *spirit*' (Rutt, iii. 181–2); secondly, the idea that it was, in Allen's words, 'the promise of the resurrection of the body, rather than the continued existence of a nonmaterial spirit that guaranteed personal immortality'.[48] James Mackintosh fiercely attacked Hartley's attempt to 'derive intellectual operations from bodily causes' because it 'overlooks the primordial and perpetual distinction between *the being which thinks* and *the thing which is thought of*—not to be lost sight of even for a twinkling, without involving all nature in darkness and confusion'.[49] Hartley's ideas were shocking to those who, like

---

[46] See Richard C. Allen, *David Hartley on Human Nature* (Albany: State University of New York Press, 1999), xi.

[47] Robert N. Essick, *William Blake's Commercial Book Illustrations: A Catalogue and Study of the Plates Engraved by Blake after Designs by Other Artists* (Oxford: Clarendon Press, 1991), 49.

[48] Allen, *David Hartley*, 377.   [49] Quoted ibid. 378.

Mackintosh, subscribed to what Allen calls 'the standard account of human nature'. Bishop Butler provides Allen's primary example of this position. Butler, according to Allen, took the mind to be 'a self-conscious unity, aware of its freedom, that directs the body to act; the mind moves the body, but except in instances of delirium, madness, or irrationality, the body does not move the mind'.[50] This view of human consciousness had a parallel cosmology attached to it: God was a separate personality presiding over his creation as the immaterial soul was a distinctive identity that was quite distinctive from the gross body in which it resided. To collapse one into the other reduced consciousness to delirium for Butler as it did for Coleridge. Hartley rejected the idea of 'a rational agent presiding over the fabric of the body'.[51] By implication he also rejected this idea of God's relationship to his Creation. Blake's *The Book of Urizen* seems to give poetic form to both ideas in its account of the origins of the eponymous tyrant:

> Lo, a shadow of horror is risen
> In Eternity! Unknown, unprolific!
> Self-closd, all-repelling: what Demon
> Hath form'd this abominable void
> This soul-shudd'ring vacuum?—Some said
> 'It is Urizen', But unknown, abstracted
> Brooding secret, the dark power hid.

> (*BU* 3.7: E 70)

Blake's poetics, as we have seen, were much less concerned than Coleridge's to defend the spiritual life from the distraction of the senses. If his poetics retained an important role for the transports of spiritual agency, they are not defined in opposition to sensual enjoyment. On the contrary, the spiritual divided from the minute particularites of the body becomes a place of abominable voids and tyrannous abstractions.

Hartley's philosophy did not simply privilege matter over spirit as is sometimes assumed. Allen points out that far from 'advocating a material universe devoid of spirit, Hartley imagined an active, spiritual cosmos virtually empty of "inert" matter'.[52] Blake's universe

---

[50] Ibid. 179.
[51] See David Hartley, *Observations on Man, his Frame, his Duty, and his Expectations*, rev. edn. (1791), 158. For obvious reasons, I quote from Joseph Johnson's 1791 edition illustrated by Blake.
[52] Allen, *David Hartley*, 382–3.

of energy is similarly active. Because Priestley's abridgement contained only the first volume of Hartley's work, however, hostile judgements such as Coleridge's and Mackintosh's were easier to sustain, and have remained the dominant impression of Hartley's work even today. Coleridge was perfectly aware of the differences between 'the life & second Vol. of Hartley compared with the inevitable consequences (in logic) of his first Vol.' (*Notebooks*, iii. 3907), but deemed the latter far too dangerous to escape censure. The first volume of *Observations* concentrated mainly on the detail of the theory of vibrations that lay behind Hartley's theology. The second volume was more concerned with ethical and religious issues: there it is, for instance, that the influence of mystical writers such as Boehme emerges. Blake's interest in Boehme is well documented, and may even have encouraged an interest in Hartley's ideas. For Blake would seem to have known not Priestley's abridgement, but the two-volume version of Hartley that he illustrated. There Hartley's universe is revealed to be not the *dead* mechanism attacked by Mackintosh and Coleridge, but alive with energy, structured around principles of attraction and repulsion.[53] Blake may have found in Hartley an affirmation of the idea that 'Attraction and Repulsion, Reason and Energy, Love and Hate, are necessary to Human existence' (*MHH* 3: E 34). The penultimate plate of *Jerusalem* finds many anticipations in Hartley if one takes the second volume of *Observations* as the standard:

There is not an atom perhaps in the whole universe which does not abound in millions of worlds; and conversely, this great system of the sun, planets and fixed stars, may be no more than a single constituent particle of some body of an immense relative magnitude, &c. In like manner, there is not a moment of time so small, but it may include millions of ages in the estimation of some beings; and, conversely, the largest cycle which human art is able to invent, may be no more than the twinkling of an eye in that of others.[54]

Passages such as these open up the possibility of Eternity being conceived as a Blakean state of:

> . . . Expansion or Contraction, the Translucence or
> Opakeness of Nervous fibres such was the variation of Time & Space
> Which vary according as the Organs of Perception vary . . .

(*J* 98. 36–8: E 258)

[53] Allen, *David Hartley*, 94.   [54] Hartley, *Observations*, 453.

Much of the opprobrium attached to Hartley's principles resolved itself around contemporary notions of the continuation of personal identity after death. To deny the autonomy of the immaterial soul, which to survive the disintegration of the body, threatened at its very root this principle of Christianity, but Hartley took seriously the New Testament promise of the restoration of the fleshly body. For Hartley, as I have been suggesting also for Blake, the notion of personal identity made no sense if it were not to reside in the particularity of an embodied being. Leaving aside the detail of how Hartley thought this embodied identity was preserved (he speculated on the possibility of 'an elementary infinitesimal body in the embryo'), his *Observations* insisted upon the literal resurrection of the 'glorified body' promised in the New Testament.[55] Blake's *Jerusalem* concurs with Hartley's *Observations*:

> Shall Albion arise? I know he shall arise at the Last Day
> I know that in my flesh I shall see God.
>
> (*J* 62. 15–16: E 213)

For both men too, I would argue, this journey towards God pivots on the key concept of self-annihilation.

Allen finds that 'at the centre of Hartley's *Observations* is a theory of the emergence and then transcendence of self'.[56] Hartley was convinced that out of the theory of association there could be constructed an explanation of how self-interest was to be turned into ultimate benevolence by divine providence. Psychic wholeness emerged from 'a parliament of intellectual affections':[57]

The virtuous dispositions of benevolence, piety, and the moral sense, and particularly that of the love of God, check all the foregoing ones, and seem sufficient to extinguish them at last. This would be perfect self-annihilation, and resting in our God as our centre. And upon the whole, we may conclude, that though it be impossible to begin without sensuality, and sensual selfishness, or to proceed without the other intermediate principles, and particularly that of rational self-interest; yet we ought never to be satisfied with ourselves, till we arrive at perfect self-annihilation, and the pure love of God.[58]

The interactions between the characters in *Jerusalem* to some extent represent precisely such a psychic parliament, although Blake was

---

[55] See Allen, *David Hartley*, 203.
[56] Ibid. 265.
[57] Ibid. 276.
[58] Hartley, *Observations*, 473.

less convinced than Hartley that 'rational self-interest' was necessarily the starting point for human psychology.[59] Both certainly agreed in placing the idea of self-annihilation at the centre of the process of regeneration. Allen shows that Hartley was indebted to the Behmenist tradition of mysticism that insisted such annihilation had more to do with the transcendence of self-interest than of the materiality of being.[60] The influence of this aspect of Hartley's thinking was a direct presence in Coleridge's 'Religious Musings' (as Coleridge's notes to his poem acknowledge (*CPW* 176)). Human love expands towards the ideal sphere of divine goodness and secures infinite happiness in the love of God through the process of self-annihilation:

> All self-annihilated it shall make
> God its Identity: God all in all!
> We and our Father ONE!
>
> (*CPW* 177–8; ll. 43–5)

In Chapter 3 I suggested that even in 'Religious Musings' Coleridge seems to hang back from full absorption into the divine being. Too sudden a claim to such absorption would have looked like the kind of transport associated with the distractions of enthusiasm (the kind of transport that contemporaries would have seen behind Plate 3 of *Jerusalem*). Coleridge's concern with self-annihilation was part of a lifelong search for 'something *one* & *indivisible*' (Griggs, i. 349) that would deliver him from the exigencies of the body. 'Judgment ever awake and steady self-possession' (*BL* i. 17), in Coleridge's poetics, had always to watch over his own desire for 'enthusiasm and feeling profound and vehement' less the latter become confused with mere bodily desires. Coleridge's desire for such vehemence should not be underplayed, but he was constantly guarding against it becoming mired in sensuality and overwhelming the autonomy of the subject. Boehme's quietism came to seem to him to have relatively more safeguards in this respect than Hartley's philosophy. The latter took him too close to the distractions of the body. Even if it claimed ultimately to transcend 'sensuality', it began and ended with an idea of the spiritual life intertwined with physical being. Blake's idea of Boehme's enthusiasm was altogether different. His

[59] In *Jerusalem*, 80 (E 80), Gwendolen weaves 'self interest & selfish natural virtue' around her father.
[60] See Allen, *David Hartley*, 338–9.

delight in Law's illustrations to Boehme seems to have resided in
the fact that they did not abstract his mysticism from the particularity of the body. Like de Marsay and Hartley, Blake's idea of self-
annihilation remains committed to the continuation of 'the physical
or natural Sense', but Blake goes rather further down this track than
Hartley. There is little idea in Hartley of the sexualized Divine Body continually found in Blake's *Jerusalem*. Hartley found a role for sensual
desires in coming to a union with the divine, but these he believed
were gradually overcome by the developing moral sense on the road
towards God. No less than for Shaftesbury or Coleridge, contemplation and meditation are the key virtues on the road to self-
annihilation. The latter for Hartley has more to do with the
transcendence or sublimation of sensual associations than their
intensification. Perhaps providing another reason why Blake was
suspicious of his judgement, Hartley shared the widespread
eighteenth-century suspicion of spiritual ecstasies, sudden transports, and any other of the vulgarities of enthusiasm:

Enthusiasm may be defined a mistaken persuasion, that he is a peculiar
favourite with God; and that he receives supernatural marks thereof. The
vividness of the ideas of this class easily generates this false persuasion in
persons of strong fancies, little experience in divine things, and narrow
understandings (and especially where the moral sense, and the scrupulosity
attending its growth and improvement, are but imperfectly formed), by giving a reality and certainty to all the reveries of a man's own mind, and
cementing the associations in a preternatural manner. It may also be easily
contracted by contagion, as daily experience shews; and indeed more easily than most other dispositions from the glaring language used by enthusiasts, and from the great flattery and support, which enthusiasm affords to
pride and self-conceit.[61]

The quietistic aspect of Hartley's writing, as Allen points out, also
supplied little warrant for the political appropriations of
Observations by Priestley, Godwin, and initially at least Coleridge.
Hartley's emphasis was on a gradualist '*process* of reintegration'
(my italics).[62] Priestley, Godwin, and in the 1790s even Coleridge
were all committed to the idea that radical interventions could be
made in the process of human improvement. Hartley's idea of slow
unconscious growth had no room for political intervention or

---

[61] Hartley, *Observations*, 289–90.   [62] Allen, *David Hartley*, 395.

paradigm leaps of any kind. If the improvements of Godwin and Priestley were made in the name of Reason, although with tinctures as we have seen of 'enthusiasm' as well, they shared with Blake a sense of the possibilities of radical transformations in the personal and the political. What Hartley called the 'pure disinterested love of God' was for Blake a potentially apocalyptic transformation at every level of human experience: 'whenever any Individual Rejects Error & Embraces Truth a Last Judgment passes upon that Individual' (*VLJ*: E 562).

So are there any limits to Blake's enthusiasm? Does he put all identities into hazard in the interests of garnering the rewards of Eternity? Without suggesting that there are no continuities of plot or structure or language in *Jerusalem*, it does seem that the possibility of radical transformation remains open at all these levels. Characters morph into other characters. There are sudden disruptions and abrupt endings in particular narratives and radical shifts in perspective. Particular words and images seem capable of carrying both redeemed and unredeemed significances. Anne K. Mellor's influential account of the poem, however, suggests some issues at the level of masculine and female identities that I would like to end by addressing. Mellor takes the view that Blake's demonization of the Female Will in the poem suggests an anxiety about the pressing power of female identity. What I want to address particularly is the suggestion that Blake participates in what Mellor sees as a defining feature of the masculine sublime. Taking Kant's aesthetics as her model, she notes that it 'erases the body, and hence, the female, altogether'.[63] We have already seen that the scandal of fleshly seeing was particularly associated with women in the discourse on enthusiasm. To this extent, at least, her general thesis is potentially analogous to my claim that the discourse of the sublime in poetics was one of several mechanisms for regulating the excesses of enthusiasm. The desire to 'transcend the realm of bodily sensation and physical nature' is an intrinsic part of attacks such as Hunt's on ecstasies such as Mrs Barker's.[64] Leaving aside the general question of Mellor's totalizing category of male Romanticism, obviously her account of Blake is impossible to square with my sense of his enthusiasm, but we have also seen that Blake is a long way from Kant on these matters. Far from seeking to transcend the body, *Jerusalem*

---

[63] Anne K. Mellor, *Romanticism and Gender* (Routledge, 1993), 88.
[64] Ibid.

does everything it can to bring it before the viewer. 'The sensible presentation of what cannot be seen by the naked eye', as Marilyn Butler puts it, is essential to Blake's idea of the 'spiritual body'.[65]

Looked at from this point of view, Blake seems to be attacking precisely the gendered version of the sublime as the regulation of sensual reveries that is also Mellor's target. The presence of St Teresa in Blake's poem provides an interesting case in point, and may represent another intersection with attacks on enthusiasm in the *Examiner*. St Teresa appears in *Jerusalem* as one of the five guardians of the southern gate of Los. Significantly in terms of Blake's argument with the Hunt brothers, Whitefield is one of the others (*J* 72. 50: E 227). Both are being honoured by the task. Hunt, in contrast, includes St Teresa's ecstasies in his discussion of the 'Indecencies and Profane Raptures of Methodism' (where he also describes Whitefield as 'a great sensualist') (H 55). Her 'sensual reveries' are brought forward by Hunt as an example of the inability of women to be 'sufficiently noble or self-commanding to act without the bodily feelings' (H 57). Writing in his notebooks in 1810, Coleridge adduced as the first of the reasons explaining St Teresa's enthusiasm: 'She was a *Woman*' (*Notebooks*, iii. 3911, Coleridge's italics). Although he is not without sympathy for these 'cravings of sensuality' (iii. 3937), the discussion of the saint scattered through the succeeding pages of the book makes it clear that he sees such transports as a particular danger to the gullible pious, and especially women. A few pages later he praises the 'Plotino-platonic philosophy', because 'it never suffers, much less causes or even occasions, its Disciples to forget themselves, lost and scattered in sensible Objects disjoined or *as* disjoined from themselves' (iii. 3935). Where Coleridge looks for a saving power out of the body, Blake's work has less fear of becoming 'lost and scattered in sensible Objects'. Nor does he seem to think that their 'sensual reveries' exclude St Teresa or Whitefield from Eternity. My aim here is not to suggest that Blake's work is totally free of gender blindnesses that might be construed as limits to his enthusiasm. What I do want to claim is that they do not include the denial of sublimity to embodied forms through an equation of femininity and the sinfulness of the body.

I would like to end this chapter by a very brief consideration of the gains and costs of Blake's commitment to 'mere enthusiasm'.

---

[65] Butler, 'Blake in his Time', 25.

Although in many ways the revaluation of enthusiasm that sustains this book has its origins in my training as a Blake scholar, my purpose has not been to present him as its hero. Blake is a good case for raising the question of whether the disavowal of the discourse of public reason leads to the death of communication. The discourse of regulation that Blake's illuminated books seem to transgress was for Shaftesbury a means of ensuring that the conversation of culture could be sustained outside the authority of the Church and State.[66] However exclusive Shaftesbury's own version of this conversation may have been, regulation of the self in the extrapolations of his ideas undertaken in the eighteenth century need not necessarily have meant regulating others or excluding those others from the conversation. Most of those who followed Shaftesbury did continue to suggest that there were certain kinds of people who were incapable of regulating their enthusiasm (and so had to be kept outside the conversation). Few writers in this period did not want to harness the power of enthusiasm to their own ends, but most were anxious as to the destructive possibilities even of their own desires in this respect, and distrusted them in socially excluded others even more. Some were ready to grant the power of regulation to groups previously excluded from Shaftesbury's conversation. And some of these groups claimed it for themselves. These groups, including many members of radical associations in the 1790s, were not necessarily subscribing to the principles of exclusion in their suspicion of 'mere enthusiasm', but saw the question more in terms of who had the right to regulate whom. Self-fashioning may be a form of resistance, or at least provide for different kinds of moral autonomy within a dominant discursive network: Foucault has shown us this much. But Blake's enthusiasm seems to constantly seek an outside to the discourse of regulation, a perspective from Eternity that reveals even space and time to be relative values capable of sudden interruptions and subversions.[67] History in Blake's prophecies is blown apart by his apocalyptic enthusiasm. Against 'the homogeneous empty time' of the same dull round, Blake offers, like Walter Benjamin's work, the continuing possibility of an unworlding

---

[66] Lawrence E. Klein, *Shaftesbury and the Culture of Politeness: Moral Discourse and Cultural Politics in Early Eighteenth-Century England* (Cambridge: Cambridge University Press, 1994), 8–10.

[67] Edward Said, 'Foucault and the Imagination of Power', in D. C. Hoy (ed.), *Foucault: A Critical Reader* (Oxford: Blackwell, 1986), 153, but see n. 8 in Chapter 4.

wherein both the individual and the nation are 'blasted out of the continuum of history'.[68] The continuities of identity cherished by Coleridge may have to be abandoned entirely in the interests of regeneration Blake suggests. One might ask whether Blake's disavowal of regulation went so far as to produce an enthusiasm so dangerous as to be incapable of sustaining a conversation? Is his idea of 'Mental Fight' too arduous and extreme to allow any kind of exchange in the public sphere? Is there a price paid in terms of comprehensibility and accessibility by Blake's 'mere enthusiasm'? Perhaps the gouged Plate 3 of *Jerusalem* is the sign of someone driven by exclusion to announce a poetics that brooked no response. Yet his constant calls to the public in the poem seem to hope that his 'Mental Fight' would arouse some kind of answer. His prophetic books are continually exhorting his readers to reply. The radicalism of his prophetic books may lie in their refusal to moderate the exchange before it has even begun.

[68] Benjamin, *Illuminations*, 263.

Conclusion
Enthusiastic Misreadings

WHERE DOES THIS account of the poetics of enthusiasm leave our understanding of romanticism? My inclination is to regard enthusiasm as the larger and more capacious term. Used more precisely in historical criticism it has the potential to overcome some of the specious divisions made between eighteenth-century and Romantic cultural phenomena; to alert us to some of the ambivalences at work within what we have come to think of as Romantic ideology; and, finally, to enable us to see the contested nature of divisions between literary and other kinds of discourse in the period. In terms of the first of these points, by taking enthusiasm as a compass, important continuities between the eighteenth and early nineteenth century's anxieties about the power of affect and the democratization of culture are revealed. To reverse the polarities, so too one can see how deeply and how early in the eighteenth century was the yearning articulated for the transformative power of 'enthusiasm' still today routinely thought of as Romantic. For all that I am at odds with its methodology and some of its conclusions, Irlam's account of the rehabilitation of enthusiasm is surely at least valid to the extent that it makes this last point very clear. In terms of the Romantic ideology, the fate of enthusiasm should allow us a more nuanced account of the urge to transcendence. The distaste for the enthusiasm of the crowd at the centre of the discourse on enthusiasm had a flip side in the desire for an unworlding power that was not necessarily as conservative or as unwordly as, for instance, the novelistic tradition would sometimes paint it. Indeed the association made by Burke and others between religious enthusiasm and revolutionary *transparence* had to do with the idea that both encouraged men and women to see the possibility of the world being utterly different from its present state. Both were also linked together by the idea of reaching beyond the self to some broader constitution of human collectivity than a developing commercial society seemed to allow.

Novelists had much more of an investment in representing the development of the individual subject in the context of a commercial society. Whatever their individual attitudes to the latter, however much they might yearn for a system of relationships beyond getting and spending, this kind of worlding was from early on seen as definitive of the novelist's medium. What was much more acutely at issue for poets in the period was the question of the limits of the unworlding power of affect (and who controlled those limits). Whatever the anxieties articulated by Wordsworth and Coleridge among others, poets came to view the enthusiasm that reached beyond the self as integral to their art. If Coleridge, for instance, increasingly defined the object of this yearning in terms of a unity that resided on the far side of sensual form, it would be misleading to ignore the strength of the desire he sometimes disavowed. If enthusiasm is the object of disciplinary regulation, it seems constantly to be running beyond the control of the producer. This endless power of semination was both a source of fascination and horror. Literature and especially poetry in the Romantic period presented itself in some respects as an answer to this dissemination in the broader cultural context. Never quite a discipline in any strict sense, not governed by explicit rules nor many institutions, it presented itself as a site where the fountains within could play with relative freedom. Simon Jarvis wants to defend against the New Historicism the claims of poetry on this basis:

There are historical objects which often claim a more than historical truth; particular objects which often claim a universal meaning; they are things which almost claim the dignity of persons, things which claim to have not just a fixed price but an unmeasurable worth.[1]

This eloquent plea is not to be dismissed lightly, but whether or not Wordsworth's poetry respects it is another matter. At the same time that literature was articulating the idea of a realm of enthusiasm beyond particular historical interests, it was constantly on the guard against the intrusions of those it deemed incapable of understanding these freedoms. Hunt's attacks on Methodism, Wordsworth's 'Preface', and Coleridge's *Biographia* were all attempts by writers

[1] Simon Jarvis, 'Wordsworth and Idolatry', *Studies in Romanticism*, 38 (1999), 1–27.

who believed in the therapeutic powers of enthusiasm but wished to quarantine it from the vile bodies of the crowd. They wished to insulate its unworlding effects so as to prevent it overwhelming the subjectivity it was meant to be saving. I would suggest that this response was one that wanted to secure a fixed price for what it also presented as an immeasurable worth. Poetic enthusiasm was constantly being defended against the inflationary pretensions of the enthusiastic crowd. Yet the constant entailment of these enthusiasms in each other meant that the aesthetic sphere could never quite secure itself a definitive cultural position. Even those who brought forward taste as an implicit barrier against such encroachments were never entirely convinced that they themselves were not the inlets of murkier waters. Literature was a category that brought with it hidden guarantees of purity and exclusivity, but precisely because they remained hidden, these guarantees offered little by way of protection from those who confused taste with appetite. Only a power out of the self, Burke had insisted, could regulate this kind of person. For someone such as Coleridge, this problem came to mean that literariness had to find institutional guardians of the sort provided for in his idea of a clerisy. Literature by itself was too unstable and insubstantial a compound to guarantee that it was not a poison rather than an inoculation. Ironically the very thing that made literature different, its lack of firm disciplinary boundaries, meant that it offered little protection at all. Perhaps the continuing popularity of Romanticism resides in this confusion. If the Romantic ideology insists on the authenticity of the Imagination, there will always be enthusiastic readers who understand the poetry to offer a more open realm of possibilities.[2]

---

[2] For two discussions of these issues that have profoundly influenced this book, see Steven Knapp, *Personification and the Sublime: Milton to Coleridge* (Cambridge, Mass.: Harvard University Press, 1985), and the 'Epilogue' to John Barrell's *Imagining the King's Death: Figurative Treason, Fantasies of Regicide 1793–6* (Oxford: Oxford University Press, 2000). I am also grateful to Peter McDonald for various discussions, especially in relation to Jacques Derrida's essay 'Before the Law', in *Acts of Literature*, ed. Derek Attridge (Routledge, 1992), 181–220.

Select Bibliography

I. PRIMARY SOURCES

(a) Manuscript Sources

Public Record Office:
Treasury Solicitors Papers
(Prosecution of Lee) 837/2832
Privy Council Papers
(Powell letters to Richard Ford) PC 1 23/38A

(b) Published Sources

Place of publication London unless stated.

AKENSIDE, MARK, *The Poems of Mark Akenside, M.D.* (1772).
—— *The Pleasures of Imagination*, ed. with a critical essay by Anna Letitia Barbauld (1795).
AUSTEN, JANE, *Persuasion*, ed. John Davie, introd. Claude Rawson (Oxford: Oxford University Press, 1990).
BARBAULD, ANNA LETITIA, 'Thoughts on the Devotional Taste, on Sects, and on Establishments', in *Devotional Pieces, Compiled from the Psalms and the Book of Job* (1775).
—— *An Address to the Opposers of the Repeal of the Corporation and Test Acts*, 4th edn. (1790).
—— *Sins of Government, Sins of the Nation; or, A Discourse for the Fast Appointed on April 19, 1793* (1793).
—— 'Essay on Akenside's Poem on the Pleasures of Imagination', in Mark Akenside, *The Pleasures of Imagination*, ed. Anna Letitia Barbauld (1795), pp. i–xxxvi.
—— *The Female Speaker; or, Miscellaneous Pieces, in Prose and Verse, Selected from the Best Writers, and Adapted to the Use of Young Women* (1811).
—— *The Works of Anna Laetitia Barbauld. With a Memoir by Lucy Aikin*, 2 vols. (1825).
—— *The Poems of Anna Letitia Barbauld*, ed. William McCarthy and Elizabeth Kraft (Athens: University of Georgia Press, 1994).
BICHENO, JAMES, *Signs of the Times; or, The Overthrow of the Papal Tyranny in France, the Prelude of Destruction to Popery and Despotism, but of Peace to Mankind* (1793).

BICHENO, JAMES, *A Glance at the History of Christianity, and of English Nonconformity* (1798).

BINNS, JOHN, *Recollections of the Life of John Binns* (Philadelphia, 1854).

BLAKE, WILLIAM, *The Complete Poetry and Prose of William Blake*, ed. David V. Erdman, rev. edn. (New York: Anchor-Doubleday, 1988).

BOGUE, DAVID, and BENNETT, JAMES, *History of Dissenters, from the Revolution in 1688, to the Year 1808*, 4 vols, (1808–12).

BROWNING, ROBERT, *Poetical Works 1833–1864*, ed. Ian Jack (Oxford: Oxford University Press, [1970] 1980).

BURDON, WILLIAM, *Various Thoughts on Politics, Morality, and Literature* (Newcastle upon Tyne, 1800).

BURKE, EDMUND, *The French Revolution 1790–94*, ed. L. G. Mitchell (Oxford: Oxford University Press, 1989), vol. viii of *The Writings and Speeches of Edmund Burke*, gen. ed. Paul Langford.

—— *The Revolutionary War 1794–7*, ed. R. B. McDowell (Oxford: Oxford University Press, 1991), vol. ix of *The Writings and Speeches of Edmund Burke*, gen. ed. Paul Langford.

BUTLER, JOSEPH, Bishop of Durham, *Analogy of Religion, Natural and Revealed, to the Constitution and Cause of Nature* (Dublin, 1736).

COLERIDGE, SAMUEL TAYLOR, *Aids to Reflection*, ed. John Beer (Princeton: Princeton University Press, 1993).

—— *Biographia Literaria*, ed. James Engell and W. Jackson Bate, Bollingen Series, 2 vols. (Princeton: Princeton University Press, 1983).

—— *Poetical Works*, ed. J. C. C. Mays, Bollingen Series, 3 vols. (Princeton: Princeton University Press, 2001).

—— *The Friend*, ed. Barbara E. Rooke, Bollingen Series, 2 vols. (Princeton: Princeton University Press, 1969).

—— *The Collected Letters of Samuel Taylor Coleridge*, ed. E. L. Griggs, 6 vols. (Oxford: Oxford University Press, 1956–71).

—— *Lectures 1795 on Politics and Religion*, ed. Lewis Patton and Peter Mann, Bollingen Series (Princeton: Princeton University Press, 1971).

—— *Lectures 1808–1819 on Literature*, ed. R. A. Foakes, Bollingen Series, 2 vols. (Princeton: Princeton University Press, 1987).

—— *Lectures 1808–1819 on the History of Philosophy*, ed. J. R. de J. Jackson, Bollingen Series, 2 vols. (Princeton: Princeton University Press, 2000).

—— *The Notebooks of Samuel Taylor Coleridge*, ed. Kathleen Coburn, Bollingen Series (Princeton: Princeton University Press, 1957–).

—— *On the Constitution of the Church and the State*, ed. John Colmer (Princeton: Princeton University Press, 1976).

—— *The Statesman's Manual, Lay Sermons*, ed. R. J. White, Bollingen Series (Princeton: Princeton University Press, 1972).

—— *Table Talk*, ed. Carl Woodring, Bollingen Series, 2 vols. (Princeton: Princeton University Press, 1990).

—— *The Watchman,* ed. Lewis Patton, Bollingen Series (Princeton: Princeton University Press, 1970).

DENNIS, JOHN, *The Critical Works of John Dennis,* ed. E. N. Hooker (Baltimore: Johns Hopkins University Press, 1939).

A Dissuasive against Enthusiasm: Wherein the Pretensions of the Modern Prophets to Divine Inspiration and the Power of Working Miracles are Examined and Confuted by Scripture and Matter of Fact (1708).

DOUGLAS, JOHN, *An Apology for the Clergy* (1755).

DRAKE, NATHAN, *Literary Hours, or Sketches Critical and Narrative* (1798).

DUFF, WILLIAM, *Essay on Original Genius* (1767).

DUTTON, THOMAS, *The Literary Census: A Satirical Poem with Notes* (1798).

ENFIELD, WILLIAM, *Sermons on Practical Subjects* (1798).

GIBBON, EDWARD, *The Letters of Edward Gibbon,* ed. J. E. Norton, 3 vols. (Cassell, 1956).

GISBORNE, THOMAS, *An Enquiry into the Duties of Man in the Higher and Middle Classes in Britain,* 2 vols, 2nd edn. (1795).

GODWIN, WILLIAM, *Political and Philosophical Writings of William Godwin,* gen. ed. Mark Philp, 7 vols. (William Pickering, 1993).

The Gospel of Reason by J. J. Rousseau, Citizen of Geneva (n.d. [1795]).

HARDY, THOMAS, *Memoir of Thomas Hardy* (1832), in David Vincent (ed. and introd.), *Testaments of Radicalism: Memoirs of Working Class Politicians 1790–1885* (Europa Publications, 1977).

HARTLEY, DAVID, *Observations on Man, his Frame, his Duty, and his Expectations,* rev. edn. (1791).

HAYS, MARY, *Memoirs of Emma Courtney,* ed. Marilyn L. Brooks (Peterborough, Ont.: Broadview, 1999).

HAZLITT, WILLIAM, *Complete Works of William Hazlitt,* ed. P. P. Howe, 21 vols. (J. M. Dent, 1930–4).

HOBBES, THOMAS, *Leviathan,* ed. With an introd. by C. B. Macpherson (Harmondsworth: Penguin, 1985 repr.).

HOW, SAMUEL, *The Sufficiency of the Spirit's Teaching without Human Learning,* 8th edn. (1792).

HUME, DAVID, *Philosophical Essays Concerning Human Understanding,* 2nd edn. (1750).

—— *The History of England, from the Invasion of Julius Caesar to the Revolution in 1688,* 8 vols., 2nd edn. (1778).

—— *Essays Moral, Political, and Literary,* ed. T. H. Green and T. H. Grose, 2 vols. (Longmans, Green & Co., 1875).

—— *The Letters of David Hume,* ed. J. Y. T. Greig, 2 vols. (Oxford: Clarendon Press, 1932).

—— *A Treatise of Human Nature,* ed. L. A. Selby-Bigge and P. H. Nidditch, 2nd edn. (Oxford: Clarendon Press, 1978).

HUNT, LEIGH, *An attempt to shew the folly and danger of Methodism. In a series of essays first published in the . . . Examiner, and now enlarged with a preface and . . . notes. By the editor of the Examiner* (1809).
—— *Autobiography of Leigh Hunt*, ed. J. E. Marpurgo (Cresset, 1949).
HUTCHESON, FRANCIS, *An Essay on the Nature and Conduct of the Passions and Affections* (1728).
JERNINGHAM, EDWARD, *Enthusiasm: A Poem in Two Parts* (1789).
—— *Edward Jerningham and his Friends: A Series of Eighteenth-Century Letters*, ed. Lewis Bettany (Chatto & Windus, 1919).
JOHNSON, SAMUEL, *A Dictionary of the English Language: in which the WORDS are deduced from their ORIGINALS, and ILLUSTRATED in their DIFFERENT SIGNIFICATIONS by EXAMPLES from the best WRITERS*, 2 vols. (1755).
—— *The Works of Samuel Johnson, Ll.D*, ed. A. Murphy, 12 vols. (1806).
KANT, IMMANUEL, *Critique of the Power of Judgment*, ed. Paul Guyer, trans. Paul Guyer and Eric Matthews (Cambridge: Cambridge University Press, 2000).
KEATE, WILLIAM, *A Free Examination of Dr. Price's and Dr. Priestley's Sermons* (1790).
LACKINGTON, JAMES, *Memoirs of the Forty-Five First Years of the Life of James Lackington*, 7th edn. (1794).
LAVINGTON, GEORGE, Bishop of Exeter, *The Enthusiasm of Methodists and Papists Compared*, 3 parts (1759–61).
LEE, RICHARD 'Citizen', *Flowers from Sharon; or, Original Poems on Divine Subjects* (1794).
—— *King Killing* (n.d. [1795]).
—— *On the Death of Mrs. Hardy, Wife of Thomas Hardy, of Piccadilly; Imprisoned in the Tower for High Treason* (n.d. [1794]).
—— *The Death of Despotism and the Doom of Tyrants* (n.d. [1795]).
—— *Proposals for publishing by subscription, sacred to truth, liberty, and peace, songs from the rock, to hail the approaching day, . . . by Richard Lee* (n.d. [1795?]).
—— *Songs from the Rock, to hail the approaching day, sacred to truth, liberty and peace. To which is added, the tribute of civic gratitude; a congratulatory address to Thomas Hardy* (n.d. [1795]).
A Letter to the Rt. Hon. Charles James Fox (1793).
LOCKE, JOHN, *An Essay Concerning Human Understanding*, ed. Peter H. Nidditch (Oxford: Clarendon Press, 1979).
London Corresponding Society, *Selections from the Papers of the London Corresponding Society 1792–1799*, ed. Mary Thale (Cambridge: Cambridge University Press, 1983).
LUDLAM, THOMAS, *Four Essays on the Ordinary and Extraordinary Operations of the Holy Spirit; on the Application of Experience to Religion; and of Enthusiasm and Fanaticism* (1797).

MACKENZIE, HENRY, *Works*, 8 vols. (Edinburgh, 1808).

MACKINTOSH, JAMES, *Vindiciae Gallicae: A Defence of the French Revolution and its English Admirers against the Accusations of the Right Hon. Edmund Burke* (1791).

MATHIAS, THOMAS, *Pursuits of Literature: A Satirical Poem in Four Dialogues*, 8th edn. (1808).

MERRY, ROBERT, *Diversity: A Poem* (1788).

—— *The Laurel of Liberty* (1790).

—— *Ode for the Fourteenth of July, 1791, the Day Consecrated to Freedom: Being the Anniversary of the Revolution in France* (1791).

MORE, HANNAH, *The Works of Hannah More*, 8 vols. (1801).

—— *Practical Piety; or, The Influence of the Religion of the Heart on the Conduct of Life*, 2 vols. (1811).

—— *The Letters of Hannah More*, ed. R. Brimley Johnson (1925).

NOTT, GEORGE F., *Religious Enthusiasm Considered* (Oxford, 1803).

ONESIMUS [Garnet Terry], *Letters on Godly and Religious Subjects*, 2 vols., 2nd edn. (1808).

PAINE, THOMAS, *Rights of Man*, ed. Eric Foner (Harmondsworth: Penguin, 1985).

PARR, SAMUEL, *A Spital Sermon, Preached at Christ Church, upon Easter Tuesday, April 15, 1800* (1801).

PLACE, FRANCIS, *Autobiography of Francis Place*, ed. Mary Thale (Cambridge: Cambridge University Press, 1972).

Politics for the People, 2 vols. (1793–5).

POPE, ALEXANDER, *The Correspondence of Alexander Pope*, ed. George Sherburn, 5 vols. (Oxford: Clarendon Press, 1956).

—— *The Poems of Alexander Pope: A One Volume Edition of the Twickenham Pope*, ed. John Butt (Routledge, repr. 1996).

PRESCOT, BENJAMIN, *An Explanatory Address to the Public on the Character & Prophecies of Richard Brothers and his Mission to Recal the Jews* (Liverpool, 1798).

PRICE, RICHARD, *A Discourse on the Love of Our Country, Delivered on Nov. 4 1789, at the Meeting House in the Old Jewry, to the Society for Commemorating the Revolution in Great Britain* (1790).

PRIESTLEY, JOSEPH, *The Theological and Miscellaneous Works of Joseph Priestley*, ed. J. T. Rutt, 25 vols. (1871).

REID, W. H., *The Rise and Dissolution of the Infidel Societies in this Metropolis: Including, the Origin of Modern Deism and Atheism; the Genius and Conduct of those Associations; their Lecture-Rooms, Field-Meetings, and Deputations; from the Publication of Paine's Age of Reason till the Present Period* (1800).

REYNOLDS, Sir JOSHUA, *Discourses on Art*, ed. Robert R. Wark, 3rd edn. (New Haven: Yale University Press, 1997).

SALTMARSH, JOHN, *Free Grace: or The Flowing of Christ's Blood Freely to Sinners*, 11th edn. (1792).

SHAFTESBURY, ANTHONY ASHLEY COOPER, Third Earl of, *Characteristics of Men, Manners, Opinions, Times*, ed. Lawrence E. Klein, Cambridge Texts in the History of Philosophy (Cambridge: Cambridge University Press, 1999).

SIBLEY, MANOAH, *The Genuine Trial of Thomas Hardy for High Treason, at the Sessions House in the Old Bailey, from October 28 to November 5, 1794*, 2 vols. (1795).

SMITH, ADAM, *The Theory of Moral Sentiments*, ed. D. D. Raphael and A. L. Macfie (Oxford: Oxford University Press, 1976).

—— *An Inquiry into the Nature and Causes of the Wealth of Nations*, gen. eds. R. H. Campbell and A. S. Skinner, textual editor W. B. Todd (Oxford: Oxford University Press, 1976).

Some Remarks on the Apparent Circumstances of the War (1795).

SOUTHEY, ROBERT, 'Art. LXXI: Periodical Accounts Relative to the Baptist Missionary Society, for propagating the Gospel among the Heathen', *Annual Review*, 1 (1802), 207–18.

—— 'Art. LXIII: A Chronological History of the People called Methodists. By William Myles', *Annual Review*, 2 (1803), 200–13.

—— *Letters from England*, ed. Jack Simmons (Cresset, 1951).

—— 'Art. XVII: *Periodical Accounts Relative to the Baptist Missionary Society*. Major Scott Waring-Twining, *Vindication of the Hindoos*, &c. &c.', *Quarterly Review*, 1 (1809), 193–226.

—— *The Life of Wesley; and the Rise and Progress of Methodism*, 2 vols. (London, 1820).

—— 'Lives and Works of our Uneducated Poets', in *Attempts in Verse, by John Jones, an Old Servant* (1831).

—— *New Letters of Robert Southey*, ed. Kenneth Curry, 2 vols. (New York: Columbia University Press, 1965).

SPENCE, THOMAS, *Pig's Meat*, 3rd edn., 2 vols. (n.d. [1795]).

STYLES, JOHN, *Strictures on Two Critiques in the Edinburgh Review on the Subject of Methodism and Missions; with Remarks on the Influence of Reviews in General on Morals and Happiness in Three Letters to a Friend* (1808).

SWIFT, JONATHAN, *A Tale of the Tub: To which is Added The Battle of the Books and the Mechanical Operation of the Spirit*, ed. A. C. Guthkelch and D. Nichol Smith, 2nd edn. (Oxford: Clarendon Press, 1958).

TAYLOR, THOMAS, *An Essay on the Beautiful from the Greek of Plotinus* (1792).

THELWALL, JOHN, *The Peripatetic, or Sketches of the heart, of nature, and society; in a series of politico-sentimental journals, in verse and prose, of the eccentric excursions of Sylvanus Theophrastus*, 3 vols. (1793).

—— *The Trial at Large of John Thelwall, for High Treason*, ed. John Newton (1794).

—— *Political Lectures (No. 1) on the Moral Tendency of a System of Spies and Informers, and the Conduct to be Observed by the Friends of Liberty during the Continuance of such a System*, 2nd edn. (1794).

—— *Peaceful Discussion and not Tumultory Violence the Means of Redressing National Grievances* (1795).

—— *Political Lectures, Volume the First—Part the First: Containing the Lecture on Spies and Informers and the First Lecture on Prosecutions for Political Opinion* (1795).

—— *The Tribune: Consisting Chiefly of the Political Lectures of John Thelwall*, 3 vols. (1795–6).

—— *Poems chiefly written in retirement. The fairy of the lake, a dramatic romance; Effusions of relative and social feeling; and specimens of The hope of Albion.* (Hereford, 1801).

—— *A letter to Francis Jeffray [sic] . . . on certain calumnies . . . in the Edinburgh Review* (Edinburgh, 1804).

—— *Mr. Thelwall's reply to the calumnies . . . contained in the anonymous Observations on his letter to the editor of the edinburgh review* (Glasgow, 1804)

—— *The Politics of English Jacobinism: The Writings of John Thelwall*, ed. with introd. and notes by Gregory Claeys (University Park: Pennsylvania State University Press, 1995).

—— *The Peripatetic*, ed. Judith Thompson (Detroit: Wayne State University Press, 2001).

THOMASON, THOMAS, *An Essay Tending to Prove that the Holy Scriptures, Rightly Understood, do not give Encouragement to Enthusiasm or Superstition* (1795).

A Treatise on Inspiration; in which the Pretence to Extraordinary Inspiration, is Considered, and Clearly and Fully Refuted (York, 1799).

TRIMMER, SARAH, *A Review of the Policy, Doctrines and Morals of the Methodists* (1791).

WAKEFIELD, GILBERT, *An Enquiry into the Expediency and Propriety of Public or Social Worship*, rev. edn. (1792).

—— *A General Reply to the Arguments against the Enquiry into Public Worship* (1792).

WALPOLE, HORACE, *The Yale Edition of Horace Walpole's Correspondence*, ed. W. S. Lewis, 48 vols. (New Haven: Yale University Press, 1937–83).

WARTON, JOSEPH, *Essay on the Writings and Genius of Pope*, 2 vols. (1756).

WESLEY, JOHN, *The Works of Rev. John Wesley*, ed. T. Jackson, 14 vols., 3rd edn. (1831).

—— *The Journal of the Rev. John Wesley, A.M.*, ed. N. Curnock, 8 vols. (1909–16).

WESLEY, JOHN, *The Letters of the Rev. John Wesley, A.M.*, ed. J. Telford, 8 vols. (1931).
—— *The Works of John Wesley*, ed. F. Baker et al. (Oxford: Oxford University Press, 1975–84; Nashville: Abingdon, 1984–): vols. i–iv, *Sermons*, ed. A. C. Outler (Nashville, 1984–7); vol. xi, *The Appeals to Men of Reason and Religion*, ed. G. R. Cragg (Oxford, 1975); vols. xxv–xxvi, *Letters*, i–ii, ed. F. Baker (Oxford, 1980–2).
WOLLSTONECRAFT, MARY, *Vindication of the Rights of Woman* (Harmondsworth: Penguin, 1975).
—— *Political Writings*, ed. Janet Todd (Oxford: Oxford University Press, 1994).
A Word of Admonition to the Right Hon. William Pitt (1795).
WORDSWORTH, WILLIAM, *The Poetical Works of William Wordsworth*, ed. E. de Selincourt, 2nd edn. (Oxford: Oxford University Press, 1952).
—— *The Letters of William and Dorothy Wordsworth: The Early Years, 1787–1805*, ed. Ernest de Selincourt, 2nd edn. rev. Mary Moorman (Oxford: Clarendon Press, 1969).
—— *The Letters of William and Dorothy Wordsworth: The Middle Years, 1806–1811*, ed. Ernest de Selincourt, 2nd edn. rev. Mary Moorman (Oxford: Clarendon Press, 1969), part 1.
—— *The Letters of William and Dorothy Wordsworth: The Later Years 1821–1853*, ed. Ernest de Selincourt, rev. Alan G. Hill, 4 vols. (Oxford: Clarendon Press, 1978–88).
—— *Peter Bell*, ed. John E. Jordan (Ithaca, NY: Cornell University Press, 1985).
—— *The Prelude: The Four Texts (1798, 1799, 1805, 1850)*, ed. Jonathan Wordsworth (Harmondsworth: Penguin, 1995).
—— *The Prose Works of William Wordsworth*, ed. W. J. B. Owen and J. W. Smyser, 3 vols. (Oxford: Clarendon Press, 1974).
—— *The Borderers*, ed. Robert Osborn (Ithaca, NY: Cornell University Press, 1982).
—— and COLERIDGE, SAMUEL TAYLOR, *Lyrical Ballads*, ed. R. L. Brett and A. R. Jones (Methuen, 1963; repr. 1968).
YOUNG, EDWARD, *An Extract from Dr Young's Night Thoughts on Life, Death, and Immortality*, ed. John Wesley (Bristol, 1770).
—— *Night Thoughts*, ed. Stephen Cornford (Cambridge: Cambridge University Press, 1989).

2. SECONDARY MATERIALS

ABRAMS, M. H., *Natural Supernaturalism: Tradition and Revolution in Romantic Literature* (New York: W. W. Norton & Co., 1971; repr. 1973).

—— 'Constructing and Deconstructing', in Morris Eaves and Michael Fischer (eds.), *Romanticism and Contemporary Criticism* (Ithaca, NY: Cornell University Press, 1986). 127–82.

ALLEN, B. SPRAGUE, 'Godwin's Influence upon John Thelwall', *PMLA* 37 (1922), 662–82.

ALLEN, RICHARD C., *David Hartley on Human Nature* (Albany: State University of New York Press, 1999).

ANDREW, DONNA T. (ed.), *London Debating Societies, 1776–1799* (London Record Society, 1994).

ASHFIELD, ANDREW, and DE BOLLA, PETER (eds.), *The Sublime: A Reader in British Eighteenth-Century Aesthetic Theory* (Cambridge: Cambridge University Press, 1996).

BARKER-BENFIELD, G. J., *The Culture of Sensibility: Sex and Society in Eighteenth-Century Britain* (Chicago: University of Chicago Press, 1992).

BARRELL, JOHN, *English Literature in History 1730–1780: 'An Equal Wide Survey'* (Hutchinson, 1983).

—— *The Birth of Pandora and the Division of Knowledge* (Basingstoke: Macmillan, 1992).

—— *Imagining the King's Death: Figurative Treason, Fantasies of Regicide 1793–6* (Oxford: Oxford University Press, 2000).

BENJAMIN, WALTER, *Illuminations*, ed. Hannah Arendt (Fontana, repr. 1982).

BENTLEY, G. E., Jr., *Blake Records* (Oxford: Oxford University Press, 1969).

—— *Blake Records Supplement* (Oxford: Oxford University Press, 1988).

BEWELL, ALAN, *Wordsworth and the Enlightenment: Nature, Man, and Society in the Experimental Poetry* (New Haven: Yale University Press, 1989).

BLOCH, ERNST, *The Principle of Hope*, trans. Neville Plaice et al. (Oxford: Blackwell, 1986).

BRANTLEY, RICHARD E., *Wordsworth's 'Natural Methodism'* (New Haven: Yale University Press, 1975).

—— *Locke, Wesley, and the Method of English Romanticism* (Gainesville: University of Florida Press, 1984).

BUTLER, MARILYN, 'Blake in his Time', in Robin Hamlyn and Michael Phillips (eds.) *William Blake* (Tate Publishing, 2000).

CAFARELLI, ANNETTE WHEELER, 'The Romantic "Peasant" Poets and their Patrons', *Wordsworth Circle*, 26 (1995), 77–87.

CHAKRABARTY, DIPESH, 'Radical Histories and the Question of Enlightenment Rationalism: Some Recent Critiques of Subaltern Studies', *Economic and Political Weekly*, 8 Apr. 1995, 751–9.

CHANDLER, JAMES K., *Wordsworth's Second Nature: A Study of the Poetry and Politics* (Chicago: University of Chicago Press, 1984).

CHASE, MALCOLM, *'The People's Farm': English Radical Agrarianism 1775–1840* (Oxford: Oxford University Press, 1988).

CLARK, TIMOTHY, *The Theory of Inspiration: Composition as a Crisis of Subjectivity in Romantic and Post-Romantic Writing* (Manchester: Manchester University Press, 1997).

COLEMAN, DEIRDRE, 'Firebrands, Letters and Flowers: Mrs. Barbauld and the Priestleys', in Gillian Russell and Clara Tuite (eds.), *Romantic Sociability: Social Networks and Literary Culture in Britain, 1770–1840* (Cambridge: Cambridge University Press, 2002), 82–103.

COPLEY, STEPHEN, 'Commerce, Conversation, and Politeness in the Early Eighteenth-century Periodical', *British Journal for Eighteenth-Century Studies*, 18 (1995), 63–77.

COX, JEFFREY N., *Poetry and Politics in the Cockney School: Keats, Shelley, Hunt, and their Circle* (Cambridge: Cambridge University Press, 1998).

DART, GREGORY, *Rousseau, Robespierre and English Romanticism* (Cambridge: Cambridge University Press, 1999).

DAVIE, DONALD, *A Gathered Church: The Literature of the English Dissenting Interest, 1700–1930* (Routledge & Kegan Paul, 1978).

DE BOLLA, PETER, *The Discourse of the Sublime: Readings in History, Aesthetics, and the Subject* (Oxford: Basil Blackwell, 1989).

DERRIDA, JACQUES, *Of Grammatology*, trans. Gayatri Chakravorty Spivak (Baltimore: Johns Hopkins University Press, [1974] 1976).

—— *Writing and Difference*, trans. Alan Bass (Routledge, [1967] 1978).

—— *Acts of Literature*, ed. Derek Attridge (Routledge, 1992).

DUFFY, EDWARD, *Rousseau in England: The Context for Shelley's Critique of the Enlightenment* (Berkeley and Los Angeles: University of California Press, 1979).

DWYER, JOHN, *Virtuous Discourse: Sensibility and Community in Late Eighteenth-Century Scotland* (Edinburgh: John Donald, 1987).

ELEY, GEOFF, 'Nations, Publics, and Political Cultures: Placing Habermas in the Nineteenth Century', in Craig Calhoun (ed.), *Habermas and the Public Sphere* (Cambridge, Mass.: MIT Press, 1992), 289–339.

ELLISON, JULIE, 'The Politics of Fancy in the Age of Sensibility', in Joel Haefner and Carol Shiner Wilson (eds.), *Re-visioning Romanticism: British Women Writers, 1776–1837* (Philadelphia: University of Pennsylvania Press, 1994), 228–55.

ERDMAN, DAVID V., *Blake: Prophet against Empire*, 3rd edn. (Princeton: Princeton University Press, 1977).

ESSICK, ROBERT N., *William Blake's Commercial Book Illustrations: A Catalogue and Study of the Plates Engraved by Blake after Designs by Other Artists* (Oxford: Clarendon Press, 1991).

EVEREST, KELVIN, *Coleridge's Secret Ministry: The Context of the Conversation Poems 1795–1798* (Hassocks: Harvester, 1979).

FAVRETTI, MAGGIE, 'The Politics of Vision: Anna Barbauld's "Eighteen Hundred and Eleven" ', in Isobel Armstrong and Virginia Blain (eds.), *Women's Poetry in the Enlightenment: The Making of a Canon, 1730–1820* (Basingstoke: Macmillan, 1999), 99–110.

FOUCAULT, MICHEL, *The Archeology of Knowledge*, trans. Alan Sheridan Smith (Routledge, [1969] 1991).

——*Discipline and Punish*, trans. Alan Sheridan (Harmondsworth: Penguin, [1975] 1979).

——*The History of Sexuality: An Introduction*, trans. Robert Hurley (Harmondsworth: Penguin, [1976] 1981).

——*The Care of the Self*, trans. Robert Hurley (Harmondsworth: Penguin, [1984] 1986).

——'Of Other Spaces', *Diacritics*, 16 (1986), 22–7.

FRASER, NANCY, 'Rethinking the Public Sphere: A Contribution to the Critique of Actually Existing Democracy', in Craig Calhoun (ed.), *Habermas and the Public Sphere* (Cambridge, Mass.: MIT Press, 1993), 109–42.

FRYE, NORTHROP, *Fearful Symmetry: A Study of William Blake* (Princeton: Princeton University Press, 1947).

GALPERIN, WILLIAM H., *The Return of the Visible in British Romanticism* (Baltimore: Johns Hopkins University Press, 1993).

GARRETT, CLARKE, *Respectable Folly: Millenarians and the French Revolution in France and England* (Baltimore: Johns Hopkins University Press, 1975).

GIBBS, WARREN E., 'An Unpublished Letter from John Thelwall to S. T. Coleridge', *Modern Language Review*, 25 (1930), 85–90.

GOLDBERG, BRIAN, ' "Ministry More Palpable": William Wordsworth and the Making of Romantic Professionalism', *Studies in Romanticism*, 36 (1997), 327–47.

HABERMAS, JÜRGEN, *The Structural Transformation of the Public Sphere: An Inquiry into a Category of Bourgeois Society*, trans. Thomas Burger with Frederick Lawrence (Cambridge, Mass., 1989).

HAMMOND, BREAN, *Professional Imaginative Writing in England 1670–1740: 'Hackney for Bread'* (Oxford: Oxford University Press, 1997).

HARGREAVES-MAWDSLEY, W. N., *The English Della Cruscans and their Time, 1783–1828* (The Hague: Martinus Nijhoff, 1967).

HARRISON, J. F. C., *The Second Coming: Popular Millenarianism 1780–1850* (Routledge & Kegan Paul, 1979).

HARTMAN, GEOFFREY H., *Minor Prophecies: The Literary Essay in the Culture Wars* (Cambridge, Mass.: Harvard University Press, 1991).

HAWES, CLEMENT, *Mania and Literary Style: The Rhetoric of Enthusiasm from the Ranters to Christopher Smart* (Cambridge: Cambridge University Press, 1996).

308 *Select Bibliography*

HEMPTON, DAVID, *Methodism and Politics in British Society 1750–1850* (Hutchinson, 1984).

HEYD, MICHAEL, 'The Reaction to Enthusiasm in the Seventeenth Century: Towards an Integrative Approach', *Journal of Modern History*, 53 (1981), 258–80.

—— *'Be Sober and Reasonable': The Critique of Enthusiasm in the Seventeenth and Early Eighteenth Centuries* (Leiden: E. J. Brill, 1995).

HOPKINS, JAMES K., *A Woman to Deliver her People: Joanna Southcott and English Millenarianism in an Era of Revolution* (Austin: University of Texas Press, 1982).

HOPKINS, MARY ALDEN, *Hannah and Her Circle* (New York: Longmans, Green, and Co., 1947).

HUET, MARIE-HÉLÈNE, 'The Revolutionary Sublime', *Eighteenth-Century Studies*, 28 (1994), 51–64.

IRLAM, SHAUN, *Elations: The Poetics of Enthusiasm in Eighteenth-Century Britain* (Stanford, Calif.: Stanford University Press, 1999).

JACOBUS, MARY, *Tradition and Experiment in Wordsworth's Lyrical Ballads (1798)* (Oxford: Oxford University Press, 1976).

JANOWITZ, ANNE, 'Amiable and Radical Sociability: Anna Barbauld's "Free Familiar Conversation"', in Gillian Russell and Clara Tuite (eds.), *Romantic Sociability: Social Networks and Literary Culture in Britain, 1770–1840* (Cambridge: Cambridge University Press, 2002), 62–81.

JARVIS, SIMON, 'Wordsworth and Idolatry', *Studies in Romanticism*, 38 (1999), 1–27.

JOHNSON, BARBARA, *A World of Difference* (Baltimore: Johns Hopkins University Press, 1987).

JONES, CHRIS, *Radical Sensibility: Literature and Ideas in the 1790s* (New York: Routledge, 1993).

KEACH, WILLIAM, 'Barbauld, Romanticism and the Survival of Dissent', *Essays and Studies*, 51 (1998), 44–61.

KEEN, PAUL, *The Crisis of Literature in the 1790s: Print Culture and the Public Sphere* (Cambridge: Cambridge University Press, 1999).

KITSON, PETER, ' "Sages and patriots that being dead do yet to us speak": Readings of the English Revolution in the Late Eighteenth Century', in James Holstun (ed.), *Pamphlet Wars: Prose in the English Revolution* (Frank Cass, 1992), 205–30.

KLANCHER, JON P., *The Making of English Reading Audiences, 1790–1832* (Madison: University of Wisconsin Press, 1987).

KLEIN, LAWRENCE E., *Shaftesbury and the Culture of Politeness: Moral Discourse and Cultural Politics in Early Eighteenth-Century England* (Cambridge: Cambridge University Press, 1994).

—— 'Sociability, Solitude, and Enthusiasm', *Huntington Library Quarterly*, 60 (1998), 153–77.

——and LA VOPA, ANTHONY J., 'Introduction', *Huntington Library Quarterly*, 60 (1998), 1–5.

KNAPP, STEVEN, *Personification and the Sublime: Milton to Coleridge* (Cambridge, Mass.: Harvard University Press, 1985).

KRAMNICK, ISAAC, *Republicanism and Bourgeois Radicalism: Political Ideology in Late Eighteenth-Century England and America* (Ithaca, NY: Cornell University Press, 1990).

KUCICH, GREG, 'Ironic Apocalypse in Romanticism and the French Revolution', in Keith Hanley and Raman Selden (eds.), *Revolution and English Romanticism: Politics and Rhetoric* (Hemel Hempstead: Harvester, 1990), 67–88.

LA VOPA, ANTHONY J., 'The Philosopher and the *Schwärmer*: On the Career of a German Epithet from Luther to Kant', *Huntington Library Quarterly*, 60 (1998), 85–115.

LIU, ALAN, *Wordsworth: The Sense of History* (Stanford, Calif.: Stanford University Press, 1989).

LOWES, JONATHAN LIVINGSTON, *The Road to Xanadu: A Study in the Ways of the Imagination* (Constable, 1927; 2nd edn. 1951).

LYOTARD, JEAN-FRANÇOIS, *Lessons on the Analytic of the Sublime*, trans. Elizabeth Rottenberg (Stanford, Calif.: Stanford University Press, 1994).

MCCALMAN, IAIN, *Radical Underworld: Prophets, Revolutionaries, and Pornographers in London, 1794–1840* (Cambridge: Cambridge University Press, 1988).

——'New Jerusalems: Prophecy, Dissent and Radical Culture in England, 1786–1830', in Knud Haakonssen (ed.), *Enlightenment and Religion: Rational Dissent in Eighteenth-Century Britain* (Cambridge: Cambridge University Press, 1996).

——'Mad Lord George and Madame La Motte: Riot and Sexuality in the Genesis of Burke's *Reflections on the Revolution in France*', *Journal of British Studies*, 35 (1996), 343–67.

——'Newgate in Revolution: Enthusiasm and Romantic Counterculture', *Eighteenth-Century Life*, 22 (1998), 95–110.

McCANN, ANDREW, 'Politico-Sentimentality: John Thelwall, Literary Production and Critique of Capital in the 1790s', *Romanticism*, 3 (1997), 35–42.

McCARTHY, WILLIAM, ' "We Hoped the *Woman* was Going to Appear": Repression, Desire, and Gender in Anna Letitia Barbauld's Early Poems', in Paula R. Feldman and Theresa M. Kelley (eds.), *Romantic Woman Writers: Voices and Countervoices* (Hanover, NH: University Press of New England, 1995), 113–37.

McGANN, JEROME, *Towards a Literature of Knowledge* (Oxford: Oxford University Press, 1989).

——*The Poetics of Sensibility: A Revolution in Literary Style* (Oxford: Clarendon Press, 1996).

MAISON, MARGARET, ' "Thine, Only Thine": Women Hymn Writers in Britain 1760–1835', in Gail Malmgreen (ed.), *Religion in the Lives of English Women: 1760–1930* (Croom Helm, 1986), 11–40.

MAKDISI, SAREE, *William Blake and the Impossible History of the 1790s* (Chicago: Chicago University Press, 2003).

MARSH, ROBERT, 'Shaftesbury's Theory of Poetry: The Importance of the "Inward Colloquy" ', *ELH* 28 (1961), 54–69.

MEE, JON, *Dangerous Enthusiasm: William Blake and the Culture of Radicalism in the 1790s* (Oxford: Clarendon Press, 1992).

—— 'Is there an Antinomian in the House? William Blake and the After-Life of a Heresy', in Steve Clark and David Worrall (eds.), *Historicizing Blake* (Basingstoke: Macmillan, 1994), 43–58.

—— 'Anxieties of Enthusiasm: Coleridge, Prophecy, and Popular Politics in the 1790s', *Huntington Library Quarterly*, 60 (1998), 1–25.

—— 'The Strange Career of Richard "Citizen" Lee: Poetry, Popular Radicalism, and Enthusiasm in the 1790s', in T. Morton and N. Smith (eds.), *Radicalism in British Literary Culture, 1650–1830: From Revolution to Revolution* (Cambridge: Cambridge University Press, 2002), 151–66.

—— ' "Reciprocal Expressions of Kindness": Robert Merry, Della Cruscanism and the Limits of Sociability', in Gillian Russell and Clara Tuite (eds.) *Romantic Sociability: Social Networks and Literary Culture in Britain 1770–1840* (Cambridge: Cambridge University Press, 2002), 104–22.

—— ' "As portentous as the written wall": Blake's Illustrations to *Night Thoughts*', in Sandy Gourlay (ed.), *Prophetic Character: Essays on William Blake in Honor of John E. Grant* (West Cornwall, Conn.: Locust Hill Press, 2002), 171–203.

MEEHAN, MICHAEL, *Liberty and Poetics in Eighteenth Century England* (Beckenham: Croom Helm, 1986).

MELLOR, ANNE K., *Romanticism and Gender* (Routledge, 1993).

—— 'The Female Poet and the Poetess: Two Traditions of British Women's Poetry, 1780–1830', in Isobel Armstrong and Virginia Blain (eds.), *Women's Poetry in the Enlightenment: The Making of a Canon, 1730–1820* (Macmillan, 1999), 81–98.

MITCHELL, W. J. T., 'Visible Language: Blake's Wond'rous Art of Writing', in Morris Eaves and Michael Fischer (eds.), *Romanticism and Contemporary Criticism* (Ithaca, NY: Cornell University Press, 1986), 46–95.

MIZUKOSHI, AYUMI, *Keats, Hunt, and the Aesthetics of Pleasure* (Basingstoke: Palgrave, 2001).

MOORE, C. A., 'Shaftesbury and the Ethical Poets in England, 1700–1760', 31, *PMLA* (1916), 264–325.

MORROW, JOHN, *Coleridge's Political Thought: Property, Morality and the Limits of Traditional Discourse* (Basingstoke: Macmillan, 1990).

MULLAN, JOHN, *Sentiment and Sociability: The Language of Feeling in the Eighteenth Century* (Oxford: Clarendon Press, 1988).

NEWLYN, LUCY, *Reading, Writing, and Romanticism: The Anxiety of Reception* (Oxford: Oxford University Press, 2000).

PALEY, MORTON D., 'Cowper as Blake's Spectre', *Eighteenth-Century Studies*, 1 (1968), 236–52.

—— *The Continuing City: William Blake's Jerusalem* (Oxford: Oxford University Press, 1983).

—— *Apocalypse and Millennium in English Romantic Poetry* (Oxford: Clarendon Press, 1999).

PASCOE, JUDITH, *Romantic Theatricality: Gender, Poetry, and Spectatorship* (Ithaca, NY: Cornell University Press, 1977).

PHILP, MARK, *Godwin's Political Justice* (Duckworth, 1986).

—— 'The Fragmented Ideology of Reform', in Mark Philp (ed.), *The French Revolution and British Popular Politics* (Cambridge: Cambridge University Press, 1991), 50–77.

POCOCK, J. G. A., *Virtue, Commerce, and History: Essays on Political Thought and History, Chiefly in the Eighteenth Century* (Cambridge: Cambridge University Press, 1985).

—— 'Edmund Burke and the Redefinition of Enthusiasm: The Context as Counter-Revolution', in *The Transformation of Political Culture, 1789–1848*, vol. iii of François Furet and Mona Ozouf (eds.), *The French Revolution and the Creation of Modern Political Culture* (Oxford: Oxford University Press, 1989), 19–43.

—— 'Enthusiasm: The Antiself of Enlightenment', *Huntington Library Quarterly*, 60 (1998), 7–28.

RATCLIFFE, EVAN, 'Revolutionary Writing, Moral Philosophy, and Universal Benevolence in the Eighteenth Century', *Journal of the History of Ideas*, 54 (1993), 221–40.

RIEDE, DAVID G., *Oracles and Hierophants: Constructions of Romantic Authority* (Ithaca, NY: Cornell University Press, 1991).

RIVERS, ISABEL, 'Shaftesburian Enthusiasm and the Evangelical Revival', in Jane Garnett and Colin Matthew (eds.), *Religion and Revival since 1700: Essays for John Walsh* (Hambledon Press, 1993), 21–39.

—— *Reason, Grace, and Sentiment: A Study of the Language of Religion and Ethics in England, 1660–1780*, Cambridge Studies in Eighteenth-Century English Literature and Thought, 2 vols. (Cambridge: Cambridge University Press, 1991–2000).

ROE, NICHOLAS, *Wordsworth and Coleridge: The Radical Years* (Oxford: Clarendon Press, 1988).

—— *John Keats and the Culture of Dissent* (Oxford: Oxford University Press, 1997).

ROGERS, PAT, 'Shaftesbury and the Aesthetics of Rhapsody', *British Journal of Aesthetics*, 12 (1972), 244–57.

ROSTON, MURRAY, *Poet and Prophet: The Bible and the Growth of Romanticism* (Faber & Faber, 1965).

RUSSELL, GILLIAN, *The Theatres of War: Performance, Politics, and Society 1793–1815* (Oxford: Clarendon Press, 1995).

RYAN, ROBERT, *The Romantic Reformation: Religious Politics in English Literature 1789–1824* (Cambridge: Cambridge University Press, 1997).

SAID, EDWARD, 'Foucault and the Imagination of Power', in D. C. Hoy (ed.), *Foucault: A Critical Reader* (Oxford: Blackwell, 1986), 149–55.

SCHWARTZ, HILLEL, *The French Prophets: The History of a Millenarian Group in Eighteenth-Century England* (Berkeley and Los Angeles: University of California Press, 1980).

SCRIVENER, MICHAEL, 'John Thelwall and the Revolution of 1649', in Nigel Smith and Timothy Morton (eds.), *Radicalism in British Literary Culture: From Revolution to Revolution* (Cambridge: Cambridge University Press, 2002), 119–32.

SEMMEL, BERNARD, *Methodist Revolution* (Heinemann, 1974).

SHAFFER, ELINOR, *'Kubla Khan' and the Fall of Jerusalem: The Mythological School in Biblical Criticism and Secular Literature 1770–1880* (Cambridge: Cambridge University Press, 1975).

—— 'Secular Apocalypse: Prophets and Apocalyptics at the End of the Eighteenth Century', in Malcolm Bull (ed.), *Apocalypse Theory and the Ends of the World* (Oxford: Blackwell, 1995), 137–58.

SIMON, IRÈNE, 'Swift and South on Enthusiasm', *Swift Studies*, 5 (1990), 113–16.

SISKIN, CLIFFORD, *Historicity of Romantic Discourse* (New York: Oxford University Press, 1988).

—— *The Work of Writing: Literature and Social Change in Britain 1700–1830* (Baltimore: Johns Hopkins University Press, 1998).

SITTER, JOHN, *Literary Loneliness in Mid Eighteenth-Century England* (Ithaca, NY: Cornell University Press, 1982).

SMITH, NIGEL (ed.), *A Collection of Ranter Writings from the 17th Century* (Junction Books, 1983).

STAFFORD, BARBARA MARIA, *Body Criticism: Imaging the Unseen in Enlightenment Art and Medicine* (Cambridge, Mass.: MIT Press, 1991; repr. 1997).

STAROBINSKI, JEAN, *Jean-Jacques Rousseau: Transparency and Obstruction*, trans. Arthur Goldhammer, introd. Robert J. Morrissey (Chicago: University of Chicago Press, 1988).

STOREY, MARK, *Robert Southey: A Life* (Oxford: Oxford University Press, 1997).

THOMPSON, EDWARD, *The Making of the English Working Class*, rev. edn. (Harmondsworth: Penguin, 1968).

—— *Customs in Common* (Harmondsworth: Penguin, 1993).

—— *The Romantics: England in a Revolutionary Age* (New York: Norton, 1997).

THOMPSON, JUDITH, 'An Autumnal Blast, a Killing Frost: Coleridge's Poetic Conversation with John Thelwall', *Studies in Romanticism*, 36 (1997), 427–56.

TUCKER, SUSIE I., *Enthusiasm: A Study in Semantic Change* (Cambridge: Cambridge University Press, 1972).

TUVESON, ERNEST, 'The Importance of Shaftesbury', *ELH* 20 (1953), 267–99.

TYERMAN, L. *The Life and Times of the Rev. John Wesley M.A., Founder of the Methodists*, 3 vols. (1870–1).

VALENZE, DEBORAH M., *Prophetic Sons and Daughters: Female Preaching and Popular Religion in Industrial England* (Princeton: Princeton University Press, 1985).

VARGO, LISA, 'The Case of Anna Laetitia Barbauld's "To Mr C(olerid)ge" ', *Charles Lamb Bulletin*, 102 (1998), 55–63.

VISCOMI, JOSEPH, *Blake and the Idea of the Book* (Princeton: Princeton University Press, 1993).

VON MALTZAHN, NICHOLAS, 'The Whig Milton, 1667–1700', in David Armitage et al. (eds.), *Milton and Republicanism* (Cambridge: Cambridge University Press, 1995), 229–53.

WALSH, JOHN, ' "Methodism" ' and the Origins of English Speaking Evangelicalism', in Mark A. Noll, David W. Bebbington, and George A. Rawlyk (eds.), *Evangelicalism: Comparative Studies of Popular Protestantism in N. America, the British Isles, and Beyond, 1700–1900* (New York: Oxford University Press, 1994).

—— ' "The Bane of Industry"? Popular Evangelicalism and Work in the Eighteenth Century', in R. N. Swanson (ed.), *The Use and Abuse of Time in Church History*, Studies in Church History 37 (Woodbridge: Boydell & Brewer, 2002), 223–41.

WEBB, R. K., 'Rational Piety', in Knud Haakonssen (ed.), *Enlightenment and Religion: Rational Dissent in Eighteenth-Century Britain* (Cambridge: Cambridge University Press, 1996), 287–311.

WHELAN, M. KEVIN, *Enthusiasm in the English Poetry of the Eighteenth Century (1700–1774)* (Washington, DC: Catholic University of America, 1935).

WHITE, DANIEL E., 'The "Joineriana": Anna Barbauld, the Aikin Family Circle, and the Dissenting Public Sphere', *Eighteenth-Century Studies*, 32 (1999), 511–33.

WILLIAMS, RAYMOND, *The Long Revolution* (Harmondsworth: Penguin, 1961; repr. 1981).

WRIGHT, PATRICK, *On Living in an Old Country* (Verso, 1985).

WU, DUNCAN, *Wordsworth's Reading 1770–99* (Cambridge: Cambridge University Press, 1993).

Index

Abrams, M. H. 131, 132, 144, 239, 240, 282–3
Addison, Joseph 13, 25, 27, 35, 56, 80
Aikin, John 146–7, 154, 182, 184, 190, 204, 257–8
Aikin, Lucy 183, 213
Akenside, Mark 17, 156, 191–7, 208, 210, 211, 212, 218, 236, 241, 282
and Coleridge 149, 154, 155
Allen, Richard C. 284–5, 287, 289
Analytical Review 57–8, 65, 94–5, 97, 98, 110, 143 n. 14
Arnold, Matthew 181, 262

Barbauld, Anna Letitia 15, 139, 154, 155, 173–213, 215, 229, 239, 262, 265
'Address to the Deity' 186, 187, 188–9, 191, 194, 198
Address to the Opposers . . . 191, 198–9
['A Character of Joseph Priestley'] 175, 180
'Corsica' 176, 195–8, 208, 210, 212
Eighteen Hundred and Eleven 177, 207–13
'Epistle to Wilberforce' 191, 200
The Female Speaker, 176, 184, 188, 206–7, 211
'Hymn I' 190
'Hymn: "Ye Are the Salt of the Earth"' 204–5
'The Invitation' 196
'On Romances' 196
Remarks on . . . Wakefield's Enquiry 201–3
Sins of Government, Sins of the Nation 182, 198, 200
'A Summer Evening's Meditation' 191–4, 208
'Thoughts on the Devotional Taste' 177–90
'To Dr. Priestley' 205
'To a Great Nation' 200
'To the Poor' 205
'To S. T. Coleridge' 139, 204–5
'[William Enfield]' 183

Barker-Benfield, G. J. 49, 50, 63
Barrell, John 98, 156; *see also* taste
Benjamin, Walter 11, 268, 292–3
Bennett, James 72, 266
Bentley Jr., G. E. 270
Bewell, Alan 222, 226
Bicheno, James 97–8
Binns, John 115, 119
Blair, Robert 270
Blake, William 19, 36–7, 71, 106, 128, 137, 177, 201, 208, 250, 257–93
'Auguries of Innocence' 260
The Book of Urizen 261, 285
Descriptive Catalogue 258, 281
Jerusalem 258, 260, 261, 264, 265, 273, 274–83, 286–91
The Marriage of Heaven and Hell 259–60, 261, 277, 286
Milton 258, 274, 281
There is No Natural Religion 259
Vision of the Last Judgment 290
Bloch, Ernst 250
Boehme, Jacob 34, 167, 170, 171, 272, 286, 288–9
Bogue, David 72, 266
Brantley, Richard 70, 240 n. 56, 241 n.
Brothers, Richard 27, 57, 65, 94–9, 108–9, 143, 144, 150, 164
Browning, Robert 23
Burdon, William 114
Burke, Edmund 24, 31, 59, 81, 83–93, 97, 106, 114, 116, 117, 122, 151, 153, 218, 236, 258, 296
and opinion 85–6, 89, 111, 226, 227, 234–5
and religious Dissent 86–7, 89, 136, 143, 148, 178–9, 199, 210
and Rousseau 8, 47, 90–2
and *transparence* 8, 44, 47, 86, 89–93, 143, 232; *see also* Pocock
and universal benevolence 16, 17, 90–1, 110, 112
Butler, Joseph, Bishop 168, 285
Butler, Marilyn 279, 291

316 *Index*

Campbell, Colin 49
Carey, William 66
Casaubon, Meric 28
Chakrabarty, Dipesh 93
Chandler, James 247
Charles I 43, 55, 86
Chase, Malcolm 105
Clark, Timothy 4 n. 10, 53–4, 58, 60
Coleridge, Samuel Taylor 13, 37, 60,
    76–7, 89, 92, 131–72, 177, 180,
    215, 216, 220, 233, 236, 238,
    245, 247, 251, 252, 256, 257,
    259, 268, 271, 272, 273, 282,
    283, 285, 293
  and Akenside 149, 154, 155
  and Boehme 167–8, 170, 171, 288
  and enthusiasm/fanaticism 19, 32,
    34, 164–72, 221–2, 263
  and Hartley 136–8, 142, 151, 152,
    160, 167, 261, 286, 288, 289
  and imagination/fancy 11–12,
    171–2
  and Luther 9, 36, 92, 165, 232
  and Rational Dissent 96–7, 136,
    142–4, 146–8, 154, 156, 164, 177,
    204–5, 208
  and Rousseau 9, 36, 92, 148, 165,
    232
  and St Teresa 291
  and Shaftesbury 135–6, 148, 152,
    155, 164, 165–6, 170, 171, 218
  and Thelwall 124–5, 147–9, 151,
    154–5, 159, 161, 164, 169, 218
  Aids to Reflection 168
  'The Ancient Mariner' 161
  Biographia Literaria 133, 151, 152,
    165, 167, 169, 170, 172, 234,
    288, 295
  Conciones ad Populum 138–40
  'Destiny of Nations' 132
  'Eolian harp' 152–3
  The Fall of Robespierre 133
  'Fears in Solitude' 161
  The Friend 8–9, 19, 165, 166, 170,
    251
  'Frost at Midnight' 150, 158–60
  'Kubla Khan' 161, 162–4, 199
  Lay Sermons (*Statesman's Manual*)
    165, 166, 168
  'Mahomet' 162–3
  'Monody on the Death of
    Chatterton' 136
  A Moral and Political Lecture 138

'Ode on the Departing Year' 151
'Reflections on Having Left a Place
    of Retirement' 156–8, 160, 204
'Religious Musings' 133, 136–8,
    142, 144–6, 147, 149, 150, 152,
    156, 164, 186, 193, 248, 288
Coleridge, Sara 152–3
Cooke, John 106
Cowper, William 29
Cox, Jeffrey N. 80
Croker, J. W. 207, 208, 210, 211
Cromek, Robert 270
Cromwell, Oliver 67, 149, 178
Cumberland, George 274

Dart, Gregory 1 n., 8 n. 22, 90; see
    also *transparence*
Davie, Donald 181, 261–2, 265, 271
de Bolla, Peter 2. n. 2, 8 n. 15, 55, 63
Della Cruscanism 56–7, 227, 233,
    235, 255
Dennis, John 11, 17, 53, 55–6, 127,
    236
Dissuasive against Enthusiasm 29
Doddridge, Philip 31, 40, 60, 181,
    183, 185, 195
Douglas, John 26
Drake, Nathan 11–12
Dryden, John 53
Duff, William 54, 56, 57
Dyer, George 139, 144

Eaton, Daniel Isaac 106
Edgeworth, Maria 18
Enfield, William 182, 183–5, 190
Essick, Robert N. 284
Evangelical Magazine 77–80, 97, 103
Everest, Kelvin 153, 154, 155, 160, 255

Favretti, Maggie 208, 210
Fielding, Henry 18
Fifth Monarchists 27, 87
Foucault, Michael 3, 5, 17, 48, 176,
    292
Fox, Charles James 108
Frend, William 96

Galperin, William 13, 216
Gibbon, Edward 67, 258
Gisborne, Thomas 92
Godwin, William 83, 84, 86, 109–20,
    122, 126, 133, 140, 141, 142,
    151, 185, 246, 253–4, 289–90

and reading 62, 63–4, 114
and literature 63–4, 114, 117
and sympathy 62, 113, 116–17,
 139, 226
Goldberg, Brian 76
Goldsmith, Oliver 59
Gordon, Lord George 99–100, 108,
 117
Gordon Riots 67

Habermas, Jürgen 30, 59, 72
Hammond, Brean 60–1
Hardy, Thomas 27, 105
Hartley, David 48, 136, 138, 142,
 150–1, 152, 153, 160, 167, 186,
 215, 220, 228, 234, 261,
 285–90; *see also* Allen
and self-annihilation 137, 242,
 287–8
Hartman, Geoffrey 24–5, 79
Hawes, Clement 73, 81, 262
Hayley, William 264
Hays, Mary 19
Hazlitt, William 120
Heyd, Michael 26, 30
Hill, Rowland 108
Hobbes, Thomas 3, 32, 33, 38
Hodgson, Richard 107–8, 109
Howard, John 156, 157, 158, 160,
 204, 208
Hume, David 5, 7, 12, 26, 43–7, 48,
 49, 87. 88, 112, 113, 139, 151,
 195, 258, 266
'Of Superstition and Enthusiasm' 6,
 10, 28, 138, 171, 187, 230–2
Hunt, J. H. L. (Leigh) 3, 4, 5, 29, 34,
 35–6, 50, 65, 71–2, 73, 80–1, 108,
 241, 264–82, 295
Hunt, Robert 36, 241, 264, 271, 272,
 273, 282
Huntington, William 29, 74, 79, 108
Hutcheson, Francis 16, 44–5, 47, 48,
 110, 112, 195, 254, 256

Irlam, Shaun 4–5, 7, 17, 25, 53, 70,
 131, 133, 144, 164, 194, 215,
 217, 294

Janowitz, Anne 182, 190, 198, 204
Jarvis, Simon 229–33, 247, 250, 254,
 295; *see also* New Historicism
Jeffrey, Francis 50, 76–7, 125, 214,
 225–6, 231, 237, 238, 251–2

Jerningham, Edward 56–7, 228
Johnson, Barbara 220
Johnson, Joseph 104, 182, 198, 206,
 258
Johnson, Samuel 10, 11, 74, 195, 212
Jones, Chris 45, 90, 220, 254
Jordan, J. S. 104

Kant, Immanuel 12–13, 166, 290
Keach, William 204
Keate, William 199–200
Keen, Paul 24, 244
Kippis, Andrew 195
Klancher, Jon 227
Knapp, Steven 166
Kramnick, Isaac 126, 127

Lackington, James 34–5, 65
Lavington, Bishop George 67–8, 214
Law, William 14, 16, 31, 32, 34, 272,
 289
Lee, Richard 'Citizen' 77–81, 90,
 103–8, 116, 127, 144, 145, 159,
 160–1, 236, 249, 250
Lindsey, Theophilus 185
Liu, Alan 238, 248, 249
Locke, John 3, 6–7, 10, 12, 16, 37, 38,
 39, 48, 51, 70, 71, 259, 270, 277,
 278
London Corresponding Society (LCS)
 27, 81, 93, 99, 103, 106, 107–8,
 115, 116, 119, 127, 132
Lowth, Robert 57, 208
Ludlam, Thomas 32, 34
Luther, Martin 8, 9, 11, 36, 92, 140,
 149, 165, 232

McGann, J. J. 227, 255; *see also*
 Romantic ideology
Mackenzie, Henry 50–53, 64, 73, 90,
 174, 179, 180–1
Mackintosh, James 87, 92, 106,
 284–5, 286
Madan, Martin 2–3
Maxfield, Thomas 68
Meehan, Michael 255
Mellor, Anne K. 290–1
Memoirs of Pretended Prophets 26–7,
 95
Merry, Robert 227–9, 233–6, 242,
 245, 246
Methodist Magazine 64, 269
Milton, John 55, 56, 142, 172

Mitchell, W. J. T. 271, 273
Mizukoshi, Ayumi 80
Mohammed 162, 163
Monthly Magazine 156, 204–5, 271
Moody, Christopher 160–1
Moore, C. A. 17
More, Hannah 16, 62, 194, 211
More, Henry 28
Mullan, John 44, 233
Murray, James 105

New Historicism 1, 132, 238, 248, 295
Newlyn, Lucy 196, 197, 207
Newton, Isaac 98, 142
Nott, George 43

Paine, Thomas 33, 62, 82, 99, 103,
    104, 106, 107, 114, 143, 257
Paley, Morton D. 144, 155
Parr, Samuel 110, 111, 112, 114, 115,
    142, 150, 159, 186
Piozzi, Hester Lynch 228, 233
Pitt, William (the Younger) 96, 103
Place, Francis 108, 109
Pocock, J. G. A. 8, 9–10, 15, 27, 43 n.,
    47 n., 51 n., 84 n., 86, 89, 232
Pope, Alexander 55, 60, 61
Powell, James 107
Prescot, Benjamin 97
Price, Richard 9, 27, 40, 41, 45, 83,
    86, 87, 89, 92, 97, 143, 178, 180,
    199
Priestley, Joseph 15–16, 24, 34, 83,
    92, 97, 98, 137, 142, 151, 152,
    153, 167, 194, 196, 202–3, 205–6,
    215, 233, 242, 261, 289–90
    abridgement of Hartley's
    Observations 284, 285
    and Barbauld's 'Essay on the
    Devotional Taste' 174–5, 177–90,
    262
    and superstition 180–1, 230

Radcliffe, Ann 52–3
Reid, Thomas 110
Reid, William Hamilton 79, 104, 107,
    109
Reynolds, Sir Joshua 220, 257
Riebau, George 95, 99
Riede, David 134, 137, 150, 168, 215,
    237, 241
Robespierre, Maximilien 9, 138–9,
    142, 162, 164–5, 232

Roe, Nicholas 80, 145, 253
'Romantic ideology' 1, 2, 13, 294, *see
    also* McGann
Romantic irony 36, 145
Rousseau, Jean-Jacques 8, 11, 36, 90,
    92, 121, 148, 149, 165, 166, 232

Sacheverell, Henry 30
Said, Edward 176
St Teresa 291
Schiller, Friedrich von 2, 131
self-annihilation 137–8, 171, 180, 187,
    189, 193, 194, 215, 229, 233,
    242, 258, 260, 278, 283, 284,
    287–9; *see also* Hartley
Semmel, Bernard 67
sensibility 2, 19, 45, 49–53, 121, 198,
    210, 212
    and religion 51–3, 174–5, 178, 181,
    183, 186, 189–90, 191, 193,
    202–3
Shaffer, E. S. 248
Shaftesbury, Antony Ashley Cooper,
    Lord 7, 18–19, 38–46, 48, 58, 62,
    83, 85, 110, 187, 289; *see also*
    taste; transports (of emotion)
    and Akenside 17, 154, 156, 192,
    194, 195, 212
    and Barbauld 176, 183, 185, 195,
    206, 211, 212
    and Coleridge 133, 135–6, 139,
    140, 148, 155, 156, 158, 164–66,
    172, 218
    and Dennis 55–6
    and Godwin 110–13, 115
    and Locke 37–38, 51
    and the moral sense 16–17, 38,
    44–5, 140, 172, 217
    and 'regulation' 3, 17, 39–40, 55,
    88, 133, 135, 136, 292
    and 'retirement' 39–40, 63, 154,
    158
    and Rousseau 90 148
    and self-fashioning 49, 61, 75
    and Thelwall 121, 122, 124, 126,
    148
    and Wesley 67
    and Wordsworth 39–40, 133,
    217–21, 226, 228, 235–6, 241–3,
    246–7, 254–6
Shakespeare, William 151, 172
Sheridan, Richard Brinsley 108
Siskin, Clifford 17, 48, 76, 237, 240

Smith, Adam 12, 46–7, 48, 50, 88,
    110, 112, 142, 186
Smith, Nigel 28
Smollett, Tobias 18–19
Southcott, Joanna 50, 58, 99, 211
Southey, Robert 14, 31, 65–6, 75–7,
    80, 150, 223, 241, 247, 259, 268
    Life of Wesley 69–70, 76, 102, 141,
    239, 264, 266 n. 15
The Spectator 25, 63
Spence, Thomas 99, 105–6
Spencer, Henry 96, 108–9
Stafford, Barbara 13, 258, 272
Steele, Sir Richard 25, 80
Stillingfleet, Bishop Edward 266
sublime, the 1–2, 8, 11, 37, 53–60,
    127, 146–7, 180, 189–95, 196,
    198, 213, 240, 248, 272–3, 290–1;
    see also de Bolla
superstition 28, 172, 181, 187, 189,
    230, *see also* Hume
Swedenborg, Emanuel 257, 261–2,
    271, 277
Swift, Jonathan 4, 30–1, 35, 43, 59,
    60, 84, 168, 220, 269

taste 40, 49–50, 61, 73, 75–6, 133,
    134, 140, 167, 170–2, 217–22,
    224–6, 296
    in religious matters 52–2, 64, 175,
    177–81, 185, 190, 262, 265
Taylor, Isaac 32
Taylor, Thomas 163, 164, 272
Terry, Garnet 74, 95, 104, 105
Thelwall, John 77, 83, 92–3, 94, 109,
    115–27, 132, 139, 140, 226, 236,
    245, 246, 265
    and Coleridge 124–5, 147–9, 151,
    154–5, 159, 161, 164, 166, 169,
    204, 218
    and Jeffrey 76, 125–6, 238, 243–4
Thomason, Thomas 33, 57
Thompson, E. P. 73, 94
Thompson, Judith 125, 154, 161, 204;
    see also Thelwall
Thomson, James 17, 218
Tooke, John Horne 108, 124
Towers, J. L. 98
transparence 8–10, 11, 18, 36, 106,
    127, 142, 143, 144, 216, 247–57,
    294
    and Burke 8, 44, 47, 86, 89–93,
    143, 232; *see also* Pocock

transports (of emotion) 7–8, 19, 42,
    52–3, 54, 55, 74, 156, 161, 179,
    189–90, 214, 216, 240, 246–247,
    255, 264, 283, 285, 288–9
Trimmer, Sarah 72

Valenze, Deborah M. 35
Viscomi, Joseph 283
Volney, Constantin 99, 103, 106, 107,
    257
Voltaire (François-Marie Arouet) 258
von Maltzahn, Nicholas 56

Wakefield, Gilbert 42, 201–3, 204
Walpole, Horace 84, 85, 200, 234
Warrington Academy 146, 173–5,
    179, 182, 183, 185, 191
Warton, Joseph 54, 283
Watson, Richard, Bishop 284
Watson, Robert 108
Watts, Isaac 31, 181, 183, 206–7
Webb, R. K. 15–16, 33, 181
Wesley, Charles 261–2
Wesley, John 14, 16, 32, 64, 67–74,
    77, 102, 141, 239, 259, 264, 266,
    268, 274
    and 'extraordinary calls' 69, 70,
    214, 240–1
White, Daniel E. 15, 182, 183, 185
Whitefield, George 71, 264, 266,
    274–5, 280, 291
Wilberforce, William 224
Williams, Helen Maria 200
Wollstonecraft, Mary 60, 85 n. 7
Woodfall, William 197–8, 210, 212
Wordsworth, Dorothy 247
Wordsworth, William 5, 11, 36, 60,
    64, 76–7, 89, 167, 171, 214–56,
    257, 259, 269, 272–3, 276–7, 279,
    282
    and Godwin 109, 226, 246, 253–4
    and Jeffrey 76–7, 214, 225, 226,
    237, 238, 243
    and 'sensuous incarnation' 179,
    181, 260, 271
    and Shaftesbury 39–40, 133, 217,
    218, 220–1, 226, 235, 236, 241–7,
    254–6
    and 'spots of time' 219, 238–41,
    247, 250
    and taste 75, 171, 220–1, 226
    and Thelwall 124–5, 131, 161, 226,
    236, 238, 243–4, 245

Wordsworth, William (*cont*):
  and Wesley 77, 214, 239–41, 245
  'The Baker's Cart' 229
  The Borderers 231–3
  'Essay, Supplementary to the Preface'
    217, 218 n.5, 221–2
  An Evening Walk 228, 236
  The Excursion 214, 225, 237, 276
  'Lines written on a Yew Tree' 245–6
  Peter Bell 218, 222–5
  'Preface' to *Lyrical Ballads* 39–40,
    75, 214, 215, 217, 218–22, 223,
    225, 226–7, 236, 243

'Preface' to *Poems* (1815)
    229–30
The Prelude (1805) 158, 214, 216,
    217, 219, 222, 225, 229–30,
    236–56, 272, 276, 295
'The Recluse' 226
'The Ruined Cottage' 229
'Tintern Abbey' 216, 222
Wotton, William 43
Wright, Patrick 250, 279

Young, Edward 70, 191, 194, 212,
    264